BY MATTHEW GOODMAN

Paris Undercover: A Wartime Story of Courage,
Friendship, and Betrayal

The City Game: Triumph, Scandal, and a Legendary Basketball Team

Eighty Days: Nellie Bly and Elizabeth Bisland's
History-Making Race Around the World

The Sun and the Moon: The Remarkable True Account of
Hoaxers, Showmen, Dueling Journalists, and Lunar
Man-Bats in Nineteenth-Century New York

Jewish Food: The World at Table

PARIS
UNDERCOVER

PARIS UNDERCOVER

A WARTIME STORY OF COURAGE, FRIENDSHIP, AND BETRAYAL

Matthew Goodman

BALLANTINE BOOKS

NEW YORK

Published in the United States by Ballantine Books, an imprint of Random House,
a division of Penguin Random House LLC, New York.

BALLANTINE BOOKS & colophon are registered trademarks
of Penguin Random House LLC.

Library of Congress Cataloging-in-Publication Data
Names: Goodman, Matthew, author.
Title: Paris undercover : a wartime story of courage, friendship,
and betrayal / Matthew Goodman.
Other titles: Wartime story of courage, friendship, and betrayal
Description: New York : Ballantine, [2025] | Includes bibliographical
references and index. |
Identifiers: LCCN 2024042974 (print) | LCCN 2024042975 (ebook) |
ISBN 9780593358924 (hardcover) | ISBN 9780593358931 (ebook)
Subjects: LCSH: Bonnefous, Kate, 1886–1965. | World War, 1939–1945—
Underground movements—France—Paris. | World War, 1939–1945—Prisoners and
prisons, German. | World War, 1939–1945—France—Paris. | Shiber, Etta. |
World War, 1939–1945—Women. Escapes—France—History—20th century. |
Shiber, Etta. Paris-underground. | Paris (France)—History—1940–1944. |
Shiber, Etta. Paris underground.
Classification: LCC D802.F8 B6164 2025 (print) | LCC D802.F8 (ebook) |
DDC 940.53/44092 [B]—dc23/eng/20240927
LC record available at https://lccn.loc.gov/2024042974
LC ebook record available at https://lccn.loc.gov/2024042975

Printed in the United States of America on acid-free paper

randomhousebooks.com

2 4 6 8 9 7 5 3 1

First Edition

Book design by Caroline Cunningham
Frontispiece: Adobe Stock/Светлана Аношина (Svetlana Anoshina)

For Cassie, *toujours*

The stars are dead. The animals will not look.

We are left alone with our day, and the time is short, and

History to the defeated

May say Alas but cannot help nor pardon.

—W. H. Auden, "Spain," 1937

Contents

Kate Bonnefous's Escape Line, 1940

Occupied Zone   Unoccupied Zone   Forbidden Zone

0   MILES   200

0   KM   200

ENGLAND   NETHERLANDS

GERMANY

Calais • Dunkirk
**FORBIDDEN
ZONE**   • Lille   BELGIUM
Conchy-sur-Canche •   • Doullens

English Channel

LUX.

Paris ⭑

O C C U P I E D   Z O N E

• Orléans

Line of Demarcation

• Châteauroux

ATLANTIC
OCEAN   F R A N C E   SWITZER-
LAND

Libourne
Bordeaux • Castillon-sur-
Dordogne
Civrac-sur-   ITALY
Dordogne   Pujols-sur-   U N O C C U P I E D
Dordogne   Z O N E

Marseille •

ANDORRA

S P A I N   Mediterranean Sea

PARIS
UNDERCOVER

Prologue

June 1, 1942

THE STATUE OF LIBERTY, that great gift of France, glowed dimly in the thin morning light as the mercy ship entered New York Harbor. The day had broken gray and damp and unusually cool for the beginning of June, and in the distance the limestone towers of lower Manhattan brooded with a sense of incompleteness, the peaks of the taller skyscrapers having vanished into low-hanging clouds. At the start of the new work week the city was stirring to life, and in the streets the heavy smell of frying oil mixed with the sharp salt tang of sea air, and coffee brewing in Automats and luncheonettes, and smoke that was already drifting in from factories uptown and across the Hudson. Drivers of vans bearing newspaper logos with ornate antique typefaces tossed string-tied bundles against the sides of wooden kiosks; within moments the strings would be cut and the papers stacked in piles under cast-iron weights or hung up with clothespins like wash on a line.

The front pages that day brought news of an air raid conducted two nights earlier against the German city of Cologne; more than one thousand bombers of the Royal Air Force, an armada with a destructive force greater than any the world had yet seen, had dropped 1,500 metric tons of high-explosive and incendiary bombs on the city, reducing much of its historic center to ruins. In New

York, the papers gave special attention to an American navigator flying along with the RAF, Brooklyn's own Charlie Honychurch, of whom it was noted, inevitably, that he was "nuts" about the Dodgers. Honychurch told the reporter from the United Press that his crew had been part of a later wave, and by the time they arrived overhead, Cologne had been turned into a vast sea of fire; it was, he said, "like looking down the mouth of hell."

Entering the harbor, the *Drottningholm* made a ghostly shimmer in the mist; the ship was entirely white but for the painted blue and yellow bands and the words SVERIGE and DIPLOMAT in black letters thirteen feet high on the hull. Once a luxury liner of the Swedish American Line, with plushly appointed salons and arched skylights and polished woodwork that gleamed in the light, the *Drottningholm* had recently been chartered by the U.S. State Department to carry out a series of civilian exchanges with Germany. Unlike other ships on the high seas in a time of war, the *Drottningholm* had sailed in the most conspicuous possible manner, with specially installed floodlights that blazed through the night to alert enemy submarines that this was a repatriation voyage—a protected mission derived from the rules of the Geneva Conventions and delicately negotiated between Germany and the United States through intermediaries from Switzerland and Sweden. The ship was returning now from ten days at sea, having just crossed the North Atlantic from Lisbon. She carried 908 passengers, including diplomatic personnel, foreign correspondents, civilian internees, and refugees and their families, released by the German authorities in exchange for a comparable number of citizens of the Axis powers who had been held in detention camps in the United States and Latin America.

One of the passengers on this voyage, Etta Shiber, was still asleep when the Statue of Liberty came into view. She would say later that she regretted missing that first treasured glimpse of home, but the fact was she had a lot of sleep to catch up on, having only recently endured eighteen months on narrow prison mattresses stuffed with straw, plus untold weeks of fitful, anxious nights before that. In 1942 Etta was sixty-four years old, and though she had never had children she would invariably be described by journalists as "grandmotherly." She wore a pair of horn-rimmed spectacles over her large brown eyes with their heavy brows; she had a long nose and a smile that turned up slightly on one side, and her hair was newly cut, colored, and permed. Her skin was still sallow, though, and there were lines in her face that she did not recognize. She had lost more than twenty-five pounds while in prison, and with it much of the plumpness that had vexed her since college; but this was weight loss, she well understood, that fatigued rather than invigorated, born of food that was repugnant rather than healthful: dreary meals of thin soup and stale crusts of bread, occasionally supplemented by slices of dried meat that tasted as if it had been produced in one of Germany's famed chemical plants.

In prison, half-starved, she had often dreamed of lavish meals; now, freed, Etta was surprised by the modesty of her own body's demands. As in the Yiddish story of the good peasant who, allowed any wish by the Heavenly Tribunal, asks only for a warm buttered roll, so too did she find that it was not caviar or pâté, or a thick steak, or Paris's jewel-like pastries that she most craved, but simply butter, good butter made from real cream, and in the mornings aboard ship she found herself almost overcome with pleasure in eating the buttered toast that arrived alongside her eggs and sausages.

A filling meal, a hot bath, shampoo: such were her newfound luxuries. Thinking about the life ahead of her, Etta looked forward to the prospect of going to a movie or attending the theater all by herself; solitude, which had been such a misery when her husband died, now seemed another luxury, having been denied her for so long. While she was waiting for the *Drottningholm* to set sail, one of the officials from the American consulate had suggested to Etta that she was the Edith Cavell of this war—Edith Cavell being the English nurse who had helped Allied soldiers to escape from occupied Belgium during the First World War. The man had meant it sincerely, and had been kind in his intentions, but Etta couldn't accept the sentiment. For her bravery, Cavell had been executed by a German firing squad, whereas she, Etta, was sailing home safely, eating roast chicken and potatoes with gleaming silverware, a snow-white linen napkin on her lap. If anyone was the new Edith Cavell (in the coming months she would insist on this over and over, though hardly anyone seemed to be listening), it was her friend Kitty, like Cavell an

English worker for the Red Cross in occupied territory: Kitty, whose firm voice and imperious manner could intimidate even Nazi border guards; Kitty, who hummed to herself as she assembled a package of chocolate and silk stockings to bribe a German officer; Kitty, whose beautiful slender hands, the last time Etta saw her, were pitted with the dark craters of cigarette burns.

Kate Bonnefous—"Kitty" to her friends—was nine years younger than Etta; born Kate Robins into a prosperous English family, she had married a French wine merchant named Henri Bonnefous in 1926 and opened a small dress shop in Paris's ninth arrondissement. That was where Etta first met her, on one of her yearly trips to France, and almost immediately the two became close friends. At the time Etta was living on the Upper East Side of New York with her husband, Bill, and her cousin Irving, but in 1933 Irving died from a chronic heart condition, and three years later, William Shiber, too, died of a heart attack. Suddenly Etta was all alone in that New York apartment, consumed by grief, thrown for the first time upon herself. She would later write that she had always depended on Bill and Irving to look out for her, "and without them I was lost." The following year, Kate wired Etta suggesting that they live together in Paris, and Etta immediately accepted; it was there that the two women intended to spend the remainder of their lives.

Between Etta's savings and the trust left Kate by her father, they seemed to have everything they could need. Their apartment was not far from Parc Monceau, where they walked their three beloved cocker spaniels; they browsed books and old magazines at the stalls run by the *bouquinistes* along the Seine, haunted the city's antiques shops and flea markets. The two women were intelligent and well-read, and they shared a love of food and wine and all things Parisian. In personality, though, they were very different: Kate was sociable where Etta was retiring, self-confident where Etta was anxious, daring where Etta was cautious. To anyone who knew Etta Shiber, she was about the last person who would be the subject of the biographical index card that the Associated Press made for her:

Is second American woman to be held by Nazis in France, 13/12/40[*]
Taken into custody by Germans in occupied France, 14/12/40
Released by Germans after arrest in Paris, 24/12/40
Arrested again in Paris; charged with "escape" plot, 14/2/41

All of that, however, had indeed happened to her (in fact she was the first American woman to be held by the Nazis in France, not the second), and any time Etta was asked about it, she confessed to being more astonished than anyone else.

It was almost eight in the morning when the *Drottningholm* docked at Pier F in Jersey City. Despite wartime restrictions the pier was crowded with some three hundred guests, on hand to see their loved ones after so long, and the scene assumed a festive atmosphere as the excited relatives pressed close to the railing, waving at the ship, straining to catch a glimpse of a familiar face. Newsreel cameramen from Paramount and *The March of Time* carefully positioned and repositioned their tripods, seeking the best vantage point to capture the moments of reunion; longshoremen hauled down luggage from the ship as if it were a day's catch from the sea, in giant nets. For more than an hour the disembarkation was unaccountably delayed, and the anticipatory clamor of the relatives on shore began to give way to a murmur of impatience and bewilderment as they stood waiting in the drizzle; then without warning the rope at the top of the gangway was unhooked and the crowd hushed, as at the raising of a theater curtain, and the first passenger stepped out. This was Adm. William D. Leahy, the United States ambassador to Vichy, who had been summoned to Washington for a consultation with President Franklin D. Roosevelt. Unlike that of the other passengers, the admiral's voyage had been an especially sorrowful one, as he was bringing with him the body of his wife, who had died just a few days before the departure from France. A Navy honor guard stood at at-

---

[*] The Associated Press used the European convention of listing the day before the month.

tention as the black-shrouded casket was placed in a hearse; then the admiral, silent and ashen-faced, got into the car waiting to carry him to Pennsylvania Station.

Once Admiral Leahy had departed, the rest of the passengers began streaming down the gangway; they had on their best clothing, the men in suits and ties with overcoats draped over their elbows, many of the women wearing white gloves, nearly everyone, including the children, in hats. Most of the children clutched dolls or stuffed animals. The pier was now alive with a hubbub of languages, of shouts and cries and tearful embraces, as port officials and workers from the Travelers Aid Society helped to translate instructions and locate suitcases and direct passengers to the correct entry points while Red Cross volunteers hurried about offering cups of milk to the children. Several of the more important-looking men were immediately surrounded by reporters with little notepads; diplomats discussed the morale of the people in the occupied territories; refugee workers warned of the worsening famine in Greece and the fate of the French naval fleet in unoccupied France.

Etta knew little about any of that ("What could I have told them," she would ask in a newspaper article the following year, "after being shut away from the world for so long?"), and she was surprised to be approached by a reporter from the *Daily News,* who wanted to know about the Nazi military tribunal that had sentenced her. "I shall never forget the judge's eyes," she told him. "They were blue and as hard and cold as frozen steel. I shall never forget the cruel, calculating voice of the prosecutor as he demanded the death penalty. I was stunned, yet not afraid. I thought, 'Well, I hope they get it over with quickly. I've lived 63 years already. I guess that's enough.'" The reporter couldn't help but note that despite her ordeal she told the story well and easily, while steadfastly denying her own importance in it. Her voice was cultured, the vowels long and perfectly formed and without any trace of a New York accent, the diction old-fashioned, in the style of Mrs. Roosevelt.

On the pier Etta was met by her nephew John Kahn, who drove her to the hotel in which she would spend the night. The next day she was scheduled to board a train from Grand Central Terminal bound for Syracuse, where she was to stay with her brother and his wife while she recuperated. Before leaving the city she would unexpectedly find a photo of herself on the front page of the *Daily News*, looking happy but exhausted, waving at the camera in the lobby of her hotel with a large American flag in the background.

Among those who saw the newspaper story was a Hungarian émigré named Aladar Farkas, who had arrived in New York one year earlier under the auspices of the Emergency Rescue Committee, an organization working to relocate journalists trapped in occupied Europe. Farkas hoped to use Etta's wartime experiences as the basis for a novel; however, Farkas's agent, Paul Winkler, decided that the book would be more successful as a memoir, and that it should be put together by the literary syndicate he had founded, Press Alliance, Inc. After several months of interviews with Etta, the result was a manuscript that would be published under the title *Paris-Underground*.

Credited to "Etta Shiber, in collaboration with Anne and Paul Dupre" (Paul and Anne Dupre were the pen names of Paul Winkler and his wife, Betty), the book would bring Etta a kind of fame that she could never have imagined possible for someone as resolutely ordinary as herself. Published by the prestigious New York house Charles Scribner's Sons, *Paris-Underground* would sell more than half a million copies, remaining on the *New York Times* bestseller list for eighteen weeks. The book was a main selection of the Book-of-the-Month Club and appeared in condensed form in *Reader's Digest;* an illustrated newspaper strip based on it was serialized in papers around the country. Its publication was met with universally rapturous reviews, including one on the front page of *The New York Times Book Review* that called the book "poignant," "remarkable," and "moving and wonderful." A half-hour radio drama adapted from *Paris-Underground* was presented on the NBC program *Words at War,* with Etta herself appearing at the end of the show to address listeners directly. The film option was sold for $100,000, equivalent to more than $1.5 million in today's currency—as much as had ever been paid for a nonfiction book. The movie, released under the same title, would appear two years later; perhaps not surprisingly, the screenwriters added a love interest and a good deal of Parisian glamour. Reviewing the film in *The Nation,* James Agee noted that it provided "enough handsome young men, in various postures of gallant gratitude, to satisfy Mae West in her prime."

Etta Shiber, in a publicity
photo for the 1943 book
Paris-Underground

As it turns out, though, the film was not the only version of *Paris-Underground* that took liberty with the historical facts; so did the book itself. Other than Etta Shiber, all of the book's central characters were given pseudonyms, and an author's note explained that a few details had been recast or omitted, so that the German authorities could not make use of the book against anyone described in it. Still, *Paris-Underground* was presented unambiguously as a work of nonfiction: The first sentence of the author's note reads, "The basic facts in this book are a matter of record." The renowned author and educator Dorothy Canfield Fisher, a member of the committee that selected *Paris-Underground* for the Book-of-the-Month Club, observed: "It is not only literally, factually true, it sounds true. The author just sets down what happened, with a singularly honest absence of any effort to dramatize the facts or to make herself out a heroine."

This was the accepted account of *Paris-Underground* for the better part of a century. It is not, however, the actual account as it is to be found in French, British, and American archives; in contemporaneous newspaper reportage; and perhaps most revealingly, in Etta Shiber's own letters to her brother and sister-in-law back home in the months leading up to and immediately following the German occupation of Paris. While the work that Kate Bonnefous and Etta Shiber did in support of the Allied war effort was very real, unquestionably heroic, and transformative for both of them, the full picture turns out to be more complex than the one presented by Shiber's ghostwriters: Several of the book's most important scenes never happened in the way they were depicted, and these changes, it seems clear, were made not for security reasons but for narrative ones. Certain other distortions are the result of omission, silences that come to haunt the story. Bonnefous and Shiber, for instance, conducted their operations in Paris while it was under Nazi occupation, amid rising anti-Semitic attacks and governmental decrees designed to isolate Jews and remove them from all aspects of civic life—and yet, remarkably enough, *Paris-Underground* withholds the fact that Etta Shiber herself was Jewish.

The most important omission, however, was unavoidable. *Paris-Underground* was published in September 1943, nearly two years before the end of the Second World War. In publishing the book when she did, at a time when the war's outcome was still far from certain, Etta Shiber hoped that it would help raise American morale and solidify public support for the war effort; in this worthy goal it manifestly succeeded. At the time of the book's publication, however, Etta did not know—and indeed never did fully discover—what had become of Kitty: That story remained to be told.

PART ONE

Paris Is a Dead Planet

C'est la nuit qu'il est beau de croire à la lumière.

[It is at night that it is beautiful to believe in the light.]

—EDMOND ROSTAND, as inscribed on the wall
of cell number 144 in Fresnes prison, 1941

1

FOR SO LONG ETTA SHIBER had lived the most circumscribed of lives: Until the age of fifty-nine she had lived in four apartments, none of them outside a radius of sixteen streets and three avenues on the Upper East Side of New York. She had married William Noyes Shiber, manager of the telegraph department for William Randolph Hearst's New York newspapers, in 1901, when she was twenty-three; she stopped teaching kindergarten three years later and didn't hold a paying job ever again. She had never learned to drive, had never registered to vote, had never appeared in the pages of a newspaper. Most days she cooked and kept house, did her marketing among the bakeries and fruit stands and German butcher shops around the neighborhood; almost nightly she accompanied her cousin Irving Weil, one of New York's most prominent music critics, to the symphony or the opera, or otherwise stayed home to knit and listen to the radio, or perhaps read a novel by Dickens or Tolstoy or Dostoyevsky. "For almost thirty-five years," a reporter would later write, in some wonderment, "this quiet pattern comprised Mrs. Shiber's daily existence."

Hers was an exceedingly comfortable, predictable routine, one almost medicinal in its regularity—for it was that very predictability, Etta found, that best held at bay her true constant companion: the nervousness that had afflicted her since she was a girl. Most of the time the feeling was like the low, persistent call of a fire alarm in the distance; it was always there, but she did what she could to ignore it and focus on whatever was in front of her. On other days, though, the bad ones, the alarm was close and loud in her ears, as if the fire were right outside her door, and she could feel herself growing hot and her heart quickened and sometimes, more worrisomely, it pounded out an irregular rhythm, and there was nothing she could do to concentrate on anything else and she had to lie down. By the time she was in her middle years Etta was suffering from hypertension, a condition that the doctors of the time still found maddeningly difficult to treat; she knew she should lose some weight, but she found that hard to do, which only increased her anxiety.

Etta had been prone to anxiety for as long as she could remember, had always been very shy, self-conscious about her appearance, and almost reflexively self-effacing; she recoiled at the notion of ever calling attention to herself. "One thing I have learned," she once observed, "is not to be a fussmaker." Early on she seems to have decided that the best path lay in being unfailingly polite and always following the rules—at Grammar School No. 1 she won medals not only for scholarship but also for "deportment"—and while she was a kind and sympathetic listener and was liked by everyone, she still found it painfully difficult to socialize with people she did not know well. At the Normal College of the City of New York,* where like many smart young women of her time she studied to become a teacher, she did not belong to a single club or fraternity (as they were called, even though all of the students were female); she did not read Shakespeare and Swift with the Phoebean Literary Society, did not observe robins and warblers and wrens in Central Park with the Bird Club, nor sing with the Glee Club, nor help organize the annual "pink tea," in which pink chrysanthemums were strewn over the top of each brewing pot—which actually contained hot cocoa, as tea was considered too mature a drink for college girls.

In the photograph of the graduating class of 1901, which shows several rows of young women in white shirtwaists and black velvet

---

* Today it is Hunter College, part of the City University of New York.

neck ribbons, their long hair swirled into pompadours in the "Gib-
son Girl" style of the time, Etta stands at the edge, ever so slightly
apart from the rest of the group, like an island just off the mainland;
in the *Normal College Echo* for 1901, the sole reference to her is the
description provided by the yearbook staff: "Rather inclined to be
good."

The Normal College of the City of New York graduating class of 1901.
Twenty-three-year-old Etta Shiber, wearing a long neck ribbon,
is at the extreme right of the photograph, standing
in the fourth row from the bottom.

In the yearbook, as in the college's grading books, she is identified
as "Henrietta" Kahn, a name that seems to have been a kind of way
station on the path to Americanization; four years later, in 1905, she
gave her name to census officials as Etta, and that is how she would
be known for the rest of her life. Her parents had named her Jennett,
after her father's late mother Jeanette Lowe Kahn, in accordance
with the Jewish tradition of naming children for deceased ancestors.
The Kahns were immigrants from the Alsatian town of Eguisheim,
where a Jewish community can be traced as far back as the early
eighteenth century. Etta's grandfather Benoit Kahn had arrived in
New York in 1845, among the small percentage of Alsatian Jews who
emigrated to a foreign country after they were granted the right of

mobility; likely he sensed an opportunity in the United States, for he had been trained as an optician in Alsace and when he opened B. Kahn & Co. on lower Broadway in 1850, he was only the second optician in the city.

Benoit and Jeanette had two daughters and five sons, three of whom went into the family business, but only one of whom, the eldest, worked not as an optician but instead as a "traveling agent"— that was Jacob Kahn, Etta's father. Etta's mother, Julia Roth, was herself the descendant of German Jewish immigrants, and though she had been born in New York she grew up speaking German as her first language. She gave birth to Etta on January 20, 1878, nine months to the day after her marriage to Jacob; three years later the couple had a son, Chester Arthur Kahn, born just six weeks after Chester A. Arthur, another New Yorker from the East Side, became president.

Jacob died while Etta was still in school, leaving the family in straitened circumstances, and for many years afterward, Julia Roth Kahn took in boarders to help pay the rent. The Kahns lived on the top floor of a four-story walk-up apartment house on Lexington Avenue at Fifty-fourth Street, above a funeral parlor and a French restaurant. The avenue was lined with buildings like that, four or five stories of stone or brick, simply corniced at the top, housing little shops or restaurants beneath cheerful awnings on the ground floor. Here and there, on more substantial corner lots, institutional buildings looked as if they had been dropped in from Europe: dark, austere churches from Germany and Sweden, synagogues in the Moorish style, a safe-deposit bank with the crenellated towers of a medieval castle, Second Empire rounded mansard roofs adorning the Hospital for the Ruptured and Crippled. From the street came the constant whir and clop of horse carriages and the occasional clang of a trolley car; every few minutes the Third Avenue elevated train rumbled in the distance like thunder. Just up the avenue was the Normal College of the City of New York, a tuition-free institution that provided most of the female teachers for the public schools of the city. Bookish and unmarried, without a father and with a younger brother still at home, and living only two trolley stops away, it was natural that Etta would attend the Normal College, and she applied and was accepted to enter in 1898.

Etta was still enrolled when she met and married William Noyes Shiber, who was living seven doors south of her on the very same block of Lexington Avenue. Born in Pennsylvania, Shiber had grown up in the small town of Olean in western New York, where his father made barrels for Standard Oil; as a young man he came to New York City and found a job as a Western Union operator before getting hired in the telegraph room of William Randolph Hearst's New York newspapers, the *Evening Journal* and the *American*. By 1896, at the age of twenty-four, he had already become the manager of the telegraph room—an exceedingly responsible position for someone so young, as telegrams were the chief means by which the paper's employees communicated with far-flung correspondents, not to mention with Hearst himself, who was generally three thousand miles away in California but who took a regular interest in the workings of all his newspapers and magazines. William Shiber was highly esteemed in the trade for his ability to oversee an efficient telegraphic service, but he was also understood to be honest and politically independent and he was trusted by labor and management alike. "Shiber is one grand fellow," *The Commercial Telegraphers' Journal* once noted. "That's why everybody on the *Journal* from W. R. Hearst on down is stuck on him."

For Etta Kahn, born and raised in an immigrant neighborhood in Manhattan, Bill Shiber must have seemed something like America itself: large and athletic, gregarious, outdoorsy (he was an avid rower and an enthusiastic nature photographer), and with a charmingly small-town demeanor. He was also not Jewish; unconventionally for the time, Etta had married outside the faith. She had been raised in a family with little in the way of religious strictures (her brother Chester's wife, Helen, was Catholic), and though Etta herself believed in God, she didn't observe Jewish holidays nor keep kosher, and their wedding had been held not in a synagogue, nor for that matter in a church, but at the Society for Ethical Culture, which ran the progressive private school where Etta was then receiving her postgraduate training. No less a figure than Felix Adler himself had performed the ceremony.

Born in Germany in 1851, Felix Adler had immigrated to New York with his family at the age of six. He was the son of a rabbi, and was himself expected to enter the rabbinate, but in his twenties he chose a different path, founding the Society for Ethical Culture. It was an unusual sort of religious movement, one that dispensed with prayer and most ritual—and left the question of a supernatural force open to individual belief—and instead sought to cultivate a universal morality that drew from a wide range of philosophical sources and promoted the cause of social justice. The society quickly developed a strong following in New York, especially among the city's Jewish population, many of whom had fled religious oppression and who understood from their own experience how religion could be used to foment hate and division, and now wanted to shed traditions that they saw as antiquated and inadequate to the demands of the modern world.

In 1878 the society established the first free kindergarten in the United States, and two years later the school expanded to include all of the elementary grades. It was called the Workingman's School (later the name would be changed to the Ethical Culture School), and its foundational principle, that the children of the poor deserved a high-quality free education, was revolutionary. This was where Etta Shiber, in 1901, undertook her postgraduate work to become a kindergarten teacher. As a teacher in training, she would have been in the audience when Adler delivered his famous lectures to the faculty of the school. He told them that the school's primary aim was not some vague notion of "character building," but rather the development of a particular *kind* of character: "The ideal of the school is not the adaptation of the individual to the existing social environment," he declared. "It is to develop persons who will be competent to change their environment to greater conformity with moral ideals; that is, to put it boldly, to train reformers." Etta trained with the school for only a single year, but she remained ever devoted to its ideals, and despite her constitutional aversion to joining societies, she served for eight years as the secretary and treasurer of the Alumnae Association of the Ethical Culture School: good work, and done for its own reward, as Felix Adler had always advised.

Though William Shiber was twenty-eight when they married and had a well-paying job, the couple did not move into a place of their own; instead, he simply relocated half a block uptown, moving in with Etta and her mother. They lived there for the next quarter century, with a shifting constellation of relatives, among them Etta's cousin Irving Weil,* who was six months younger than Etta and with whom she was so close that she thought of him as another brother. After graduating from the City College of New York, Irving had continued his studies at the Sorbonne in Paris; back in New York, he wrote about classical music for a variety of publications, and in 1910 he was named the chief music critic of the *New York Evening Journal.*

He was slender and pale and had the intent, scrutinizing aspect of a bank teller counting out bills, with pince-nez spectacles that magnified his eyes, a thin mustache, and wispy hair parted in the center that had turned gray by the time he was forty. A diffident, slightly stooped, entirely unprepossessing figure, he was the sort of man who could easily get lost in a crowd—unless that crowd happened to be inside one of New York's concert halls and opera houses, where he was well known and deeply respected among the artists and impresarios for his discernment, his intelligence, and the breadth of his knowledge. As much as William Shiber exemplified cheerful small-town America, Irving seemed to inhabit an older European world in New York City, a world of music teachers and opera coaches calling themselves Madame and Maestro, of elderly men with indeterminate accents arguing on park benches over Stokowski and Toscanini, of exiled Russian quartets and dramatic sopranos who advertised their services in the back pages of *Musical America.* Irving was, in the genteel phrase of the time, a "confirmed bachelor," and so it was Etta who usually accompanied him to performances; she was thrilled to enter this captivating world with her cousin as her guide, able to lose herself for an evening in the beauty and power and melancholy of the music, Irving beside her with the grave absorption of a spiritualist as he closed his eyes and concentrated on the vibrations of a violin string in the air.

---

* Irving's mother, Isabella Kahn Weil, was the sister of Etta's father, Jacob Kahn.

It wasn't until 1930 that Etta and Bill finally moved out, relocating with Irving to an apartment house just a few blocks away on East Fifty-second Street. By then Etta had given up kindergarten instruction. After receiving her teaching license and professional certificate she had been hired at Public School 147 on the Lower East Side, but overseeing a large class of excitable five-year-olds wasn't an ideal fit for someone of such a nervous temperament: Etta's teaching license expired after three years, and she didn't seek to renew it.

For most of the next decade Etta volunteered with the Ethical Culture School, but eventually that too fell away and by the time she was in her midthirties she had confined herself to an even narrower routine, centered mainly on domestic tasks; in later years a journalist would call her life "unusually sheltered," and Etta, too, once referred to herself as "just a sheltered housewife, looking forward to a quiet old age." Most evenings she had dinner with Bill and Irving, generally something simple that she had prepared, before she and Irving set out for Carnegie Hall or the Metropolitan Opera House; or on more special occasions, perhaps bouillabaisse at Prunier's or chicken Divan at Divan Parisien, the three of them in a banquette having a glass of wine and a cigarette as Bill laughingly shared the latest instructions from "the Chief" to purchase the entire library of some English manor house, from the ceiling beams right down to the fireplace, for his new castle at San Simeon, or as Irving discoursed on the influence of Buxtehude on Bach's chorales or why the English horn was neither English nor a horn. Etta saw her brother and his wife whenever they came into town from upstate, but generally when she socialized it was with Bill's friends from work, and she also enjoyed meeting other music devotees through Irving before a performance or during intermission. She was almost entirely dependent on the two of them for her companionship; she did, though, have one close friendship that she had made on her own—with Kitty.

The two had first met in 1926, in the shop that Kate Bonnefous had recently opened on rue Rodier, a picturesque little street in the ninth arrondissement. "A deep sympathy developed between us immediately," Etta would later write. "I sensed a natural liking for me entirely unconnected with the desire of the shopkeeper to please a customer, and I reciprocated it." After that the women spent time together whenever Etta came to Paris on vacation. Unlike Etta, with her sharply delimited life experience, Kitty had lived in England, Italy, and France, and was running a business of her own. "I admired her as a woman of the world," Etta said, "as well as a person of kind and sympathetic character." Kitty was always eager to hear all of Etta's news, yet Etta detected in her friend a certain reserve, a reticence—British, perhaps—about sharing much in the way of personal information. She told Etta about her son, Len, who had been born in Rome in 1911, but she spoke little about the circumstances of his birth, nor about her own family back in England. There was time in her past that seemed unaccounted for, certain gaps that only slowly got filled in. She had, for instance, introduced herself to Etta in the shop as "Mrs. Robins," her maiden name and the one she used for business, and it was some years before Etta even knew that Kitty's husband was French.

In 1932 Etta, Bill, and Irving moved again, to a modern two-bedroom, two-bath apartment with beamed ceilings and wrap-around corner windows on East Sixty-eighth Street near Second Avenue. Irving had always been frail, but by this time he was in genuinely poor health, weakened by a condition that doctors diagnosed as lesions on his heart. In June 1933 he and Etta sailed from New York on the ocean liner *Lafayette,* bound for France; their destination was Aix-les-Bains, a picturesque spa town that during the summer season received some forty thousand foreign visitors, among whom it was jocularly known as Aches and Pains. Etta had booked rooms for them at the Hôtel Splendide-Royal, an alabaster palace overlooking the Lac du Bourget at the foot of the Alps. Wealthy patrons, often in ill health, came to the Splendide-Royal to "take the waters," following a supervised regimen of diet and moderate exercise along with a variety of thermal treatments from hot springs rich in sulfur and calcium.

The stay at the Splendide-Royal, though, seems to have done little to ameliorate Irving's cardiac conditions, and by the end of June he and Etta had relocated to Paris, to the Hôtel Bristol on the rue du Faubourg Saint-Honoré. Sometime that summer he developed pneumonia; Kate arranged for the best medical care for him, but as the summer wore on his condition worsened, and on August 26, 1933, Irving passed away at the age of fifty-five. His death was reported in all the New York newspapers, and widely mourned among the city's music community. "It was a privilege and a stimulus to enjoy Irving Weil's friendship," observed Robert Simon in *The New Yorker*, "and those of us who had that privilege learned much not only about music and its people but about any subject which might have interested a wise, entertaining, and kindly gentleman."

Ever competent, Kate oversaw all of Irving's funeral arrangements (he was cremated and his ashes buried in Père Lachaise, Paris's best-known cemetery) and took a room for herself at the Hôtel Bristol so that she could care for her grieving friend until William arrived to take Etta back home. He reached Paris on September 7, having booked the first Atlantic passage he could, and he made sure that their return trip, on the SS *Paris*, was in a first-class cabin.

Not long after their return to New York, shockingly, Bill too started to experience shortness of breath; then came worrisome chest pains that upon examination the doctors attributed to myocarditis, an inflammation of the heart. Eventually his kidneys began to fail, and the next two years felt to Etta like a long, ghastly smash-up, one collision leading inexorably to the next. There would be no more vacations for them in the Adirondacks or the White Mountains, no more cruises to Bermuda or France; eventually Bill had to stop going to work, unable to make the daily commute downtown to the Hearst offices on Catherine Slip, as he had for as long as she had known him. His world grew progressively smaller, until it had been reduced to the size of their apartment. Sometime after midnight on April 24, 1936, Bill suddenly collapsed. Though the Shibers lived only a block from New York Hospital, by the time the medics arrived it was too late. The time of death was recorded as one A.M. He was sixty-three years old.

They had been together for thirty-five years, and his absence felt like an amputation. At first, half-crazed with grief, Etta imagined that she could still hear Bill's laughter filling the apartment; worse was when the sound faded, to be replaced only by silence. The apartment in which she had once been so comfortable now felt oversized,

as if she were wearing one of Bill's old overcoats, constantly enveloped by its weight. There were papers to sign, phone numbers to locate, meetings with attorneys, bankers, insurance agents; overnight
she had transformed from wife to widow and executrix. She wandered through it all in a kind of haze, long hours punctuated only by
a newly lit cigarette; her interest in the things she had cared about
before—books, music, food, the news of the day, even talk itself—
withered from lack of nourishment. She was grateful for the sympathy offered by friends and relatives, but she heard it only dimly, as
though from the end of a long hallway; she was entering what she
would later call "a year of loneliness."

She had, of course, wired Kate the terrible news. Kate was much
too far away to provide the kind of firsthand attention she had given
to Etta in the days after Irving's death, and her own life was going
through something of an upheaval: Four years earlier she had closed
her dress shop to become the director of the American Business
College, a school near the Champs-Élysées. Now, at the age of fifty-
three, she had left that position and was working as a freelance editor
and translator. What was more, she and her husband, Henri, had
separated after twelve years of marriage; they had decided that he would
keep their apartment in the ninth arrondissement, and she would
move to a new one in the seventeenth, on rue Balny-d'Avricourt, not
far from the Arc de Triomphe. It was a large apartment, with two
bedrooms; early in 1937 Kitty wrote to Etta suggesting that she
come live with her in Paris.

In the weeks that followed Etta slowly began to function again,
animated now by a single idea. She sold off or gave away whatever
she could, books, furniture, cooking equipment. Like her ancestors,
she was reducing her life to what she could carry aboard a transatlantic ship. She left Bill's heavy photo albums with an old friend of his;
later in France she would regret leaving them behind, but as she told
her sister-in-law, "I was so crazy at the time that I nearly left myself
behind."

On the morning of April 24, 1937, at the pier on West Forty-
eighth Street, Etta boarded the *Ile de France,* bound for Le Havre; it
was one year to the day after the death of her husband.

2

KATE BONNEFOUS'S APARTMENT AT 2 rue Balny-d'Avricourt
was on the top floor of a six-story building made of massive
blocks of cream-colored limestone with a steeply sloped roof and
filigree wrought-iron balconies as intricate as lace; the front door,
too, was garnished with flowering vines exquisitely rendered in iron.
Upstairs, the apartment had parquet floors and decorative plaster
moldings and expansive windows that let in the morning sun; a small
antique mirror hung in the front hallway, an ideal spot to adjust a hat
or check one's lipstick before going out. In the center of the apartment, a large drawing room held cases with books in several languages, many of them the British adventure stories that Kate liked;
it also had a long leather-covered divan, a few comfortable armchairs,
a coffee table with a dial telephone (a recent innovation, still rare in
the country outside Paris), and a heavy wooden desk at which she
wrote letters and did her work. Scattered around the apartment were
several engraved silver and enamel boxes that held the cigarettes she
always smoked—Player's Navy Cut, made in Nottingham. She was,
as the old phrase had it, English to the tips of her fingers.

By nature Kate Bonnefous was a whirlwind, but a whirlwind that
left a neater, cleaner, better-organized world in its wake. When she
wasn't working she seemed always to be preserving quinces or mak-

ing chocolate fudge, or cooking waffles (a remarkable food that she had discovered on holiday in the States; she loved them so much that she had brought a waffle iron back with her), or tracking down just the right man in Paris to fix a broken fountain pen or turn an old sealskin stole into a winter hat. She was always bustling through rooms to straighten up just a bit, while whistling or humming some tune to herself, throwing open windows when the weather was warm, declaring to anyone within earshot that she felt positively claustrophobic when the windows were closed. Her natural manner was direct, the sort of practical, no-nonsense attitude that tends to inspire confidence in those of waning energy or wavering conviction. She had never attended university, but she was fluent in three languages and had run a school that offered classes in seven. She claimed to be widowed, but she was not; she claimed not to be divorced, but she was. At a time when women rarely drove a car, much less owned one, she did both—and drove an ambulance as well. In private she was charming and sociable, a generous hostess; in public she spoke quietly but firmly, with the fine manners and plummy tones she had been taught in a finishing school on the coast of Kent, where the English Channel empties into the sea.

The name on her birth certificate was simply Kate Robins, although her friends called her Kitty, and to her family she was always Kay. She stood five foot six, which was tall for a woman of the time, and she was slender, with wavy chestnut-brown hair now tinged with gray, cut at her ears and curled slightly at the ends in the modern style. She had a long oval face with a straight nose and a firm set to her mouth, and heavy-lidded, penetrating brown eyes. Her French was nearly impeccable, but she spoke the language with a noticeable English accent. She dressed simply but stylishly, her outfit often set off by a single strand of pearls; sometimes when the weather was cool she wore tweeds, which, with her even temperament and dignified bearing, gave her something of the appearance of a country squire's wife.

In fact she had been born into a prosperous English family, though it was one of newfound rather than ancestral wealth: Her father, Charles Henry Robins, a printer and stationer, was himself the son of a printer. He was a man of the age, however, hard-driving and well connected, a member of one of London's oldest Freemason lodges; eventually Charles became a partner in the successful printing and lithography company of Palmer, Sutton and Robins, and by the time his first child, Kate, was born on August 5, 1886, in the London suburb of Brentford, he was able to list his profession on the birth certificate as "Gentleman." Charles had not married until he was forty-four years old, literally to the girl next door, twenty-nine-year-old Emily Harper, the daughter of a music professor and his wife. The couple would have two more daughters as well as a son, and in the course of Kate's childhood the Robins family would occupy three houses in the vicinity of London, each one progressively grander, until finally they were living in a large house with a name—Hawthorn Bank—that stood behind a high stone wall on a quiet street lined with ancient trees and newly installed electric streetlamps, with three servants (a cook, a housemaid, and a nursemaid) on hand to attend to the family's needs.

At the age of fourteen Kate was sent away to a boarding school called Thanet Hall, in Margate at England's southeastern tip, which advertised itself as a "home school for young ladies" having the "finest sea air in England." She was one of thirty-six girls in the school, ranging in age from seven through seventeen, with proper English names like Winifred and Constance and Violet and Nellie; they wore high-necked lace dresses with button boots and their long hair carefully plaited atop their heads, and they lived under the direct supervision of a headmistress and one French and one German governess in a rambling brick villa that was said to assure its young residents "thorough ventilation and the absolute exclusion of draughts." It was the close of the Victorian era (the queen had passed away that very year), but for girls of Kate's social class a school such as Thanet Hall still existed primarily to instill the virtues as well as the practical skills of domesticity; the teaching of advanced mathematics or physics or classical literature was considered to be wasted on the female mind, washed away like sand through a sieve with not enough gold left behind, and the curriculum centered instead on subjects such as needlework, drawing, English composition, music, basic math and science, religious (by which was meant Christian) thought, and of course etiquette, with a sprinkling of the romance languages that would prove useful during summer tours of the Continent.

An undated photograph of the
young Kate Robins

Sadly, her mother, Emily, died while Kate was still attending Thanet Hall, of an unspecified illness, when she was only forty-eight years old; Charles died two years later, in 1904, thus orphaning the four Robins children at the ages of seventeen, thirteen, ten, and eight. None of her parents' siblings, however, were willing to care for Kate's younger brother and sisters, and at seventeen she had to arrange for them to be taken in by friends of her father who lived in Kent, not far from her school; the experience would embitter her toward her extended family for the rest of her life.

Charles Henry Robins left an estate worth £51,105—well over $8 million today—with trusts in place for all of his children. Her father's money allowed Kate to live an independent life once she came of age; like the vast majority of Englishwomen of the time, she didn't attend university, nor did she go into a settled profession, and in the collective memory of subsequent generations of the family she does not reemerge until 1911, when she suddenly appears in Rome, having given birth to a son, Leonardo. The boy's father was an Italian named Antonio Sales, who was, as the story goes, the man Kate married before she subsequently married Henri Bonnefous in Paris. As it turns out, however, Antonio Sales was not her first husband, nor even her second; he was not her husband at all.

In the life of Kate Bonnefous, one single period exists in which she attempted to live according to conventional dictates, to conform to the sort of life that had been expected of her as the daughter of a member of the rising English business class, who had grown up in solidly Conservative districts and attended an expensive finishing school on the southern seacoast. The attempt did not go well.

In March 1908, twenty-one years old and still living in Kent, Kate Robins married a man named James O'Brien Tufton Walsh, who lived in Oxford, about a hundred miles away. He was exactly the sort of husband who might have been anticipated for her: four years older than his bride, part of a prominent local family of long standing, a graduate of the prestigious Charterhouse public school, a solicitor who was himself the son of a solicitor, whose mother was the daughter of the local vicar. Though his father, Percival, maintained an extensive legal practice, James himself seems not to have been especially distinguished in the field; even after Walsh's death in 1947, a local judge could only bring himself to observe, "While it would be an insincerity—which he would be the first to decry—to say he was a great lawyer, a deep knowledge of the law is not an essential to being a good advocate, and James Walsh was a good advocate."

What James Walsh did have was a large and powerful family, who eased the way for him at every turn. His father was the very definition of the well-connected man, and likely it was through his intercession that the newly married James Walsh, despite a conspicuous lack of professional achievements, managed to secure a consular post with the British embassy in Rome. He and Kate lived there on via della Rotonda, a cobblestone street of ancient stone houses washed in sunny oranges and yellows and pinks; it was next to the Pantheon, and not far from the neighborhood known colloquially as the English ghetto, the center of British life in the city. Though only a few thousand British officials and expatriates were then living in Rome, an extensive society had been established to cater to them, comfortable and entirely insular: One could be cared for by English doctors and dentists, have prescriptions filled by an English chemist, save one's money in English banks and spend it in English specialty stores, pray at the All Saints' Anglican church (and be buried in the English cemetery), take high tea at Babington's Tea Room, and, for the women in the community, have one's hair done at the Ladies' Toilet Co., all of it without ever having to speak a word of Italian. It was one of the peculiar privileges of empire: the privilege of insensitivity, the right to live at home even when in a foreign country.

How Kate Robins Walsh navigated her new role as a young embassy wife is unclear, but her home life couldn't have been a very pleasant one, for within two years, in 1911, James Walsh was back in Oxford, where he moved in with one of his brothers; his wife, however, was still living in Rome. It's not difficult to see what instigated the break, though, because Kate, now twenty-four years old, had become pregnant by another man.

The neighborhood around via della Rotonda retained a medieval flavor, the narrow, winding streets lined with artisans' shops selling handmade baskets, hats, pots and pans; one of these, a shoe shop, was owned by a tall, dapper forty-four-year-old widower named Antonio Sales, the son of a family of wealthy spice merchants from Naples. The Italian birth certificate for Leonardo Antonio Federico Sales, born at home with a midwife on July 21, 1911, states that Antonio Sales was the father, "from his natural union with a woman to whom he is not married, nor a relative or with any such ties as would block the recognition of the birth." The mother's name was given as "Caterina Robins"—not Walsh.

One can only imagine the indignant, not to say condemnatory, reaction among the close-knit English community in Rome to the news that the newly arrived young woman had separated from a British consular official to have a child out of wedlock (a bastard son, as per the English parish registers of the time) with an Italian shopkeeper nearly twice her age. Nevertheless Kate stayed in Rome, maintaining her relationship with Antonio Sales, though they kept their own residences a few blocks from each other; in the years that followed she raised her young son and seems to have fully immersed herself in the local life, as within a few years, unlike so many of her countrypeople, she had become fluent in Italian.

Kate Robins in Rome in 1912, with
her infant son, Leonardo Sales

Antonio Sales died in March 1919 of the Spanish flu that was then cascading through Europe. He left behind a young son and a grieving woman, a widow in all but name; there was now no reason for Kate to remain in Rome, and she did not. She loved England, and would always consider herself English, but she didn't return there: Perhaps that country was still too redolent of the deaths of her parents, the unkindness of her aunts and uncles, a failed marriage to a man who wasn't the father of her child. It was one of the things of which Kate never spoke, even to those closest to her; all her life she

maintained a strong sense of personal discretion, believing that certain things were best for only her to know.*

Instead Kate went with her son to Paris, where she rented an
apartment at 29 rue Rodier, a narrow five-story whitewashed stone
building with wooden shutters. Two years later she filed for divorce
from James O'Brien Tufton Walsh, and it was granted without opposition. (Divorce was rare in England at the time, and still carried a
heavy social stigma; 2,588 divorces were obtained for the whole of
England in 1922—compared to well over one hundred thousand per
year today—and only about a third of those were initiated by the
wife.) Sometime after that Kate met Roger-Henri Bonnefous, who
lived near her in the ninth arrondissement and whom she married at
the local *mairie* in 1925; afterward, she would change her surname to
Bonnefous and become a naturalized French citizen.

Henri, as he was known, was a year older than Kate, a successful
wine merchant with a specialty in the wines of Bordeaux; he was
short—at five foot three he was three inches shorter than his wife—
and had straight black hair parted on the side, blue eyes behind round
steel-framed glasses, and a thick mustache, and he often wore a
double-breasted suit on his stocky frame. According to Etta, Henri
was "a fascinating companion, a good talker, who seemed to know a
little about everything, and who always managed to learn what was
going on within a few minutes of arriving anywhere." He must also
have been an unusually broad-minded man, or at least one who was
willing to brook popular disapproval, because for his first marriage
he had chosen to wed a divorced thirty-nine-year-old mother of a
teenaged son, who was, moreover, a foreigner and not a Catholic and
who harbored a desire to run a shop of her own.

The idea of a woman earning her own livelihood was then highly
suspect in France, especially among the more privileged classes, for
whom the income was not strictly necessary and for whom, as Eugen
Weber noted in *The Hollow Years,* his history of France in the 1930s,

---

* Etta Shiber, for instance, would later say that Kate had married young (which
was correct) and had a son with her husband before he died (which was not); Kate's
son, Len, would say that his father was Antonio Sales (which was correct), who was
her mother's first husband (which was not).

"it was ill considered to have a wife who worked—at least, who worked for money. Among the upper classes, volunteer work was perfectly all right; income-producing labor was for the men alone." The French republic had been born of long and bloody struggle, and its citizens prided themselves on the country's guarantee of social rights for all, but in regard to women's rights, France was lagging behind many of the other industrialized Western democracies. Not only were Frenchwomen still denied the vote (they did not gain full suffrage until 1944), but a married woman in France could not maintain a bank account in her own name, nor control property without her husband's permission. So Henri Bonnefous must have been unusual in this regard as well: He must also have been supportive of Kate's insistence on financial independence. At the time of their marriage in 1925, Kate was listed as *"sans profession,"* but within the year, the Paris census identified her as the sole proprietor—not co-proprietor—of a clothing shop.

An undated photograph showing Kate Bonnefous behind the wheel of a car. Her husband, Henri Bonnefous, is sitting on the running board to the right, with an unidentified figure, likely a relative, beside him.

Kate kept the shop open for only a few years, though, because in 1932 she accepted the position of director of the American Business

College, a vocational school that offered day and evening classes in typing, accountancy, and shorthand, taught by French, English, Spanish, German, Italian, Russian, and Norwegian instructors. Given her energy, organizational skills, and facility for languages, she was well suited to the position, and in her four years as director she oversaw the relocation of the school to larger quarters in the New York Herald Tribune building, a modern nine-story "skyscraper" on rue de Berri. As she reached the age of fifty, though, she found herself ready to make some changes. First she left the school to work at home as a part-time translator and editor, and then the following year she moved to an apartment of her own on rue Balny-d'Avricourt.

After twelve years of marriage, it was a most amicable separation: Kate had decided that she simply preferred for them to lead separate lives (much as she had with Antonio Sales), and in this Henri seemed perfectly willing to oblige her. They maintained a strong friendship— the two never divorced, Kate never shed her married name, and she never stopped wearing her wedding ring—and they often spent time together when Henri was in town, clearly still charmed by each other's company. Three years after moving to rue Balny-d'Avricourt, Etta was struck by how close Kitty and Henri were: "They seemed deeply in love with one another, although they had been separated for years. Ever since I had lived with Kitty, she had always talked of him most affectionately—yet much of the time she didn't even know his address. His business as a wine merchant required him to do a good deal of traveling, and sometimes months passed without his turning up, or even writing a letter. But whenever he did come to town, the day was a holiday for both of them."

Kate Bonnefous's apartment house was in the quartier Monceau, the more elegant residential section of the seventeenth arrondissement. From the building's top floor, Etta's window looked out over the horizon of Paris, a landscape of domes and turrets and terra-cotta chimney pots atop silvery roofs that reflected the shifting patterns of the sky, the light changing from pink to buttery gold and back again as the day went on, thinning and strengthening with the passage of the seasons, as in one of Monet's studies.

Often Etta and Kate did their marketing in the mornings, bringing their large market bags, sometimes just to one of the nearby *boulangeries* for bread and a *laiterie* for milk for Kate's coffee, and sometimes to the covered market on rue Bayen, a vast warren of food stalls such as Etta had never seen, clusters of dried sausages hanging overhead like tropical fruit, terrines shimmering with aspic, wooden barrels full of dried lentils and split peas and fava beans, pyramids constructed of tins of *jambon* Olida and tuna packed in oil, wheels of Gruyère as large as automobile tires, cylinders of Cantal that smelled of fresh cream and straw and sometimes bore traces of the mold that the French referred to admiringly as *fleur de bleu:* There was nothing better melted onto boiled potatoes, with sliced apples on the side. Sometimes Kate sliced apples to make fritters for breakfast, or made waffles or buckwheat cakes on the electric griddle, and as Etta sat at the dining-room table with her breakfast and black coffee, talking with Kate about their plans for the day, New York seemed a distant memory. In a letter to her sister-in-law, Helen (written in the large, flowery script she had been taught in Grammar School No. 1, with a stylographic pen as always, in the same dark blue ink on light blue paper), Etta observed that she was feeling "very much happier"—but then, worried that she might be sounding selfish, hastened to add, "I say I am happier, well, that only means I am less unhappy. What I really am is contented and not actively grieving and that is at least something to be grateful for."

When Etta moved in, Kate owned a small black cocker spaniel named Nanette; later they acquired two matching puppies, whom they named Winkie and Micky. Kate and Etta walked the dogs on a leash that split into three at the end, most often in the nearby Parc Monceau; when the weather was good they bundled the dogs into the car and drove to the Bois de Boulogne, a vast wooded park of lawns and lagoons and sun-dappled bridle paths, which in earlier times had been a hunting ground for royalty. Everywhere Paris seemed a kind of palimpsest, one text written atop the traces of another. So much of the city had once been something else: The Louvre had been a palace, the Panthéon a church, Cherche-Midi prison a convent. They strolled by mansions where Chopin had composed his études and Molière his plays, drank coffee at a table where Trotsky had played chess; they ate onion soup at the Café de la Paix on the place de l'Opéra, where Maupassant had drunk his absinthe in the evenings after work. Often Etta visited Irving's grave site, nestled amid the greenery of Père Lachaise; nearby was the sarcophagus of the doomed medieval lovers Abelard and Héloise, lying side by side forever. Over time, it seemed, every surface in Paris had acquired depth, complexity; walls bulged and cracked from the weight of centuries, marble steps were bowed at the center, the stone eroded by endless waves of footsteps. Modern high heels clicked like castanets on ancient cobblestones. In their section of the seventeenth arrondissement, which had been incorporated late into Paris and retained a certain village flavor, wandering bands of street musicians with accordions and drums played for coins, like the ones she had read of in Chaucer. Paris sometimes seemed to Etta a kind of history museum, or a stage set, too gorgeous to be real.

3

ON THE FIRST DAY of September 1939, Germany invaded Poland and the Second World War began. The previous one, of course, was well within living memory: A baby born on the final day of World War I would have been prime draft age, twenty years old, on the first day of World War II. Nowhere were the losses of that earlier war still felt more acutely than in France.

Beginning in August 1914, French soldiers had been killed at the rate of about one thousand per day over the course of the entire fifty-one months of the war, a percentage of the population higher than that of any other Western nation. More than half of the soldiers who survived the war had been wounded, and about one in four was permanently disabled, living now in wheelchairs, on crutches, in hospital wards, victims of what the poet Blaise Cendrars, who had himself lost his right arm in combat, called "all the anonymous, demonic, and blind machinery of war"; an association was established in France specifically to care for the many soldiers who had been left with disfiguring facial injuries—these men were known as *les gueules cassées,* or "the broken mugs." Nearly one and a half million Frenchmen had died in the war; most of them were young, and they left behind them a generation of babies who would never be conceived. Between 1900 and 1939, France's population grew by only 3 percent, almost entirely

as the result of immigration; during that same period, the population of Germany grew by 36 percent, Italy 33 percent, and England
23 percent. France now had the oldest population in Europe, as well
as the greatest numerical disparity between men and women—more
than 130 women for every 100 men. Every city and town in France
had a memorial bearing the names of its own war dead; in each place,
there were women who had not yet taken off the veils and black
dresses worn in memory of a lost husband or son or father. As France
entered the Second World War, it did so as a country still in mourning.

The general mobilization began in France on the day after the
German invasion, even before war had been officially declared. Young
men once again reported to their local induction centers to receive
their orders; railroad stations were crowded with soldiers off to join
their units, most of them headed to the north and east of the country,
to be positioned along the Maginot Line. Constructed throughout
the 1930s, and spanning France's eastern border, from Italy up
through Switzerland, Germany, and Luxembourg to the southeastern corner of Belgium, the Maginot Line comprised a series of concrete fortresses, reinforced by observation towers, machine-gun posts,
troop bunkers, and tunnels, and among the French public the faith in
its impregnability was nearly absolute. All through the fall and winter the armies of France and Germany faced each other on opposite
sides of the line, embedded in what seemed a perpetual stalemate.
For months on end French soldiers dug trenches for communica-
tions lines, stretched barbed wire, camouflaged artillery, greased their
guns and fed their horses, waiting for something to happen. Recalled
Jean Dutourd, a writer then serving in the infantry: "The gunners
settled down in the Maginot Line like apartment-house janitors,
trailing about the corridors in their slippers, playing innumerable
games of cards under the silent guns, yawning from morning to
night." This was the period that came to be known as the *drôle de
guerre,* or "phony war."

Though Paris was hundreds of miles from the front, the city was
still vulnerable to attack from the air, and a blackout was instituted
for nine o'clock each evening. Like the rest of their neighbors, Kate
and Etta draped heavy blackout curtains over their windows each

night; during air raid alerts, when the sirens began to wail, they tramped down to the building's cellar with the other tenants (the dogs had to stay behind, as no pets were allowed in shelters) to await the three-part tone of the all-clear.

Kate was, in Etta's description, "incapable of inaction," and at the start of the war she began volunteering for the *défense passive;* she was one of the female defense wardens who drove around Paris at all hours of the day and night, outfitted in rubber suit and gloves and a steel helmet, long-snouted gas mask at the ready, with a machine beside her that monitored for the presence of gas in the event of attack. She worked a grueling schedule: She was on day duty (seven A.M. to seven P.M.) twice one week and three times the next, and night duty (seven P.M. to seven A.M.) also twice one week and three times the next. Because of the blackout, the streets of Paris were very dark at night and the traffic was light, and some drivers took advantage of that to speed recklessly. One rainy night in early October, a car suddenly came bearing down at her; it skidded on the wet pavement, slammed into her front end, turned over twice, and landed right side up again. Remarkably, the man was able to drive away under his own power, while Kate had to take a taxi home and leave her car there to be towed to a garage the next morning. The repairs ended up costing 7,000 francs—when she had purchased the car three years earlier for only 23,000. The other driver, Kate believed, had lost his head when he saw her and stepped on the accelerator instead of the brake; fortunately, she had kept hers, or they both would have been killed.

By December, Kate had begun volunteering at the American Hospital of Paris, which was located in the suburb of Neuilly, not far from their apartment. It was a private hospital, founded in 1926 to provide medical care for Americans living in Paris and traveling in Europe, but at the outset of the war its board of governors agreed to convert it for use as a military hospital. Sandbags were piled around the building, windows striped with paper to prevent shattering in the event of an explosion; temporary barracks were constructed in the hospital's gardens; windows were painted blue, in accordance with blackout orders, and blue lightbulbs were installed throughout the building. A huge gasoline storage tank was placed deep underground, to make sure that fuel would be available for the hospital's ambulances even in the event of an air attack. The hospital had ten full-time ambulance drivers on staff, but it was in the process of raising money to establish the American Hospital Ambulance and Transport Service, which would be staffed entirely by female drivers. Kate served at the hospital three days a week, seeing to whatever tasks needed to be done. There was never a shortage of work— helping the nurses on their rounds, performing clerical duties in the purchasing and supply departments, stocking the English-language library with French books in anticipation of French wounded—but still she hoped that eventually she would be enlisted to serve as one of the drivers.

Kate's son, who was now twenty-nine years old, had joined the French navy and was on submarine duty, stationed at a base near Cherbourg. She fretted about Len constantly ("Mothers, it seems, are the same the world over," Etta noted wryly in a letter), and she visited him whenever she could, often bringing warm clothing; every week she put together a package to mail to him containing anything she thought he might want: chocolate, magazines, and especially pipe tobacco, which was now too expensive for him to afford. The tobacco shops had begun a "cigarette for the front" campaign, urging customers to donate one cigarette from each purchase; their counters had wooden collection boxes on them with signs that read DONNEZ UNE CIGARETTE! C'EST POUR CEUX DU FRONT! Dozens of groups in the city were now engaged in charitable work on behalf of the war effort. One organization sent letters and packages to soldiers who had no families; another sent books and journals to mobilized students; a Catholic organization sent chaplains and officers clothing that had been knitted by religious congregations. In railroad stations the *dames de charité,* wearing their distinctive blue capes, poured hot wine into the canteen cups of soldiers waiting to join their units. The Société des poètes français provided an emergency fund for mobilized poets; the Fédération française de football sent soccer balls to soldiers on the front; the Oeuvre du théâtre du soldat organized free theatrical performances for soldiers quartered in Paris. An organization that sent packages to wounded aviators was called Les ailes brisées, or "The Broken Wings."

On weekends, when Kate wasn't working at the hospital, she and

Etta volunteered for the Foyer du Soldat, bringing food and clothing to soldiers on short leave near the front; they drove in Kate's car (paying for the gas themselves, not an insubstantial expense) to the group's social centers along the eastern front, in Sainte-Menehould, Nancy, Metz, wherever they were directed to go. The roads in France were often rutted and pocked with potholes, and even the car's comfort tires and modern shock absorbers could not prevent the constant buffeting and jarring; when they got out of the car, their joints were invariably achy and their muscles stiff with tension, as if they had been riding a bucking bronco. One Sunday morning they set out for Metz at 7:45 and didn't return home until 8:45 that night, having stopped only for lunch in Verdun and then for tea on the way back; Etta later calculated that, accounting for breaks, Kate had driven for ten hours that day. Etta sat beside her plotting out the routes with the blue-and-orange Michelin maps unfolded on her lap: red lines for the *routes nationales,* yellow for the secondary roads, black for byways. She was seeing a France she hadn't known before, older-seeming even than Paris, a country of snow-capped stone walls bordering neat fields of winter wheat, of mossy stone farmhouses, rows of pollarded willows with their strange tufts of branches like shaving brushes, sawmills and silos and horse-drawn carts, thatch-roofed cottages delicately perched alongside rivers like water birds: a harsh but beautiful landscape, and one that seemed wholly unaffected by the passage of time or the workings of armies.

While Kate was working at the hospital, Etta did her part at home by crocheting woolen mufflers for soldiers on the front. The work was pleasant enough, but she found that she couldn't put in more than a few hours at a time because too much of it made her edgy. The onset of the war had Etta feeling nervous in a way she hadn't been since New York. Like much of the rest of France, she placed her faith in the Maginot Line, and believed that the French and British armies would prove victorious, as in the Great War; still, she couldn't help but worry and she was always eager for encouraging news. Her French was improving but still spotty, and fortunately the radio on her bedroom nightstand received both medium- and short-wave broadcasts from England. Often she tuned in to as many as five news programs a day, including the Overseas report from London on short wave and London Home Service on medium wave; there were news bulletins at 11:30 A.M. and 9:00 P.M., and she had found an English-language broadcast on a local French station that she listened to every night in bed at 9:45. Then she turned off the radio and read the Paris editions of the English-language newspapers, the *Herald Tribune* and the *Daily Mail,* for a while before going to sleep, with one of the dogs curled up next to her for warmth.

It was an exceptionally cold winter throughout much of Europe, and in Paris there was little snowfall to relieve the gloom. All day long the sky cast only a dull gray light, the sun rarely emerging from behind its veil of clouds; from Etta's window, the roofs of the city looked like a dark, roiled sea. Sometimes when Kate was at work and she was alone in the apartment, Etta read the tarot cards, as a friend had once taught her how to do. She was a little embarrassed about doing it, not generally going in for that sort of thing, but she found even the slightest prospect of advance knowledge nonetheless comforting. Her interpretations were not sophisticated, she understood; still, she knew what the arrangements of the cards meant, the future they were supposed to foretell. "Sometimes it's good, other times not," she wrote in a letter to her brother. "But almost always there is the loss of a friend."

After the cold, dreary winter, the spring of 1940 was especially glorious in Paris, imbued with a golden light that made the city almost preposterously beautiful. Each day, it seemed, morning showers gave way to warm sunshine that dried the moisture on the grass and released its scent into the air; all of central Paris seemed a public flower show, daffodils and hyacinths and a rainbow of tulips blooming in the Luxembourg Gardens, an explosion of geraniums behind Notre-Dame and in front of the Louvre. Women wore dresses in floral shades, lavender, jasmine, dusty rose, cut into the slim silhouettes with padded shoulders that were the fashion that season. Zinc roofs shone in the sun as though newly polished. In the Bois de Boulogne, swans glided on the lake beneath the feathery green of the cypress trees and the delicate white pyramids of the horse chestnuts. The *terrasses* in front of the cafés were as crowded as ever, the briskly efficient aproned waiters with heavily laden silver trays still performing their ballet around the little marble-topped tables, the air filled with the smell of Gauloises and coffee and women's perfume. People lined up to hear Maurice Chevalier sing at the Opéra and Josephine Baker at the Casino de Paris. The walls of the city were plastered with advertisements for a new movie musical called *Chantons quand même...* [*Let's Sing Anyway . . .*], about a soldier who falls in love with a beautiful young innkeeper while stationed near the front. In May the swifts returned from North Africa, as they always did, joining clusters of sparrows and swallows and martins on roofs and in the trees; at night they chirped and trilled like chanteuses in the open air.

Yet there was something disquieting about the extraordinary beauty of Paris in the spring of 1940, as with an ill person made radiant by fever. Everywhere were signs of danger, the air seeming to hold the invisible tension of a tightening coil. The picturesque sunsets over the Seine were punctuated by the strange sight—at once comforting and unsettling—of thousands of huge balloons being raised into the sky, trailing behind them not strings but heavy cables, forming a curtain around the city meant to ensnarl the propellers of low-flying planes carrying bombs or canisters of poison gas. Ornate streetlamps, shaded for the nightly blackout, emitted only the faintest coronas of light; the dark blue discs that glowed like sapphires in the darkened streets were the painted headlights of cars. In the thin glow of lamplight, the buildings appeared desolate and lonely; the night sky silhouetted the domes and turrets of the apartment houses, darkness etched by a greater darkness. The city's residents had been issued gas masks in long cylindrical containers with straps, which were to be carried at all times; in quintessentially Parisian style, boutiques offered gas mask boxes in leather or satin, and in various colored fabrics to coordinate with a woman's outfit. Métro stations and apartment house cellars were converted into air raid shelters; sandbags were piled around the city's monuments and important buildings, and an antiaircraft gun positioned atop the Arc de Triomphe.

The *drôle de guerre* was finally shattered on May 10, when the German army launched an invasion of the Low Countries of Belgium,

Luxembourg, and the Netherlands, a carefully coordinated attack of massed Panzer tank units supported by Stuka dive-bombers. Three days later they invaded France, shocking the French high command, who had staked their careers, and more significantly the security of their country, on the Maginot Line. In fact, the Germans skirted the line entirely by attacking to the west of it, through the hilly, densely wooded Ardennes forest (French military leaders had not believed such an attack was possible) into northern France, in so doing slicing the French army in half. Suddenly the reliance on a great wall, built at a cost of billions of francs, seemed emblematic of an elderly military command that had not kept up with the advances in modern technological warfare (in the fifth decade of the twentieth century, the French army was still spending four times as much on horse feed as on gasoline) and had committed itself to a stationary, defensive posture that seemed, in hindsight, far more suited to the previous war than the current one.[*]

This portion of the war—May and June 1940—would become known in France simply, and expressively, as *la débâcle.* In a matter of weeks the German army was marching through French towns in which it had never set foot during the entirety of World War I. Refugees brought reports of endless gray columns of Wehrmacht soldiers, lines of trucks and tanks and armored cars that stretched past the horizon; the lines looked to be converging on Paris. Like dreams that render anxieties in fantastic forms, wild rumors began to appear, seemingly from out of nowhere. German paratroopers, it was whispered, had landed in Paris disguised as priests and nuns—in one version of the story, they had come as an entire ballet troupe. Only four days after the German attack, word had already gotten around that paratroopers had landed, or perhaps were just about to land, right on the Champs-Élysées, and that morning clusters of people could be seen all along the avenue, gazing worriedly up at the skies.

---

[*] Not everyone in the French army believed this to be the correct approach. A group of younger military officers advocated instead an offensive-minded strategy that emphasized speed and mobility and relied extensively on the use of massed tank units; chief among them was a young colonel by the name of Charles de Gaulle.

The next day, *Le Figaro* felt obliged to run the story: PARIS HAS NOT BEEN VISITED BY PARACHUTISTS.

On the morning of June 11, 1940, the residents of Paris awoke coughing, shocked to see their faces and hands smeared with soot, walls and furniture discolored overnight. The air was filled with a strange greasy smoke, flecked with tiny black particles that settled everywhere and, as in some Grimm tale, refused to come off when wiped. The smoke was so thick, reported Quentin Reynolds of *Collier's* magazine, "you could reach out and grab a piece of it in your hand," so thick that for hours it blotted out the sun, giving the world the muted, blurry look of an underdeveloped photograph.

Like many others in the city, Reynolds believed that the smoke had been released by French civil-defense teams to hide the railroad stations from German planes; conversely, according to another theory, the smoke had been laid down by German planes to hide an imminent infantry attack. The real answer, when it emerged, turned out to be equally bleak: French troops had been ordered to set fire to the oil depots on the outskirts of Paris to keep them out of the hands of the German army, now within twenty miles and advancing quickly.

By that point the French forces were everywhere in disarray; there were still pockets of scattered resistance, but almost all of the army was either dead, dispersed, or captured. France had fallen much as Hemingway once described a man going bankrupt: gradually, and then suddenly. Officials of the Foreign Ministry were seen burning papers on the Quai d'Orsay, not a sight to instill confidence in the stability of the government. Dozens of hurriedly arranged trains rolled south out of the capital, evacuating more than forty thousand women, children, and elderly people; among them were fourteen trains filled entirely with government records. Next came word that the government itself had fled to Tours, southwest of the city; in a matter of days it would relocate again, farther south to Bordeaux.* On June 13, the French government declared Paris an "open city"— the city would not be defended against enemy invasion, so as to pre-

---

* Before long the government had moved once more, to the spa town of Vichy, the place-name that would become synonymous with collaboration.

vent it from being destroyed in battle. That was the day Parisians could hear, for the first time, the low throb of distant cannon fire.

In Paris, as they waited anxiously for the Germans to arrive, people began to notice a terrible silence: The smoke from the oil depots, full of thousands of tons of burning naphtha, had killed the birds in the trees; it would be the first June without birdsong.

4

By June 1940, Kate Bonnefous had been working for several months as one of the American Hospital's female ambulance drivers. Though the French Red Cross had set strict preconditions for their *conductrices*—no one older than forty-eight, and married women could serve only with the consent of their husbands—there were no such requirements for the American Hospital of Paris, and Kate, who was fifty-three and separated from her husband, joined the Ambulance and Transport Service, donning the khaki uniform of the unit; of the twenty-six drivers, she was the second oldest.

According to the hospital's own publication, *Ambulance and Transport Service: The American Hospital of Paris in the Second World War*, "The work of the women ambulance drivers was varied, fatiguing, and often dangerous. . . . They drove repeatedly to the refugee hospital at Châteauroux and the base hospitals at Étretat and Angoulême. They aided in the evacuation of civilians and soldiers, and later carried supplies to prison camps. Frequently, their missions took them through regions under bombardment, and at times they were obliged to drive without lights at night along roads crowded with refugees." The work was almost never-ending, and it seemed only to intensify: The ambulance service as a whole traversed 1,670 miles in January 1940; by May that number was 10,327.

On May 11, the day after the German attack on the Low Countries, Kate received word from the American Hospital that she should have a suitcase packed and be ready to leave at a moment's notice for the Belgian border. Ultimately the hospital dispatched six other drivers to help evacuate Brussels, providing first aid and transporting residents to the safety of the countryside; in the meantime, Kate and the other *conductrices* had been working around the clock to carry Belgian refugees from Paris's Gare du Nord railroad station to reception centers that had been set up around the city.

The refugee trains arrived almost hourly, pulling into the station always off schedule and with little notice. The passengers emerged from the cars dazed with hunger and fatigue and terror, having just passed through a kind of haunted landscape: woods aflame, bombed trains flung from tracks like children's toys, the blackened shells of burned-out cars lying by the roadside. Some had held themselves together for the length of the trip, and then collapsed or burst into sobs upon stepping down to the platform. Inside the vast skylit shed of the terminal, Red Cross nurses in white bustled about, distributing baguettes and cups of hot wine; French Boy Scouts lugged baggage, much of which consisted of bedding and household items tied up in sheets or tablecloths. (One man and his son had brought with them only their gas masks, a tennis racket in its wooden press, and a violin.) The station evoked the constant noiseless hubbub of a silent movie. A *New York Herald Tribune* reporter noted: "Occasionally a tiny baby cries, or a woman starts to weep, but for the most part they are silent, as if the life had been drained out of their tired bodies."

With their tattered clothing and their bundled belongings and their tales of German military might, the refugees from the north seemed both relics of the past and emissaries of a terrifying future. Kate and Etta had seen newsreel footage of the disaster that had been inflicted on helpless civilian populations in Guernica, Madrid, Warsaw; had sat in darkened movie houses watching with horror the soundless scenes of burning buildings, collapsed houses, crews of workmen shoveling out bodies. The danger was steadily nearing: German planes were now bombing towns in the north of France in which Kate and Etta had earlier delivered packages to soldiers. Kate returned home each day looking pale and worn; her face was drawn, her shoulders not as straight as usual, her step not as brisk. That month, for the first time, she broached with Etta the possibility of her returning to the United States.

It would not have been difficult for Etta to do. Her passport was up to date, she had sufficient money in her account at the Paris branch of the Central Hanover Bank,* and there was opportunity to depart. The Special Division, a newly established office within the U.S. State Department, had been tasked with repatriating all American citizens who wished to leave Europe; it did so with remarkable speed and efficiency, commissioning six transport ships and arranging for additional voyages to be made by commercial transatlantic steamers. At the beginning of the war, in September 1939, some hundred thousand Americans were living in Europe; by the spring of the following year more than eighty thousand had been returned to the United States. In May 1940, with France now engaged in active combat, the American ambassador to France, William Bullitt, informed the remaining Americans that they could return home on the SS *Washington*, which would be departing from Bordeaux on June 4.

Etta understood that Kitty was protecting her, as she had always protected her, was still trying to care for her as she had cared for her in the Hôtel Bristol after Irving died. Kitty had taken her in after the deaths of her cousin and her husband, had thrown a line to the shipwrecked woman and pulled her to safety; Etta couldn't imagine abandoning her now—and in any case, what would she do if she returned to New York? Nothing was left for her there. Her life was in Paris, with Kitty and the dogs; she would stay despite the danger, much as an owner might hold on to a beloved home though it exists on a flood plain. Etta was well aware of the gentleness of her own appearance, but she also understood that there was a determination—she thought of it as a stubbornness—at her core. She was deeply loyal to those who were loyal to her; for all of her

---

* The U.S. government expected nongovernmental civilians in Europe to cover the cost of their repatriation to the United States. A special flat-rate fee had been negotiated with the shipping lines, which, as one historian of the repatriation voyages has noted, "proved rather contentious because the standard of accommodation on the ships, as in peacetime, varied considerably by class."

anxiety, she was resolute in that. Perhaps it *was* the anxiety that caused her to dig in her heels, to remain steadfast rather than disrupt the life she had painstakingly created for herself. And Kitty had no one else on whom she could depend, other than her brother, Leonard, in London—which these days, what with all the regulations imposed on foreign travel, might as well be across the Andes as the English Channel. Also, Len had been placed on active service aboard a French submarine and was now at sea for weeks at a time. "I only hope that nothing happens to that boy," Etta wrote to her brother, Chester. "I dread to think what it would do to his mother. You will very easily understand that just now I could not possibly think of leaving Kitty. . . . That would be too cruel."

By that time most of the thirty thousand or so Americans living in Paris had already left or were preparing to go; those who had decided to stay for the duration—no more than a few thousand—exchanged addresses, updated wills, transferred funds to more secure locations. Between May and June, the city had been slowly but noticeably emptying out, especially in wealthier arrondissements such as the seventeenth. Each day, it seemed, more houses were locked up tight, another shop closed without warning. There had been a run on the banks; in the month of June, the banks of Paris returned to their depositors more than 1.2 billion francs. The vast gold reserves of the Bank of France had been shipped overseas to French colonies such as Senegal and Martinique. For three days thousands of desperate Parisians had besieged the Gare d'Austerlitz, hoping to find seats aboard a southbound train; finally the station had been gated shut and gendarmes called out to disperse the crowd. The city's schools had closed on June 8, to provide an opportunity for children to evacuate to safer locations. Long convoys of buses, their windows covered and with policemen stationed on their rear platforms, had transported the prisoners of Cherche-Midi and La Santé to jails in the countryside. Newspapers had either stopped publishing or were doing so in sharply reduced form. The newspaper with the largest daily circulation in all of Europe, *Paris-Soir,* had been cut from four to two pages, and then ceased publication entirely on June 11; the paper's editor in chief, twenty-six-year-old Albert Camus, drove out of Paris with the manuscript of his first novel, *L'étranger*, in the trunk of his car.

Each day was stranger than the one before. Paris existed in a state of confusion and neglect, uncollected garbage piling up in the street, normally bustling avenues now empty. "There never has been anything like the eerie atmosphere in Paris during the two days between the departure of the French government and the arrival of the German troops," recalled Robert Murphy of the American embassy. On June 12, a herd of cows was seen wandering on the place de l'Alma, at the bottom of avenue George V. "The creatures were hungry and their bellowings echoed sadly in the deserted quays," wrote one Swiss journalist. "Occasional passersby scarcely bothered to turn and look at this astonishing sight." It was at that moment that the journalist decided it was time to leave Paris.

Early the next morning, June 13, Kate Bonnefous sat at her desk phoning friends to ask for the latest news. With each call, though, she got only a dull buzzing on the other end, the sound of a phone ringing in an empty room. All of their friends had fled Paris, she told Etta finally; it seemed they were the only ones left.

At nine o'clock Etta called the American embassy; an official there gave her the shocking news that Paris had been designated an open city and would not be defended. The official urged Etta to leave, and now the women agreed it was time to go. In a flash they had opened closet doors and armoire drawers, pulling out clothes and tossing them into the trunk; together they packed a few assorted bags with food, bank notes, medications, and other necessities. Kate thought they might be of use in Châteauroux, where the American Hospital of Paris had constructed one of its field hospitals; she had been dispatched there for a week in April and knew a hotel where they might stay. The women carried their bags into the elevator; then they gathered up Nanette, Winkie, and Micky and took a last look around the apartment before closing the door and locking it. The steel elevator door swung shut behind them, and with a press of the button the elevator slowly rumbled down to the lobby. Kate's car was parked right outside.

The car was a beauty: a black Peugeot 402. With its long, elegant chassis, the 402 had been marketed as the epitome of affordable luxury; the interior was a confection of Art Deco styling, the dashboard trimmed with chrome and displaying an array of switches and knobs in brown Bakelite, the front seat couch-like in tufted maroon velvet. In keeping with Peugeot's leonine emblem, there was a snarling lion's-head hood ornament, a lion's-head mascot on the front grille, and stylized silver lions' manes that adorned the rear fender skirts. Thanks to its independent front wheels and hydraulic shock absorbers, the 402 was touted as being especially comfortable to drive, and Peugeot targeted some of its advertising at female drivers like Kate Bonnefous, including one full-page magazine ad that featured a woman at the wheel, her hair swept back by the breeze: "Drive for hours without effort or worry," the ad copy urged, declaring that the 402 was "the car that knows how to be forgotten!"

A 1937 magazine advertisement for the Peugeot
402, "the car that knows how to be forgotten!"

Unusual for its time, the Peugeot 402 had twin windshield wipers powered by their own motor (the double windshields could be pushed open slightly to provide a cooling breeze), twin sun visors, recessed door handles, and semaphore indicators that clicked out from the side of the car like tiny red flags to signal a turn. The 402 also had one especially unusual feature: The luggage compartment did not open at the back of the car, where a spare tire was stored, but rather from beneath the back row of seats. It was a small, covered, inconspicuous space, nearly invisible from the outside.

On the southern outskirts of the city they turned onto the N20 national road. A line of refugees was already stretched out as far as the eye could see; some came from Paris, while others were rural families fleeing from the north, employing every manner of conveyance imaginable, from cars and bicycles to tractors and carts and rickety farm wagons pulled by horses and mules and oxen. It was as though three centuries of French history had merged into a single tragic caravan. The wagons were piled high with furniture and bedding, pots and pans dangling from their sides; many of the cars had mattresses tied to their roofs. Parents and children trudged wearily along the roadside, some pushing elderly relatives in baby carriages or wheelbarrows. Some carried the most unlikely of items, which apparently they could not bear to leave behind: washbasins, salad bowls, birdcages. Bands of ragged, unshaven soldiers marched alongside the civilians, their presence a bitter and humbling reminder of national defeat.

The sky was a crystalline blue, the sun reflecting mercilessly off the dark asphalt. The day was already very hot, but many of the women along the side of the road, unable to carry all they wanted in suitcases, were wearing what looked to be their entire wardrobe: layers of coats over additional layers of blouses and skirts, their bulky silhouettes like that of the Michelin man. In the stifling heat the road was clogged with stalled, steaming cars, which further impeded progress and provoked a cacophony of useless horns and shouting; it was preferable to focus on a recalcitrant horse or broken-down car than on the imminent fall of France. The line moved forward a few feet at a time, then stopped; then another few feet, or a few hundred, and then more waiting, over and over. Kate had to keep letting the clutch in and out, changing gears constantly—the best way to wreck an engine, but there was nothing to be done about that.

Etta sat with the map unfolded on her lap, staring at the same baffling village names inside the same creased rectangle: Longjumeau, Saulx-les-Chartreux, Montlhéry. Châteauroux was 170 miles south of Paris; normally they could be there by midafternoon, but now there was no telling when they would arrive. She was comforted to recall the great gas efficiency of the Peugeot 402, as trumpeted in all the advertisements. Now and again they smoked cigarettes, leaving the ends in the little pull-out ashtray on the dashboard. At long stops they took the opportunity to walk the dogs among the poplars that lined the roadside, squinting against the sun's glare at the vast slow-moving river that extended to the horizon in both directions.

Sometimes drivers turned off the highway onto unfamiliar back roads, in search of a less obstructed course, and then sometimes, frustrated, rejoined the main route; everywhere, though, the tide flowed in only one direction, as if the enormous plate of France had been tipped up at its northern edge. One of the refugees would later describe it as "a Dantesque vision of a people in exile." For most of the travelers there was no knowing what the final destination was, other than a place safer than the one they had left; urban or rural, they shared a single animating belief, that nothing they might encounter on the road could be as difficult or as menacing as what awaited them back home. Aviator and author Antoine de Saint-Exupéry, whose flights over the North African desert would inspire his book *The Little Prince,* was then performing military reconnaissance missions above France; looking down on the line of refugees from far overhead, he observed that it was as if "a great boot had smashed into an anthill in the north, and the ants were on the move." At least six million and perhaps as many as ten million people were then on the road, nearly a quarter of the entire population of the country; it was, to date, the largest migration in recorded history. In France, those days in June would come to be known simply as *l'exode*—the exodus.

The road was increasingly strewn with discarded items: empty bottles, punctured car tires, broken suitcases, pieces of clothing no longer wanted. Slowly the interminable column moved forward; it could take an hour to reach any point on the horizon. At this rate,

they were clearly not going to reach Châteauroux by nightfall. Orléans was much closer, and that fabled city, where Joan of Arc once led
an army, became their new destination.

Among those on the road to Orléans that day was a Jewish couple
in flight from Paris, hoping to board a ship at Bordeaux that would
take them to the United States. Their names were Hans and Margret
Rey, and they were riding bicycles that Hans had managed to con-
struct the night before from parts he found in their local bicycle
shop. Just before setting out that morning, Margret had thrown into
her satchel the drawings for a new children's book on which the two
were then at work, about a monkey named Fifi. Later, after they had
arrived in New York, the monkey was given a new name, and the
book would be published as *Curious George*.

Eventually the sun began to set; the western sky bruised red, then
purple. When darkness fell the women had been on the road for
more than twelve hours. The moon was almost full and it shone in
the cloudless sky, silvering the fields that they passed. It was very late
by the time they reached Orléans, and the narrow streets along the
Loire river were choked with traffic. In every hotel they entered, exhausted travelers lay stretched out on the floor, resting their heads on
suitcases, and the women had to step carefully over them to reach the
front desks. The clerks were apologetic but firm: There was no available room, at any price. Outside, people were sprawled on benches in
the brasseries, in chairs on sidewalks, on mattresses they had untied
from the roofs of their cars. The Paris-based *New Yorker* writer A. J.
Liebling also came through Orléans on his flight from Paris, and he
would later report that he could not find a room anywhere in the
town; he even called at some of the local bordellos, thinking of the
abundance of beds there, but those establishments too were crowded
with earlier arrivals. "They are so tired," one of the madams told him
sympathetically, "that some of them are actually sleeping."

Liebling ended up spending the night in his Citroën; Kate and
Etta also slept that night in the car, dozing fitfully in their seats, the
dogs curled up in their laps.

· · · · · · · · · · · · · · · ·

The next day, terrible news was passed among those on the road: The German army had entered Paris. Etta said later that she received the news like a slap in the face. Kate crouched over the wheel, her eyes set grimly on the road, lips clenched tight. Grief and despair had now compounded the general misery of hunger and exhaustion. Elderly women sat weeping on the roadside, unable to go any farther. It was a scene of almost unendurable suffering.

Once again the sky was crystal clear, a blue so bright it almost hurt to look at it. There would be more sun in France that June than in any June of the previous forty-seven years. Even after so many hours at the wheel Kate still handled the Peugeot expertly, navigating among the obstacles that appeared on both sides of the car. Little by little the line seemed to be thinning out. The surface of this stretch of the N20 was atrocious; going fast seemed somehow even worse than the constant stop-and-start, because the incessant bumping made one almost seasick. Their muscles ached from sitting for so long; sleeplessness gave every object a blurred quality, even in the strongest sun. It began to seem that they had always been driving. They passed rows of green wheat, stone houses with red-tiled roofs; occasionally the carcass of a horse festered on the side of the road, flies circling around it. Clusters of unarmed soldiers sat quietly smoking, no longer having anywhere to go.

At a roadside restaurant they bought a small piece of cheese with some buttered bread to share with the dogs. The proprietor was charging an inflated price for the food, and Etta argued with Kate that it was ridiculous to pay that much; Kate laughed at the notion that prices had any meaning at that moment. It was a kind of new-found alchemy: bread turned into gold. All along the exodus, some were taking the opportunity to cheat and exploit their countrymen. A few especially enterprising families had set up tables in front of their farmhouses, selling glasses of water to the parched passersby. There had been numerous reports of looting in northern towns, of soldiers who broke into empty houses and ransacked them, to eat but also just to steal; one observer called it "an atmosphere of riot." Another noted that "people carrying empty bags go into houses, people carrying full bags come out. . . . Not a single officer, not a soul tries to stop this shameful behavior." Yet Etta had also seen soldiers sharing food from their packs with children; and whenever a car broke down, she noted, a soldier always seemed on hand to help fix it. Some local officials had set up canteens on the outskirts of their towns to provide food and water to those who passed along the way; in some towns, farmers had brought provisions to refugees stranded on stuck trains; some shopkeepers, in fleeing a town, had intentionally left their doors open for those arriving later. "Base men show their baseness," Saint-Exupéry would write. "Looters reveal themselves as looters. Institutions crumble." But the reverse was true as well: Some among them demonstrated reserves of kindness and generosity even when they were hungry and exhausted and afraid. Power, it has been said, reveals character; but so, in its way, does powerlessness.

In arriving at Châteauroux, Kate and Etta had reached almost the geographical center of France. It was an old manufacturing town perched on the Indre River, the skyline dominated by a double-spired church in the Gothic style. Normally Châteauroux had about 35,000 residents; now, as a stopping place along the exodus, it was stuffed with five times that number. A local newspaper characterized the streets as "an indescribable disorder," in which "refugees fleeing the invader and soldiers having lost their regiment mingled with the population going about their business." Here, too, the hotels were already at capacity; one proprietor, though, remembered Kate from her earlier work at the hospital and made special arrangements to accommodate them.

The Châteauroux field hospital, with forty beds, had been set up in a large stone building that had previously been used as a medical clinic. On the day that Kate and Etta arrived, the hospital received even more grim news: the death in Paris of Dr. Thierry de Martel, the chief of the American Hospital's department of brain surgery. At the age of sixty-five, Martel was a witty and debonair man about town, but he was increasingly heartsick about the state of the war, and in particular the prospect of the hospital being occupied by the German army; his own son had been killed in the First World War, and he had vowed never again to speak to a German. As the Germans closed in on the city, Martel went to United States ambassador William Bullitt, the American Hospital's honorary president, to ask for permission to leave his post by evacuating from Paris. Bullitt reminded Dr. Martel that the hospital was doing invaluable work and said that men of his skills were critically needed in the operating room.

Martel asked quietly if that was a direct order. Bullitt smiled and patted him on the shoulder. "If you wish," he said, "but the friendliest one in the world."

"Very well," Martel replied. "I will stay."

The next morning, June 14, Thierry de Martel awoke in his elegant townhouse on rue Weber near the Bois de Boulogne. He shaved and dressed; then he entered his second-floor study, removed the two boxes of phenobarbital that he had prescribed for himself, and injected himself with a fatal dose. His final note was addressed to Ambassador Bullitt: "I promised you not to leave Paris. I did not say if I would remain in Paris alive or dead. To remain living in Paris would be a cashable check for our adversaries. If I remain here dead, it is a check without funds to cover it. Adieu."

Fourteen residents of Paris committed suicide that day, unwilling to see their city occupied by German troops.

On June 17, the newly installed French chief of state, Philippe Pétain, went on the radio to declare, "It is with a heavy heart that I say we must cease the fight. I have this night applied to our opponent to know the conditions on which he is prepared to agree to a cessation of hostilities." Marshal Pétain, who was known as the Lion of Verdun for his service in the First World War, was now eighty-four years old. His voice was thin and reedy, regularly punctuated by a cough; the writer Arthur Koestler described him as sounding like "a skeleton with a chill." In Châteauroux, as in towns all over France, people gathered around their radios, trying to fathom the full import of his words: Were they supposed to stop fighting now, or only when an armistice was signed? Had Great Britain also agreed to a cease-fire? Was the war already over? "We had all heard the same speech," a

British medic in France would write, "yet no one had rightly understood. It was a masterpiece of ambiguous phraseology."

The following afternoon the crowd in the town's streets heard a buzzing in the sky, as from a vast cloud of insects, which slowly grew into a hum and then the roar of plane engines. "For the refugees and soldiers," noted one newspaper, "whose long and sad exodus had familiarized them with this sound as a precursor to great misfortune, there was no doubt about what was going to happen." Over the next two days the Luftwaffe unleashed several waves of bombings on Châteauroux; by the time the bombardment had ended, sixteen people were dead and 144 buildings had been totally or partially destroyed.

Kate and Etta endured the bombings in the hotel's shelter, hurrying downstairs whenever the air raid siren sounded. The explosions registered less as noise than as concussions that filled the chest and left muscles taut and quivering, the vibrations seeming to come from every direction at once, as in an earthquake. When they emerged onto the street, the air reeked of smoke, and large buildings had been reduced to piles of rubble and charred wood. It was the terrible magic of modern warfare: a home turned to debris in an instant. Why one building was destroyed while the one next to it remained untouched seemed the product of nothing more than pure chance. A few inches of altitude, a split second in a bomb release, a slight breath of wind—that spelled the difference between life and death.

Kate and Etta assisted in the field hospital until June 22, when German troops were on the verge of entering Châteauroux, and once again they took to the road. Margot, the maid who worked for Kate, had fled Paris for her home village on the western coast of France, and they decided to head in that direction.

After a day of driving they reached Poitiers, southwest of Châteauroux. There, too, all of the hotels were full, and once more they had to sleep in their car. It was increasingly difficult to cope with the three dogs, who were hot and restless and seemed to perceive the tension in the air, constantly whimpering and squirming in the back seat. Other than one day of rain in Châteauroux, the sun had been relentless, and the air in the car was suffocating even with the windows open. As they headed west, the traffic abated a bit, and it was possible to drive in a more normal fashion. The foliage here was a deeper green, the landscape more rugged, marked by ruined castles and Roman walls and medieval stone windmills with conical turrets like witches' hats. At La Pointe de Chémoulin the road ran along a line of cliffs looking out on the Bay of Biscay: At last they had reached the edge of the continent.

Margot was staying with her family in a little village not far from there. She had begun working for Kate and Henri twelve years earlier, not long after they married; now that the two had separated, she worked for Henri in the mornings and Kate in the afternoons. She was overjoyed to see Kate and Etta and the dogs, who capered excitedly around her; she suggested that they try the nearby town of Guérande, where she had heard that rooms were available.

Sitting on a plateau above the salt marshes, Guérande was a charming Breton town of stone houses and narrow cobblestone lanes—entirely enclosed by a fifteenth-century stone wall, nearly a mile in length, constructed to defend against attacks from the north. There they found a small hotel that had two rooms available for them. In the following days, they felt themselves living in a kind of no-man's-land, not of space but of time—the brief span between French and German rule. Entirely enclosed by that high wall, the town seemed like the setting of a medieval fairy tale; almost always there was the sense of waiting for something to happen. Guérande had no local newspaper and its telephones were not functioning, which further deepened their sense of seclusion. They had little information other than the sure knowledge that the German army was coming ever closer, would continue rolling westward until it had reached the sea.

Still, they could not help but feel a sense of shock when one day they heard a rumbling like thunder, and from the distance, beyond the walls, came a long line of German motorcycle troops. Surely these soldiers had also been in battle, and yet they were clean-shaven and their uniforms were spotless, not dusty and threadbare like those of the French soldiers Kate and Etta had passed on the road; the riders looked cold, mechanical, like modern centaurs, half-man, half-machine.

After months of dread and weeks of flight, it was here: The future had finally arrived.

With the Germans now in control of nearly the whole of France, Kate and Etta decided that they might as well return to Paris. They and the dogs would be more comfortable in their own apartment, and they could better manage their expenses at home, where they wouldn't have to pay for hotel rooms and meals in restaurants. That same week, the French historian Henri Amouroux wrote in his journal: "After the flow of the exodus, France is going to know the ebb of the exodus." Slowly the tide was moving back in the opposite direction, emptied towns and cities beginning to fill again. Shockingly, the Germans had already posted directional signs on the roads, black-bordered arrows with German words and French place-names in angular German lettering. Several times Kate and Etta were stopped by German soldiers on the road, at bridge entrances and other locations that the Germans deemed sensitive, but Kate produced the *sauf-conduit* [safe-conduct pass] that had been issued to her by the American Hospital, and after a brief inspection they were allowed to go on their way. The guards did not seem especially concerned about any security risk posed by two older women and their cocker spaniels.

Back in the city, Etta was surprised to feel her spirits lifting, as they always did when she returned to Paris. The deep blue of the afternoon sky silhouetted the noble form of the Arc de Triomphe, the symbol of French military victory; coming closer, she felt her heart constrict when she saw the Nazi flag flying from it, the place de l'Étoile having been turned into a staging area for military vehicles emblazoned with swastikas.

Silently Kate and Etta took in the appalling scene. It wasn't primarily anxiety that Etta was feeling, born of the fear of an indeterminate future. Instead she realized how exhausted she was—owing to innumerable nights without proper sleep, of course, but also to the unremitting sense of helplessness and anger and frustration that she had been carrying. In the span of three weeks Etta had seen how frail a thing even a well-ordered life really was, like those seemingly sturdy houses leveled in an instant, saw how a life could be upended by decisions made by unknown men hundreds of miles away. Everyone was vulnerable, everyone could be made a refugee—even, in Etta's own description, "two middle-aged respectable women of sheltered background."

The Peugeot 402 rounded the corner and pulled up to rue Balny-d'Avricourt. There was the wrought-iron front door, entirely unchanged from before. The elevator still worked, the key still fit in the lock, and inside, everything was just as they had left it, yet nothing looked quite the same. The house they had left behind, in a free Paris: That was gone.

5

On June 17, 1940, it was announced that all the clocks of France would be moved forward by one hour: France was now running on German time, and each day began in new and unfamiliar darkness. In his journal, Henri Amouroux wrote that Paris in the summer of 1940 was "a dead planet, occupied by an army to which the eye has not yet become habituated." In countless ways the Germans were already branding the city, making it their own. Enormous swastika flags and banners and streamers were draped from French monuments and government buildings; a German marching band played each day at noon on the Champs-Élysées as detachments of soldiers goose-stepped along behind it, and free concerts were given in the Tuileries by bands representing various motorized divisions. The *bouquinistes* along the Seine reported that the books in greatest demand were French-German dictionaries and language manuals, as well as guidebooks and maps of the city—presumably to be put to use by the German newcomers. The plushest among the city's restaurants printed German-language menus to cater to the Nazi diplomats and army officers who had become the core of their clientele; the storefront ENGLISH SPOKEN HERE signs that had been widespread since the end of World War I were replaced by ones that read MAN SPRICHT DEUTSCH.

Within a week of the start of the occupation, a poster appeared around the city that showed a smiling German officer, broad-shouldered and handsome, his high-crowned military cap removed to reveal a head of perfectly coiffed blond hair, holding a delighted child in the crook of his elbow as a pair of other children gazed up jealously. POPULATIONS ABANDONNÉES, the poster read, FAITES CON-FIANCE AUX SOLDATS ALLEMANDS! [Abandoned populations, trust in the German soldiers!] The initial detachments of occupying troops seemed to have been selected for their charm and good looks (among Parisians, they would come to be known as "the chorus line"), and they strolled cheerfully through the city's streets and public gardens like conquering heroes, chatting up women and coochie-cooing babies in their carriages, ostentatiously giving up their seats to the elderly on the Métro. *Ils sont corrects,* the city's residents marveled about them over and over: "correct" not meaning right or accurate, but rather that they were behaving in a proper manner. Thus far, at least, Paris had been spared the carnage unleashed on Warsaw; in large part, of course, this was because Nazi ideology esteemed France in a way it did not Po-land, while Paris itself was viewed, from Hitler on down, as a city to be enjoyed rather than one to be destroyed.

German soldiers seemed to have been issued cameras along with their rifles and canteens, as they were constantly seen snapping pho-tographs in front of the Eiffel Tower, the Louvre, the Arc de Tri-omphe, and the city's other famous sights, like a vast throng of heavily armed tourists. (Indeed, German soldiers stationed in Paris were issued a guidebook describing the highlights of the city, includ-ing officially sanctioned restaurants, nightclubs, and bordellos.) Shortly after the fall of France, Hermann Göring himself had em-barked on a Parisian shopping spree, ordering a selection of gowns and furs for his wife from Maison Paquin, followed by a stop for jewelry at Cartier.* The German authorities had set the currency ex-

---

* The shopping trip began inauspiciously: Göring had asked the maître d' at Maxim's—the luxurious restaurant that was a favorite of Nazi brass—for recom-mendations, and the maître d' had offered to escort the Reich Marshal personally to the salon Molyneux; Göring, though, had to cancel that visit midtrip after he learned that "Molyneux" was Edward Molyneux, a British designer. The next desti-nation was no better: the salon Heim, which turned out to belong to the designer Jacques Heim, descended from Polish Jews.

change at the highly favorable rate of 20 francs to the reichsmark; flush with power and overvalued money, they indulged themselves in luxuries. Up and down rue de Rivoli and the Champs-Élysées, German officers in their trim gray uniforms and polished boots could be seen carrying daintily ribboned boxes labeled Chanel or Guerlain or Lanvin. One of the mordant jokes told in Paris that year was about the two Frenchmen who attempted to cross the border by disguising themselves as Wehrmacht officers, but were found out because they were not carrying any packages.

One year earlier, Parisians could choose among two hundred newspapers and magazines; now there were just four newspapers, in the pages of which France's enemy had switched, virtually overnight, from Germany to Great Britain. (*Paris-Soir* was now being edited by the building's former elevator operator, an Alsatian who was the only collaborationist among the paper's employees and who performed his editorial duties while wearing the uniform of a German army officer.) At least initially, the newspapers published only two pages per day, much of which consisted of reprints of Hitler's speeches and German military communiqués, as well as articles decrying English generals and Jewish bankers, and praising American isolationists such as Charles Lindbergh and Henry Ford. The second page consisted primarily of classified advertising, many of the job notices responding to the sudden demand in the city for German-speaking chauffeurs, maids, cooks, stenographers, translators, and tutors. A new subsection of the classifieds was the *Renseignements Recherchés:* postings from French people seeking information about family, friends, fellow servicemen, or important documents (with rewards offered) lost amid the chaos of the recent weeks. It was said that ninety thousand children had become separated from their parents in the course of the exodus, and each day the classifieds contained heartbreaking appeals from parents looking for their own lost children:

Please give news of Robert Prevost, 15 years old, seen Pont de Sully, 16 June, 10 am

*Request information on Marie, Elise, Annie Page, lost trace at Gien, in
the direction of Corrèze*
We are seeking Marie-José Philippe, 6 years old, lost Bourges 16 June

The trauma of the exodus—those indelible images of a frightened
people in headlong flight—only intensified the sense of shock and
horror at the unexpected military disaster that had befallen France.
The army that after five years had prevailed in the First World War
had succumbed in the second in scarcely a month; now some 90,000
French soldiers were dead, another 200,000 wounded, and 1.8 million more had been taken prisoner. (To put that number in perspective: 1.8 million represented 4 percent of the entire population of
France.) Perhaps most humiliating of all, the armistice signed between Nazi Germany and France's new Vichy government had established a "line of demarcation" through France; it extended from
Switzerland in the northeast to Spain in the southwest and was
patrolled by German and Vichy security guards at control posts established up and down the line. The configuration of the line of demarcation was, of course, highly advantageous for Germany: About
three-fifths of France—including the majority of the country's population and agricultural and industrial resources, as well as its entire
Atlantic and Channel coastlines—fell into the Occupied Zone to
the north and west of the line, and though nominally under the control of the French Vichy government, this section was overseen by a
German military administration based in Paris. Below the line of
demarcation, the Unoccupied Zone was administered by the Vichy
government.

The line of demarcation was, in the words of Henri Amouroux,
"the new border that separates France from France."

The population of Paris, normally about three million, had fallen to
some 700,000 during the exodus; by the middle of July, it had crept
back up to just over one million. Life in the city was slowly returning.
Etta's bank had evacuated to Nantes during the exodus, but she anticipated that it would be back soon; if not, she could always send her
brother a check on her New York bank account and have him wire

her francs via the American embassy. Money was not yet a problem, and in any case Kate and Etta didn't have many expenses beyond rent and food. The two of them went shopping in the mornings, Kate to the large market, Etta to the little shops for bread and fruit, and cake on the days it was sold. A system of food rationing had been instituted in Paris (a substantial portion of the most desirable resources was being siphoned off to feed an occupying army), and the city's *pâtisseries* and *chocolatiers* were now closed four days a week, along with the butcher shops. Fresh fruit, though, was still plentiful and very good, especially the raspberries, and peaches and melons were beginning to arrive in the markets, and apples were abundant if Kate wanted to make fritters. Lots of vegetables were available as well, and lettuce for salads. Milk was about the only item in short supply—that didn't matter much to Etta, as she took her coffee black, but Kate would not drink hers without milk and sometimes she stood in line for up to an hour to get a quart.

Kate's son had sent word that he had managed to avoid capture and was now staying in London with her brother, Leonard; that was an enormous relief, except when she read in the newspapers of bomb strikes being readied against England. In the evenings now, Kate would sit in the drawing room with the French papers; English-language newspapers were no longer permitted in the city, and most of the time Etta contented herself with a book or turned on the radio to listen to a classical music concert or news of the war. In that regard, the French radio stations were now little better than the French newspapers—so much of the reporting was out-and-out German propaganda—but it was still possible to get the BBC; Etta especially liked the broadcasts relayed to London from the United States by the commentator Raymond Gram Swing, who had long been warning Americans of the dangers posed by Nazi Germany. It was advisable, of course, to listen to the BBC with the volume turned low, in the unlikely event that any informers happened to be passing by, and afterward to retune the dial to a French station, just in case the apartment was ever inspected by the police.

There wasn't much else to do in the evenings anymore: German newsreels now played in the cinemas, and one always faced the possibility of sitting next to a soldier there, which was not a very pleasant prospect. Kate and Etta hadn't seen a movie since before the exodus, when Etta had insisted that they go out for an evening to take Kate's mind off ambulance work. (They went to see *Goodbye, Mr. Chips,* a loving tribute to traditional English virtues.) In any case, the two of them hadn't been, as Etta put it, "gadders" even in the best of times, and especially not now, when the streets were full of Germans in uniform and an eleven o'clock curfew was strictly enforced. Cafés and restaurants had to close by 10:30, and at ten o'clock proprietors all over Paris alerted their customers to the time by dimming the lights with pieces of blue or black cloth, a kind of microcosm of the blackout itself. The Métro stopped running at 10:45, and just before that Kate and Etta could open a window and hear the anxious clatter of footsteps from the street below: people who had lost track of time and were now hurrying to get to the nearest station before the gates shut for the night.

The streets of Paris were quieter than Etta had ever known them. The German military administration had banned the use of all civilian vehicles, with the exception of police cars, ambulances, fire trucks, and cars belonging to those in the medical professions or those providing necessary supplies; on Sundays private cars were forbidden altogether. In accordance with the newly issued traffic regulations, Kate had registered her car with the local police prefecture shortly after their return to Paris. Given her service work with the American Hospital and the Foyer du Soldat, she was provided with the rare and valuable sticker known as an S.P.—for Service Publique—that was to be displayed on the windshield at all times, showing the number of the car and the official stamp of the prefecture that had provided it. As the distribution of gasoline was banned to all vehicles not covered under the regulations, she had also put in a request for a gasoline ration card at the Service Publique office on place Denfert-Rochereau. In a matter of days she had been issued a card that allowed her to receive a coupon book each month at the *mairie* of the seventeenth arrondissement; with the coupons, she could purchase forty liters (about ten and a half gallons) of gasoline per month, good for about three hundred miles of driving.

After their return to Paris, Kate and Etta had continued their occasional work with the Foyer du Soldat, delivering parcels to soldiers—except that now their destinations were not social centers but the prisoner-of-war camps that had been set up throughout the north of France. The Foyer du Soldat office was on avenue de l'Opéra, on the second floor of an ornately carved stone building with a mansard roof, in the Haussmannian style. The office itself was rather dreary, described by one observer as "a poorly lit room with a sad aspect," staffed by volunteers whose main activity was reading and sorting the letters that arrived each day appealing for information about sons or husbands who had disappeared. Most heartbreaking were the letters that contained a photograph of the loved one, as though he might be recognized among the nearly two million men taken prisoner; invariably the photo showed him smiling at the camera in happier times, having no idea of the use to which that photo would later be put.

In addition to her work with the Foyer du Soldat, Kate was volunteering part time with the Croix-Rouge française. A Red Cross emblem was painted on the side of her car, and she was issued a Red Cross armband to wear while working. Over the course of the war some twelve hundred women would so volunteer; they were, in the description of a Croix-Rouge history of that period, "French women who were not nurses and who wanted to serve. They were athletic, they were courageous, some had their own cars." Kate carried supplies including bread, chocolate, tinned meat, jam, and packs of cigarettes, setting out for Verdun, Metz, Toul, Nancy, wherever she was sent, leaving early in the morning so that she could be home by nightfall. The eastern landscape still bore the scars of recent combat: crumbled walls, burned-out cars and trucks. Here and there a broken artillery piece listed to one side, its barrel staring blindly at the sky; planted along the roadside, homemade wooden crosses, some adorned with flowers, added a funereal air.

Primitive camps had been set up in barracks, fortresses, stadiums, wherever very large groups of men could be held efficiently at gunpoint; in the words of one of the prisoners, the camps "oozed improvisation, ignorance, inexperience, and misery." They were a portrait of wretchedness and squalor; dysentery was rampant, and a foul smell lay heavily over everything. The prisoners—a mix of white and colonial North African and black African troops—were gaunt, weakened by illness, their expressions dulled by hunger and fatigue; they still wore the uniforms in which they had been captured, the clothing almost colorless now beneath layers of dust and mud. That few ever tried to escape was due in large part to their severely weakened physical condition: "When one reaches an advanced stage of exhaustion," one prisoner noted later, "planned thinking becomes almost impossible and all one wants is to stick with one's friend and go on doing what everyone else is doing almost automatically." Besides, the prisoners generally believed that because an armistice had been signed— and thus a condition of war no longer existed between France and Germany—they would be released shortly anyway. Their captors constantly assured them that they would be back home before long, perhaps in just a matter of days, and under those circumstances it seemed foolhardy to hazard an escape attempt, when the chances of success were low and the potential consequences so grim. In one camp, for instance, a soldier from colonial North Africa was killed while trying to escape, and his corpse was left for an entire day at the entrance to the camp, to serve as an example to the other prisoners.[*]

Of course, some French prisoners did hope to escape—often to join the Free France army then being raised by Charles de Gaulle in London—and some French civilians were willing to risk their safety to help them. Many were women, especially those rare women who drove their own cars; in 1940, as one French historian has observed, at a time when so many men were captured or in exile, women "were in the first rank" of resisters, "constantly at work, intrepid and ingenious."

In July 1940, Kate Bonnefous was not yet helping prisoners to escape. French by marriage rather than birth, she might have felt some hesitation in joining herself so actively with the French military struggle. Still, Kate could not help but feel enraged and deeply saddened by the piteous state in which she found the French prison-

---

[*] As a rule, the Nazis treated colonial troops far more harshly than white ones. Soldiers of black and Arab origin were singled out for abuse during the forced marches and were routinely harassed in the camps; sometimes they were goaded into attacking a guard so that they could be shot. On numerous occasions the Germans refused even to accept surrender from colonial troops and simply murdered them outright; the number of troops killed in this manner is known to be at least fifteen hundred and might well be twice that.

ers, and it was not difficult for her to see her own son in them. Len (whom Kate affectionately called Sonny) had grown up to be a strikingly handsome young man, tall and muscular, with piercing blue eyes and slicked-back dark blond hair and the louche smile of a silent movie idol. She could only imagine what Sonny would look like now, as a prisoner, had he not been fortunate enough to find refuge with her brother in Great Britain. Would she have been one of those mothers sending desperate appeals to the Foyer du Soldat? Many of the photographs enclosed with the letters were accompanied by brief descriptions meant to help identify the prisoner. One mother had written simply, "You see, my son is handsome and has an elegant look"; Kate herself could have written the same.

On July 18, 1940, Kate and Etta had been back in Paris for exactly two weeks. It was late in the evening and the two women were sitting in the drawing room after dinner with cigarettes and cups of tea; Kate was on the leather divan reading *Le Matin*, and Etta in one of the armchairs with a book. They did not plan to stay up much longer, because they had to get up early the next morning to visit four prisoner-of-war camps for the Foyer du Soldat. As Etta would later recall the moment, Kate suddenly gave a brief exclamation and then handed the paper to Etta.

"Etta," she said, indicating one of the items, "isn't that interesting?"

She had been reading the *Renseignements Recherchés*. There, near the top of the page, was a ten-line announcement that gave the names of sixteen wounded officers recently admitted to the hospital in Doullens, a town well north of Paris.

Etta glanced at the paper. There was nothing exceptional about that, she said. Announcements like that one appeared in the papers every day—captured soldiers wanted their relatives to know where they were.

Yes, Kate agreed, but Etta should look more closely: Among the obviously French names in the notice—Guillot and Prévost and Delafond and the like—there was this: "Lt. Hunter." She had been looking at the classified advertisements for days, she told Etta, and this was the first time she had ever seen an English name.

Etta began to feel slightly panicky, a hum rising dimly inside her; she understood at once what it meant that Kitty had been scanning the classifieds searching for English names. "There are Frenchmen with English names, you know," she said. "You're English, but you've got a French name."

"I married mine," Kate replied. "I doubt he got his that way." Besides, his regiment was also listed there: "Cameron H.G.H." That sounded British as well, not like the simply numbered infantry regiments of the other officers.

That might be the case, Etta acknowledged; but still, even if this Lieutenant Hunter was English, they were in no position to do anything for him. Doullens was a military hospital, which meant he was under armed guard. Even if they worked out some scheme to help him escape, they would likely be caught red-handed—and then what would become of them?

The world beyond the heavily curtained windows was almost silent, as though the two of them were sitting in a farmhouse somewhere rather than in an apartment in one of the world's great cities. Soon the curfew would go into effect; a few minutes before eleven, they would hear the nightly announcement coming from speakers mounted atop police cars—*"Allo! Allo!"*—a loud, disembodied voice warning that all persons found on the street after curfew would face arrest. "Oh, I suppose you're right," Kate said finally. She would do just one thing, she assured Etta, and it was perfectly safe: She would answer Lieutenant Hunter's advertisement, offer to bring him something if he wanted. Surely there was no harm in that. They were permitted to take packages to wounded soldiers, she pointed out—indeed, at the Foyer du Soldat they were supposed to. What did it matter if they took a package to a soldier of their own choosing rather than someone else's?

Etta had to concede that this was true; still feeling uneasy, she went off to bed. Kate would too, but she had one thing left to do. That night she stayed up long enough to write a letter to Lieutenant Hunter, care of the military hospital in Doullens.

6

S ECOND LT. COLIN D. HUNTER, intelligence officer with the 4th Territorial Battalion of the Queen's Own Cameron Highlanders, was on a beach in France when the shell exploded in front of him. The Camerons were among the British Expeditionary Force units that had been ordered to stay behind during the Allied evacuation of France of May 1940, fighting rear-guard actions to buy time for the embarkation of more than 300,000 troops from the beaches of Dunkirk and the nearby coastline. Outmanned and outgunned, they took up defensive positions to slow the German advance, detonating bridges and railways when they could, then falling back to a new position. Day after day the men retreated west, passing charred vehicles and staring corpses and bombed-out villages where tall columns of stone chimneys stood solitary amid the rubble of the wooden houses that had once surrounded them. The weather remained confoundingly gorgeous, the afternoon skies so clear and blue that forever after Colin Hunter would think of fair, clement days as "Dunkirk weather."

By June 12, the remaining members of the 4th Camerons had reached France's western shore, near the fishing village of Saint-Valery-en-Caux, where they hoped an evacuation boat might pick them up. On the beach at Veules-les-Roses, the broad expanse of sand was crowded with the bodies of the dead and wounded. Wehrmacht gunners on the nearby cliffs raked the beaches with machine-gun fire, and the men took cover in a cave at the foot of the cliffs. When the firing from above became more sporadic, the company commander, Capt. Derek Lang, organized a group of volunteers, Colin Hunter among them, to gather up their weapons and make a dash for a small British rescue ship that had run aground on the sand. The ship would not be able to sail until high tide arrived again several hours later, but at least from there they would have an angle on the German gunners.

The Camerons had been aboard the ship for only a few minutes when they saw German tanks rolling into position on the cliffs facing them. The first shell from a tank exploded at the ship's bow, the deafening burst sending up a shower of metal fragments, and all at once the air was thick with smoke and noise. Another shell blasted a hole in the keel, sending a dreadful vibration through the frame of the ship, like an animal shiver of pain; one more landed directly on the deck, and the world seemed to come apart. Something struck Hunter just above the left eye, knocking him backward; dazed and bleeding, he managed to crawl down into the ship's hold, where he threw himself onto a bunk and lost consciousness.

The next thing he remembered was Derek Lang's voice calling from up on deck: "Colin, are you down there?"

Dimly he came to; his head was aching, one eye blinded by blood and swelling. He understood that he needed to rejoin the battle, and he collected his helmet and strapped on his gun belt—somehow he had taken it off before collapsing—telling himself, *Last man, last round, here we go.* When he reached the deck, though, he was greeted by a large German officer brandishing a pistol. "Congratulations," the officer said in English, "for you the war is over."

The men were forced to surrender their weapons, field glasses, and compasses, and at the point of bayonets they were marched onto the beach, where German medics gave them water and treated their wounds; then all of the British soldiers who had been captured that day were formed into squads and directed up the cliff path. Colin

Hunter would say later that it was the most depressing moment of his life; from then on, he said, "I had one aim and one object, and that was to escape."

A photograph published in the Nazi propaganda magazine *Signal* showing British prisoners who had been captured on the beach at Veules-les-Roses in 1940. Second Lt. Colin Hunter can be seen at the right of the photo, wearing a bandage over his left eye.

The prisoners were put aboard trucks and driven to a temporary staging camp in the interior of France, where they joined four thousand other prisoners. The men there were ragged and unwashed; some had supplemented their uniforms with pieces of civilian clothing, and they wore dented tin plates or mugs around their waists, giving them the look of tramps. After several days, the wound above Colin Hunter's eye turned septic and his face swelled badly; he was examined by a medic, who determined that a shell fragment had lodged under his skin. On June 19, he was transferred to the nearby town of Doullens, where a French civilian hospital had been requisitioned by the German army. The next morning a doctor arrived at his bedside with surgical instruments and a small pair of scissors, and after some effort removed what turned out to be an inch-long splinter of metal. Hunter was permitted to remain in the hospital while the incision healed. "I had a priceless asset," he would say later. "I had a wound." He knew that once he had recovered, he would quickly find himself in a prisoner-of-war camp; his only hope, such as it was, lay in delay, and for the next several weeks he did whatever was necessary to make sure that his wound remained open.

One day in July a young woman arrived at the hospital; she was a sales agent for the newspaper *Le Matin,* and she asked the wounded officers on the ward if they would like to take out a notice announcing their whereabouts. Ten lines in the paper would cost the not-insignificant sum of 300 francs, but the French officers eagerly agreed, and in a burst of high spirits they insisted that their British comrade add his name to theirs. Unlike them, he didn't have any family in France who might see the notice, nor was he keen on spending his money unnecessarily, but he did so, simply to please the men in the other beds. "Really, it was a joke," he said years later. "I never thought any more about it."

Before the week was out, the French officers had begun to receive letters and parcels. "There was always tremendous excitement when the postman came," Hunter recalled. "And then one day there was an absolute whoop of joy, and the French officers all came rushing over, saying, 'Colin! *Une lettre, une lettre!'* I opened it with trembling fingers."

The letter writer, a Madame Bonnefous, said that Lieutenant Hunter didn't know her, but she worked for the Red Cross and hoped to visit him in the hospital, and if he wanted, she would do her best to bring along anything he might need. From his hospital bed, Colin Hunter composed a letter in reply, brief and circumspect because, as he was a prisoner, his mail would be inspected before it was sent. She was very good to write to him, he said; he was looking forward to her visit, and he would be very grateful if she might bring him a pair of pajamas.

Doullens was about 125 miles directly north of Paris. The round trip to the hospital would consume just about all of the gasoline that Kate Bonnefous had been provided for the month; indeed, it wasn't clear that she could even make it to Doullens and back, more than six hours of driving, on what was less than two-thirds of a tank of gas. Kate, though, had already planned for this—although exactly how she did so is a matter of some disagreement. By Etta Shiber's account, Kate managed to procure extra gasoline for their first trip to Doullens from some physician friends of theirs, who as medical professionals were also allowed a ration of gas from the Service Publique.

As for the subsequent trips, Kate herself would tell a British prisoner of war that she had arranged a deal with the German commandant of the nearby military prison in Doullens—the venerable fortress known as the Citadel—by which he allowed her to bring the Citadel's prisoners of war provisions from the Foyer du Soldat in exchange for gifts of chocolate and silk stockings that Kate herself gave to his guards; the commandant was said to be so taken with her directness of approach, and so intent that she be able to follow through on her proposal, that he provided her with a supply of gasoline, and on one occasion personally escorted her to a nearby fuel depot to obtain fifty liters' worth. One prisoner of war would recall the transactions slightly differently, saying of Kate, "She even used to go to the German aerodromes and get petrol for her trips by exchanging silk stockings and chocolates," while Colin Hunter noted simply that she loved to go out and "kid" (in the sense of "fool") the Germans. The appendix of a lengthy prisoner-of-war report given to British MI9 investigators stated simply: "German soldiers could not get chocolate. Mme. Bonnefous gave them chocolate as bribes for extra petrol for her visits to hospitals." Any of these scenarios might be true; in any event, it seems clear that Kate Bonnefous had figured out a means of supporting her trips to Doullens—by using gasoline that had been provided to her by the German army.

Etta Shiber would say later that she decided to accompany Kate to Doullens because she wanted to see that Kitty stayed out of trouble, and there was a great deal of trouble involved in what Etta knew she was contemplating. Almost immediately after the Germans occupied Paris, a proclamation had gone up on the walls of the city assuring those who conducted themselves peacefully that they had nothing to fear from the occupying authority; on the other hand, individuals who committed any prohibited activities would be subject to the judgment of a military tribunal and "punished most severely." There followed a list of seven classes of such activities, the very first one of which was: "All assistance provided to non-German military located in the occupied territories."

One morning at the end of July the two women put together a package for Lieutenant Hunter that included the pajamas he had requested, as well as cigarettes and bread and a few other items they thought he might like. They put the parcels in the back of the Peugeot and settled into the plush front seat; once more Kate pressed the starter and they headed off.

Before long they had passed through the Porte de la Chapelle at the north of the city, then left behind the industrial area of Saint-Denis. As they drove uphill through the woods of Montmorency the morning sunlight seemed to dance on the glossy leaves of the beech trees and twinkled like stars on the dark still water of the ponds. Often no other vehicles were to be seen anywhere; the only sound was the low rumble of the car's engine, the whir of the tires on the road. They descended into a valley near Presles, the sun making a composition of shadow and light on the craggy foothills in the distance. Soon the silvery ribbon of the Oise had come into view. Here the landscape became more level, plains neatly divided into a patchwork quilt of farm plots. Farmers working plow horses were dressed as they must have been for generations, in berets and collarless blue shirts with rolled-up sleeves, handkerchiefs tied around their necks to absorb sweat. Wheat fields rippled in the breeze like a pale green sea. Despite everything, Etta thought, France was still beautiful. As always, she marveled at Kitty's skill at the wheel, the briskness of her movements with scarcely a moment's hesitation. The two of them spoke occasionally, filling time as they drove, about the recent news from Kitty's daughter-in-law, Mireille, that Sonny had left London and was now in Casablanca; about Margot, who had just returned to Paris and begun working for them again; about how the dogs were doing in the hot apartment; about what Lieutenant Hunter might be like. At one point, Kitty mused aloud about whether he wondered if they were coming at all—whether he simply took her for some sort of nosy old lady, charitable but frivolous, who would pry into his troubles but wouldn't do anything about them.

The sun beat down on the shimmering fillet of asphalt. They crossed a bridge spanning the river Somme; there they encountered one of the checkpoints that seemed to have gone up in France overnight, the guardhouse flying the swastika flag and giving orders to halt in two languages. A German military policeman strode up to the car, wearing the uniform of the Feldgendarmerie with its intimidating gorget, the silver crescent that displayed the Nazi eagle hanging from a heavy chain around his neck. Under his scrutiny Etta could not help but feel guilty, despite having done nothing wrong. He inspected their transit papers, noting the Red Cross emblem on the side of the car, the S.P. on the windshield, the Red Cross armbands they both were wearing, and then inspected the car, rummaging briefly through their packages, before waving them on.

Past Amiens, they turned onto the N25 national road for the remaining twenty miles to Doullens. They were now inside the *zone interdite,* the "forbidden zone," the two departments of the Nord and Pas-de-Calais at the extreme north of the country. This region—of special importance to the Nazi hierarchy, because it had been chosen as the launching point for a planned invasion of England—was the most tightly controlled in all of France, and the most isolated, with the densest concentration of German troops. In the *zone interdite* the nightly curfew began at nine o'clock, two hours earlier than in Paris, and extended until six the next morning. Fines were levied for the slightest of offenses, including not tipping one's cap to the local commandant as he passed by. Any property, it seemed, could be requisitioned, taken by the Germans simply as they wished: cars, bicycles, trucks, horses, garages, barns, bedrooms. It was now illegal to own hunting rifles, or indeed guns of any kind, even antique heirlooms that no longer fired. It was illegal to own a radio. It was illegal to keep passenger pigeons, which might be used to deliver messages; pigeon breeding and racing had long been passionate pursuits in the north, and many owners wept as they destroyed their prized birds. Farmers were ordered to hand over to the German authorities one-tenth of their assets, and inspectors came to weigh the grain and count the livestock; the scale of the burden began to take on an almost biblical quality.

In 1941, an emissary from Marshal Pétain's Vichy government would remark that the *zone interdite* bore the same relation to the rest of occupied France as occupied France did to Free France. In Vichy, he said, life was peace; in Paris, occupation; in Lille, war.

In Doullens, *l'exode* had begun on May 17; almost overnight, a town of six thousand had nearly emptied, with only a few dozen residents remaining in their homes. By July still only about a third of the residents had returned, and as Kate and Etta drove in, Doullens exuded the particular melancholy of a market town without its market. The town drowsed in the afternoon heat, high sun reflecting off whitewashed walls; everywhere shutters were closed, turning a blank face to narrow cobblestone streets that opened onto plazas where farmers had once brought their pigs for sale. Rows of attached houses lined the avenues, many of them half-timbered in the northern style, others with the steeply sloped mansard roofs and frilly ornamental flourishes of the Second Empire.

The Hôpital-Hospice of Doullens was a large three-story brick building with a mansard roof and carved stone clock tower; the hospital grounds were entirely surrounded by a high brick wall, bare but for a single spreading oak tree around the back. Though operated by its French medical staff, like all of the municipal buildings in Doullens the hospital was under the command of the local Kommandantur, the German military authority. Visitors passed through the iron front gate under the gaze of a pair of helmeted German soldiers; Kate and Etta, though, barely merited the notice of the guards. Over time Etta would come to understand that their natural appearance—the lined faces, the eyeglasses, the gray in the hair—concealed them more effectively than any wigs or false noses, providing almost a cloak of invisibility: For a woman, it seemed, old age was the best disguise.

The Hôpital-Hospice of Doullens

The hospital's chief of staff was a French physician by the name of Jules Ponthieu. In his office Dr. Ponthieu cursorily inspected their entry papers and parcels, then granted them permission to wander through the hospital without being trailed by German soldiers, and to speak directly to the patients—privileges strictly denied to Kate Bonnefous on her visits to prisoner-of-war camps. Nearly two hundred soldiers, most of them French, were being held in various wings of the hospital; the wards were crowded but clean, with tall windows that allowed sunlight to fall on the rows of narrow beds that lined the walls. Doctors in gowns made their rounds, assisted by the Daughters of Charity of Saint Vincent de Paul, instantly recognizable by their billowing gray habits and the large white-linen *cornettes* they wore on their heads, the twin starched flaps extended outward like goose wings.

Kate and Etta found Lt. Colin Hunter sitting alone on a bench in the hospital's back garden, wearing the long, sack-like nightshirt and felt slippers that served as the standard garb of French military hospitals. Hunter was twenty-six years old, with dark hair and bright blue eyes—one of them heavily bandaged—and a brush mustache under a hawkish nose. He had an appealingly wry smile and, despite being a member of a Scottish unit, a posh English accent, the sort of diction in which the word "really" sounds like *rally;* as it turned out, he was descended from a large cattle-farming family up in Angus, and often spent summers and holidays on his grandfather's estate on Loch Lochy, but he had been raised in the north of London. His family home in Hadley Court was only a few miles from the suburb of Stamford Hill in which Kate had lived as a girl, and though they were a generation apart they shared a number of landmarks, had grown up in similarly quiet, leafy neighborhoods filled with tall, dignified townhouses built of sturdy London Yellow Stock brick. Etta watched Lieutenant Hunter intently as he talked about his family, his work as a "stock jobber" in his father's firm in the City, marveling at how sociable and outgoing he was despite his difficult situation, and how he managed to maintain a sense of optimism through it all. She thought about how proud she would be if he were her own son; she could not help but think of Colin's mother. Etta was sure that if she were in her place she wouldn't be able to sleep for worry, knowing that her son had been wounded and captured; or perhaps she didn't know what had become of him, which might well be worse.

Etta asked how he had been wounded, and Hunter described the circumstances of his capture, the ghastly scene on the beach at Veules-les-Roses and how he had been hit with a piece of shrapnel and was sent here to have it removed. He had been on the officers' ward for five weeks; a doctor came around each day with a little hammer and tapped lightly on his forehead, and in his best French he expressed the great pain he was feeling, and when no one was around he did what he could to work on the stitches and try to keep the wound open. In fact he was perfectly fit to leave, he told them, but he was stalling for time until he could figure out what to do. Even if he could get over the wall, he wouldn't get far in that hospital outfit. He supposed that was what the Germans counted on—that, and their being ill and weak. Otherwise they would watch the patients more closely than they did. A French clerk called the roll only twice each day, he said, first in the morning and then again at six o'clock in the evening. He didn't know what would happen to him once he was deemed fit to go—probably sent to the Citadel first, and from there marched to some grim prison camp in Germany to sit out the remainder of the war.

That was when Kate said in a low voice: "Would you like me to take you to Paris?"

Later Etta would note the "cold terror" that had coursed through her just then; it was one of those awful moments when life seemed to soften, distorting itself into the exact shape of her fear.

He was desperate to escape, Colin Hunter acknowledged, but he didn't see how it could be done. While the hospital was not as closely watched as the Citadel—there was little enforced discipline and most of the time one did as one liked—armed guards were stationed at the front gate and some others patrolled the interior of the build-ing, and occasionally the hospital received a visit from a German officer and then security became tight indeed. And even if Kate did manage to get him out, they would have to pass through various military checkpoints on the way to Paris, while German motorcycle patrols on the highways were authorized to pull over and inspect any car they deemed suspicious.

Kate replied in a cool, firm voice that he was mistaken, that she was sure she could get him out if he was willing to try. It was a single sentence that implied the existence of many others, and Etta sud-denly understood that Kitty had already been thinking about this, on her own, perhaps in her bed at night while Etta was in hers searching the dial for comforting news on the radio, and it struck her that Lieutenant Hunter, and Dr. Ponthieu, and surely the Germans as well, viewed her merely as a do-gooding charity lady in pearls, when in fact she was a woman who had arranged for the guardianship of her orphaned siblings while still a teenager herself, who spoke three languages and had run two businesses and raised a son mostly on her own, who had volunteered to drive ambulances and watch for enemy gas attacks, who was sturdy and determined and clever, and resource-ful enough to use their biases to her own advantage.

They would be back to see him, Kate assured Colin Hunter, but not right away.

In the days after their visit to Doullens, Etta found it difficult to put Lieutenant Hunter entirely out of her mind, remembering his face with that lopsided grin and the one shining blue eye, remarking to herself how brave he was, and modest in that English way, how he tossed off the nights he slept on the ground during the forced march as "not so bad, really." She understood that Kitty was determined to do everything in her power to help Colin Hunter escape, regardless of any objections Etta might raise; worse, she knew that Kitty was willing to do so without ever discussing it, would perhaps even adjust her activities to shield Etta from knowledge of them—thus adding layers of complication and danger to something already too complicated and dangerous. How, Etta wondered, could she continue to live in that apartment, walking the dogs and going to the market and having dinner together, discussing the latest events of the war, knowing that Kitty was risking herself for others when Etta would not?

"Such an infinitely important thing it is to do the right!" Felix Adler had exhorted the faculty of the Ethical Culture School. "Our worth as human beings, the success or failure of our life, so utterly depends upon this." When a ship is foundering, he liked to remind them, you don't ask if you should try to reach the land, but instead where the land lies and what the best means of getting there might be: And this was as true in moral as in maritime questions. When the world was turned upside down, one had to adjust one's bearings to maintain any sense of balance; it wasn't possible simply to act as before, not at a time when even a good meal seemed selfish and laughter on the street rang of coldheartedness. It seemed a lifetime ago that she had had the luxury of deciding simply between pork chops and chicken for dinner or what novel to read before bed. These days she had too little attention for literature, her mind wandering before she reached the end of the page. She was finding that a quiet life could no longer blunt her anxiety, that the notion of a predictable routine struck her as absurd in a world that seemed to reconstruct itself daily. She felt better when she was distributing food, visiting hospitals, opening mail at the Foyer du Soldat; her anxiety, like the occasional ache in her back, seemed to diminish with movement.

Etta did make clear her concerns about what Kate was planning to do; now, however, it was not pleading—as when Kate had first showed her the classified ad in *Le Matin*—but more of a sounding, as a diver might test the depths of the water before plunging in. She reminded Kate, sensibly enough she felt, that even if they managed

to get Lieutenant Hunter back to their apartment, they had no idea
what to do with him once he was there. Paris was still inside the Occupied Zone, it was impossible to cross the line of demarcation without the proper papers, and they knew no one who might help them.
To whom would they pass off Colin Hunter on his way to the Unoccupied Zone, and from there onward to England?

When pressed, Kate admitted that she hadn't yet figured out the
answer to Etta's questions; in Paris, though, Colin Hunter at least
stood a chance of reaching freedom, which he never would have in
that hospital. She assured Etta that she was going to be very careful,
and that she did not intend to get caught. Her voice was solemn, her
features as composed as marble. She simply believed that she knew
how to get this young man out (Kitty had absolute faith in her ability
to solve problems; that was the lesson her life had taught her), and no
one in her position had the right to leave the responsibility of helping to someone else.

Etta was reminded of the Underground Railroad, those small
groups of courageous Americans who had risked their safety to help
deliver runaway slaves to freedom, often by sheltering them in their
own homes before leading them to the next stop on the line. At the
time she first learned of that secret escape line, as a girl, many of its
"conductors," as they had been called, were still alive; they were not
mythical heroes from an ancient Greek tale, but people one might
meet in the course of a day without even being aware of it: just ordinary people, most of them, who had managed to do extraordinary
things. Now Kitty was conceiving a kind of Underground Railroad
of her own—knowing the first and last stops but not yet the places
in between.

7

Kate and Etta went to Doullens again two weeks later, this time bringing with them, as Colin Hunter described it, "a magnificent amount of food, clothes, sheets, medical stores, and books." On that visit they met another British serviceman, Cpl. Gordon Hood-Cree of the 5th Royal East Kent Regiment (known as the Buffs), who was in a ward designated for junior officers. Hood-Cree was thirty-three years old, tall and slim, with round metal-rimmed military glasses and a debonair pencil mustache like David Niven's. He had been wounded outside Doullens at the end of May, more seriously than Colin Hunter had been, with a bullet having shattered his tibia and a piece of shrapnel lodged in his ribs that would remain there for the rest of his life. Two months after the battle, his leg was still in poor condition and he struggled to walk. He, too, though, expressed an eagerness to escape. Kate informed him that she could take only one soldier at a time; she planned to help Lieutenant Hunter on their following visit, and she would come for him after that.

In making her approach to the British soldiers in the hospital, it seems clear that Kate Bonnefous was capitalizing on the French tradition of the *marraine de guerre*, literally "war godmother." The tradition dates to the early years of the First World War, when

Frenchwomen—mostly older, generally well-to-do—began to send letters to wounded soldiers who had been captured by the Germans, as a way of boosting their morale. Over time, the letters were often supplemented by gifts from the *marraine,* who would knit warm clothing and provide food and other treats to her adopted *filleul* [godson], sometimes in personal visits to hospitals in German-occupied northern France.

In her book *French Women and the First World War,* the historian Margaret H. Darrow noted, "The *marraines de guerre* were a peculiarly French creation without close parallels in Britain or Germany," and in the French popular imagination, the kindly, patriotic *marraine* became something of a personification of the motherland herself, as well as a narrative device used in novels, plays, and films (most of which turn on the notion of a secret identity, the *marraine* ultimately revealed as a long-lost mother or estranged wife, or a beautiful young woman posing as an older one). In a society in which women could neither vote nor control their own bank accounts, "charity" was seen as uniquely women's work, in which, Darrow writes, "their natural 'maternal solicitude' made the care of the wounded, displaced, and grieving their particular province. The desire to comfort, feed, clothe, even spoil the soldiers with canteens and care packages came from the same natural instinct." The gendered division of labor extended even to letter writing, which was seen primarily as women's responsibility; the French novelist Lucien Descaves observed that for men, "the pen is heavier than the rifle."

According to Catherine Bergin, a historian of British escape organizations in the Second World War, the role of the *marraine de guerre,* original to World War I, was resurrected in occupied France as early as the summer of 1940. In the Second World War, Bergin writes, "the concept of the *marraine de guerre* was crucial in establishing connections between potential helpers and men seeking a means of escape. . . . Despite the paucity of research on the movement, the evidence suggests that the *marraine* shaped the experiences of wounded British prisoners and in some cases the *marraines,* by their escape activities, were drivers of early resistance (1940–42). The work of the *marraine* was facilitated by the German authorities' willingness to turn a blind eye to civilians visiting the wounded. Visits became an acceptable part of life in hospitals."

On the morning of Wednesday, August 28, two weeks after their second visit, Kate and Etta prepared to set out once more for the Hôpital-Hospice of Doullens. Kate assembled another pile of provisions, including books and mail that had been supplied by the Foyer du Soldat, supplemented by other items they had obtained on their own, including one parcel wrapped in plain brown paper. On their first visit, Kate had noticed that the pajamas for Colin Hunter were not seized by the guards—as a rule, civilian clothing was banned from prisoner-of-war camps—and on their second visit they had brought additional items of clothing that likewise were allowed in. Watching her pack, Etta understood once more that no detail had been lost on her, that all along she had been taking the measure of the hospital: bringing in the clothing as a kind of practice run, using the first two visits to acclimate the guards and hospital staff to their presence, learning the roll call schedule, inspecting the hospital grounds. It was something like one of those English locked-room mystery stories that Kate enjoyed reading, except that in this case she was not trying to figure out how the perpetrator had escaped from the locked room, but rather how she might engineer the escape for someone else.

A week earlier, the Germans had begun to seize privately owned automobiles in Paris, claiming that the additional vehicles were needed for the planned invasion of Great Britain. Thus far, at least, they seemed to have a fondness not for Peugeots but for Citroëns; still, Kate could not help but wonder how long the S.P. affixed to her windshield would protect her, how long she would be permitted to continue her missions of charity at Doullens. Events had been moving quickly. Two weeks earlier, the Vichy government had issued a decree banning so-called secret societies, an order clearly directed at Masonic organizations (Kate's brother was a Freemason, as their father had been), and within days "spontaneous" demonstrations against Jews and Freemasons had broken out in Vichy, Toulouse, and Lyon. Next the government repealed the Marchandeau Decree of 1939, which made it illegal to incite hatred against any group of people based on their racial or religious origins. Later that same week, a mob of young men in uniform, members of the fascist group Jeune Front, had rampaged down the Champs-Élysées in broad daylight, smashing the plate-glass windows of Jewish-owned shops, shouting *"À bas les juifs!"* ["Down with the Jews!"].

In Paris, all foreigners over the age of fifteen had been ordered to register with the local authorities; completed registration forms had to be submitted to the foreigners' landlords or concierges within one week, which were then to be conveyed to the French police. There was a growing emphasis on documentation, on proving one's proper status; wherever one looked, it seemed, a wall poster was asking ÊTES-VOUS EN RÈGLE?—"Are your papers in order?"

After the cool, rainy spring, France had been experiencing an unusually dry summer; some parts of the country had not received any rain at all in more than a month, and the fair weather that had once been such a delight began to seem more like an affliction. Every morning, farmers cast gloomy looks up at the cloudless sky, waiting for the winds from the west that were reliable harbingers of rain. In Doullens the streets were hot and dusty, flowers drooping in the wrought-iron window boxes. Approaching the hospital with Etta, Kate turned onto a cobblestone side street and parked around the back of the building, by the high brick wall near the spreading oak, across the street from a Mobil service station with a large blue-and-white wall advertisement for Dubonnet. Once again, the women gathered up their packages and set off. At the front gate, Kate waved their entry papers at the sentries and the two of them proceeded into the hospital.

Inside, having registered with the official on duty, Kate began to pass through the wards delivering mail to the wounded soldiers, taking time to talk and joke with them in French, Etta following along behind. In the ward for junior officers, Kate paused for a moment at the bedside of Cpl. Gordon Hood-Cree, one of her English "godsons." If it was possible, she murmured, he should arrange to be on the officers' ward that evening at six o'clock. Hood-Cree had already informed her that the evening roll call was not especially careful, as the hospital authorities did not anticipate any escape attempts during daylight hours, and sometimes one or two of the men were elsewhere, receiving treatment or for some other reason; the morning roll call was the one during which all of the men had to be in their beds. Gordon Hood-Cree spoke excellent French, and he and Kate arranged that when Colin Hunter's name was called that evening, he would tell the French clerk that Colin had taken ill and gone to the toilet—that explanation would likely suffice for the clerk, as Hunter had been in the hospital for more than two months and by this point could not have been viewed as a security risk. His absence would surely be noted in the morning, though, and it would be assumed that he had somehow slipped out overnight.

While Kate spoke with the men, Etta wandered around the ward, striking up a conversation with any German soldiers who happened to enter, as she had promised Kate she would. Etta was far from fluent in German, but it had been her mother's native tongue and she used to hear it around the apartment growing up; though in recent years she had come to hate the sound of the language, there was something about having to concentrate while speaking it that she found calming, that bolstered her for the fearsome task of diverting the attention of enemy soldiers. Besides, after a moment's confusion the guards all turned out to be delighted to find this grandmotherly American who spoke to them in German, because of course they knew that the United States was neutral in the war and lots of isolationist Americans distrusted England and were sympathetic to Germany, and in the ensuing conversation Etta would scarcely have failed to mention that her mother was originally from Baden-Baden and that she herself had grown up around the German neighborhood of Yorkville—the headquarters of the pro-Nazi German American Bund, which had more than twenty thousand members and its own family camp on Long Island (the Long Island Rail Road featured "Camp Siegfried Specials" on summer weekends), and had filled Madison Square Garden for a "Pro American Rally" held against the backdrop of a giant portrait of George Washington under a Nazi eagle. If Etta wanted to ingratiate herself with the guards, she had plenty of material from which to draw, and later she would admit to Kate that she was shocked by how open the guards were with her about their intense hatred for the British and their frustration over delays in the promised invasion of England.

On the officers' ward, Kate distributed the mail and the provisions she had brought from Paris, including the package wrapped in brown paper for Lieutenant Hunter. There was a pair of shoes wrapped in overalls in that package, she told him quietly, sitting at his bedside; he should go to the toilet and put them on without being seen, leaving his hospital clothes somewhere out of the way, where they would not be found for at least a few hours—and he must be absolutely sure to remove his bandage. That way, if any Germans happened to see him, they would simply take him for one of the many French workmen who were always coming and going around the hospital, making deliveries, cleaning the floors, fixing windows or lights, tending the plants in the gardens. In the far corner of the back garden, Kate went on, he would see a single tree with several low branches, its trunk partly camouflaged by a row of bushes; when no one was looking, he could shinny up one of the branches and leap over the wall. Her car, a black Peugeot 402, was parked directly beneath that tree, and she had left it unlocked. Behind the back seat he would find the latch for the luggage compartment; he should get into it, close the latch behind him, and wait. It would be a tight squeeze, but she believed he would fit.

Colin Hunter nodded wordlessly. "He seemed," Etta would note later, "too moved to speak."

Kate told him not to be nervous if they were slow in coming; they were going to stay for another ten or fifteen minutes, to make sure they were seen with other prisoners before they left.

The three of them shook hands and said goodbye, as though parting until the next visit; leaving Colin Hunter with his parcel, Kate and Etta went back to their rounds, which Etta would call "one of the hardest things I ever did in my life . . . stopping to talk to patients as though nothing had happened. I tried to appear calm and natural, but I didn't feel as though I were succeeding. I forced a smile to my lips, where it seemed frozen in place; and then I found I didn't know how to stop smiling. It seemed to me that I must be walking through the wards like a hideous grinning gargoyle." At one point Etta whispered to Kate that they had waited long enough and for God's sake they should get out of there, but Kate replied in a low voice that he might not be ready yet, and it was better to allow too much time than too little, so the thing to do was to stop looking terrified and say hello to the men in the next ward, and with that she swept off down the hallway.

Again the sentries at the front gate paid them little mind as they exited. Etta forced herself through the gate and onto the sidewalk, her legs unsteady, heart skittering like a trapped bird inside her chest. At the corner of the hospital they turned and started up the side street, keeping to what felt a normal pace; still, the far end of the brick wall seemed as if it would never arrive, and at any moment a scene would erupt as in one of the American crime movies they used to see in Paris, when a prison escape has been detected and suddenly sirens are blaring everywhere, baying hounds straining at their leashes as they follow the scent of the prisoner. But the street remained absolutely quiet and they turned another corner and there, under the spreading oak, was the Peugeot 402 with its distinctive reverse-teardrop front grille and close-set headlights. Opening one of the rear doors, Kate leaned into the car to lock the luggage compartment, taking a moment as she did so to quietly reassure Colin Hunter that all had gone well and that soon they would be safely in Paris.

Slowly Kate navigated through the streets of Doullens, trying not to attract the attention of the German soldiers who loomed at crosswalks, who stood guard by the École Jeanne d'Arc and at the town hall where the swastika flag now hung above the front door. Finally they were back on the N25 heading south. Gazing out the window, Etta felt almost dazed with fear and by the sheer strangeness of it all: the notion that on a hot summer's day she would be driving along a highway in the north of France, toward a German checkpoint, with a British soldier hidden in the rear. Thinking of that poor young man lying motionless inside that cramped box, it was difficult not to picture the long black car as a hearse. There was no way to tell for certain if he had enough oxygen back there, if the exhaust pipe wasn't somehow pumping a stream of poisonous gas into the luggage compartment. The car was hot and stuffy even with the windows open, the ride over bumpy roads uncomfortable even on velvet seats—Etta could scarcely imagine what it would feel like inside a small metal container suspended above the back wheels. They tried calling out to Lieutenant Hunter, but he seemed not to hear them; the silence from the trunk grew worrisome enough that at one point, when they could see no other cars on the road, Kate pulled over and ran to the back of the car to make sure he was all right; to her relief, a muffled call in return came from the depths of the car's interior.

Within the hour, the Amiens bridge appeared in the distance; just before the entrance to the bridge, the gate arm of the German guard-house extended across the road, barring passage. Kate slowed the car as they approached the security check, and a military policeman stepped out; he was the very picture of state authority, sidearm strapped to his belt, the heavy steel plate of the Feldgendarmerie around his neck, his uniform trimmed with gold braid and adorned with various indecipherable emblems. Striding to the car, the guard ordered them to produce their papers. Etta fought down her growing panic; presenting her American passport and French identity card, she willed her hands not to tremble.

After a few moments the guard returned their papers, then took a step back and opened one of the car's rear doors, peering into the interior: His head was now no more than two feet from Colin Hunter's. Etta held her breath, praying for silence. She waited for the guard to ask Kate to open the trunk; if he did, their only hope was that he would see the vertically anchored spare tire and not notice the compartment behind it, tucked away between the tire and the rear seat, just large enough to hold a man.

The seconds passed. Finally the guard shut the door, and with scarcely a word he motioned for the gate to be raised and waved them on.

Back in Paris, Kate pulled the car over in front of their apartment building and turned off the engine. After unlocking the luggage compartment she sat back down, turning to speak to Colin Hunter. She and Etta would go inside first, she told him quietly; he should wait there for a minute, until they were no longer in sight, and then come in. He should just act naturally and not hesitate—if someone caught sight of him entering the building, he would seem to be just a workman there to make repairs.

When the street was clear, Kate briskly opened the car door and stepped out, and Etta did the same. The two of them entered the elevator, and after what seemed an eternity Colin Hunter hurried in beside them. Kate pressed the button, and the elevator rumbled slowly upward to the sixth floor; then she stepped out, fitted her key into the lock, and pushed open the apartment door to the excited yapping of the dogs, who greeted them as if they had been gone for days rather than hours.

With the front door closed and locked, the three of them collapsed in the drawing room, exhausted but exultant; Colin Hunter was flushed and perspiring from his difficult journey but otherwise looked none the worse for wear. Etta was relieved to be safe inside their apartment, surrounded by familiar belongings, with a cocker spaniel squirming contentedly in her lap, but still she felt shaken by the events of the day: This was a future she could not possibly have read in her cards. How she wished they were simply coming home from one of their annual car trips south, like the one the year before, when they had vacationed with Etta's brother, Chester, and his wife, Helen, in Nice. Everything that week had been beautiful, the flower show and the dog show and the gems in the jewelry-shop windows and the graceful palm trees with their feather-duster crowns. With Kitty and Colin Hunter, she could never return to a life that allowed for that sort of pleasure, just as in visiting Nice with Kitty and the others she could not return to the untroubled life she had once lived with Bill and Irving. She had always been the sort of woman who never attracted much attention, who felt most comfortable standing in the shadows, who could never bring herself to be—as she thought of it—a fussmaker; in school she had taught herself that success came from being polite and following the rules, and now, at the age of sixty-two, she had broken the most serious rule she had ever encountered.

Etta watched Kitty as she chatted with Colin Hunter. Soon, she knew, Kitty would be busying herself again, whistling a little tune as she put a kettle on the electric plate, rummaging in the icebox for something to serve for tea; later she would go into the hall linen closet to find towels and sheets and pillows to make up the divan for their guest. Kitty was taking things one step at a time, the way she always did, and it had gotten them this far. Still, Etta couldn't help but wonder what was next, how on earth they were going to procure an identity card for an escaped British soldier in the midst of German-occupied Paris—one that was genuine-looking enough to fool Nazi officials—and figure out how to transport him across the line of demarcation to the Unoccupied Zone, while in the meantime feeding him and finding him a set of clothes and men's razors and a shaving brush and who knew what else, and making sure he never answered the telephone or the door or stood too long by an unshuttered window. They had gotten him out of one locked room; now they had to get him out of another.

8

THAT MONTH—AUGUST 1940—a mimeographed pamphlet began appearing around Paris, surreptitiously placed in mailboxes, slipped under doors, left behind on the Métro. Entitled *Conseils à l'occupé* ["Advice to the Occupied"], it offered Parisians thirty-three suggestions for passively resisting the Nazi occupation. Though the Germans were purchasing street maps and phrasebooks, and waves of them were descending daily on Notre-Dame and the Panthéon, and though "not one of them has not got a camera to his eye," the pamphlet proclaimed emphatically "THEY ARE NOT TOURISTS." They were conquerors, and while current circumstances forced Parisians to be "correct" with the Germans, it was not necessary to go beyond that, to offer them anything other than a studied, unhelpful politeness.

If one of them speaks to you in German, make a sign of incomprehension and be on your way.

The man from whom you buy your suspenders has put a sign in his shop: "We speak German." Go to another shop.

If they think it is useful to spread defeatism among the citizens by offering concerts in public places, you are not obliged to go. Stay at home or go to the countryside and listen to the birds.

You complain because you have to be home by 11 P.M. Don't you understand that this allows you to listen to the English radio?

And most important of all: "Display total indifference, but privately nurture your anger. It will serve you well."

The spirit of the *Conseils à l'occupé* can be found in the story that circulated at the time about the painter Jean-Gabriel Daragnès, who early one morning was lolling in the sun in front of his house in the Montmartre section of Paris. A German soldier came by and asked him how to get to the nearby Sacré-Coeur Basilica. "I don't know," replied Daragnès, still wearing his bathrobe. "I don't live in the neighborhood."

One of the Parisians who was heartened to discover the anonymous pamphlet was the art historian Agnès Humbert. That summer she had become one of the founding members of an early resistance group called Le Réseau du Musée de l'Homme [The Network of the Museum of Man], after the Paris museum at which several of them worked; composed primarily of writers and intellectuals, the group sheltered British soldiers, passed military information to England, and published an underground newspaper entitled *Résistance*. On August 18, 1940, Humbert wrote in her diary: "Will the people who produced *33 Conseils à l'occupé* ever know what they have done for us, and probably for thousands of others? A glimmer of light in the darkness. . . . Now we know for certain that we are not alone. There are other people who think like us, who are suffering, and organizing the struggle."

Those in occupied Paris, in the summer of 1940, who were engaging in the earliest anti-Nazi activities, including giving aid to escaped British soldiers, did so furtively, in loosely organized small groups, and they were heartened by the signals sent out occasionally by others of similar conviction, flares burning for only a few moments in the darkness: a flyer placed in a library book or a bouquet at a war memorial, a bit of graffiti chalked on a wall (the Cross of Lorraine, the emblem of de Gaulle's Free France, could be produced with just three quick strokes). Relatively few Parisians were actively collaborating with the Nazi regime, beyond a certain class of politician, or journalist, or industrialist, or petty criminal; and other than out-and-out fascists and anti-Semites, few viewed the Nazis as their liberators, despite what the local newspapers were telling them each day. But neither could most Parisians bring themselves to imagine a homegrown resistance to the Nazis—not when even the supposedly mighty French army had been so thoroughly routed only months before. The vast majority, of course, hoped that Great Britain would eventually prevail, despite the recent setbacks on the battlefield. (According to Florence Gilliam, an American then living in France, the early months of the occupation brought the witticism that France was divided into Anglophiles and Anglophobes: "The Anglophiles hoped the brave and noble English would win the war. The Anglophobes hoped the English sons-of-bitches would win the war.") In the meantime, they would pin their hopes on the venerable Marshal Pétain to provide their nation the most favorable possible armistice. Stunned, powerless, mourning, traumatized by defeat, most French people, in Paris and throughout the country, adopted the carefully detached posture that came to be known as *attentisme:* They would wait and see.*

Kate Bonnefous had loved the sea ever since she was a girl on the coast of Kent, had talked of one day living in a sunny cottage somewhere along the Riviera; she enjoyed nothing better than to walk the dogs in the Bois de Boulogne, even in the wind and the rain, wearing a pair of high rubber boots. That had been a primary motivation for purchasing her own car as well—the sense of freedom it offered, the chance to escape the city as one wished, to feel oneself a part of the sunshine and the breeze and the "white wool sack clouds sailing," in the words of the old English poem, contentedly smoking a cigarette and humming a little tune with the road slipping by barely noticed beneath the wheels, deciding in a moment to turn right for a medieval castle or left toward a harbor with yachts bobbing at anchor and fishing nets hung out to dry. Now, with an escaped British soldier under their roof, she and Etta were living an almost cloistered exis-

---

* The term is taken from the French verb *attendre,* meaning "to await."

tence. They had shared their secret only with Kate's maid, Margot, who had returned to Paris at the end of July. Margot had been working for Kate and Henri Bonnefous for twelve years, ever since Kate first hired her as a seventeen-year-old Breton girl new to the city, and Kate trusted her as a French patriot and a loyal friend. Margot came to the apartment in the afternoons to help out with the dogs and the cleaning and shopping, which had become increasingly difficult and time-consuming—there was even a cigarette shortage now, and one sometimes had to walk to ten or more tobacconists to find any.

Henri was in the Unoccupied Zone, near Marseille; though he was fifty-five years old, he hoped to make his way to London, to join de Gaulle's forces there. Before that he had been in the region around Bordeaux, scouting out ways of crossing the line of demarcation. Henri knew that particular region of France very well, having long done business with many of the local vineyards for his wine distributing business, and eventually he had been introduced to a vineyard worker who conducted passages for a local clandestine group. Kate had written to him carefully explaining their situation and asking for advice about how to proceed, but thus far she had not received a reply.*

The German presence in their neighborhood was intensifying daily; it was impossible now to walk even a few blocks without feeling oneself observed by soldiers. All around their apartment house, buildings had been requisitioned by the Germans, especially auto garages, which were being used for the storage and repair of military vehicles. Seemingly all of the nearby hotels were now lodging German troops, and even the modern red-brick primary school on boulevard Berthier had become a barracks, the uniformed boys who used to attend having been dispatched to some other location, who knew where. Jewish-owned homes had been seized and given to German families who came with the army to live in Paris; reports circulated of mansions being ransacked, of soldiers getting drunk and shooting at paintings for fun, tossing priceless objects into sacks and making off with them, like marauders out of the Dark Ages. Increasingly the German army was requisitioning foodstuffs as well: Eggs and pasta

---

* The Nazis were able to intercept and read only a small percentage of the mail that French people sent each day.

had become almost impossible to find, milk was available only in the afternoons, the famous abundance of cheese (it was often said that France had as many types of cheese as days in the year) had been reduced solely to Gruyère, and, most shockingly, the sale of croissants and pastries had been banned to save on butter. Even the Bois de Boulogne had been closed, after two nighttime incidents on the grounds; no one knew exactly what had happened, but gunshots had been heard from the street.

Colin Hunter was eager to notify his family that he was all right, and Kate assured him that she was working on that; it wasn't so simple to send messages from France to England, which was currently enduring the most intense bombardment of the war to date. The German-controlled French papers reveled in the "rain of steel" that poured daily on England, destroying ports, aerodromes, factories. A more balanced view could be found only on the news programs of the BBC, including one they listened to nightly at 9:15.* That program was called *Les Français parlent aux Français* ["The French Speak to the French"], and it began each evening with the Morse code signal for the letter *V,* for *Victoire—dot dot dot dash.* That also happened to be the opening of Beethoven's Fifth Symphony, and hearing those immortal notes each night, Etta could not help but recall the countless evenings she had spent with Irving in concert halls listening to the work of Beethoven and other composers, transported by the power and beauty of the music. Kate was always there to listen to the evening program, though she was often away in the afternoons. Occasionally she left the apartment for hours at a time and afterward did not say where she had gone or what her plans were, other than that they would soon be going back to Doullens to get Corporal Hood-Cree; she had promised that she would get him out, and this was a promise she meant to keep. "Madame Bonnefous," Colin Hunter was to say later, "was British to the backbone. If you

---

* It was estimated that as much as half of the French population regularly listened to that broadcast. In a joke told widely that year, one Parisian asks another, "Did you hear what happened last night? At 9:20, a Jew killed a German soldier, cut him open, and ate his heart." The other Parisian replies, "Impossible, for three reasons: A German has no heart. A Jew eats no pork. And at 9:20, everyone is listening to the BBC."

were British, she would do anything to help you. It didn't matter what your rank was."

On the morning of Monday, September 9, Kate and Etta set out once more for Doullens, inside the *zone interdite*. Even in September, the summer showed no signs of receding. Beyond the city the air was filled with the drone of insects, the deep coffee-like aroma of warm earth. Most of the vehicles they passed on the road were the greenish gray of the Wehrmacht, an ominous color, like smoke or the sky before a storm. When they arrived in Doullens Kate parked at an intersection several blocks from the hospital, and the two of them waited together uneasily in the front seat, hoping to remain as inconspicuous as possible in a sleek black car with a large Red Cross emblem painted on the side. Kate had arranged with Gordon Hood-Cree that she would pick him up at noon, and she and Etta had left plenty of time to spare—it would not do to leave the young Englishman standing around waiting for a ride—and as the minutes crept by Etta kept checking her watch, sometimes at such short intervals that she had to convince herself it hadn't stopped. Finally, from somewhere, came the sound of bells tolling the hour.

It was only a few minutes past twelve when they caught sight of Gordon Hood-Cree in the distance.* He was limping down the street, all six foot two of him, his right foot turned in noticeably, and as she watched him Etta thought wildly that he could not possibly wedge himself into that small luggage compartment; it had been a very tight fit even for Colin Hunter, who was shorter and did not have a badly wounded leg. Hood-Cree was wearing the clothing that Kate had procured for him, including a brown jacket over a yellow shirt, and he had removed his round steel-framed eyeglasses, which

---

* According to the escape report he provided to interrogators from the British agency MI9 on March 18, 1941, Gordon Hood-Cree had escaped from the hospital the day before, September 8, and then stayed overnight at "Mme. B's flat in the town." There is no evidence that Kate Bonnefous herself had a flat in Doullens, and it is possible that she had arranged with a local resident to shelter him overnight. (In one account, Hood-Cree refers to a young local woman named "Yvonne" who delivered the clothing to him inside the hospital.) Hood-Cree did not mention the flat in his other accounts of the escape, but it would not have been possible for Bonnefous and Shiber to have picked him up on September 8, as that was a Sunday and private vehicles were banned from the roads on Sundays.

could give him away as a British soldier; getting those lenses put into a civilian pair of frames was another task that would need to be undertaken in Paris.

Down the street, Hood-Cree stopped at a corner and stood there gazing into the distance, as though waiting for a bus or struck by a sudden thought; Kate started the car and they set off in his direction. As they approached the corner Hood-Cree waved at the car, gesturing for them to stop, and then leaned toward the car to ask loudly in French if they might give him a lift to the next town. When they agreed, he thanked them politely, as a grateful stranger would, and got into the back seat; then, once they were out of Doullens, Kate pulled over again to the side of the road and turned off the engine, and Gordon Hood-Cree got out of the car while she came around to open the luggage compartment.

In a 1952 essay entitled "Escape from France," Gordon Hood-Cree would write, "I was picked up by the two brave women in their car. . . . The best place for me was out of sight, so I folded up my six feet of skin and bone (German P.O.W. diet is not conducive to body-building) and disappeared into the luggage-boot behind the rear seat." He slid in feet first, like a miner going down a shaft, and though it was painful to maneuver, what with his sewn-up leg wound and a piece of shrapnel still lodged in his ribs, after some effort he managed to wedge himself into that small space, curled into something like a fetal position, his head facing toward the back of the car and his legs extending beneath the rear seat. "I was lying on my side," Hood-Cree recalled, "cramped up, with my nose some six inches from a very hot and smelly exhaust pipe which ran under the boot." Kate shut the compartment after him, and a few seconds later he heard the dull thud of the driver's door closing. Then everything began to vibrate around him as the engine was turned on, and in another moment, with the brief stomach-lurching sensation of an elevator quickly ascending, Hood-Cree felt the car begin to move.

The compartment was suddenly filled with a humming, like the cockpit of a small propeller plane; his skin tingled from the constant vibrations, his bones were jostled by every bump in the road, a throb of pain occasionally shot out from the shard of metal lodged in his rib cage. It was impossible for him to judge time with any sense of precision, but not long after they set off he was alarmed to feel the car unexpectedly slow down and then come to a stop. He lay there silently in the sweltering darkness, wondering what had happened, and then from the side of the car he heard two men's voices, speaking loudly, in a French thickly accented by German. After a moment he heard a woman's voice; then he heard the sound of the rear doors opening, first one, then another, and with a sickening feeling Hood-Cree understood that the men were getting into the car.

Kate and Etta were about fifteen miles from Doullens when they saw the pair of German officers, in full dress even on a day in late summer, dark uniform with high collar and wide leather belt and brilliant silver braid. Until that point everything had been proceeding just as planned, and if all continued to go well the women expected to be rejoining Colin Hunter in Paris by midafternoon. In the past they had driven by innumerable uniformed Germans as they made their rounds of the prison camps and hospitals, of all ranks and branches of the military, and none seemed to have paid them any particular mind. On this occasion, though, the officers called to them from the side of the road while pointing at their car, clearly indicating that they should pull over.

In an instant Etta could picture what was about to happen—search, arrest, prison—but after Kate stopped the car the officers approached with friendly expressions and addressed the women in "correct" tones. Of course, they did not know that Etta understood German and so they spoke in French, as was common for German officers stationed in the Occupied Zone. They explained that the car for which they had been waiting had not yet arrived, and it was now quite delayed and they were anxious to be on their way, and they hoped that the two ladies would be so good as to give them a lift to their destination, which was directly on the way to Paris.

The very idea of it was unthinkable, but Kate understood that she was in no position to refuse these men, and so she consented to their request, mustering up all the graciousness she could manage. The two officers thanked her politely and, as it was a very hot day and the car's rear windows were open, it was no trouble for them simply to reach in themselves and pull down the little Bakelite knobs that unlocked the doors and then step inside, settling themselves comfortably in the back. Kate and Etta could do nothing but wait for the groan, the gasp, the tremor of movement from beneath the seat that would alert the two German officers to the presence of someone else inside the car. But there was only silence, and after a few more agonized moments Kate released the hand brake and directed the car back onto the road.

Etta felt that she could barely breathe; her heart was beating too fast, her head roaring with anxiety, and as she fought to regain her bearings she silently marveled at how Kitty was managing to work the clutch and the gears and keep the car on the road, her left hand clenched tight on the wheel, all the while keeping up a conversation with the Germans. The conversation was going on in French, punctuated by occasional laughter from the back seat, and Etta was not paying close enough attention to understand what was being said, other than to recognize that Kitty was doing everything she could to keep the men talking, because as long as they were talking they might not notice any sound coming from the luggage compartment. All Etta knew for certain was that things had spun wildly out of control, in a way no one could have anticipated, although she was clearheaded enough to recognize that at least now they did not have to worry about being searched at the upcoming checkpoints, nor pulled over by any motorcycle troopers, as long as they had a pair of German officers sitting in the car with them. She could only imagine the consequences the officers would face if they were found to be driving in a car with an escaped British serviceman hiding at their feet.

Trapped beneath them, Gordon Hood-Cree was horrified to realize that the weight of the Germans pressing down on his knee had burst the stitches and that his leg wound had now reopened. He felt blood beginning to trickle down his shin, just at the spot where the bullet had entered. The leg felt as if it were on fire; inside that suffocating space his skin was burning, his clothes damp with sweat. Every bodily instinct told him to move, to cry out, to gasp for breath, but he did not: Everything in the future now depended on silence. He had lost all sense of time, felt the world reduced simply to heat and darkness and the pain in his leg. On and on they drove; he had no idea where the car was going or why, whether the two women had been arrested or not. All he knew was that he had no alternative but to wait, and as the car sped onward he kept his eyes clenched tight in the blackness of the compartment and willed himself not to make a sound.

Etta could not fathom the utter silence from beneath the floorboard. Was it possible that Gordon Hood-Cree had died en route? She could not bear the thought of it, nor bring herself to imagine what on earth they would do with him if he had. In the past Etta had sometimes felt that Kitty drove too fast for her liking, but now the car seemed achingly slow. After what seemed an interminable length of time—it had actually been no more than half an hour—one of the Germans called out from the rear seat with directions to their destination, and eventually Kate pulled the car to a stop. Once the officers had thanked them for their kindness and disappeared inside the building, Kate leaped from the car; leaning inside, as though looking for something in the back seat, she called to Gordon Hood-Cree to make sure that he was all right. They were deeply relieved to hear his voice, sounding tired but well enough under the circumstances, and with no further delay Kate got back in the car and they sped off toward Paris.

On the northern outskirts of the city, perhaps twenty miles from home, they suddenly heard a loud bang and the car skidded and rumbled to a stop. "Did they shoot at us?" Etta recalled asking, in fright and shock.

No, Kate told her, turning off the engine, but one of the tires had gotten a puncture and would have to be changed.

Almost disbelievingly, the two of them stepped out to investigate the situation, and after a brief inspection of the flat tire, Kate unlocked the boot and together they hauled out the spare tire and the jack. The car's underframe, Kate knew, had a square hole located at the midpoint of the chassis, just beneath the hinge of the front door, and the lever arm of the jack was designed to fit into it. By rotating the jack handle one was supposed to be able to raise that side of the car to free the damaged tire, but this was not easy to do even on the best of occasions, much less with the weight of a large, if underfed, man lying directly above it, and as they struggled they heard Gordon Hood-Cree's voice coming from the luggage compartment offering to help, but Kate just leaned into the car and hissed at him to be quiet, for goodness' sake, Germans were passing by all the time. In changing the tire they could not help but feel as if they were trying to defuse a ticking bomb, because eventually, they understood, one of the passing German soldiers would notice the two older women bent over the side of the car, and he would gallantly volunteer his services to them, and if he tried to rotate the jack handle himself he might wonder why a seemingly empty car felt so heavy, and they simply couldn't have that. So Kate waited until the street was clear and then called to Hood-Cree to come out of the car, quickly, and somehow he managed to extricate himself from the luggage compartment and get out of the car, and after quickly filling his lungs with fresh air, drenched with sweat and crouching gingerly on his gamy leg, he set to work. As he would later write, "I found myself fixing the tyre in a main street while German soldiers and airmen strolled by, little thinking that the ragged type working on the car was a corporal of the Buffs, escaped . . . only two hours before."

There was one especially delicate moment when another German officer pulled up in a car to ask if they needed any assistance, but Hood-Cree remained bent over his work with his back to the street, and Kate thanked the officer kindly and assured him that there was no need, the job was just about finished, and with that the officer nodded and drove off.

Finally the tire had been replaced and Gordon Hood-Cree returned to the luggage compartment for the remaining portion of the journey back to rue Balny-d'Avricourt. "And so," he wrote later, "to a haven of peace and rest and good nursing at the home of these two ladies."

9

F OUR STORIES TALL, EMBELLISHED with neoclassical columns and balustrades, and built from creamy local stone selected to complement the surrounding buildings, the American embassy in Paris carried the serene, dignified aspect of an eighteenth-century noble mansion, but in fact it had opened only in 1931. It stood in one of the most prestigious locations in the city, by the northwest corner of the place de la Concorde, facing the avenue Gabriel and the picturesque Jardins des Champs-Élysées—and directly across a narrow side street from the Hôtel de Crillon, which in June 1940 had been requisitioned by the Nazis to serve as the headquarters of the German army in the city; from certain windows of the embassy, one could look out across the street and see German officers at their desks inside the hotel, bent over their work of conquest.

Sometime during the month of September 1940, Kate Bonnefous entered the American embassy. In those first chaotic months of the occupation, the embassy received hundreds of visitors daily (one memo from the First Secretary, Cecil M. P. Cross, referred to visitors "besieging the Embassy"), and the information desk on the right-hand side of the entrance hall would have been surrounded by desperate refugees of many nationalities waiting to be directed to the proper office, or perhaps, if they were more fortunate, to be received by an embassy staff member upstairs, not all of whom actually represented the American government. Since the evacuation of the British embassy on June 10, the American embassy had provided offices for a skeleton staff of British employees. Certainly the most colorful of these employees was a large, well-dressed Englishman by the name of Cecil Shaw. He was the man Kate Bonnefous had come to see.

Born in 1871, Col. Cecil A. Shaw was a career military man, a veteran of the second Boer War and World War I. He had long since retired from active service, after which he had married an extremely wealthy American woman (Sylvia de Grasse Fox, of the Philadelphia Foxes), and now lived in a suite at the Hôtel Ritz and drove through the city in the back of a chauffeured limousine. With his enormous frame, fringe of white hair surrounding a pinkish pate, and large nose perpetually reddened by drink, Cecil Shaw could not help but call to mind another superannuated British colonel, the popular cartoon character Colonel Blimp, but in fact, Shaw was a highly respected figure among the British community in Paris—"a tower of strength," in the words of one of his many friends—a war hero decorated many times over for his service with the 9th Lancers and 7th Dragoon cavalry regiments and the newly established Royal Air Force. Shaw had also worked in British military intelligence in India, South Africa, and Rhodesia, and although he did not have an official position with the British Interests Section, he was a regular presence in the American embassy in the early months of the occupation and could often be found in an upstairs office, from which he oversaw the dispersal of funds to British citizens in need of them.

As it happened, a vast portion of these monies came from Shaw's own accounts, which granted him a good deal of latitude about how they were to be distributed; at least some ended up in the pockets of escaped British prisoners of war on the run from the Germans. Reports from numerous servicemen, given to the British escape agency MI9 upon their return to London, mention Colonel Shaw as the embassy representative in Paris who sympathetically listened to their harrowing tales of capture and escape, offered to send word home to their families, suggested possible means of reaching the Unoccupied Zone, and provided money to help defray the costs of the journey. Anthony Richardson's 1950 biography of Basil Embry, an RAF wing commander who escaped from a German prisoner-of-war camp in the summer of 1940, described how Embry came to the American embassy seeking help and was advised to see Colonel Shaw. Embry found Shaw there "without any difficulty," wrote Richardson. "The Colonel appeared to know his business and his views were concise." Shaw said to Embry,

> "Here are three hundred francs, Wing Commander, to help you on your way. I suggest that you do not leave Paris as you've been advised to do. Instead, you should report to the Salvation Army hostel in the Rue Cantagrel. Here is the address." He scribbled on a slip of paper and handed it to Embry. "You will find the Salvationist in charge an excellent fellow. The position is this. The War Cemetery gardeners—I speak of the Fourteen-Eighteen war—are coming in from the outlying districts and are being collected at the hostel in order to be returned home. They are all British, of course. Mix in with them and pass yourself off as one of them and get back to England as a repatriated gardener."

Several of the MI9 reports indicate that Cecil Shaw directed escaped British servicemen to the local branch of the Salvation Army, but that was just one of the service organizations in Paris to which he had close ties. "In 1940," an obituary of Shaw would later note, "he used his close connection with the French Red Cross to assist British officers and men left stranded to get back to Britain." Undoubtedly it was through her own volunteer work with the Croix-Rouge française in occupied Paris that Kate Bonnefous first heard about the assistance that Shaw was providing to escaped British soldiers. In the late summer and fall of 1940 she would regularly visit Cecil Shaw in the American embassy, waiting to be received by him in the lobby with its decor of a much earlier period, the oil portraits of Presidents Washington and Monroe, the black marble columns topped by busts of Washington and the Marquis de Lafayette, the brass lanterns with the eagle finials—all set off by that emblem of modern American ingenuity, a watercooler.[*]

Neither Kate Bonnefous nor Cecil Shaw ever recorded what was said during that particular September meeting in the American embassy, but when she returned to the apartment on rue Balny-d'Avricourt, Kate informed Colin Hunter and Gordon Hood-Cree that she had been able to send messages home to their families in London reporting that they were well and "with friends." She had also brought back 1,750 francs (worth about $800 in today's currency) that Colonel Shaw had given her for the men's journey to unoccupied France.

How exactly they were going to get there she had not yet figured out. Thus far there had not been any reply from Henri; indeed, Kate didn't even know whether he had received her letter. In the meantime, Hunter and Hood-Cree could remain in their apartment; Hood-Cree in particular would need the time to let his leg wound heal.

Complicating matters enormously, a new system of food rationing had just been introduced in France. Sharp limits were set on a wide range of basic foodstuffs, including bread, meat, cheese, eggs, oil, rice, and sugar; it was estimated that a typical French person could now consume only about 1,300 calories per day, less than half the average consumption before the war. Parisians were instructed to present themselves at their local *mairie,* or town hall, to register for their monthly ration books; the books contained little colored squares called *tickets* that permitted the purchase of specific items and amounts, to be snipped off by shopkeepers, for whom a pair of scissors around the neck had become a symbol of vested state power. In the seventeenth arrondissement, where Kate and Etta lived, the *mairie* had installed the local food office inside "a rather sordid-looking garage and store" on rue Jacquemont. Residents had to endure a wait of an hour or longer to receive a blank application, followed by an-

---

[*] One escaped British prisoner of war who came to the embassy that summer seeking help would later note that he had only ever seen a watercooler in Hollywood movies; despite his thirst he resisted the temptation to use it, because he didn't know how it worked and feared drawing undue attention to himself.

other extended wait after completing it, at which point they could submit the application to the scrutiny of one of the local officials on duty, most of whom were bureaucratically imperious if not overtly hostile, and seemed to avail themselves of every opportunity to demand additional information, ordering the applicant once more to the back of the line. "Any responsible, good-natured French citizen who turns up at the rue Jacquemont," one resident noted, "leaves three or four hours later with a snarl on his lips and loathing in his eyes, boiling with a destructive hatred of present-day France and the incorrigible, pernicious stupidity of her administration."

Making things worse for Kate and Etta, they now had four mouths to feed but only two ration books. It was therefore imperative to stretch the allotments just as far as they could go, and the two women spent a large portion of their time waiting alongside other women outside the food shops with which they had registered as customers, hoping that a grocer's assistant or butcher's boy would not be rude or, worse, that the proprietor would not give short weight or hand over some rotten onions or a shriveled bunch of carrots. Given the intense demand for even the most dismal of foodstuffs, and the force of the crowd pressing impatiently behind her, a customer had little recourse but to submit to the petty tyranny of the shop, for fear of being removed from the books and having to return once more to the *mairie* to register for a different one, where the service and supply would likely be much the same. "Nobody crosses his vegetable store owner these days," one local journalist observed during the occupation; another asked a friend what she would do when the war was over, to which she replied: "Personally, I shall set fire to my grocer's store."

Somehow, though, scraps of leftover meat and some lowly root vegetables, moistened with broth and enlivened by a few dashes of vinegar, could be turned into beef Miroton; there might be a salad with chunks of beets red and shining as garnets, or cabbage goulash if that had been the vegetable available that day, and in the mornings, a baguette topped with Kate's homemade jam, or fritters made possible by the twenty kilos of sugar she had presciently laid away before the occupation. (Tins of "prewar sugar," declared one correspondent for *Les nouveaux temps,* were now "worth their weight in gold.")

Later Colin Hunter would enthuse to a reporter about Kate Bonne-fous, "She had a colossal sense of humor—and could she cook!"

Still, even with Kate's cooking skills, and her well-stocked pantry, and the hours spent waiting outside the shops, it's inconceivable that Kate and Etta could have fed themselves and their British servicemen for an extended period simply on the provisions allowed them; like many other Parisians, they would almost certainly have had to resort to the black market—especially as Kate had already gone outside regular channels to obtain gasoline for her trips into the "forbidden zone." It wasn't especially difficult to locate a source, if one really wanted to: a shop that kept some boxes in the back containing extra items sold at a markup; a neighbor with a cousin who occasionally brought in eggs and butter from the country, or perhaps even a slab of bacon or a chicken. These were not the widely despised profiteers who traded sugar and rice and olive oil by the ton, or the smaller-scale crooks who asked extortionary prices or watered their milk and cut their tobacco with bits of dried grass; it was not the sort of high-end black market that enabled luxury restaurants like L'Aiglon, Fouquet's, and La Tour d'Argent to keep a steady supply of oysters and rabbits and bouillabaisse on hand for their wealthy and well-connected patrons, French and German alike. As a neighbor explained to the expatriate American writer Gertrude Stein, there was a distinction between the black market and "finding" something: "To 'find' is when you find a small amount any day at a reasonable price that will just augment your diet and keep you healthy. Black traffic is when you pay a very large sum for a large amount of food—that is the difference."

Everyone, it was said, was looking for "BOF" (*beurre, oeufs, fromage*), and at a certain point everyone had to confront the question of what he or she was willing to do, and under what circumstances, to obtain more food: whether one would break the law, or betray one's own conscience, to surreptitiously purchase products that were not available to others, or buy up someone else's ration tickets, or ask for ration tickets as a wedding present, or use tickets that one suspected might have been forged—especially if one had, say, an ill parent or an underfed child, or an escaped soldier, waiting at home. The black market, as it turned out, contained many shades of gray, and it was just one of the means by which many Frenchwomen under occupation pursued the resourceful, improvisatory way of life—scrounging, stretching, substituting—known widely as *"le système D,"* after the French verb *se débrouiller,* meaning to manage or to cope.

An occasional excursion into the black market seems to have been one among the many "errands" that Kate Bonnefous was then beginning to undertake—errands of which it was better not to know too much. "Food in Paris was extremely short even then," Gordon Hood-Cree would recall of Kate, "but somehow she always managed to bring something back. Where she got it, I don't know. We never asked."

There was yet another errand that Kate had to run, and for this one she needed Colin Hunter and Gordon Hood-Cree to accompany her. For each of the men, it was the first time they were sitting upright inside the Peugeot 402, their first opportunity to see Paris from anything beyond a sixth-floor window. After three months of occupation, the city seemed already sapped of vitality. Everywhere shops stood quiet behind locked gates and latched shutters, blind eyes turned to the street; the ones that remained open—especially food shops—could immediately be identified by the lines outside them. Sometimes a line was the scene of shoving and arguments, as when a pregnant woman might attempt to cut to the front; reports began to circulate of women pretending to be pregnant by stuffing pillows under their dresses or coats. From everywhere came darkly muttered complaints and accusations about who was responsible for the shortages; some, as always, blamed the Jews. All of the major intersections now had street signs posted in German, black-bordered arrows stacked one on top of another. High-pitched police sirens wailed in the distance, rising and falling just at the edge of consciousness; planes buzzed ceaselessly over the rooftops. Parisians were living these days in a city they no longer entirely recognized, like one in a dream, familiar but changed in ways that were strange and deeply unsettling.

Kate and the two servicemen drove past the Tuileries, where one of the Nazis' first acts had been to blow up the marble bas-relief honoring Edith Cavell, the British relief worker executed by the Germans for aiding in the escape of Allied prisoners from Belgium in World War I. Traffic was light, but no route was direct anymore: Streets were unaccountably blocked off with white barriers, gendarmes waved cars away from intersections seemingly at random. Along the sidewalks, Nazi officers relaxed at café tables. The city's prefect of police, Roger Langeron, noted in his diary that month that he admired the "perfect dignity of the passersby," who gazed straight ahead as they walked, as if the enemy were invisible; among the German occupiers, Paris would become known as *die Stadt ohne Blick*—"the city without a glance."

Kate parked the car and together they made their way through the crowd to a set of stone and cast-iron buildings clustered between rue de Rivoli and the Seine. One of them, an immense structure with sinuous balconies in the Art Deco style, displayed the store's name atop the roof in tall white letters: SAMARITAINE. Kate had brought them there because La Samaritaine offered one of the city's few Photomaton booths—the while-you-wait photo machines popular with young couples and others wanting a souvenir of a cheerful moment, and, more soberly, with those who needed personal identification for official documents. To use the Photomaton, the customer sat down inside the booth behind its heavy black curtain, turned the wooden stool to adjust it to the proper height, and then, after placing five francs in the coin slot, pressed a rubber bulb and posed as a series of flashes went off over the course of sixteen seconds; eight minutes later, the machine delivered a thin paper strip, still slightly damp, containing six small black-and-white photographs. Hunter and Hood-Cree were wearing civilian clothing, of course, and by this time they had shaved their mustaches, in order to look less British; but while both men spoke reasonably good French, neither felt that he could actually pass as a Frenchman if put to the test, and so for an interminable eight minutes they had to pose as shoppers, feigning interest in displays of underwear and watches while trying to avoid making conversation with the counter staff. "It was terrifying," Colin

Hunter would later say. "I thought that everyone knew we were English and that everyone was going to denounce us. But nobody took the slightest notice."

Estimates vary as to how many British servicemen remained in France after the evacuations from Dunkirk and surrounding regions in the spring of 1940. Lt. Jimmy Langley, who had himself escaped from a military hospital in France—and who would subsequently become an important figure in the British escape agency MI9—noted in his report of March 1941: "I consider that about 2,500 British soldiers are in hiding north of the Seine; some of these have married French girls and settled down. Of these probably 2,000 would, if contacted and helped, get out." The French estimate, according to Langley, was closer to 3,500. Whether or not they planned to escape, or to stay in France for the duration of the war, all of these soldiers needed identity cards. Possession of an identity card was necessary for a wide variety of functions, and during the occupation anyone was subject to an identity check at any time.

Finding a blank identity card was no problem, as they were available for purchase at stationery shops and department stores, and the photograph for the card could be taken at a Photomaton or made at home with a small box camera. Still, a completed identity card was useless if it did not also display an imprint from an authorized stamp, which in most cases was to be obtained only at the local town hall or other government office.*

In Paris, a government employee named Gustave Rackelboom was hoping to furnish forged identity cards to those who needed them. Rackelboom, a World War I veteran, worked in the Ministry of Pensions for the Fédération Nationale des Voluntaires de Guerre,

---

* For those with no access to such a stamp, some improvisation was required. A simulacrum of a stamp, for instance, could be produced by making cuts very carefully with a razor blade in the rubber heel of a shoe; if one did not have a stamp pad to provide the ink, then the incised heel could be rubbed on a piece of carbon paper before pressing it onto the completed identity card. Alternatively, a cold hard-boiled egg could be rolled over the inked stamp on an authentic card; the imprint made on the albumen could then be transferred by rolling the egg over the would-be card.

an office that provided assistance to former soldiers; in the summer of 1940, he established a reception center for newly demobilized French soldiers. To obtain provisions for the men served by his center, he sought assistance from another government office in Paris—overseeing "hygiene, work, and social welfare"—where the *chef de secrétariat* was a Parisienne named Jeanne Monier. Over the course of weeks the two colleagues came to know each other, and by the end of August, Rackelboom had learned that Monier was authorized to supply transit vouchers to those who needed them—free railroad passes that enabled the holder to travel from one station to another within the Occupied Zone. In principle, these vouchers were reserved for refugees from *l'exode* who wished to return to their former homes. Rackelboom, however, sensed an opportunity to help escaped soldiers he had heard about through his work, and at that point he decided he would take the step of confiding in Jeanne Monier—regarding, as he would later phrase it, "men in an irregular situation vis-à-vis the occupiers (that is to say, escaping prisoners of war), who wanted to pass into the Unoccupied Zone." Rackelboom's idea was to provide vouchers that would allow these former prisoners to travel from Paris to a railroad station near the line of demarcation; there, they could make contact with one of the *passeurs,* the French locals who surreptitiously brought those fleeing Nazi rule across the line into the Unoccupied Zone.* There was still the matter of forged identity cards, though; travel vouchers were of little use without identity cards to accompany them.

Jeanne Monier, for her part, was in contact with another government employee, a man named Henri Grimal. Grimal was a clerk in the Préfecture de la Seine, the state organization overseeing administrative services in Paris, and as such had access to official stamps. After the war, Grimal would attest that he had conducted numerous acts of resistance, including "aid in the escape of French and British prisoners of war," by means of "fake papers" and "fake identity cards." Thus the chain began to be put together, stretching from Henri Grimal (who had forged identity cards) to Jeanne Monier (who had

---

* It was possible to take a train directly from the Occupied into the Unoccupied Zone. However, this was a risky endeavor, as German scrutiny of passengers at the border was particularly severe.

forged travel passes) to Gustave Rackelboom (who had the service-men who needed them).

Only a few weeks later, in September 1940, Kate Bonnefous made contact with Gustave Rackelboom. The organization for which she volunteered, the Foyer du Soldat, had for many years established and supplied reception centers for French soldiers, just as Rackelboom did through his own office, and the two of them would likely have met in the course of their work. Etta Shiber later indicated that Kate did in fact know Gustave Rackelboom through the Foyer du Soldat, and that one day in the summer of 1940 she returned to the apartment excitedly reporting that she had just run into him in the Métro. (As it happened, Rackelboom's office was located only two blocks from Kate and Etta's apartment.)

By the middle of September, then, Kate Bonnefous had procured identity cards and travel passes, as well as 1,750 francs in spending money, for Lt. Colin Hunter and Cpl. Gordon Hood-Cree. She felt confident that she could now bring the men up to the line of demarcation—but she still did not know how to get them across.

It was just around this time that the letter arrived from Henri Bonnefous.

10

S HAPED BY ICE AND smoothed by water, the cliffs of the Périgord are now dotted with ancient castles and the villages that
cluster around them, built from stones carved out of plains of limestone and granite and slabs of primeval timber pulled from the deep
forest. In olden days the forest was said to be home to a multitude of
fantastic creatures, of deer that were larger than horses and stole children and damaged crops; or of the Striae, which had the bodies of
women but also sharp claws and leathery wings like those of a bat,
and on cold winter nights, it was said, would swoop down on an un-
suspecting poacher and tear his heart from his chest and devour it.
For those living in the timeworn remote villages of southwestern
France, the misfortunes wrought by the world were mysterious but
perhaps not entirely inscrutable; meaning might be discerned in a
flight of crows, a pattern of clouds, the sound of dry thunderclaps
rattling overhead like walnuts shaken in a bag. Otherwise one was
simply at the mercy of fate, unprotected against a life too often buf-
feted by rain and drought and frost, and beset by would-be conquerors dating all the way back to the Romans and the Visigoths.

Elie Teyssier was born in 1895 in the southwestern town of
Castillon-sur-Dordogne. Although he had been born on the cusp of
the twentieth century and would participate in two wars that in-

volved the most complex and fearsome machinery ever devised, in his daily life Teyssier was not far removed from the peasants of an earlier time, who lived in stone cottages without benefit of heat or electricity or running water, used a fireplace as their cookstove, and scratched out their existence from what they could extract from the earth. Except for the periods when he was a soldier, he was all his life a *métayer*, an old-fashioned word that is rarely used anymore and for which the closest English translation is probably "sharecropper." At the time of Elie Teyssier's birth, more than twenty thousand *métayers* labored in and around the Périgord, agricultural workers who did not own any land and, barring a miraculous turn of events, never would. Like the rest of them, Teyssier worked for an absentee owner who provided the land, the buildings, and the farm equipment in return for a share of the annual yield. The apportionment varied from place to place, and it was set out in a contract minutely detailed in its particulars—an arrangement that would seem to have put Teyssier at something of a disadvantage, as neither he nor his wife, Jeanne, could read or write, and signed their names, on the few occasions when it was required, with an *X*.

When he stood up straight, as he rarely did anymore, he measured 1.57 meters tall—just a shade under five foot two—short even for that time, but a practical height for planting roots and picking grapes and tying vines to a stake, all of which were done close to the ground. It seems likely that as a child he had lacked proper nutrition, as he had proper schooling. He had been arrested once, in his teens, on a charge of theft, and though the court sentenced him to a month in jail, he did not serve any time, and this seems to have been his only encounter with the police until the German occupation. By that time, well into his middle age, he had bought himself a boat, which he kept on the Dordogne River: nothing extravagant, just one of the flat-bottomed, canoe-like little craft called barques that were perfect for fishing the sinuous rivers and tributaries that wound through the hills and that he knew almost as well as the land. He did not speak much. In part that owed simply to the laconic tendencies of the men in the area (in the words of one local proverb, "The mewing cat gets nothing when hunting"), in part to the ease with silence imposed by many years spent in a solitary profession, but some of it, too, was surely due to ill health, in particular to the pulmonary scarring that had left his lungs as stiff as cardboard, making breathing laborious and eating an ordeal, and which inevitably impaired his voice as well. The condition was chronic and untreatable, its origin a cloud of German phosgene gas that had swept over him while he was fighting in the trenches of Verdun during the First World War.

Elie Teyssier had enlisted on August 11, 1914, one week after Germany declared war on France; four years later, with the war almost at an end, he left the army at the same rank at which he entered it, as an infantry private second-class. In that time he had received no promotions, no commendations, nothing that would in any way distinguish him from the men alongside whom he fought: He was just another *poilu*, one of the innumerable anonymous foot soldiers from the countryside who had fought bravely and endured much, and returned home damaged in countless ways. He had never graduated from any school, and when he joined the army, still in his teens, he was described on his military entry papers as a "farm worker" (the more elevated title of "farmer" having been written and then crossed out); in his twenties he resumed his *métayage,* much as before, except that now he had to work the land without ever being able to draw a free breath.

Back home, Teyssier found himself living once more in the poets' vale of enchantment, a landscape of sheer white cliffs and golden sunlight diffused through vaults of chestnut and hornbeam. Yet even in this idyllic setting, even many years later, he could still hear the sound of the guns in his ears. He would never really be free of the army: He was a member of the territorial reserve until 1929, at which point his deteriorating physical condition no longer permitted him to serve; a decade later, when France and Germany were again at war, he was called up as part of a general mobilization and assigned to a nearby agricultural depot that was being used for the storage of ammunition. It was there that he watched, in shock and horror, the abrupt collapse of the French army. Like so many other veterans of the 1914–18 war, he did not understand how a front line could crack like the shell of an egg, not when he and his comrades had held out for four years in a world of mud and shit and blood, the air filled with the roar of cannons and the moans of the wounded and dying, the ground trembling, the horizon a sheet of flame.

For former soldiers like Elie Teyssier, there was no more powerful and humiliating symbol of defeat than the line of demarcation that had been imposed on their country, dividing families, slicing towns in two, separating storekeepers from their stores and farmers from their fields. The line of demarcation stretched diagonally like a bando-lier across the chest of the country, from Jura in the east to the Basses-Pyrénées in the southwest. Extending for nearly 1,200 kilo-meters (some 750 miles, or about the distance from New York City to Chicago), the line was patrolled by Vichy police on one side and German soldiers on the other; at various places along the line, French citizens had been requisitioned to cut down trees and build the guard-houses and barriers that would separate them from their neighbors.

Not far from Teyssier's home, the line of demarcation ran north-south along the Lidoire River, then made a brief east-west turn at Castillon-sur-Dordogne before bearing north-south again along the Dordogne River, which provided a natural border between the Oc-cupied Zone on its western shore and the Unoccupied Zone to the east. Castillon was patrolled especially closely—between 250 and 300 German troops were stationed in a town of some three thousand inhabitants—as it sat directly on the line and the Unoccupied Zone could be reached from there in a number of ways: by car or bicycle over the bridge that spanned the Dordogne; by railroad; or by boat via the Dordogne itself, which passed under the bridge as it me-andered west toward Bordeaux.

Since the establishment of the line of demarcation at the end of June, Castillon and its surrounding area had served as a gathering place for those looking to cross into the Unoccupied Zone. Carefully, not knowing who could be trusted and who couldn't, they reached out to those whose jobs brought them into contact with the public— café owners, hoteliers, taxi drivers—seeking to find people who might be willing to convey them clandestinely across the line, the *passeurs*. Most of the *passeurs*, for their part, had jobs that allowed them a familiarity with the local topography—farmers especially, but also canal pilots, truckers, postmen, even poachers. Research conducted in France after the war found that about four-fifths of the *passeurs* were men; the largest percentage were in their twenties, while less than one in ten were as old as Elie Teyssier. Fully 95 percent were working in the region in which they had been born.

In the vast majority of cases, the *passeurs* were motivated by patriotic and humanitarian sentiments, reinforced sometimes by a taste for adventure, a desire to vary the monotonous daily rhythms of farm work. The extreme danger of the undertaking—the likelihood of prison or even death—was a hardship, but also a means of maintaining self-respect, a sense of dignity, in the face of national defeat. And while most of the *passeurs* were honest, a small number viewed the occupation as a windfall, the line of demarcation serving as a kind of lever to extract large sums of money from desperate people. Most gallingly, they sought to reap extraordinary profits from anti-Semitism: While a payment of 250 francs might suffice to bring a Frenchman across the line, a foreigner would typically be charged three times that amount, and Jewish refugees (including French citizens) would have to pay anywhere from 2,000 to 10,000 francs for a crossing—because these unscrupulous *passeurs* believed, often mistakenly, that Jewish refugees were wealthy, and that the especially vulnerable condition of Jews under Nazism would force them to spend lavishly for the chance to obtain their freedom.

For his part, Elie Teyssier asked only 50 francs per passenger, barely enough to cover his own expenses—although in at least some cases, it seems, he did not charge even that. Gaston Melet, the owner of a bar in Libourne and a member of a local clandestine group called Group 606, would later recall that Teyssier "worked for us purely free of charge." The two knew each other from before the war, Melet said, and "I entered into a relationship with him with the arrival of the occupants. . . . Teyssier rendered me great services. I used him principally to pass Jews and French people fleeing the occupied zone."

Before long Teyssier's work as a *passeur* would come to include escaped British servicemen as well. On September 26, 1940, the first of those servicemen, Colin Hunter and Gordon Hood-Cree, set out from Paris to meet him.

The train trip was passed mostly in darkness, save for a single bulb burning overhead, painted blue for the blackout, which cast the carriage into a permanent gloomy twilight. The third-class compartment contained a few tired, silent travelers, among them a pair of young men in berets who had taken seats on opposite ends of the car, because two men of military age traveling together might draw too much attention. In addition to a forged identity card, each one carried a ticket from Paris to Libourne, a southwestern town not far from Bordeaux; Libourne actually came three stops before Castillon, which was the closest station to the line of demarcation, but they would not go that far, as German customs officials were known to inspect the train especially closely just before it crossed the line.*

Kate Bonnefous had purchased the train tickets for them the day before, and when they all said goodbye she gave them the tickets along with the money she had obtained from Colonel Shaw. The two men entered the Gare d'Orsay shortly before their train was scheduled to depart. The immense space seemed as much palace as railroad terminal, with heroic murals of western landscapes at either end, a golden clock hanging overhead, and arches of tiled rosettes soaring to a vaulted canopy of glass and cast-iron. More than two hours remained before curfew, and the hall was still clamorous with conversation, shouts, porters' whistles; from a loudspeaker somewhere an announcer intoned station names, followed by the ringing call *"En voiture, s'il vous plaît!"* Customers pushed coins beneath ticket windows that were barred like those of a bank; then, clutching their bags, they hurried beneath the TICKET D'ENTRÉE sign toward the wrought-iron staircase that led down to the train yard, past the advertisements for chocolate, apéritifs, and soap that lined the platforms, searching for the carriage doors bearing the correct numeral.

Colin Hunter entered the train first and took a seat at the far end

---

* This was true of traffic across the bridges at Castillon as well, where inspections sometimes included the disassembly of bicycles and even cars and trucks. A Vichy police report from March 1941 described how a French Red Cross truck had been "dismantled and inspected, piece by piece, by a team of specialists. This operation lasted four hours." In June of that year, a women's auxiliary was posted at a bridge near Castillon; the female agents, it was reported, "inspected everything in detail, including hygienic napkins; they even used a speculum . . . which provoked the indignation of witnesses."

of the compartment, and Gordon Hood-Cree followed shortly afterward. For more than five hours they would speak not a word in the semidarkness of the car. The train made periodic stops but never remained at any station for long. They passed Fleury-les-Aubrais, Blois, Saint-Pierre-des-Corps, crossed the Cher, the Indre, the Isle. Beyond the windows, the French countryside rolled silently by. Under a sliver of moon the steel tracks took on a milky appearance; tiny crescent-shaped pearls bobbed on the surfaces of rivers. The night revealed only the contours of the passing landscape—the acute angle of a church steeple, the multiple arches of a viaduct, the delicate traceries of tree branches.

It was past two o'clock in the morning when the train finally arrived at Libourne, a larger station than most of the others along the line, with a stone station house and a rail shed extending over several sets of tracks. Leaping hurriedly from the train, the two men walked to a nearby hotel, where they took a pair of single rooms. Not more than a few hours later, Gordon Hood-Cree was awakened by someone knocking on his door; getting up to answer it, he was surprised to see Colin Hunter standing in the hallway. Hunter closed the door behind him. "Listen," he murmured. In the quiet of the room, they could make out the sound of German voices on the ground floor. Gathering up their clothes, the two of them crept quietly down the stairs and back onto the street, where they noticed a sign that they had missed the night before, indicating that the hotel had been requisitioned for the local Kommandantur, the German military headquarters. "The place," Hood-Cree would later recall, "was stiff with Germans."

For some time the two British soldiers walked briskly around the town, trying to look as if they had somewhere to go, until finally the hour came for them to meet their contact. "We went to see a Frenchman in Libourne," Hunter would note in his escape report, "who put us in touch with another man, who helped us to cross the line of demarcation." Neither Hunter nor Hood-Cree ever gave the name of their contact in Libourne, but the second man was Elie Teyssier.

The two British soldiers might well have been surprised to learn that they would not be waiting for nightfall to cross the line of demarcation, but experienced *passeurs* like Elie Teyssier understood that at a length of more than seven hundred miles, the line of demarcation was too long for even the Germans to guard entirely. Perhaps twenty-five hundred German soldiers were patrolling the line at any given time—that is to say, an average of about three per mile—which meant that most of the line was unwatched most of the time. (In his book *La ligne de démarcation, 1940–1944,* the French historian Eric Alary observed that "the line of demarcation was neither an uncrossable obstacle nor a totally permeable barrier.") Often it was best not to try to defy the nightly curfew, when travel within the Occupied Zone was forbidden and all movement was subject to arrest, but rather to proceed in the direction of the line in as inconspicuous a way as possible, avoiding the fixed control points, and then cross the line when no German patrols were in sight. Like the other *passeurs* of the area, Elie Teyssier knew the local topography intimately, knew exactly where the German control posts had been established and the usual hours of the patrols. The bridges around Castillon were heavily fortified with German soldiers, and so the safer route was instead to head downstream on the Dordogne, toward Civrac-sur-Dordogne, where the river briefly forks, and then proceed south on foot through the fields.

In a book-length study of Castillon under German occupation, a group of French historians noted of the local *passeurs:* "They were a link in a network of which they were often unaware. . . . They needed only to know the person who brought them their 'clients,' and the one to whom they would entrust them downstream." In the case of Elie Teyssier, the latter was a young woman from a farm family who would meet them on the other side of the Dordogne.

When all went well, the passage by boat took no more than an hour. The barque slid almost silently through the water, in the shade of the enormous trees that lined the banks of the river. The dark rippling water sparkled in the afternoon glare, color transformed into black and white; blooms of algae lay on the surface like continents on a map. Hunter and Hood-Cree perched on the wooden slats of the boat; behind them they heard the lapping of a paddle in the water, a rale of labored breath. Somewhere not far from there, they knew, German soldiers were looking for them, or others like them. Every now and again they could see a fish rise; the river was rich with trout, carp, eels. They felt a world away from Paris, with its shouts and sirens and the warplanes droning overhead, away from modern life entirely, as though the train had carried them across not just space but time.

Eventually Teyssier found what he was looking for; he directed the barque in and the three of them scrambled up the muddy bank. Before long they had emerged into a clearing of scrubby brush, where a softly undulating valley spread itself out before them, isolated farmhouses scattered here and there along the horizon. The men walked for a long time, passing meadows, ditches, streams; whenever possible they went through a cornfield, hidden from sight by the tall stalks not yet cut. There was a German lookout post located not far from where they were headed, but Elie Teyssier had made sure to spread around some of the money he collected from his passengers (bribery made up a significant portion of his expenses), inducing at least some of the young German soldiers to look the other way at the time of his crossings. Eventually Teyssier directed Hunter and Hood-Cree to one of the local vineyards, where he left them in the care of a young woman who was waiting for them with her son;* she indicated to the soldiers that they were to crawl through the vineyard, hidden by the thick vegetation, as she and the boy walked on the road alongside. On their bellies, they struggled their way through the alleys between the vines. "Soon she turned," Hood-Cree later wrote, "the signal to us that she had reached the line . . . and that it was now up to us."

After some time a German soldier rode by on a bicycle, making his patrol. When he was out of sight, the two men darted across the graveled road, scaling a fence and plunging back into the vines on the other side. By now Hood-Cree's wounded leg was aching badly, and eventually, as he crawled, he lost sight of Hunter moving up ahead. Wondering whether he had gone far enough past the line to be safe, he stood up tentatively and looked around. "Colin was a few yards away," he would recall, "sitting under a tree smoking."

* Presumably the boy's presence was meant to allay German suspicion; female *passeurs* near the line of demarcation also sometimes carried baskets filled with eggs or fruit, to create the impression of pursuing an errand.

On September 27, 1940, some four months after their capture in battle, Colin Hunter and Gordon Hood-Cree had reached the Unoccupied Zone. Up a hill, perhaps two miles away, lay the village of Pujols-sur-Dordogne, where they could stay overnight before boarding a train at La Réole bound for Marseille. The sun was just beginning its descent in the west behind them. They turned, and together they made their way slowly up the hill.

11

A WALK AROUND PARIS, WHICH for Etta Shiber had once been the greatest of pleasures, was now an ordeal, something to be endured rather than savored. The beloved *bouquinistes* with their wooden stalls along the Seine were no longer permitted to stock books by "unacceptable" authors such as Shakespeare or Thomas Mann or Virginia Woolf, or Jewish authors such as Freud or Kafka or Proust, or more than a thousand others; the books that remained on sale seemed tainted by their very acceptability. Etta could hardly bear to see the yellow signs that had recently gone up, by state order, in certain shop windows, informing all who passed by that this was a Jewish-owned enterprise; nor the repulsive anti-Semitic graffiti scrawled on walls; nor the German soldiers with submachine guns watching her closely as she went past, perhaps scrutinizing, she could not help but wonder, her eyeglasses, her long nose.

Anti-Semitism had seemed to be subsiding in France in the 1920s—in part due to the undeniably patriotic service of French Jews in the Great War*—but in the following decade it resurged with an influx of Jewish refugees from the east, fleeing poverty and

---

* Poignantly, many Jewish shopkeepers posted their combat medals and other military decorations alongside the yellow ENTREPRISE JUIVE signs, as silent testimony to their patriotism.

Nazi oppression. Right-wing politicians began propagating the trope that France had been "invaded" by a horde of immigrants who were stealing jobs, undercutting wages, importing dangerous foreign ideologies, and polluting the country's traditional culture. Once installed in power, the Vichy government and its mouthpieces took this notion a step further, suggesting that even native-born Jews were not truly French, because their loyalty was to their religion rather than their country. On October 3, the so-called Statut des Juifs removed Jews from all positions in government service and the media and set strict quotas on positions in the liberal professions, including medicine, law, and teaching. The country's German-controlled newspapers issued a constant stream of anti-Semitic invective, while running article after article purporting to reveal the longtime Jewish domination of the country's cultural and economic life. Without comment, the papers published photos of stores that had posted notices forbidding Jews to enter, houses with signs in the front window that declared, "This house is authentically French." Former cabinet ministers or businessmen who had been put on trial, or whose holdings had been seized, were now identified in the press with the phrase "the Jew" before their names.

On September 27, 1940, on the eve of the Jewish High Holidays, the German military administration in France announced that it would be undertaking a "special census" of the Jewish community. Between October 3 and October 20, all adult Jews living in the Occupied Zone were to present themselves at the nearest police station to be registered.[*]

Although Etta Shiber did not explicitly identify as Jewish, the Vichy definition of a Jew was designed to take into account assimilationists like her. According to Vichy, a Jew was someone who practiced, or had at one time practiced, the Jewish religion—or someone with at least three Jewish grandparents (or two if one had married a Jew). Ancestry determined all: Even if you had never observed any Jewish rituals or traditions—even if you had been raised as a

---

[*] The decree was expanded on October 13, when it was announced that Jews would need to have their identity cards or visas "validated"—that is to say, stamped on the front with the word *Juif* or *Juive* in red letters that measured, in typically scrupulous Nazi fashion, exactly 3.5 by 1.5 centimeters.

Christian—if your grandparents were Jewish, then you were Jewish as well. It didn't matter if you saw yourself as part of a universal religion, as Felix Adler had counseled, and found meaning not in scripture but in good works; it didn't matter if you were devoted to secular rather than sacred music and sought the divine not in a synagogue but in a concert hall, as had Etta's cousin Irving Weil. If it hadn't been clear to her before, it was now: Political power includes among its attributes the right to define others. In Vichy France, a Jew was anyone with at least three Jewish grandparents, and Etta Shiber had four: the Roths on her mother's side of the family and the Kahns on her father's. Moreover, the name Kahn (which derives from Cohen) was readily identifiable as Jewish—so much so that in 1941, the German-language newspaper *Pariser Zeitung,* celebrating the city's declining Jewish population, noted that only 477 Levys were to be found in the current Paris phone book compared to 747 in 1939; 114 Dreyfuses compared to 203; and 87 Kahns compared to 142.

Day after day, the Jews of Paris lined up at their local *préfecture* to have their cards stamped. By the end of the registration period, 149,734 Parisian Jews—some 90 percent of the city's Jewish community—had registered with the "special census"; of these, 86,664 were French citizens, and the remainder were foreigners. Etta Shiber seems not to have been among them, nor were the few other American Jews who remained in Paris. American citizens held a special status in occupied France at that time. The United States remained officially neutral, and opinion polls indicated that as much as four-fifths of the American population opposed entering the war; it was not in Germany's interest to antagonize the United States by treating any of its citizens as enemies.

Etta's brother continually urged her to return to the United States. He was a Republican and an isolationist, and she often argued international politics with him, especially after she moved to Paris and could see the Nazi threat up close. "Your views on the American neutrality act is a point of view that I cannot quite understand," she had written in one letter, regarding U.S. military aid for the Allies. "Being so far from the actual scene accounts for it. Use your imagination, Chet. . . . Help *now,* help all you can." She had refused to return even when such a return was feasible, when the American embassy in Paris would have helped her. Now who even knew how to find the way back? It was easy enough to cast her mind across the ocean, back to that modern Sixty-eighth Street apartment with the fireplace and exposed-beam ceilings, where she had spent contented years with the two men whom she loved the most. But the men were gone now, the apartment lived in by others. Remarkably, it had been four and a half years since she last saw Bill, seven years for Irving. She had moved to Paris to live out the rest of her life in ease and friendship, but she had lost that simple vision of the future; it had blurred like a window in the rain. New York was a city for the young, with its pace and energy and its constant, churning reinvention of itself; she might not even recognize it anymore, or recognize herself in it. Paris was a grande dame, mature and cultivated; Etta had come to feel at home there—yet now she was exempt from Paris's police registry only because, officially at least, she still belonged to New York.

So Etta Shiber came face-to-face with the contradiction of her current life: She wanted desperately for the United States to enter the war against the Nazis, but it was only the country's neutral status that protected her.

By that point hundreds, perhaps even thousands, of British servicemen had managed to survive uncaptured for months behind enemy lines; as the prospect of winter drew closer, though, many felt the need to embark on their journeys southward. British evaders and escapers* were still arriving at the American embassy in Paris, seeking help in reaching the Unoccupied Zone. Among them was a twenty-seven-year-old captain from the Cameron Highlanders, Derek B. Lang, who had escaped from the Germans not just once but twice, the second time from a prisoner-of-war camp at Tournai, accompanied by a younger comrade from the Camerons, 2nd Lt.

---

* The British intelligence agency MI9 divided the soldiers who returned from behind enemy lines into two categories: *evaders* and *escapers*. An evader was a soldier who had never been captured by the enemy; an escaper was a former prisoner of war who had escaped. According to Airey Neave, a top intelligence officer with MI9 in the later years of the war, a soldier had to be in enemy hands for only a few minutes to be classified as an escaper.

John F. N. Buckingham. For months the two men had hidden in the French countryside, trying to find some organization that could help them get to unoccupied territory. Eventually a French Red Cross worker provided them a pair of bicycles, and together they rode to the nearby city of Lille to meet another Red Cross worker, Sally Siauve-Evausy.

Sally was thirty-five years old, with short dark hair and a sturdy frame. In Lille she oversaw a network of escaped prisoners of war hiding in various houses throughout the city; she secreted Lang and Buckingham in a friend's attic, but after they were accidentally seen by a neighbor she moved them into her own home, a gated stone mansion on rue Solférino. Her husband, Georges, a distinguished surgeon, had been in charge of a hospital but resigned because he could no longer bear taking orders from Nazis; his greatest wish, he informed the two Englishmen, was to escape France to join de Gaulle's forces in London.

In October, Georges told them that he had made contact with a newly formed escape organization in Lille, which had arranged for him and the Englishmen to be met by an agent in Paris and transported into unoccupied France. Later that week two anonymous women appeared at their door on rue Solférino bearing a pair of forged Polish passports, and on Friday, October 11, the three men took a train to Paris, arriving at the Gare du Nord just after ten P.M. Alarmingly, though, the agent who was supposed to meet them never showed up, and with the clocks of Paris sounding the curfew they could do nothing else but find a hotel near the station where the desk clerk would not look too closely at their papers.

The next day, when they were still unable to make contact with their agent, the men decided to seek assistance from the American embassy; as Derek Lang would later write, "America was not yet in the war and preserved her diplomatic relations with Germany. We could not believe, however, if we threw ourselves on their mercy that there would not be some way in which they could help us." In the embassy, Lang and Buckingham managed to find an American official who was willing to meet with them, but he seemed flustered to learn that they were escaped prisoners of war and promptly ushered them out, saying that an elderly Englishman kept an office there and would, he was sure, give them excellent advice. Thus the two men were directed to the office of Col. Cecil A. Shaw.

With his expensively tailored clothes and martial bearing, and his impressive bulk of a sort not often seen in wartime Paris, Cecil Shaw seemed the very picture of British solidity as he leaned forward in his chair to listen to his visitors' story; after just a few moments, though, he interrupted to complain about how difficult things had gotten around the embassy. His deputy consul had been arrested by the Gestapo that very weekend and sent off to prison on charges of being a spy. The whole thing was ridiculous, Shaw said regretfully, but he would be unable to provide any assistance—without the deputy, there was no one left to countersign the receipts, as the Americans were now demanding. At one time, the Americans themselves had been prepared to advance a bit of cash to those who needed to quit the Occupied Zone *tout de suite,* but that money had since dried up.

The next morning Lang and Buckingham returned to the embassy, joined this time by Georges Siauve-Evausy, who waited outside while the two Englishmen went in search of help. Once more, though, they were refused, politely but firmly, and finally they had to concede that they had reached a dead end. Disheartened, and at a loss about how to proceed, the two were heading to the front door when they heard a voice say, "I hear that you are escapers and need some help."

Turning, they saw a middle-aged woman, tall and slender and neatly dressed in autumn tweeds. Before they could recover from their surprise, she bundled them off into an empty room nearby and began to ply them with questions. Her name, she said, was Kate Bonnefous, though they could call her Kitty. Upon hearing that the two had a Frenchman waiting for them outside, she had him sent for, and for reasons of security (in an English-speaking venue) the rest of the conversation was conducted in French. Kitty's manner was brisk and her voice was clear and robust, and even in French it carried the broad *a*'s and clipped *t*'s taught to young women in English finishing schools. Derek Lang would later write, "Kitty had an air of directness and determination which did much to reassure us. When we told her that we had been refused money she was highly indignant and immediately offered to do battle for us herself. She made it clear that this was not the first time she had come across a situation like ours."

Within fifteen minutes, plans were being set in motion. The men were to come to Kitty's flat later that afternoon; in the meantime, she said pointedly, she would do what she could to get the money.

Kate Bonnefous in 1940

At three o'clock the bell rang from downstairs, and a few moments later two young men in suits and ties appeared in the doorway. One of them (Etta would learn that this was Derek Lang) was dark and handsome, standing just a bit under six feet tall, with a cleft chin and eyes shadowed by fatigue; he was wearing a slouch beret tilted nonchalantly to one side. The other, John Buckingham, had wavy strawberry-blond hair and a pinkish complexion and looked as if he was barely out of his teens. They were accompanied by an older man, Georges Siauve-Evausy, whose suit jacket displayed a row of colorful military ribbons above the breast pocket.

"You must be starving!" Kate exclaimed, ushering them into the apartment, where a lavish spread of cakes and buns had been laid out on the dining room table. She introduced them to her American friend, Mrs. Shiber, and they all sat down; soon Margot, in her black maid's uniform and white cap, brought each of the men a plate of bacon and eggs from the kitchen. While the men ate, Kate talked with them about the current situation in the city. After the occupation of Paris, she said, there had been a great deal of apathy, which was understandable when the situation looked so hopeless, but lately she could sense the people regaining their spirits; the Parisians, she said cheerfully, were developing "a healthy loathing for the Germans." Even the slightest encouragement from Great Britain could stiffen their resolve even further—just a few days earlier, a British warplane had flown over the city and traced out the word COURAGE in smoke; that single act, she said, had undone months of German propaganda.

Etta knew that Kitty expected her to join in, but she found herself barely able to keep track of the conversation. Her longtime companion anxiety had returned, her ears starting to ring. What if the Gestapo had followed these men from the hotel and were standing right outside the door? Their home address must have gotten around among the patients at Doullens, because one day, while Hunter and Hood-Cree were still with them, a French officer who had escaped from the hospital showed up unexpectedly at their door; he had stayed for several days, until Kate managed to get him smuggled inside a truck bound for Avignon. Etta had been unnerved by the idea of their address circulating among prisoners of war—how could they ever be sure that none of them was a spy or informer?

To Derek Lang, the older American lady seemed the very opposite of Kitty Bonnefous. "She was a bundle of nerves," he would write years later, "and, although she attended our discussions with Kitty, [Etta] was clearly something of an irritation and embarrassment to her."

In the course of the conversation, Kate told the men about her activity with the Red Cross, how it provided excellent cover for the secret side of her work. She and Etta had driven to prison camps and military hospitals all over the north of France; one of the places they visited regularly, she said, was the hospital at Doullens, from which they had helped some British officers to escape. Out of curiosity, Derek Lang asked her if she could remember their names, and the first one she mentioned was Lt. Colin Hunter.

But that was remarkable, Lang exclaimed—Colin Hunter was one of his closest comrades! Colin had been his intelligence officer with the Camerons; the two of them had been captured together at Veules-les-Roses, after fighting the Germans side by side aboard a beached British warship. The men listened raptly as Kate described how she and Etta had smuggled Hunter to Paris in the boot of their car, and then had done the same with another wounded officer named Gordon Hood-Cree—how they had picked up a pair of Nazi officers, and how one of their tires had been punctured outside Paris and had to be changed. "These tales of her various activities," Lang would later write, "convinced us that we had struck gold and could trust her completely."

Eventually the table was cleared and cigarettes were passed around; Kate's voice lowered as she outlined her plan, describing a path that in the coming days would take them from Paris to Libourne, across the line of demarcation to Pujols and finally to Marseille. Her contact in Libourne still had to be alerted, and so it was agreed that the men should spend the night in their hotel and return to the apartment the next day, at which point she would drive them to the station to meet their train. As they stood to leave, Kate pulled Georges Siauve-Evausy aside and pressed a 1,000-franc note into his hand. It was not her money, she explained—she had "bullied it out of an American official" after they left the embassy that morning.

The next day, after another big meal, Kate drove the men to the train station. They embraced her warmly as they parted, still not quite believing their good fortune in her having found them when they were at such a low ebb. Kate Bonnefous was "heroic," Derek Lang would say later, "another Nurse Cavell in every way, who would stop at nothing to help the British."

Meanwhile Margot finished cleaning up and returned home, and Etta was left alone once more with the dogs. The house was quiet now; pale October sunlight slanted through the front windows. Soon the colder weather would arrive and Paris's autumn colors would drain away, leaving behind a gray that would last all winter.

There had been, of course, no secret policemen in black leather trench coats standing outside their door, no one waiting to seize Kitty and the men before they stepped into the elevator. Etta could not help but feel a kind of shame, remembering the admiration she saw in the men's eyes when they gazed at Kitty, the indifference when their glance happened to rest momentarily on her. She had felt out of place at the table, a civilian who had wandered into a council of war. If Kitty had hidden any of her actions—and why, after all, had she even been in the American embassy that morning?—it was because she knew that Etta would disapprove of them, would try to persuade her to act otherwise. Yet Etta also believed that helping Allied soldiers to escape was the most important work either of them could do. Legally she might be a neutral, but morally she was not. She wanted nothing more than for Great Britain to emerge victorious, for the Nazis to be disgorged from Europe once and for all; it was why she listened to the radio every night before bed, hoping for a scrap of good news that she could nibble on as she lay anxiously awake in the dark. Over the course of a lifetime, she recognized, her anxiety had become habitual, requiring little more thought than a leg that jerked reflexively when a hammer struck the knee in the right spot. Lots of drugs were available to treat it, capsules in every color of the rainbow, but in truth, anxiety itself functioned as a kind of drug: a numbing agent, most often leading to inertia. In her heart she was a partisan, but when left to her own devices she was an *attentiste*, passively waiting to see how things turned out.

In 1933, when Bill had arrived in Paris to get her after Irving's death, he had said to Kitty: "If anything ever happens to me, will you look out for Etta?" and Kitty had just laughed and said, "Of course I will." Later, that moment had come to seem to Etta like a kind of premonition, as if Bill already sensed the weakness developing in his heart. Kitty herself had brushed it off lightly, but when the time came, she had indeed taken over from Bill, rescued Etta from her solitary life. Sixty-two years old, Etta thought, was old enough to no longer need protection; she would try, instead, to gather her resolve—to project herself, as she later wrote, "into a new course," from which she would not thereafter be able to escape.

12

FALL HAD COME TO the Pas-de-Calais since the last time Etta had driven there with Kate, the hillsides mostly russet now, wheat fields arrayed in the shimmering golds and greens of a van Gogh painting. Fallen leaves accumulated against stone walls like snow drifts; newly harvested fields held piles of sugar beets, brown and muddy as stones. The light seemed softer than before, and here and there the air carried the tang of wood smoke. It was so difficult to imagine that placid countryside as a war zone; somewhere out there, Etta knew, escaped British soldiers were sheltered in barns or attics, holed up in abandoned brickyards, living in rudimentary huts in the woods. The Peugeot rumbled quickly northward, almost always the only car on the road. They passed herds of staring cows, sagging wooden gates, white stone farmhouses; some of the meadows were dotted with fallen apples.

The village of Conchy-sur-Canche, where they were headed, was fifteen miles northwest of Doullens, in the *zone interdite*. They were on their way to meet the parish priest there, whose name had been given to Kate by Sally Siauve-Evausy. Georges Siauve-Evausy had confided in Kate about the work his wife was doing with escaped British prisoners in Lille and suggested that the two of them might want to talk. As it turned out, the women had a great deal in common: Both were Red Cross volunteers, both had driven ambulances during the war and had delivered supplies to prisoners for the Foyer du Soldat; both were practical and independent, calm under pressure, "whose front of cool efficiency," Derek Lang once noted, "covered a very warm-hearted personality." Sally Siauve-Evausy, too, was doing everything in her power to aid the British cause. She regularly sent reports back to England via short-wave radio, containing information given her by a network of contacts she had developed through the Red Cross. Of late she had heard about a Catholic priest in the little village of Conchy-sur-Canche; he was in contact with a number of escaped British prisoners hiding nearby and was looking for someone who could get them all the way across the line of demarcation into the Unoccupied Zone.

The N16 national road rose to a plateau, then descended into the valley of the Canche; at Frévent they turned left onto a smaller road heading northwest. Entering Conchy-sur-Canche, they turned onto the main street. Towering above a row of low brick buildings stood the Catholic church, the Église Saint-Pierre, an unadorned, medieval-looking structure of weathered gray stone, with arched windows, a broad slate roof, and a hexagonal steeple. Kate pulled the car over and the two of them got out; they walked briefly around the church grounds, hoping that they might encounter the priest, but no one was in sight. Kate said that she would look for him inside, and Etta went back to the car.

Conchy-sur-Canche had a stillness about it that seemed unusual even for a country village in the middle of the day. As she waited, Etta couldn't help but scan the street for the long black Citroëns favored by the Gestapo, the sleek sedans that appeared out of nowhere, shark-like and menacing; seeing them glide into view, one could only pray that they kept moving. She was keenly aware that she and Kate had taken no provisions with them this time, had no nearby prisons or hospitals to visit, no good explanation for why they were parked in front of a church in an isolated village three hours north of Paris.

After several minutes Kate emerged from the church with a priest walking beside her. Etta had imagined him as an old man with a bald pate and a long white beard, along the lines of Tolstoy, but in fact he looked to be scarcely thirty, with gleaming black hair parted neatly on the side, darkly expressive eyes, and a strikingly aquiline nose. "He was," Etta would later write, "one of those Frenchmen whose classic profiles, passed through generation after generation down the centuries, remind the foreigner that France was once part of the great Roman Empire." He stood five foot ten—tall in France at a time when the average height for a man was five foot six—and walked with an easy, athletic stride, his slim frame hidden beneath a simple black cassock cinched at the waist by a wide horsehair belt. Speaking in French, he suggested that they walk over to the rectory, where he had an office; it would be safe to talk in there.

Edouard Régniez had been named curé of Conchy-sur-Canche in February 1937, when he was twenty-seven years old. According to the historical parish register produced by the diocese of Arras, "He was welcomed with a delirious joy by all of the population. . . . Young and full of energy, he energized the population, organizing processions such as had never been seen in the village." Régniez belonged to the local aviation club, the Aero-Club de la Somme, and whenever his pastoral duties allowed, he would head out to the local airfield, where he donned goggles and a leather helmet and piloted a Potez 60, a straight-wing twin-seat airplane with an open cockpit. Aviation might have seemed an unusual pastime for a country priest, but for him there was nothing odd in the notion of propelling oneself toward heaven: ascending in a few sweeping circles as the wind whipped past and the roar of man's ingenuity thundered in his ears, the neatly bordered fields of the Pas-de-Calais spread out beneath him like a quilt sewn by a great hand. At heart he was an enthusiast, blessed with a vigor and eloquence that seemed able to stir others to action. As was recalled in the parish register, "The sad and gloomy services of the former curé had given way to ones that were lively and cheerful and attracted an ever-larger portion of the population. His sermons were passionate and exciting, and he knew how to move the hearts of his parishioners." One of those parishioners was to say of him later, recalling the words of the psalmist: "He would have made us pass through the fire."

Little of this would ever have been predicted for him. Edouard had been born in Carvin, a northern industrial town of barren wind-swept streets and narrow brick row houses, where a layer of soot seemed to stain every surface. In that part of the world, the horizon was dominated by the slag heaps known as *terrils,* black pyramids of coal waste often more than one hundred meters high, less grand than the ones in Egypt but likewise a product of exploitative toil and hardship. His paternal grandfather, François, had spent his life in the mines, arriving for work in the early mornings in his coarse blue-linen smock and leather helmet, a tin can filled with water strapped to his belt; when he emerged at the end of his shift he was covered in coal dust, black from cap to clogs, as if he too was a product of the seam. François died in 1890, like most of his fellow miners too young, at the age of forty-six. Edouard's father, Emile, escaped the coal mines, making his living instead as a chauffeur and mechanic, and when World War I began he enlisted in the army; he was killed in 1915, in his first year of service, at the age of thirty-one.

Edouard was then six years old—the same age Emile had been when his own father died—and his early memories would have been ones of deprivation and grief. Carvin was among the northern French towns occupied by the Germans shortly after the onset of the First World War; almost immediately they set about shuttering most of the mines and factories, dismantling or simply smashing the ma-chinery and sending back to Germany whatever parts they could use. A large portion of the local men lost their livelihoods as a result, and in the coming months many of those civilians were deported to Ger-many to work in the industries there, a war crime that would linger in common memory long past the start of the next world war. Con-voys of French prisoners of war sometimes passed through Carvin; the images of those prisoners, gaunt and hollow-eyed, must have impressed themselves deeply on young Edouard, who had lost his own father to the men in field-gray uniforms parading around the town.

When the war was finally over, nine-year-old Edouard Régniez—like nearly one million other French children of soldiers lost in the war—was declared an *orphelin de la guerre;* from that point on, his education would be paid for by the French state. As a student of ex-ceptional promise, he was selected to attend the local junior seminary; he received his baccalaureate from the University of Lille in 1926, going on to earn a Licence de lettres classiques, studying English and German as well as French. After briefly serving as a professor in the *petit séminaire* of Arras, he was named curé of three neighboring villages, one of them Conchy-sur-Canche.

When war broke out again in September 1939, Régniez joined the 2nd Infantry Division as a member of radio company 2/82. The 2nd Division was stationed in northeastern France, and when the *drôle de guerre* was shattered by the German invasion of the Low Countries, it engaged the enemy in sustained, exceptionally hard combat. "Without a doubt," wrote Col. Robert Villate, the 2nd "was the division that was under fire the longest during the war." On June 10, Régniez's company found itself nearly encircled. "No matter the cost, we had to remain in place, hold our ground," one of the radio men would recall. "Everything was burning, the smell of gunpowder surrounded us. We thought our last hour had arrived." The next day, the order was given to fall back. The 2nd Division had sustained enormous losses: Of more than sixteen thousand men, only about fifteen hundred remained alive and uncaptured. Antoine de Saint-Exupéry, then conducting aviation missions for the 2/33 Reconnaissance Squadron, observed with horror those final days of battle; Frenchmen, he wrote, "are being sacrificed like glasses of water hurled at a forest fire."

Piled into trucks, the remaining soldiers retreated nearly two hundred miles south. There was nothing left to do but deny the enemy whatever one could: They passed scenes of French soldiers burning tanks, slashing tires, destroying the cannons on antiaircraft guns, ripping up account books and identification papers. Telegraph poles were chopped down; horses were shot. It was, recalled one soldier, "an end-of-the-world spectacle."

Edouard Régniez was taken prisoner with his company at Vitteaux on June 19. The men were assembled into rows and ordered to begin marching east, toward Germany. They tramped through villages where the inhabitants came out to watch them; most bitter was the pity the men could see in their eyes. Often women were in tears as they passed. Régniez could not have helped but recall those hungry, exhausted prisoners of war that he had seen in Carvin as a boy;

he had now become one of them himself, watched by other children in his moment of greatest humiliation. As always, he thought of his widowed mother, his ill older sister Emilie back in Carvin; they would be frantic to find out what had become of him. He couldn't bear to think that his town would be occupied by the Germans once more, the hated *Boches,* the eternal enemies. Back then, everything had been taken from them—armchairs, copper pots, cutlery, clocks, blankets, mattresses, galoshes, paper and ink, even the mercury from their thermometers. A home inspector made a mark on an inventory sheet, and another item was gone forever. They had had little to eat, no gas or electricity, not even any coal for heating—this in the rich coal basin of the French north. The Germans told them to "go out into the woods" to forage for fuel but did not allow them to cut any branches wider than seven centimeters. Rage, he knew, was not the most dangerous reaction, nor fear, nor grief, nor even despair; the one truly to be struggled against was resignation. *"La guerre est finie!"* some of the German captors had shouted at them; *his* war, he felt certain, was not yet over.

Escape was something like working the lock on a safe; one had to wait patiently, concentrating all the while, until the correct combination was found and the tumblers clicked into place: Only then could the door be opened. It was important to position oneself neither at the front nor the back of the column; then to watch for a rise in the road that would temporarily block the view of the German soldiers in the rear, with a sharp turn for the escort vehicle in the front and a corn or wheat field on the opposite side, one that had no fence and extended right up to the edge of the road, as he marched alongside fellow prisoners who knew to close the gap in the row to provide cover as he dived into the field, perhaps saying a prayer as he did so, and lay there barely breathing among the stalks as the column continued on until it was out of sight.

On June 21, somewhere on the road between Vitteaux and Dijon, Edouard Régniez escaped from German captivity. One week later, the commander of the 2nd Infantry Division, Gen. Albert-Frédéric Klopfenstein, cited him for special commendation, stating: "[He] always volunteered for missions in contact with the enemy. During the days of June 9 and 10, 1940, [he] maintained under violent bombardment the liaison that had been assigned to him. His transmitting set destroyed, [he] joined the Infantry and participated with fine courage in the defense of the position." Régniez was awarded the Citation à l'ordre de l'Infanterie Divisionnaire on June 28, 1940— the very day he arrived back in Conchy-sur-Canche to take up once more his position as parish priest.

Abbé Régniez walked Kate and Etta to the back of the rectory, past a little vegetable garden and up a set of stairs into his office, which was low-ceilinged and had thick walls of stone and mortar. Not long after his return, Régniez told them, he had learned that eight escaped British servicemen were hiding in and around Conchy-sur-Canche. For weeks on end the eight had moved from place to place, finding refuge occasionally in barns or brickyards but mostly in dugout shelters that they constructed out of wood and brush. Occasionally they would knock on the doors of farmhouses looking for food, and when one of the local parishioners had seen the same face two or three times, he began to fear the consequences of consorting with English soldiers and alerted the curé to their presence.

Since that time, Régniez said, he had done what he could for the men, procuring civilian clothing and false identity cards and arranging for them to stay with some trusted families. Two of them were now in Boubers-sur-Canche, southeast of Conchy; another group was being sheltered in a farmhouse just outside of town, where they were posing as agricultural laborers. The officer in the group had set off for Lille, where he intended to set up a network to help other escapers reach unoccupied territory. In the meantime, though, there was the matter of the servicemen still under their care. Of late the Germans had launched a crackdown in the region, arresting a number of people on suspicion of aiding the enemy; Abbé Régniez explained to Kate and Etta that he didn't want his parishioners to be taking such risks, especially the ones with children. "Now here is what I have done," Etta recalled him as saying. "I have made all the necessary arrangements to get these men out of here, a few at a time. I will take the responsibility for getting them to Paris if you can take charge of them after that."

There was no mistaking the sense of danger that lay in his words. A French guidebook to the Pas-de-Calais of the time observed that a curé "is in general respected and sometimes venerated," but then meaningfully added, "when he doesn't involve himself in politics or municipal affairs." Not even a priest was immune to being informed on; anyone could send an anonymous letter to the occupying authorities claiming that a certain individual was in league with the enemy and should be investigated. The letter of denunciation might have been intended to express a genuine "concern," but it might just as well have stemmed from an old political disagreement, or a business rivalry, or a prejudice of some sort, or it might simply have been a convenient means of settling scores with a personal enemy rather than an enemy of the state. The informer faced no risk, but for the accused the consequences could be catastrophic: jail, torture, even death. Growing up in the Pas-de-Calais, Edouard Régniez himself surely recalled the many priests suspected of having aided British prisoners during the First World War; they had been executed by German firing squads, the Our Father on their lips. Without anything needing to be said, Etta understood that this stranger was entrusting them with his life.

He had already obtained identity cards for the Englishmen, Régniez went on, which showed that they had permission to go to Paris to take jobs in war factories there; this would enable them to take a train to Paris, and he didn't anticipate that they would meet with any difficulties. But few of them spoke French, and he was not comfortable sending them off on their own. They had to be escorted by someone who could speak up for them quickly, in unforeseen circumstances—he planned to do that himself, unless it proved impossible and he had to substitute someone else. In any case, he said, he would guarantee to deliver the soldiers to Kate and Etta in Paris, if they could handle the transport at that point.

Kate assured him that they could. They had a five-room apartment in Paris, she said; he could bring the men directly there, and they would arrange for the travel papers needed to go to Bordeaux.

It was decided that, for now, the curé would arrive twice a week, Mondays and Fridays. He said that he had recently become acquainted with a local group of like-minded people, and he was sure that among them all there would be no trouble providing a ready supply of soldiers. He would be at their apartment within the week, bringing with him a pair of British soldiers—what one of his colleagues referred to as the "dangerous merchandise."

The Germans had now been in France for four months, and much of the populace was still dazed by the sudden military collapse, frightened, in pain, trying to comprehend what had happened and to gauge the extent of the damage, like a passenger waking up inside a smashed car. The French people who already understood that they had no course but to resist found themselves confronting the perennial question asked by those seeking to rid themselves of tyranny: *What is to be done?*

Within the closed-off, sharply restricted world of the *zone interdite,* the earliest resisters generally confined themselves to distributing anti-Nazi tracts, transmitting information to Great Britain via short-wave radio, and sheltering trapped British servicemen; these were the only avenues of resistance that seemed possible at the moment. Such was the case with Edouard Régniez's group in the fall of 1940. After the war one of the other members would recall of that period, "The network was in the process of being established, spontaneously, step by step, crystallizing little by little." Later the group would come to be known as Richard Coeur de Lion [Richard the Lion-Hearted], likely for one of its founders, Arthur Richards, a retired typesetter originally from Birmingham, England. As with this one, most of the earliest resistance groups were organized around a small, dedicated core of individuals. These were by no means professional spies; they were teachers, shopkeepers, tradespeople, housewives, farmers, priests. By trade they were ill-suited for conspiratorial work, having never had cause to forge identity cards, bribe officials, create aliases and code words, turn homes into refuges, hold furtive meetings in cafés and hotel lobbies. They had no experience of the compartmentalization that was required to lead one life in public and another in private,* above and underground at once, keeping

---

* Gay resisters, of course, would have had some experience with this.

secrets even from loved ones, always watchful for signs of danger, silently evaluating each new acquaintance as a possible comrade or informant: living, in a sense, as a fugitive without ever having left home.

For the most part, these early groups were operating blindly, with little guidance from British intelligence; while Great Britain had established the escape-and-evasion agency MI9 at the end of 1939, British money, equipment, and intelligence agents would not begin arriving in force in western Europe until 1941. The year 1940 thus represented what the Belgian researcher Étienne Dejonghe has called the "artisanal stage" of the escape lines: a time when everything was being made from scratch, each transport improvised to meet the demands of the moment, before the creation of the larger, more professionalized lines that eventually came to function almost as conveyor belts for the transmission of escaped and evading soldiers, stretching like a vast railroad system across much of a continent, and which ultimately would involve more than twelve thousand civilian helpers and rescue more than eight thousand Allied servicemen.

The tasks were shared by women and men alike, and as often as not, women took leadership roles within the groups.* Some of these women, like Kate Bonnefous, had begun their resistance work by serving as *marraines de guerre*—war godmothers—making contact with imprisoned soldiers while doing charitable work inside military hospitals and prison camps. About Kate Bonnefous, though, much was different: Unlike other *marraines de guerre,* she was not content simply to help prisoners of war escape from their places of confinement, but instead sought to establish a genuine escape line stretching from occupied to unoccupied territory; and she did so essentially alone, rather than as part of an already-existing group. As Catherine

---

* In Richard Coeur de Lion, for instance, one of the prime movers was Eliane Méplaux, who over the course of the war sheltered dozens of escaped prisoners from five Allied countries, on one occasion attacked German soldiers with a scythe, was arrested several times and twice sentenced to hard labor in German prison camps, and had her house blown up by a fascist French militia. Méplaux died in 1949 at the age of fifty-three, in large part as a result of the maltreatment she had suffered during her detention. In a certified declaration made at the close of the war she said, "I regret nothing at all of what I have done."

Bergin noted in her study of World War II escape lines: "While [Bonnefous's] efforts were similar to [those of] other *marraines de guerre* or charity workers, in that they were limited to a small number of men, her ambitions were much bigger. Whereas most civilian-aided escapes terminated at the demarcation line, an assessment of the escape reports suggests that Bonnefous was one of the first civilians to attempt to create an escape organization stretching from Paris to Marseille."

13

THE AUTUMN RAINS BEGAN to fall. The weather grew colder, the days shorter; the light over Paris dimmed. On the streets, the floral pastels of the glorious springtime had been replaced by muted shades of gray, brown, blue. Many Frenchwomen, of course, were still smartly dressed, wearing patterned jackets with fur pieces draped around their shoulders, complicated hats adorned with feathers and beads. Sprinkled among them in the crowds were the young German women who had been relocated to Paris to operate the wireless transmitters, telegraphs, and phone switchboards required by the occupying power; hair neatly pulled back into buns, they dressed in trim gray uniforms with peaked caps, like airline hostesses, and immediately became known among Parisians as the *souris grises* [gray mice]. Even amid the lunchtime crowds the city was subdued, listless, its usual hum gone, as though a great machine had been switched off: There was, it seemed, no melancholy as bottomless as that of a fallen world capital.

Paris, wrote Jean-Paul Sartre during the occupation, was "haunted by the memory of its grandeur." Apartment buildings unheated for lack of coal were mocked by their own resplendent exteriors; inside luxurious department stores, bare display counters had gray sheets pulled over them, like a corpse or the contents of an abandoned house. "The silence caught you by the throat," a Parisian teenager at the time would recall, "made sadness press into your thoughts. The houses had grown too tall, the streets too wide. People were separated from each other by spaces that were too big." The uncanny quiet intensified the sudden wail of a police siren or the drone of an airplane engine overhead; many, hearing the noise, privately hoped the plane was British, come to bomb their own captured city.

Under occupation Paris seemed to darken, its contours growing indistinct, shadows lengthening as if from a setting sun. The air was thick with secrets, the murk of imagined conspiracies. It was widely understood that the Nazis had cultivated a vast network of informers, French people covertly in the service of the Germans—sometimes out of political conviction, sometimes for financial gain or to protect a loved one, sometimes for reasons that remained obscure even to the informers themselves. On the street, at work, even in the privacy of one's home, no one could be sure of not being watched; the editorial director of French *Vogue* noted that the *souris grises*, as a basic function of their work, would "listen in on all suspected wires." A moviegoer might wonder, looking around at the others in the cinema, who would report him if he coughed or sneezed or read a newspaper during the German newsreels, a relatively mild form of dissent, not like those who baaed like a sheep when a collaborator appeared on the screen, or barked like a dog, or released a pigeon with the French tricolor attached to its leg.

Occupied France no longer had a sitting parliament to safeguard a citizen's basic freedoms, nor impartial courts to enforce them, nor labor unions to fight for them, nor an independent press to avail itself of them. In Paris, the least censorious of cities, where freedom of speech had long been enshrined as a fundamental right and citizens were not shy about making their opinions known—where they were, in the words of the historian Henri Michel, "accustomed to expressing themselves without fear, and consequently without reticence"— free expression had become a thing of the past. In its absence, Parisians produced a stream of rumors that flowed ceaselessly beneath the surface of public life, like the city's famed sewer system, wide-ranging, unseen, foul perhaps, but indispensable. In his book *Occupation*, Ian Ousby noted, "The phrase on everybody's lips was *on dit que* [it's said that]. . . . People exchanged gossip, embellished it, exaggerated it and helped it further on its way. Rumor quickly became the common currency."

Suspicion is the root of rumor's weed, and in the fall of 1940 it was everywhere, not just in Paris but throughout the occupied territory, in every part of society, and perhaps nowhere more than among those helping escaped British servicemen—those for whom the wrong word could mean imprisonment, torture, or death. In October, for instance, an escaped soldier named Harry Clayton became the subject of potentially fatal rumors that he was a police informer. Since his escape from a German prison camp in August, Clayton had been living in Lille, helping Capt. Charles P. Murchie in his efforts to organize an escape line to Marseille. On October 12, a British soldier hiding just south of Lille was arrested by the German security police; as it happened, Clayton had visited him just the day before, and also bore a certain resemblance to the officer who had led the raid. Quickly the rumor spread among local farmers that Clayton had "sold" the escaper to the Germans, and, in retaliation, one of the farmers denounced him to the police. Murchie and Clayton decided that it was too dangerous to remain in Lille, and with the help of a sympathetic railway worker they boarded a train bound for Paris.

One day later, they appeared at Kate and Etta's door, seeking shelter.[*]

Charles Plowman Murchie was a tall, beefy Englishman with reddish hair, a ruddy complexion, and a neatly trimmed gray mustache. He spoke loudly, drank freely, didn't mind flashing money around, and liked to cultivate an air of conspiracy around him—none of them desirable traits in a would-be secret agent. Still, for all his personal shortcomings, Murchie was deeply devoted to helping British servicemen trapped in occupied territory, and in the eleven days during which he stayed in Kate and Etta's apartment he continued to make plans for the escape line that he was envisioning. Years later—long after that escape line had become legendary—Charles Murchie

---

[*] Presumably they had received the address from Sally Siauve-Evausy in Lille.

would say that he had never forgotten the kindness of "Madame Bonnefous" (as he always respectfully addressed her); she had, he said, "treated me like a royal prince."

On October 28, Kate put Murchie and Clayton aboard a train bound for Bordeaux; in Libourne they made contact with Elie Teyssier, who brought them across the line of demarcation into the Unoccupied Zone. By November the two were in Marseille, where Murchie began working with a Church of Scotland minister named Donald Caskie. Earlier that year Caskie had taken over Marseille's venerable British and American Seamen's Mission, which quickly became a magnet for the escaped and evading servicemen who were pouring into the city. Before long Murchie had set his escape line into motion, employing *passeurs* to bring escapers from the Lille region across the line of demarcation and down to Marseille; there Donald Caskie would arrange shelter for them until Murchie could find a boat for North Africa or a guide to lead the overland trek across the Pyrenees into Spain. In a report to MI9 entitled "Helpers, Details of Evasion and Notes on Marseilles," submitted in March 1941, Lt. Jimmy Langley noted that during his escape from a military hospital in Lille "I was advised . . . to contact the Rev. D. Caskie at 36 rue de Forbin, Marseilles. This advice is given to practically everybody going down to Marseilles, including French civilians. The Rev. Caskie undoubtedly works with Capt. Murchie, R.A.S.C., in helping people out of Occupied France."

By that time Murchie had become well known around Marseille and was, as he later affirmed in a letter to the British ambassador to Spain, "arrested daily by the French on some pretext or other." As a consequence he began to restrict his activities, staying away from the Seamen's Mission and operating only through associates, until finally in April 1941 he and Harry Clayton fled Marseille for Spain, leaving the escape line in the hands of a fellow British escaper, Capt. Ian Garrow. The line that Murchie had established, though—later dubbed the Pat O'Leary Line—would go on to become one of the most important escape lines of the Second World War, rescuing some six hundred soldiers.

By November 1940, Kate Bonnefous and Etta Shiber had begun to receive a steady stream of escaped soldiers at 2 rue Balny-d'Avricourt. Though Paris lay barely 125 miles from Conchy-sur-Canche and could be reached by car in under three hours, without a car the trip took the better part of a day: first by bus to the nearby town of Frévent and then by rail, with a connection in Abbeville, through Amiens, and then on to the Gare du Nord in Paris, and finally via Métro to the Pereire station near the apartment. Very quickly Abbé Régniez came to see that the round trip was too time-consuming for him to undertake twice each week while still keeping up his pastoral duties, and on one of his first visits he informed the women that in the future he would arrive only on Fridays. The Monday deliveries would be conducted by a Mlle July Boulanger; she was a close associate of Abbé Julien Berteloot of Hauteville (another priest about whom Sally Siauve-Evausy had told Kate Bonnefous), a devout woman as well as patriotic, and they should trust her as they did himself.

Kate's escape line was now fully established, stretching nearly one thousand miles, from one end of France to the other: from Conchy-sur-Canche in the north, where Abbé Régniez was sheltering the soldiers; then south to their apartment in Paris; then southwest to Libourne, where Elie Teyssier brought them across the line of demarcation; and finally southeast to the Seamen's Mission in Marseille. The past few months had been like one of those spinning carnival rides that start slowly but gather speed, whirling ever faster until finally the world is a blur. Kate and Etta hardly went out anymore, other than to run essential errands and walk the dogs; they preferred not to socialize with friends—and certainly not to drop in on them unannounced, as they might have in the past—in order to discourage the possibility of visits in return. "If we didn't want people to come to see us," Etta noted, "obviously we had to avoid as much as possible going to see them. . . . We didn't expect that our old friends would dash to the police and denounce us even if they did catch us, of course, but we both felt that the fewer persons in on our secret, the better." If someone did happen to ring the bell when soldiers were in the apartment, the men were instructed to pile into the bathroom at once, and then one of the women would do her best to keep the visitor from entering the apartment. Quickly they hit on a technique that proved effective: If either of them was dressed in anything at all suitable for street wear, she would greet the friend at the door and exclaim, "My dear, how glad I am to see you! I was just going out. Are you going my way?"

The previous fall, when she was downstairs on her way out to walk Micky, Etta had watched gratefully as their apartment building's huge winter shipment of coal arrived. "Our flat is heated now and very comfortable," she reported in a letter to Chester. This year, though, the shipment had not come. The women put on sweaters and wore their heaviest stockings; at night Micky got under Etta's bed-covers and slept as close to her as he could.

On Monday, November 11, though, the weather turned unexpect-edly mild, and they might have opened the windows a bit in their apartment, just to get some fresh air, as they awaited the arrival of July Boulanger with her group of English servicemen. November 11 was Armistice Day in France, commemorating the end of the First World War, and since 1922 it had been a national holiday, featuring parades of uniformed military veterans. In Paris, the line of march proceeded along the Champs-Élysées to the Arc de Triomphe, the Napoleonic symbol of French military victory, under which the Tomb of the Unknown Soldier's flame eternally burned. As Armi-stice Day also celebrated the defeat of Germany—and could thus provide an impetus for the expression of anti-Nazi sentiment—the German military commander in France, Gen. Otto von Stülpnagel, had decreed that November 11 was to proceed like any other day: Schools and businesses would remain open as always, and any orga-nized ceremonies or demonstrations were strictly forbidden.

A dignified individual act of commemoration at the Arc de Tri-omphe was to be allowed by the military administration, though, and that morning a long line of Parisians stretched across the place de l'Étoile, men and women alike dressed in black hats and overcoats that gave the scene a funereal mood. Silently they filed past the Tomb of the Unknown Soldier, under the watchful eyes of the gendarmes; long an amiable presence in the city, during the occupation the gendarmes had taken on a more sinister aspect, with their long wooden truncheons and black capes like bats' wings. The air was heavy with impending rain, a sheet of dark clouds hovering overhead. At half past ten the gendarmes broke up a group of about twenty truant schoolchildren, and another, larger group just before noon. Later, when the *lycées* let out, schoolchildren began to arrive in droves. Hundreds of girls wore outfits in either red, white, or blue—an overtly oppositional act only en masse. Some children marched behind a large floral wreath in the shape of a Cross of Lorraine, the Gaullist emblem; they managed to toss it onto the Tomb of the Unknown Soldier before scurrying off with gendarmes in hot pursuit.

In the late afternoon rain started to fall. By five o'clock, university students had begun to pour out of the nearby Métro stations. French tricolor flags were unfurled; together they sang *"La Marseillaise,"* arms linked like the communards of an earlier time. A contingent of students from the Sorbonne marched with a pair of fishing rods resting on their shoulders like rifles, chanting *"Vive! Vive!"* in unison. The Germans might have been mystified by the incongruous display, like something out of a French surrealist performance, but the spectators who lined the avenue laughed and cheered, understanding at once the students' witty composition: In French, a "fishing rod" is a *gaule,* and two are *deux gaules*—thus, *Vive de Gaulle!*

As the sun began to set the temperature dropped; the pavement grew slick with rain. The darkness brought an air of menace, the sense of unknown forces gathering. At the Arc de Triomphe the crowd had swelled into the thousands. Shouts rang out from all sides: *Vive la France! Vive l'Angleterre! À bas Pétain! Merde aux Boches!* Suddenly, from somewhere, an order was given, and violence erupted with the released tension of a coiled spring. Covered military vans pushed into the crowd, pinning some demonstrators against a metal barrier; German soldiers carrying rifles with fixed bayonets poured out from the backs of the vans, as more soldiers appeared from the surrounding streets. Riot police swung their truncheons at demonstrators, landing blows again and again; soldiers smashed rifle butts against heads and faces. Students crumpled onto the wet pavement; their comrades were clubbed as they tried to help them up. Gamely they fought back, whirling and kicking and trying to push themselves free. The air was filled with shouts and groans and cries, the sickening crack of wood against bone. Police whistles shrilled; somewhere a stun grenade exploded. A group of students surrounded a lone German soldier and beat him to the ground, swearing at him with each punch. Suddenly a fusillade of rifle shots rang out. In panic the crowd scattered, demonstrators warding off blows as they tried to break their way through the lines of army and police. The two-tone pulse of sirens grew closer; gendarmes began pulling scores of bloodied young people into waiting vans.

More than one thousand demonstrators were questioned at police stations that night and then released. One hundred forty-three students were seized by German soldiers and thrown into the Cherche-Midi and La Santé prisons, where they were kicked and beaten by soldiers demanding the names of the demonstration's organizers. At Cherche-Midi, five students were selected at random, then lined up against a wall to face a mock execution. Others were made to stand in a courtyard all night in the pouring rain, their hands on their heads. Thirty would remain in prison for as much as five weeks.

The events of November 11 received no coverage in the Paris newspapers. Still, everyone knew what had happened, and the thought of the city's children being beaten and bloodied and hauled off to prison provoked a revulsion that would not be allayed; gone now was any *vie-en-rose* notion of the "correct" German soldier, the civilized occupier who loved the French people and was kind to children and the elderly. The student uprising of Armistice Day 1940 was the first collective resistance to the Nazi occupation of Paris; in the city, the memory of the occupation would forever be cleaved in two: before November 11 and after.

In June, Kate and Etta had fled Paris as the city seemed to be collapsing around them; now, in November, their apartment served as a central station on a kind of underground railroad, something like the one that Etta had learned about as a girl back in New York. Etta could not see herself as any type of heroic conductor; still, there was no denying the fact that she was helping to feed and shelter men on the run. "There were no difficulties," Etta later wrote. "The system

was working like a well-oiled machine." Sometimes Edouard Régniez or July Boulanger brought two English soldiers with them, and
sometimes they brought three; sometimes Gustave Rackelboom sent
over escaped French soldiers from his nearby reception center. Often
the men stayed only a few hours before getting put onto a train;
sometimes, depending on the timing, the men stayed with Kate and
Etta overnight.

Late at night, after turning off the radio, Etta could hear the murmur of conversation drifting in from the drawing room, the sound
of muffled laughter; the men's voices seemed to linger in the apartment, like the scent of their shaving cream, even after they were gone.
Etta found that her anxiety these days was mostly directed outward,
toward the young men themselves, all those mechanics and miners
and lorry drivers and clerks (which they pronounced *clark*, like
Gable). She didn't see how they could possibly remain safe for the
length of their remaining journey. They were too tall, too blond, too
ruddy, their posture too straight, their stride too firm: Their nation of
origin seemed to be written on their bodies.

"We arranged it," Etta would recall, "so that a French soldier and
an English soldier always traveled together, so the French boys could
do all the talking. As soon as an English boy opened his mouth, of
course, he'd be lost." In fact, some of the English servicemen spoke
French well enough to fool a German guard walking through a train
car checking papers. But sometimes there were no French soldiers,
and none of the Englishmen spoke a passable French. On those
occasions—the first one was on that notorious November 11, when
July Boulanger arrived with three English soldiers in tow—Kate decided that she herself would bring the men to meet Elie Teyssier in
Libourne, accompanying them on the train in her capacity as a representative of the Foyer du Soldat. As a Catholic priest presented a
dignified, socially respectable authority figure, so too might a well-
dressed older woman with official-looking identification; a young
German guard would scarcely expect such a person to be a cunning
conspirator. Still, to Etta, chaperoning escaped prisoners of war behind enemy lines seemed perilously close to a game of Russian rou-
lette: On each turn the odds might be in your favor, but play long
enough and eventually the wrong chamber is sure to find you. Did

Kitty really believe that she would remain safe until the war was over? It was clear that the end would not arrive anytime soon; the ink blot of the German army continued to spread across the map of Europe. Yet she still willingly put herself in danger, much like a soldier who volunteers for even the most perilous missions.

Official reprisals for the events of November 11 had begun immediately,[*] and sterner measures were sure to follow, further deprivations, restrictions, raids, arrests. There was one fact, though, in which Etta could still take the barest of comfort: No resister had been put to death in Paris; that line, at least, was yet to be crossed.

---

[*] The Sorbonne was closed for a month, the surrounding Latin Quarter was open only to authorized residents, and the city's students were required to report daily to their local police station.

14

E VEN A SENSE OF danger became routine over time; fear, unlike anxiety, was a note that could not be long sustained. It was best, Etta had found, to live from one day to the next, thinking only of the tasks that were immediately at hand. Shopping needed to be done, linens needed to be changed, dogs needed to be fed and walked: These were not abstract matters, they would not wait until the weather changed or a mood had lifted. The most important thing was to stay active, to keep moving forward as best one could.

The soldiers generally arrived at their apartment around noon, which was advantageous, as most of their neighbors were away at that hour, and there was usually time at least for lunch before the departing train. Kate and Etta felt responsible for feeding the men well while they were under their roof—no simple matter when the butcher shops in Paris regularly offered little more than tripe or a few slices of black pudding, the groceries only brussels sprouts, rutabagas, or turnips: hard times indeed, when even potatoes can seem a luxury. There was no cream or sugar for one's morning coffee; even the coffee itself had disappeared, replaced by an ill-tasting powder made from chicory and roasted acorns that had been given the grandiose name *café national,* as if drinking it was some sort of patriotic act.

These meager provisions had to be supplemented by whatever

could be obtained on the black market, and for the first time Etta became conscious of a serious financial strain. "The drain that purchases on the black market made on our small funds couldn't be remedied," she would recall. Kate's family trust was in England, and in the past she had returned to London twice a year to draw on it, but since the war began that was no longer possible; in September, Etta had sent for $1,500 from her New York bank, through the American consulate in Paris, but the money had not yet arrived. They were living on whatever savings they had accumulated before the exodus, with little relief on the horizon, and their expenses were greater now than ever before. In addition to the outlays for food (as well as for cigarettes, soap, and other necessities not easily found), they were covering the cost of the railway tickets to Bordeaux, plus the 50 francs per person charged by Elie Teyssier. Sometimes additional civilian clothes had to be purchased; sometimes Kate might note that one of the Englishmen was short of spending money and she would give him a few hundred francs of her own.

Etta could not help but observe that as the weeks passed Kate was growing increasingly tense. One afternoon July Boulanger arrived at the apartment with not two or three men in tow, but four—one pair each from two of Abbé Régniez's most dependable helpers, Madame Merly of Noyellette and Madame Duval of Lattre-Saint-Quentin. In Boulanger's description, Kate "reproached" her, saying that four was too many, she didn't have the money to send four men to Marseille. Boulanger, though, did not relent; the men had come all that way, she said, they had passed the night in a single cold room in a hotel near the Gare du Nord, and that morning she had taken the liberty of letting them go to a barber, and she wasn't about to bring them back to the Pas-de-Calais—and with that she reached into her handbag and pulled out 500 francs so that, she said, Madame Bonnefous might take all four.

"I've got to look around for some money," Etta recalled Kate telling her one day. "We'll have to give up our work for lack of funds if I don't get some assistance." If she could get to the Unoccupied Zone, she said, she knew a number of well-to-do families who would undoubtedly be glad to contribute.

Kate left by train on the evening of November 25; she would be setting out on the same path to Marseille that the young men had taken before her, intending to cross the line of demarcation with Elie Teyssier. She thought that she would be gone for two weeks, perhaps three.

That night Etta turned out the light and lay bundled beneath the bedclothes, but sleep didn't arrive. Even a silent house was full of noises: the tick of a clock, the clang of the elevator as it lurched into motion, a pane of glass rattling in the wind, one of the dogs sighing in her sleep. Well past midnight she still lay in bed with her eyes open, staring into the darkness. Finally, not knowing what else to do, Etta got up and set to work. She went through the apartment one room at a time, rifling through all of the closets and drawers, pulling out furniture to look under it, searching for any incriminating photograph or jotted note or spare identity card. She didn't return to bed until she had satisfied herself that no evidence was to be found anywhere, at which point she fell into an exhausted sleep.

When she awoke she performed her usual morning rituals of washing and dressing—how unpleasant those tasks were in a cold apartment. In the kitchen she made herself a piece of toast, which she ate standing, as she always did when she was alone; it seemed too much trouble to sit at the table for breakfast when it was just her. It was not yet eight o'clock, the city still coming to life in the strange morning darkness of German time. On the other side of the kitchen window she could see herself hanging in the air, transparent and weightless as a ghost, peering back into the lit room.

After breakfast Etta took the dogs out for a walk. November 26 was another overcast day in Paris, the sky a leaden gray, temperature hovering around the freezing mark. Before long Margot arrived to begin work. The morning's paper announced that the first oranges of the season had appeared in Les Halles, but the meat, butter, and egg stalls were closed, poultry was practically nonexistent, and almost no fish had come in beyond tins of sardines and herring. As always, the most plentiful foodstuffs were cabbages, turnips, carrots, and potatoes—bland, pallid vegetables that seemed to carry the chill of winter within them. The newspaper was the usual carnival of bad news: German warplanes, it was reported, had set off immense fires in the English city of Southampton; one hundred thousand children were to be evacuated from London that week; Hungary had signed a mutual aid treaty with the three Axis powers. The city's cabarets and music halls were open for business; the National Opera, having just completed performances of Wagner's *Der fliegende Holländer*, was about to present a new staging of Strauss's *Der Rosenkavalier.* According to the daily horoscope, Etta would find it a day of "pleasant surprises."

At noon the doorbell rang.

It rang several times, insistently. Opening the door, Etta saw two men standing in the hallway, each wearing a long coat and a fedora and holding a briefcase. She understood at once why they had come; their arrival seemed less a surprise than a confirmation.

One of the men, Etta would later recall, spoke to her in French, informing her that they were German policemen and then asking, "Where is Madame Bonnefous?"

"She's not at home," Etta replied. Behind her, she was dimly aware of Margot disappearing down the service stairs.

"When will she be back?"

"Why are you asking all these questions about Madame Bonnefous?" Without responding, the men pushed past Etta into the apartment. Though they had identified themselves only as German policemen, she knew perfectly well that they were agents of the Gestapo, the dreaded secret police, charged with ferreting out and interrogating so-called enemies of the state. It was terrifying to think that Kitty had risen to that level in the eyes of the Nazis. Silently she watched the men move around the apartment, checking each room to make sure that it was empty. Either the agents assumed that Etta didn't understand German, or they didn't care; in any event, they spoke freely to each other, disregarding her presence. They had taken charge of the apartment without hesitation; she supposed that somewhere beneath those coats they were carrying revolvers.

One of the agents located the telephone on the coffee table in the drawing room. Then, with the air of a man entirely at home in his surroundings, he picked up the phone and dialed a number; after a moment he spoke a few words into the receiver and when the connection was made Etta heard him say that they were in the apartment but that the Englishwoman was not there, only her American friend. He was silent for several moments, listening attentively to instructions from the other end of the line, and then he hung up the phone. Turning to Etta, the Gestapo agent switched back to French, telling her that she would be coming along with him. He instructed her to put a few things into a bag, and to make sure to include some warm clothing.

In a daze, Etta walked into her bedroom and began to pack a suitcase, tossing in a bathrobe, a nightgown, a pair of slippers, a few handkerchiefs, some toilet articles from her dresser. From her closet she took the caracal fur coat that she had bought with Bill before he died; the coat was one of the few things she had brought with her to Paris from New York. She made sure to pack items of identification, including her passport, issued to her by the American consul at Nice on January 11, 1939, magnificently embossed with a red wax seal like a sunburst, which evoked the imperial seals of earlier centuries and seemed to bespeak the great power of her own government.

The door to the bedroom was open, and Etta was aware of the German standing behind her, watching her every move. Desperately she tried to think of some way that she might warn Kitty that the apartment was no longer safe. She cast her mind about the building, thinking about where she might leave a message—on the front door, perhaps, or in the elevator—but she didn't see how she could possibly do it without one of them noticing.

When she finally emerged from the bedroom, she saw that the other Gestapo man had begun searching the apartment—much as Etta herself had done only a few hours earlier. Apparently his job was to remain behind and wait for anyone who arrived there, because he paid little attention as the other agent took Etta's arm and led her out of the apartment and toward the elevator.

Etta had hoped that the building's concierge, Madame Allain, might be in the front hallway, and that she might find a way of making her understand what had happened, but the hallway was empty. Etta could not help but notice that another German agent had stationed himself near the front door, in a position to observe everyone who came in or out of the building. She hoped that Margot would stay away, would not fall into the Gestapo's trap—that was what their beautiful apartment had now become, a trap—and not feel obligated to return because of the dogs.

"My dogs!" Etta suddenly exclaimed. She had to go back, she said, just for a moment; and before the agent could respond she hurried back through the lobby to the concierge's *loge* next to the elevator.

Thankfully Madame Allain was at home, and when she opened the door Etta began speaking quickly, explaining that she would be going away for a little while, she didn't know how long, and in the meantime she wondered whether Madame Allain might be able to take care of the dogs until her return.

Surely the concierge wondered why Margot would not be able to tend to the dogs, as she always had when Kate and Etta were away on an overnight trip, but she simply nodded, looking warily at the man standing behind Etta in the hallway. After a moment he took Etta's arm and directed her back outside.

One of the shiny black cars waiting on the street was for her. The Gestapo agent motioned Etta into the back seat, and he got in beside her. The driver put the engine into gear and pulled away from the curb. Etta felt herself growing panicky, her ears ringing, cheeks starting to burn; she fought to stay calm, as she had at the German checkpoints with Kitty. She had no idea where the men were taking her; she told herself that they weren't going to arrest her—she hadn't heard of any Americans being arrested in Paris, much less an older woman such as herself. She wondered how the Gestapo had been tipped off about their activities; they had been as careful as possible, but still, there was no way to be sure of everything. Their address was known among at least some of the prisoners in the hospital at Doullens; by *les abbés* Régniez and Berteloot and their helper July Boulanger; by Sally Siauve-Evausy in Lille; by Gustave Rackelboom at the demobilized soldiers' welcome center; and of course by all of the men, British and French, who had passed through the apartment in the recent weeks. When she actually thought about it, she realized with horror that dozens of people must have been aware of what they were doing. Any one of them might have been susceptible to betrayal. The Nazis, she knew, offered sizable rewards for information leading to arrests; the Gestapo and other branches of the secret police were said to pay their collaborators out of cash boxes containing money and other valuable goods seized during raids. Her own apartment's closets and armoire drawers were stuffed full of clothing, linens, jewelry. She herself had a gold ring and a pin that she had taken from her mother's bedroom after her death; there was no telling now whether she would ever see them again.

They circled the compass rays of the place de l'Étoile, then headed south toward the Seine; the river reflected the color of the sky, a dark, cheerless gunmetal gray. In the distance stood the American embassy, where Etta had renewed her passport the previous April. It was comforting to remember that, legally speaking, that tiny piece of Paris was American territory.

Finally the driver turned onto the rue de Varenne in the seventh arrondissement, pulling into the courtyard of an enormous cream-colored stone palace. Built in the eighteenth century as a private mansion, the Hôtel Matignon had later been home to the Austro-Hungarian embassy before being purchased by the French government in 1922. Like so many of Paris's most distinguished buildings, it had been requisitioned by the Germans at the beginning of the occupation, where it provided offices for the Sicherheitsdienst (SD), the Nazi intelligence service.* Etta had never been inside a building such as this one, a wedding cake of frills and gilding and ornate moldings, with carved putti and medallions and garlands everywhere and rich, thick draperies that seemed to glow in the light. The Gestapo agent led her up a grand staircase to the second floor, into a high-ceilinged room decorated with heroic paintings and dominated by a long conference table. Another man, presumably an officer of the SD, sat at a desk in the corner of the room; unlike the Gestapo agent, he wore a military uniform, brown with black patches and epaulets. The Gestapo agent gestured to Etta to sit at the table, and the Germans took seats on the other side. She felt herself begin to wilt under their gaze, self-conscious of her eyeglasses, her curved nose, the folds of skin that hung beneath her chin, as in a Nazi caricature of an old Jewish woman.

After a moment, the Gestapo agent calmly explained in English that she must not lie to them, must not keep a single word from them, that things would not go well for her if she did. There was no point in her making matters more difficult for herself by denying

---

* Today the Hôtel Matignon serves as the official residence of the prime minister of France.

things unnecessarily, they had no wish to detain a citizen of a great country such as hers, and indeed, what they wanted most of all was to be able to release her at once, and if she were a sensible woman she would tell them candidly everything that had happened.

Again, Etta fought to choke down her fear. She didn't believe they were going to beat her—the Germans, she felt sure, wouldn't dare to harm a citizen of the United States. When she hesitated to reply, the Gestapo agent pointed out that they already knew most of the story anyway. They knew that Madame Bonnefous was carrying on her activities under cover of her work with the Foyer du Soldat. They knew about her trips around the country, knew that she was smuggling English soldiers across the border. All they wanted now, he said, was for Etta to fill in a few details of the case.

Her immediate instinct was not to challenge him, nor try to outwit him, but to apologize; apologizing was almost second nature to her. She was very sorry, Etta said, but she knew nothing of these activities. If Madame Bonnefous had been doing anything of that kind, it was in secret.

The Gestapo man gazed down at the papers in front of him. She was an intelligent woman, he said finally, and she must know that she could do nothing to save her friend from the consequences of her ill-considered acts. According to their reports, he went on, Etta was not implicated in any way in her friend's activities, and the only charge they could bring against her was the very concealment in which she was presently engaged. But he was sure that the courts would be glad to overlook that matter, as she was a neutral and therefore in a different situation than a citizen of one of the belligerent nations, especially if she demonstrated that she was not an accomplice by her willingness to clarify some of those minor details.

Again Etta said that she was sorry, but she knew nothing of Madame Bonnefous's activities.

Still he persisted in his questioning, Etta in her denials. Over time the agent changed tactics, asking about their private lives, how she and Madame Bonnefous had first become acquainted, why she had come to Paris, the state of Madame Bonnefous's marriage. The afternoon wore on; she was not offered anything to eat, nor coffee, nor a cigarette. Occasionally a phone rang, or a messenger came in and out. Beyond the tall windows the sky began slowly to darken; enormous crystal chandeliers sparkled overhead, filling the room with light. How strange it was to be having this conversation amid such splendor.

Eventually the agent gathered up his papers, then instructed Etta to take her bag and come along with him. With that he led her out of the room and back down the broad stone staircase.

"Where are you taking me?" Etta asked as they stepped into the courtyard where the black car was waiting.

"Don't worry, Madame," she would recall him saying with a smile. "We're going to a good hotel."

After a few minutes the car stopped along boulevard Raspail, in Saint-Germain-des-Prés. Across the street stood the Hôtel Lutetia, its Art Nouveau façade embellished with grapevines and cherubs, the illuminated sign with the ancient Roman spelling LVTETIA. The Lutetia, though, was not the "good hotel" of which the Gestapo agent had spoken; instead, Etta was ushered out of the car toward the brick building that faced it.

The Cherche-Midi prison

The Cherche-Midi prison was a hulking structure with a mansard roof and several rows of small windows, entirely cut off from the street by a high stone wall. Originally a convent belonging to the Sisters of the Good Shepherd, after the French Revolution the building had been seized and converted into a prison, and then a factory; in the nineteenth century the building was razed and rebuilt as a military prison with two hundred solitary-confinement cells.* The most famous of the prisoners who had been held there was Capt. Alfred Dreyfus, a French army officer of Alsatian Jewish descent who in 1894 had been falsely accused of spying for Germany; found guilty, he was sentenced to a term of life imprisonment. Twelve years later, after a long campaign on his behalf, Dreyfus was exonerated; in the meantime, though, the "Dreyfus affair," as it came to be known, had revealed deep strains of anti-Semitism in France, notably among the professional military, and aggravated long-standing fault lines in French society—intellectuals, secularists, and republicans on one side, and traditional Catholics and monarchists on the other—that still remained at the time of the Second World War.

Once, after a visit to the book stalls along the Seine, Kitty had returned home with an old French pamphlet about the Dreyfus affair; on the title page, an illustration depicted Alfred Dreyfus as he was led up the steps of Cherche-Midi prison. Now Etta too was being escorted past the sentry gate, across a small courtyard, and up those very same stone steps.

Paris no longer seemed a museum, or a beautiful stage set; dazed and trembling, Etta felt herself entering history.

* In the 1960s the building was razed again; the site is now occupied by a graduate school, the École des hautes études en sciences sociales.

15

THE FIRST MOMENTS INSIDE seemed wrenched from a night-mare: trapped in a dark, tomb-like place of unwashed walls and interminable hallways. The Gestapo agent had handed Etta off to a pair of soldiers, who now led her down one of the long hallways and then turned into a room that was bare but for a pair of desks and four chairs, one wall lined with empty bookshelves. Sitting behind one of the desks, a Nazi officer pushed a pen and a piece of paper toward her, instructing her to sign it; the document stated in German that she had entered the prison on November 26, 1940, and had surren-dered all of her personal effects.

Etta signed the paper, and her keys and wallet and passport and identification card were taken from her and sealed inside a large en-velope; then she was brought into another room, where she was handed over to the matrons, rough-looking female guards in black blouses and skirts, who ordered her to undress. After a moment she removed her dress and then stood uncertainly under the lights with her arms clasped in front of her, hoping that she might be permitted to keep on her underwear, but they just shouted impatiently at her in German to hurry up, and when she still hesitated they grabbed her and pulled the remaining garments off her body, leaving her naked and shivering in the unheated room, and then subjected her to an invasive bodily inspection that seemed less a genuine search than a demonstration that she was now utterly under their control, subject at any moment to ritual humiliation and personal violations of a sort she had never imagined.

Etta was instructed to put her clothes back on, and then she was brought into yet another room, this time to have her fingerprints and photograph taken. She held herself still for two photographs, one full face and one in right profile, as in the Wanted posters she used to see on post office walls back in America, and then another soldier took her to the section of the prison in which female prisoners were housed.

As they climbed the winding stairway to the third floor, Etta began to detect an unpleasant odor emanating from somewhere; the odor grew stronger as the guard selected a key from a large ring and unlocked a steel door that opened onto a corridor that was itself lined with a row of heavy, ancient-looking wooden doors, each fastened with a heavy metal bolt. Stopping before one of the doors, he slid open the peephole (Etta would come to learn that this was known in French as a *judas,* as though it carried the idea of betrayal within it) and scrutinized whatever was inside; apparently satisfied, he opened the door and shoved Etta in. She heard the door swing shut behind her and the bolt thud back into place: She was in her cell.

Inside, the smell was so strong that it seemed to have actual weight, suffocating her like a blanket. Instantly Etta felt that she would faint or be sick; either one might have brought some relief, but her body did not comply and for a moment she just stood unsteadily, taking in the contents of the small cell. A single bulb hanging from the ceiling cast a sickly, shadowy light over everything. The whitewashed walls were stained and covered with scrawled inscriptions from over the decades; high on one wall was a tiny barred window, scarcely larger than a sheet of writing paper. Nearly all of the space in the cell was taken up by four iron bed frames, each with a straw mattress wrapped in coarse sacking and two thin horse blankets but no pillows; young women, looking pale and drawn, sat silently on three of the beds, their hands in their laps like obedient children. A reddish-brown washbasin rested on a small table; on the floor next to it, an enamel water jug stood beside a tin pail, which Etta immediately understood, with a clutching sense of revulsion, to be the source of the terrible odor. Throughout the prison there must be hundreds of those vessels, each one a kind of fouled pond that together made up a stagnant, permanent sea of waste; and in perceiving this, Etta also realized that while she was held in Cherche-Midi she would have to perform even the most private of physical functions in the direct view of her cellmates, and the effects would remain there for who knew how long, until someone came to remove the pail.

The three young women on the other beds did not speak at first, but simply gazed at her with interested expressions. Later Etta would come to understand that the arrival of a new cellmate was a significant event, as she not only brought her own personal story but was also a source of recent news from the outside, and so could relieve, if only for a little while, the dreadful monotony of the daily routine— and, even more important, provide evidence of a world that still existed beyond that high prison wall. Etta had not eaten anything since the piece of toast that morning, but she wasn't hungry; indeed, the very thought of food seemed nauseating. It dawned on her that she had a splitting headache, but at the same time she knew that no aspirin would be available to her, indeed that no care of any kind would be forthcoming, that this was her life now, and in contemplating this a wave of misery swept over her and she felt a pressure growing in her chest, a tightness in her throat, and she dropped limply onto the unoccupied bed and like a dam too long under pressure the resistance she had maintained all day suddenly gave way and she began to cry. She struggled to hold on to the last remnants of a pride that told her not to show weakness in front of strangers, but the more she tried to restrain herself the harder she cried, from fear and desperation and from the very fact of being unable not to. She had not cried so intensely since Bill died in her arms in New York, and before that, since Irving died in the Hôtel Bristol in Paris; this time, though, she was not weeping for the loss of anyone else, but of herself.

At six o'clock a guard entered the cell with the evening meal; Etta was shocked to see that it consisted of no more than a cup of ersatz tea sweetened with saccharine and half of a small round loaf of dark bread, some of which the prisoner was supposed to save, as it also served as the following day's breakfast. Between the dryness of the bread and the odor in the cell, Etta managed to choke down just a few bites; even such a meager meal, though, seemed to invite conversation, and after a while she began to speak to the young woman in the bed beside hers.

Her name was Mary Bird and she was a tall and pretty twenty-year-old, with wavy brown hair, light blue eyes, and an open, friendly manner. She came from Guernsey, one of Great Britain's Channel Islands, located about thirty miles off the western coast of France. In July 1940 Germany had captured Guernsey and placed it under strict military occupation, with a permanent contingent of hundreds of troops, seventeen machine-gun positions, and three antiaircraft posts; eventually the German army would lay some sixty thousand land mines around Guernsey's picturesque cliffs and shoreline, making them no longer accessible to the island's inhabitants. At the beginning of September, two young men from Guernsey who had joined the British army—2nd Lts. James Symes and Hubert Nicolle—were deposited on the island under cover of darkness by a Royal Navy motor torpedo boat, charged with gathering information undercover in preparation for a possible British raid. Before they could be returned to England, though, the two were arrested by the Germans; a military tribunal on the island found them guilty of espionage and sentenced them to death. At the end of October, thirteen of Symes's and Nicolle's loved ones were also arrested and held in Guernsey prison; in November, eight of them were flown to Paris to be detained in Cherche-Midi.

Mary Bird was Jimmy Symes's fiancée. Symes too had been sent to Cherche-Midi, the sentence from the tribunal having not yet been carried out, but she had received no word of his fate, didn't even know whether he was still alive. Mary said that she had been interrogated only once during her time in Cherche-Midi; fortunately she had not been beaten during the interrogation, as had many of the female prisoners. She explained that the prisoners undressed once a day to wash themselves with the water from the jug, although the water was never hot and there was never enough of it. In any case,

Mary said, this hardly seemed to matter, as the smell from the slop pail overwhelmed everything else. Far worse than the smell, though, was the cold, in large part because it made sleeping difficult—that and the hourly ringing of the prison bells.

Already Etta had become conscious of the many noises of the prison, constant and predictable, like the inner workings of an immense machine: the clicking of hobnail boots on concrete floors; the thud of iron bolts; keys jangling musically on a chain; the rasp of a peephole as it slid open and shut. The guards were encouraged to look in on the inmates as often as possible, to make sure of what they were doing at every hour of the day or night. As a result the female prisoners could not count on any privacy from their male guards, even when they happened to be using the slop pail or when they had undressed to wash themselves; sometimes the guards made inspections in their stockinged feet, the better to surprise the prisoners.

The women weren't granted any exercise time, not even a brief promenade in a courtyard; and with four beds set in a space designed for solitary confinement, there wasn't room to pace back and forth in the cell. They could not read, as books were not allowed, nor magazines, nor letters from the outside; they could not write, as paper and pencils were also not allowed. They could not knit or sew or do manual work of any kind; they could not even smoke, as cigarettes were likewise forbidden in the cell. There was simply nothing to do, hour after hour, other than sit upright on the bed—prisoners were not permitted to lie down during the day—and perhaps say a few words to one's cellmates (after a while, all topics of conversation seemed to be exhausted) and wait for the next meal, which was revolting in itself but at least provided a break in the dreary, measureless procession of time.

A fist banged on the cell door at seven thirty each morning, and ten minutes later the prisoners had to be ready for inspection, standing at attention with clothes on and beds made; a prisoner who failed the inspection would find herself removed to the punishment cell, which differed from the others in having no window and only bare concrete blocks instead of beds on which to sleep. At eight o'clock, "coffee" was distributed, which the prisoner was expected to drink with whatever was left over from the bread of the night before.

Lunch, the main meal of the day, was served in the prison corridor at eleven and was unvarying: a ladleful of thin soup that left a greasy coating on the tin cup, along with two slices of a rubbery substance that was meant to look like salami but seemed to contain no meat and left a distinct chemical aftertaste. The evening meal consisted of tea with a chunk of black bread, handed out by a prisoner serving as "bread orderly," who lugged a heavy bag containing the food rations through the corridors for distribution in the cells. An hour later, at seven o'clock, the prisoners were permitted to undress, wash, and get into bed; at eight o'clock the lights were turned out, and the next morning the dismal routine was once again set into motion. It was a regimen of forced inaction, of cold and hunger and stink and boredom, designed to reduce life to its most basic physical necessities, to dull one's mind and sap one's strength, and thus to make any sort of resistance impossible.

That first night Etta lay sleepless for hours on the straw mattress. Despite the exhausting events of the day, she found that her mind was racing uncontrollably, returning again and again to questions that did not admit of answers: what was to become of Kitty, and of Abbé Régniez and the others, and who had betrayed them to the Gestapo; and, even more confoundingly, how it was that she, the most unassuming and diffident of women, who had regulated the motions of her life with a clockmaker's precision, now found herself at the age of sixty-two inside a German military prison, her location unknown to loved ones and her future very much in doubt.

That sort of nocturnal rumination could be terrifying, but over time Etta would come to find that nighttime inside Cherche-Midi was almost pleasant when compared to the day, "allowing me to lie in its silence and blackness, as though enveloped in a heavy curtain, and float away in imagination, away from the stone walls, and iron-bound doors, and locks and keys of the prison." Aided by the light-headedness caused by lack of food, and unable to see her actual surroundings, she discovered that she could lie awake in the inky, impenetrable darkness and dream with her eyes open. Often, in that state somewhere between wakefulness and sleep, she imagined that she was lying in her bedroom in New York and that she had just emerged from a nightmare of confinement; and sometimes that feeling would persist until she fell asleep, only to awaken a few hours later to the heart-wrenching realization that it was the nightmare that was real, and the relief from it only the dream.

A few days after her arrival in Cherche-Midi, a guard came to inform Etta that he was to bring her to the warden's office, because she had a visitor. She was startled to be spoken to directly, confused at first, and then shocked to discover what an effort it was simply to move her legs to walk. By that point hunger and boredom had already reduced her to sitting listlessly on her bed, fantasizing about long-ago meals as an invalid might fantasize about long-ago adventures. She was hungry all the time now. On occasion the hunger was actually painful, a sharp contraction in her belly like a muscle spasm, but more often she experienced it as a discomfort gnawing away at her from the inside, a hollowness that slowed movement and turned limbs to jelly and clouded the mind so that nothing seemed to be of much importance anymore.

The warden's office was on the second floor of the prison. Etta was to learn that his name was Captain Liebgott, and that he was in charge of the three German-run prisons in Paris. He was large and blond, described by one acquaintance as "a tall, handsome gentleman of the old school," who greeted his visitors by bowing at the waist and could converse in French and English as well as German; he wore the field-gray Nazi officer's uniform, the metal belt buckle inscribed with the words GOTT MIT UNS, "God with us." Sitting with the warden was a man in his middle years, wearing round steel-rimmed glasses, with wavy dark hair and a thin, pleasant face. Slight of build and neatly dressed in a suit and tie, he looked like nothing so much as a small-town banker. He stood up as Etta entered the room, and in a mild voice introduced himself as Josiah Marvel, the representative of the American Friends Service Committee (AFSC) for occupied France.

Josiah P. Marvel came from a family that had belonged to the Society of Friends—more commonly known as the Quakers—since the seventeenth century. Since his graduation from Earlham College, he had pursued a varied career in museum administration and public service; among his more notable projects, he had helped Margaret Sanger to establish the country's first birth-control clinic in Brooklyn in 1916. At the onset of the Second World War he organized the Friends Sewing Room, which would ultimately send more than three hundred thousand pieces of clothing overseas. The AFSC's bureau in Paris was then being deluged with phone calls from French people who were frantic to find out where their loved ones were being held, for, as Marvel himself once observed, "to be arrested by the Gestapo is like being removed to another planet."

Marvel had arrived in France from New York only four months earlier, shortly after the armistice had been declared, and in that time he had already set up six homes for refugee children in Biarritz and Bordeaux and a maternity home in Poitiers. In Paris he was the only American permitted to enter the Gestapo prisons, and thus was often relied upon to carry out the relief work that the American embassy itself could not do. Through his negotiations with Captain Liebgott it had been agreed that he would be allowed to go from cell to cell to determine if each prisoner had sufficient clothing or was in need of medical care, though he had to be accompanied by German guards at all times and was not permitted to speak freely with prisoners. For those prisoners who did not have family available, Marvel also offered a weekly change of laundry, which was done for him at no charge by a group of nuns at a nearby convent. "I find myself running a large laundry service," he acknowledged in a letter written to his mother back home in Indiana. "However, you can imagine what it means to a prisoner, after several weeks in the same outfit, to have someone come along and say, 'Do you want to have your clothes washed?'"

The warden indicated to Etta that she should sit down. Josiah Marvel turned to her and said that as soon as he learned that an American woman was in the prison, he had hurried over to inquire about her situation.

Even in her diminished state, Etta noted the great care he had taken with his words. "Did the American Embassy send you over?" she would recall asking him, half in surprise.

Marvel smiled. "I'm sorry," he replied gently, "but I am not allowed to talk to you about anything except your physical needs. That is the condition on which I am here." Marvel asked if she had enough warm clothing; his organization kept a storeroom of clothing that had been contributed by sympathetic groups and individuals in Paris.

After a moment's thought Etta said simply that she could use some warm underwear, and Marvel assured her that he would bring her some. He would be returning to the prison later that week and would come to her cell to check on her.

With that the meeting came to an end and the guard was summoned to return Etta to her cell. She walked back through the damp, dingy prison corridors, she said, with a new energy, "almost light-heartedly." Josiah Marvel had told her almost nothing, and yet he had said so much. She didn't know exactly how it had happened, but someone out there had learned of her arrest—someone in enough of a position of authority to dispatch the felicitously named Mr. Marvel to come look after her. Surely the person worked for the American embassy, or at least was in contact with the diplomats who remained there, those few who had stayed behind while the rest of the government decamped for Vichy. And there were others, groups and individuals, who were sympathetic to her plight and wanted to help. She was no longer abandoned and alone; beyond the prison walls, she believed now for the first time, friends were working for her release. Sometime soon she would be free once more; she would see her apartment again, and the dogs, and she would find out what had happened to Kitty.

16

ON JANUARY 17, 1941, the First Secretary of the American embassy in France at Vichy, Maynard B. Barnes, sent a memo to Secretary of State Cordell Hull "in relation to the arrest and detention of Mrs. Etta Kahn Shiber by the German authorities in Paris."

The embassy, Barnes reported, "was confidentially advised on November 26 that an American citizen, Mrs. Etta Shiber, living at 2 rue Balny d'Avricourt with a friend, a Frenchwoman, had been arrested by the German authorities. It was rumored that the French woman had been active in getting military fugitives across the demarcation line. Mrs. Shiber did not, however, appear involved."

The case was immediately taken up by the embassy's consul in Paris, Edwin A. Plitt. Though a longtime Foreign Service officer (he had served in Sofia, Constantinople, and Athens before being posted to Paris in 1939), Plitt had been trained as an engineer rather than as a diplomat, and he took an industrious, problem-solving approach to addressing consular issues. In this case, his first step was to ascertain from passport records that Mrs. Shiber was indeed an American citizen, born in New York City in 1878. Next he had to determine where she was being detained, and for what reason. When informal inquiries made to German authorities proved fruitless, Plitt decided to forgo the indirect route and drove to the Cherche-Midi prison to ask Captain Liebgott himself.

With the exception of Josiah Marvel—who held a coveted *Ausweis,* or travel pass, that bore the imprimatur of the commander of the Military Administration in France—entrance to German prisons in Paris was strictly barred to Americans. Still, Edwin Plitt somehow managed to talk himself into Captain Liebgott's office (a 1952 book on American diplomatic practice says only that "he entered by a ruse"), and while the Kommandant did not allow Plitt to look for Mrs. Shiber among the prison's two hundred cells, he consented to open the inmate files, at which point Plitt found Etta Shiber's name, presumably along with her photograph and fingerprints. A United States embassy worker was then dispatched to rue Balny-d'Avricourt to procure warm clothing for the American prisoner (characterized in the Barnes memo as "an elderly lady suffering from the cold"), only to discover that her belongings were now inaccessible, as the apartment had been placed under seal by the Gestapo.

On December 6, 1940, Maynard Barnes sent a letter to the secretary of the German embassy in Paris, Count Henri Thun, informing him that the American embassy had learned of the arrest and imprisonment of the American citizen Mrs. Etta Kahn Shiber, that no member of the embassy staff had been allowed to visit her in Cherche-Midi prison, and that the embassy was now making a formal demand for her release. No response to that letter was forthcoming, but in the meantime Edwin Plitt had made contact with an attorney by the name of Jehan Burguburu. A native of Strasbourg who had relocated to Paris only the year before, Burguburu had the rare ability to speak French without a German accent and German without a French accent, and he was one of a handful of French attorneys who had been granted the right to plead before German military courts. Plitt alerted Maître Burguburu of Mrs. Shiber's arrest and advised him to get in touch with her. He then sent Josiah Marvel to Cherche-Midi prison to look after Mrs. Shiber's welfare; within the week Marvel had brought her woolen underwear, as she had requested, and some scarves and a flannel nightgown as well.

If Etta Shiber knew who had alerted the American embassy to her arrest, she never revealed it; in her book *Paris-Underground* she indicated that it was Henri Bonnefous, whom their maid Margot apparently contacted after she fled the apartment upon the arrival of the Gestapo agents. In fact the answer to the question is contained in the records of the Special War Problems Division of the U.S. State Department. Originally called simply the Special Division, this agency had been established by President Franklin Roosevelt on September 1, 1939—the day Germany invaded Poland—for the purpose of identifying Americans living in Japan and Europe who would be endangered in the event that the United States entered the war. According to the division's organizational history (which was produced by the State Department after the war), "The American Embassy first learned of Mrs. Shiber's disappearance when the doorkeeper of her apartment telephoned to say that an American woman who lived there had gone away several days before with two men who looked like secret police and had not returned."

It was the concierge, asked to care for the dogs, who had made the call.

Already the details of her previous life—home, friends, family—had begun to fade, expunged by hunger and supplanted by the ongoing routines of the prison. The single lightbulb in the cell was controlled from somewhere outside; it went on at seven in the morning and was turned off twelve hours later, although the guards switched the light back on at random times throughout the night to inspect the cell through the peephole. The bells rang hourly; the matrons made their morning inspections; the slop pail was removed in the evenings. At night, prisoners found ways to communicate by calling through cracks in the doors or tapping a spoon on a wall. Rumors circulated about new prisoners; legends were told about the brutality of certain guards, especially the head matron, a Frau Blümelein, who despite an ingratiating exterior was said to be a torturer and sadist. As the days passed, cellmates came and went, with no telling where or why. Some of the women on the corridor were being held for prostitution or theft, or black-market operations, or simply for violating the curfew, but most faced charges that were in some way political. Occasionally a prisoner might be taken elsewhere for an interrogation; some of the women said they looked forward to being interrogated, even if it meant a beating, just for the break in the monotony. The other prisoners were all much younger than Etta, and they addressed her as Mrs. Shiber or Madame Shiber. These women had their lives still ahead of them; thinking of the prison sentences that they all faced, she came to feel her age as a kind of achievement, the completed distance of a race mostly run.

As the hours passed, a small shaft of sunlight would move slowly across the wall of the cell, extinguished sometimes by a cloud or, more fleetingly, a passing bird. Over time one learned to estimate the hour simply by the position of the light on the wall, as if they had reverted to a preindustrial age. One day snow began to fall, the first of the season; the window was too high to look through, but the shadow of tiny flakes could be seen in the air. It was so strange to think that just beyond that window was Paris, where people went on about their days, while they all suffered inside, hungry and cold, just a stone's throw from the sidewalk.

Her mattress was filthy, and so old that the straw inside it had broken down into small pieces that dug into her back and hips. She could roll up her caracal coat and use it as a pillow, although if the weather grew any colder it would need to serve as an extra blanket. The cell itself was unheated, the only warm air coming in through the transom above the door. The small window admitted little fresh air or sunlight, but it had the advantage, at least, of not letting in much cold. Late at night, amid the blackness of the cell, the window shimmered in the glow of the moon. Nighttime was when the secret police came for their victims, seizing a prisoner from her bed to drive her to one of the Gestapo torture chambers tucked into grand houses on avenue Foch or rue des Saussaies.* Sometimes at night Etta could hear them coming, recognized the telltale clop of boots and jangle of keys; barely able to breathe, she'd close her eyes and silently pray that these angels of death would pass by her doorway.

---

* After the war, the Gestapo headquarters at 11 rue des Saussaies would become the headquarters of the Direction de la Surveillance du Territoire, the French counterintelligence agency; during the Algerian War (1954–62), the building served as a site for the detention and torture of Algerian nationalists.

Edwin Plitt of the American embassy soon had a new diplomatic problem on his hands. Four days after the arrest of Etta Shiber, another American woman, Elizabeth Deegan, was detained for questioning by German authorities. Deegan, who was forty years old and originally from North Carolina, worked as a clerk and receptionist at the American embassy; she was often the first person to whom visitors to the embassy spoke, and in the summer and fall of 1940 these had included a number of British servicemen seeking American help in escaping France. On the morning of Sunday, December 1, a pair of German agents showed up at her apartment while she was having a manicure and informed her that their chief wished to speak with her about the activities of Col. Cecil A. Shaw, the former British intelligence officer who maintained an office in the American embassy. Through an intermediary, the Germans sent a message to the embassy explaining that Mrs. Deegan was being held for questioning in "a comfortable hotel in Paris"; while it would be impossible for her to be at the embassy the following day, she would doubtless be able to report for work on December 3.

However, Elizabeth Deegan did not appear at the embassy that morning. By then the German authorities had come to believe that she was part of an organized effort within the embassy—an "underground railway," as one news story characterized it—to help British officers escape from German-occupied France. They claimed that Mrs. Deegan had given embassy money to escaped British servicemen, which they understood to be a violation of America's neutral status under international law; they were especially incensed that another member of the American embassy staff, First Secretary Cecil M. P. Cross, had for several months provided living space in the embassy to the British clerk Edward Sutton, who they were convinced was a spy and whom they were now holding in Cherche-Midi prison.*

On December 7, the American embassy in Berlin filed an official protest with the German government and demanded recognition of

---

* Apparently unbeknownst to the Germans, another escaped British soldier, Pvt. S.G.C. Park of the Argyll and Sutherland Highlanders, had stayed in the home of an American embassy official for nearly the entire month of November.

diplomatic immunity and the immediate release of Elizabeth Deegan. In a Washington press conference, Secretary of State Cordell Hull said that the United States government was "watching the matter closely."

For the next week, furious negotiations went on behind the scenes, until the afternoon of December 14, when Elizabeth Deegan was released from German custody. One week later, a news report announced that three staff members of the American embassy in Paris—First Secretary Cecil M. P. Cross, Second Secretary Leigh M. Hunt, and clerk and receptionist Elizabeth Deegan—were being transferred to posts outside France.

For her part, Elizabeth Deegan stoutly denied having aided any escaped or evading British servicemen or having given money to anyone whom she knew to be a British soldier. More sweepingly, H. Freeman Matthews, chargé d'affaires at the American embassy in Vichy, sent a telegram to Secretary of State Hull assuring him that whenever a British soldier appealed for help, "relief has been refused and the persons in question have been requested to leave the Embassy and not to call again. At no time, from the very outset of the occupation, have responsible officers of the Embassy tolerated the thought that relief could be given to British military refugees." The classified accounts of several repatriated servicemen, however, given to interrogators from the British intelligence agency MI9—which are among the several hundred World War II escape reports held at the National Archives of the United Kingdom—present a rather different picture.

One British soldier, for instance, Pvt. A. A. L. Lang of the Argyll and Sutherland Highlanders, who had escaped from captivity in Belgium, came to the American embassy seeking assistance in reaching unoccupied France; Edward Sutton, the clerk in charge of British interests at the embassy, was able to offer him only 50 francs, at which point, Lang reported, "Mrs. Deegan gave me another 250 francs, a map, food, and clothing. I understand that this good lady had helped a lot of British escapers on their way." Sgt. Maj. Charlie Fullerton of the Gordon Highlanders reported that he went to see Col. Cecil Shaw in the American embassy, who directed him to the local Salvation Army hostel, where eight other British servicemen were staying; the next day, Fullerton returned to the embassy and "was given 500 francs by an American lady." Similarly, Driver G. J. Thibaut of the Royal Army Service Corps arrived at the American embassy on July 20 "and there found Colonel Shaw and the British Consul, Mr. Sutton, who were unable to give me any assistance, but I was advanced 500 francs by a secretary at the Embassy." (One recalls as well Kate Bonnefous confiding to Georges Siauve-Evausy that the 1,000-franc note she was giving him had been "bullied . . . out of an American official.")

A detailed account was provided by John Forbes Christie, a signalman with the 51st Highland Division, who arrived at the American embassy in August. He informed the woman at the front desk that he was an escaped prisoner of war and that he had a companion waiting outside. She instructed him to get his companion and then to tell the doorman that they wished to see "Mrs. Deacon." Christie's testimony continues:

> Soon a lady appeared in the lobby, at some distance from the public counter, and introduced herself to us as Mrs. Deacon [Deegan]. She asked us who we were and took a note of our names and addresses. Getting down to the purpose of our visit, I told her that our need was for money to help us get into the unoccupied zone of France. . . . Mrs. Deacon came back with our money, which amounted to 600 francs each. . . . She wished us well and advised us to "beat it out of town" that night as she had prior information that the Germans were going to start a "crackdown" on all foreigners in Paris on the following day.

At the end of December, after the Deegan controversy had passed, Adm. William D. Leahy, the American ambassador to France at Vichy, sent a telegram to Secretary of State Hull informing him that the embassy in Paris had checked its records of cash payments made since the beginning of July and found that "the recipients of such payments in twenty cases were British military stragglers. The number of payments amounted to 38 and total 12,410 francs out of approximately 6,800,000 disbursed until the end of October." These payments, Leahy acknowledged, "were made contrary to standing instructions that no relief should be extended to members of the British military forces."

At eleven o'clock in the morning on Saturday, December 14, the same day that Elizabeth Deegan was released from German custody, a guard came to Etta Shiber's cell and ordered her to come with him, informing her that she was being released.

For several moments Etta remained sitting on her bed, trying to understand what he had said. Had she misheard? But when he barked at her to hurry up, she quickly embraced her cellmates, gathered up her bag—it was always packed, as she had nowhere else to keep her belongings—and followed the guard into the corridor. Her head spinning from confusion and hunger, her legs stiff as stilts, she hurried behind him as fast as she could, down the stairs to the room in which she had been photographed and had her fingerprints taken. There, an Unteroffizier handed her a release form stating in German that she had been held in Cherche-Midi prison from November 26 to December 14, and on the latter date had been freed. Another guard then took her to the warden's office, where Captain Liebgott stood to greet her as she entered. With a flourish he handed her the envelope that contained her papers and wallet, then picked up a set of keys from his desk and gave them to her. She recognized them as her own.

The warden walked Etta back to the anteroom of his office. He must have said goodbye, but she didn't notice; she walked past the twin silent guards at the entrance, then down the steps and across the courtyard to the large outer gate inscribed with the words PRISON MILITAIRE DE PARIS. At the gate, the German officer inspected her release form and returned it to her without a word; then the heavy door was pushed open, and she stepped out onto the rue du Cherche-Midi.

Paris was all around her; she could turn in any direction. Etta stopped for a moment on the corner of boulevard Raspail. She breathed in deep the cold, exquisitely fresh winter air. With her bag in her hand, she felt like a tourist, seeing the city for the first time: the undulating façade of the Hôtel Lutetia, its exterior as smooth and creamy as parchment; pedestrians walking this way and that; *vélo-taxis,* bicycles attached to brightly painted carts with cushioned seats, darting through the streets like tropical fish in a tank. It occurred to her that she could go to a restaurant if she chose to, order as much food as her ration cards allowed; she could go to a hairdresser, read a book, take a bath. Most luxurious of all was simply the notion of having privacy once again: being able to eat, dress, move her bowels, even just sit quietly without being watched by others. Already she began to feel her old life seeping back in, loved ones returning to mind, Bill once again with her but not with her. She was desperate to know what had become of Kitty, to warn her if she possibly could. Surely her own unexpected release from prison was the American embassy's doing; she would have to go there as soon as she could and find out what information they had. She could hardly bear to think that she might have been set free because the Nazis no longer needed her—because Kitty, the one they really wanted, had already been arrested.

She turned toward the Métro station, heading for home.

17

EVEN UNDER OCCUPATION, THE United States embassy in Paris maintained much of the genteel ambience of a manor house. Etta Shiber arrived at the embassy on Tuesday, December 17, three days after her release from Cherche-Midi prison; she was greeted at the front entrance by a uniformed doorman, who escorted her to the information desk in the front lobby. After filling out a visitor's card she proceeded up the main staircase, where an attendant in black formal coat and white gloves ushered her to the reception room for Edwin A. Plitt, the embassy consul.

Edwin Plitt was then forty-nine years old, though his gray hair, rimless spectacles, and stout frame gave him the bearing of an older man. He had been exceptionally busy of late, for in addition to the regular course of business he had overseen negotiations for the release not only of Etta Shiber but also of Elizabeth Deegan, in concert with German ire over the goings-on inside the embassy in Paris. To Etta's profuse expressions of thanks for his assistance, he said simply that he was very sorry about her recent unfortunate experiences but gratified that she was now free, and he hoped and trusted that she would remain so in the future. To that end, he "strongly advised" her to consult with Maître Burguburu without delay, and to leave her apartment and take a room in the nearby

Hôtel Bristol, where she would be under her government's protection.* He was also pleased to inform Etta that the Paris branch of the Central Hanover Bank and Trust Company, the New York office of which she had wired for the money, had recently deposited $1,000 with the embassy, credited to her account. That money was now hers to do with as she pleased, but he would recommend that she leave the bulk of it with the embassy, where it would be secure and available to cover any expenses involved in her return to the United States.

Etta accepted all of Edwin Plitt's suggestions, assuring him that she would go to the Hôtel Bristol as soon as she felt sufficiently recovered from her recent ordeal. At his request, before leaving the embassy she set into motion the various bureaucratic processes involved in repatriation to the United States, applying for her French exit visa and her currency export permit as well as the necessary Spanish and Portuguese visas. She also withdrew $200 against her credit, leaving the remainder with the embassy.

Two days later, First Secretary Cecil M. P. Cross sent a letter to Etta's brother, Chester Kahn, in Syracuse, who had written to the State Department some weeks earlier expressing concern for her welfare. Chester said that he had not heard from his sister since August, when she had written him a long letter describing her flight from Paris before the occupation and her return to the city two weeks later. Cross gave him the good news:

I take pleasure in informing you that the Embassy has recently interviewed your sister, who is well and preparing to return to the United States very shortly. She has received through this office sufficient funds to enable her to carry out her purpose. While she is still residing at 2 rue Balny d'Avricourt, she intends to move to the Hotel Bristol and await there the completion of the various

* The Bristol was one of the few luxury hotels in Paris that the Nazis had not requisitioned, as the United States ambassador of the time, William Bullitt, had already leased it for the use of embassy employees and other American nationals. In addition to its convenient location, the hotel was seen as especially desirable because its basement shelter was the only one in the city designed to protect against the use of poison gas.

formalities which American citizens have to comply with before leaving occupied France.

In Paris, the winter of 1940–41 would turn out to be the coldest in memory, with a record seventy days below freezing. Only those with the proper Nazi connections had enough coal or oil to heat their homes. It had been discovered that paper soaked for twenty-four hours becomes a pulp that can be formed into balls that, when dried and lit, supply a bit of temporary warmth; thus did newspapers, magazines, cardboard boxes, and even some books find their way into the stoves of Paris. The city's German-controlled newspapers were certainly fit for burning, but burning books was another matter, and uncomfortable jokes were made about which of the books on one's shelves had a literary value that was lower than their value as fuel. Parisians ate in restaurants while wearing overcoats and gloves, shivered for hours outside on ration lines. An unfamiliar sound could now be heard on the streets: the dull clop-clop-clop of wooden soles, made necessary by the shortage of leather. It was rumored that some women were wearing coats made from the pelts of dogs, cats, horses.

On the grim, overcast winter afternoons, when sunlight itself seemed a scarce resource, Etta opened the shutters and looked down at the street below, half expecting to see Kitty there; instead she saw strangers hurrying by, bundled up as best they could. Their apartment had been left in surprisingly good shape; one could barely tell that it had been searched by the Gestapo. On first arriving home she had wandered around for some time in a joyous reverie, just walking from one room to another, unable to sit calmly and rest; she turned the lamps on and off, opened the icebox, tried the hot-water faucet in the bathroom to make sure it was still working. Gratefully she collected the dogs from Madame Allain; they rushed up to her, barking frantically, jumping around her and licking her hands. There was no news of Madame Bonnefous, the concierge said regretfully. For a while the Gestapo had stationed a man by the front door around the clock, checking everyone who came in and out. They were hardly shy about it—at night he would shine an electric torch right at your face. After a few days, though, the Germans had disappeared; they must have decided she wasn't coming back.

The twice-weekly delivery of soldiers had likewise stopped, Etta didn't know why. Nor had Margot returned to work, so now it was just the dogs and her. How devoted she and Kitty had been to those dogs, how attentive their care for a tapeworm or a case of milk fever. Shortly after Etta came to live in the apartment they had gotten Winkie and Micky as puppies, joining Kitty's cocker spaniel Nanette, with the idea that they would all grow old together. What was to become of the dogs now, if she were just to pack up and leave? She couldn't take them with her: Chester and Helen's little house in Syracuse could barely hold their own family, and she wouldn't think of further imposing on them. Nor would the hotel be enthusiastic about the prospect of three cocker spaniels staying indefinitely in one of their elegant rooms. She knew the Hôtel Bristol well, that limestone mansion on rue du Faubourg Saint-Honoré with the Renaissance paintings and Gobelins tapestries in the downstairs salons, the chintz wallpaper and authentic Louis XVI furniture in the rooms. The Bristol, of course, was where her cousin Irving had died, after their return to Paris from the spa in Aix-les-Bains. It was in a room at the Bristol that she had waited for days, miserable amid the luxury, for Bill to arrive to take her home—where Kitty had promised that she would take care of Etta if anything ever happened to him.

Several days elapsed with no new information, no good ideas about what to do with the dogs. She walked them in the morning and the evening; otherwise she went out only to shop, and only when she had to. Cold winds whipped through the streets, rattling shutters and ruining umbrellas; rain drummed a tattoo on zinc roofs. Paris seemed to have lost its vitality, turned to stone like one of Medusa's victims, the populace settling in grimly for what looked to be a long occupation—five years perhaps, or ten, or twenty. After the whirlwind of the fall, life seemed now to be moving in slow motion. At night she slept beside Winkie and Micky; Nanette, who snored, slept in a basket in the kitchen. The dogs lay under the covers, whimpering unhappily; they could sense that something was wrong with her.

One day slid into the next; she felt almost overcome with lassitude, unable to think of anything to do. She had still not recovered from her time in Cherche-Midi, two and a half weeks of insufficient food, fitful sleep, and almost no activity, compounded by the constant tension that the routine of the prison seemed designed to cultivate. Now she was overwhelmed by the thought of the planning, the packing, the bureaucratic red tape that had to be negotiated before undertaking a repatriation voyage; beyond that, she could hardly even contemplate the idea of leaving France, crossing the ocean to safety, without knowing if Kitty was free or in jail, or even still alive. She recognized that the American embassy wouldn't have information about a French citizen of British birth, and by this time the British Interests Section inside the embassy had for all intents and purposes ceased to exist. She had thought that perhaps Mr. Marvel might know something, but Edwin Plitt refused to divulge his address, saying that to do so might compromise the important work being done by the Quakers. Josiah Marvel was able to maintain his unique status only because he was conscientious about observing the restrictions that had been placed on his activity: that he confine himself to the physical well-being of the prisoners and refuse ever to discuss their cases. If Etta called on him, the Germans might well suspect that he had overstepped his role and would bar him from the prisons. Plitt assured her, though, that the embassy would pass along to him her expressions of thanks for his care.

There was no possibility of stopping by friends' houses to see if they had any news of Kitty, lest she turn the attention of the Gestapo onto them; she carried a kind of contagion now and didn't want to infect anyone else with her presence. She might simply have called, but using the telephone was likewise impossible: Someone else could well be listening in on the line, wanting information as much as she did. She had not yet met with Maître Burguburu, had not contacted the Bristol to reserve a room. She cast her mind about the apartment, considering which belongings she should take along for the voyage, almost as a hypothetical proposition, like the old question about the best books for a desert island.

On the evening of December 22, 1940, she heard another unexpected knock at the door. This time only one Gestapo agent was standing in the hallway. He greeted her by name and explained that she was to come with him; he sounded almost apologetic about having to arrest her. Etta made no protest; his arrival seemed less a surprise than an inevitability. For eight days she had been waiting for something to happen, and now it had. She wondered if she had been followed during her excursions outside the house; it occurred to her that the Nazis might have freed her in the hope that she would lead them to Kitty. By a certain point they must have recognized that she would not; or—more distressing to contemplate—she was being returned to prison now because Kitty had already been captured.

Etta put on her old fur coat over the navy-blue wool dress she was wearing, then grabbed her purse and her overnight bag, which she had not unpacked since returning from Cherche-Midi; wordlessly she closed the apartment door behind her. Downstairs, she again received permission from the Gestapo man to ask the concierge to care for the dogs, and then the two of them left the building and got into his car.

It was not a long drive to Cherche-Midi prison. Etta was struck by the realization that she was not as frightened as she had been the last time she walked through that imposing front gate, passing beneath the words PRISON MILITAIRE DE PARIS engraved on the stone like an epitaph. The entry process was far less difficult than before; the guards seemed to be treating her arrival less as a new imprisonment than as a continuation of her previous one. "I seemed to reenter immediately the atmosphere I had left," Etta was to recall. "The intervening period was wiped away cleanly, as though by a sponge. Five minutes after I had set foot in the prison again, I felt as though I had never left it."

The first Nazi execution of a civilian in Paris—another prisoner at Cherche-Midi—took place within hours of Etta's second arrival in the prison. On November 10, a young engineer named Jacques Bonsergent had been arrested for jostling a German officer on a street near Gare Saint-Lazare. A group of young Frenchmen had encountered a group of drunken soldiers that evening as they returned to their barracks, and though Bonsergent seems not to have taken part in the scuffle that ensued, he was the one who was seized, and when he refused to name his companions he was thrown into Cherche-Midi. On December 5, a military tribunal found him guilty of "an act of violence against a member of the German army" and sentenced him to death. His attorney assured him that the sentence was merely a formality and would be reduced on appeal, that the führer did not wish to antagonize the people of Paris; recent events, though, including the student demonstrations of November 11, had hardened Hitler's attitudes, and he waved away the appeal without a word when it was brought to him.

At dawn on December 23, accompanied by twelve soldiers and the prison chaplain, Jacques Bonsergent was driven to the Bois de Vincennes, a park in the twelfth arrondissement; in the truck, the condemned young man sat with the priest on the pine coffin that would soon hold his body.

The German announcement of the execution of Jacques Bonsergent was posted on the walls of Paris on December 24. The novelist Jean Bruller noted that he was "transfixed" by the news, so unexpected and awful, and that all around him "people stopped, read, wordlessly exchanged glances. Some of them bared their heads as if in the presence of the dead." The German authorities had further decreed that midnight mass would be canceled that night, due to curfew regulations; on Christmas Eve 1940, for the first time ever, midnight mass in Paris was celebrated at five P.M.

In Etta's cell in Cherche-Midi, one of her three new cellmates, a young Frenchwoman whose name Etta would remember only as Genevieve, was grieving her first Christmas Eve away from her family. Despite the arresting policeman's assurance to her mother that Genevieve would be back home in a matter of days, she had now been imprisoned for three months, with no sign of being released anytime soon. That evening, after the light in the cell had been turned out, Etta heard Genevieve crying softly in her bed, and after a little while the crying died away and there was silence again in the cell, and then unexpectedly she began to sing the Latin hymn "Adeste Fideles," just as she must have on Christmas Eves with her family so many times before.

This was Etta's third night back in Cherche-Midi, and although the holiday itself held no special meaning for her (she would later observe that "I was no sadder, no more depressed on Christmas than on any other day"), she understood how difficult it was for the others to be in prison at that time of year, and even through the darkness she could sense that the carol had offered the young woman some small bit of comfort. Gently Etta encouraged her to keep singing, and so Genevieve sang a few of the traditional folk songs, simple and haunting, that had echoed through the French countryside for centuries, and which on this night rose through the cell's single barred window to reverberate in the empty prison yard and up through other barred windows; and then finally, enveloped in the darkness and quiet, she sang *"Ave Maria,"* the long, sustained notes like a bell slowly tolling, her uplifted solitary voice seeming to transform the prison into a cathedral.

Years later one of the Guernsey prisoners, Hubert Nicolle, would recall: "One of the most moving moments for me during the whole of my captivity was on Christmas Eve, 1940, when a French girl with a magnificent voice sang the Ave Maria. Her cell window was overlooking the prison yard and her voice echoed around the square. It was a very emotional occasion. . . . After that the girl was moved to a cell without windows."

By the end of the week, once more perpetually cold and hungry and with nothing to occupy herself, Etta had returned to the almost mechanical state of her previous imprisonment, with long stretches that in retrospect she could not remember at all. The slumber was broken one day when the prison warden, Captain Liebgott, came into Etta's cell during what seemed to be a routine tour of inspection. "It occurs to me," she recalled him as saying, "that perhaps you would be more comfortable if I had you placed in the same cell as another English-speaking person."

Along with her cellmates Etta was standing, as prisoners were obliged to whenever a German soldier entered their cell. She looked at the warden in some surprise—this was the first time that anyone in Cherche-Midi had expressed the slightest consideration for her—but she told him that yes, she would like that change. She was brought to a cell at the end of the corridor that had only a single occupant. This woman looked to be about the same age as herself, with short brown hair, a broad jaw, and prominent brows; her dark eyes, though, had a haunted look to them, and her mouth was a grim line. She eyed her new cellmate suspiciously, but after Etta had said hello and introduced herself, she softened somewhat and introduced herself as Mrs. Symes.* At once Etta realized who she was—she was the mother of Jimmy Symes, one of the two servicemen from Guernsey who had been captured while doing reconnaissance of the island in preparation for a possible British invasion. Her son, then, was the fiancé of young Mary Bird; and when Etta told Mrs. Symes that she had been in a cell with Mary, any suspicion melted away and tears came to her eyes, and before long she began to weep.

After some time she managed to calm herself and explain to Etta what had happened. Her husband, Louis Symes, had been caught communicating with Mary through his cell window, which happened to face hers across the prison yard. (In an account given years later, Mary Bird said that she and Louis "wrote messages on the window to each other using a rag," one letter at a time.) As a consequence he was sentenced to one month in a solitary, dark punishment cell, with only a concrete block for a bed, and on December 22 he was found there with his wrists slashed with a razor blade, dead of an apparent suicide.† Her widow's grief was as fresh and painful as an open wound, and in witnessing it Etta suddenly understood why she had been transferred: The warden didn't want another suicide among his prisoners—it was bad for morale, not to mention a blot on his own record—and he was counting on Etta's presence in the cell to prevent Mrs. Symes, in her misery, from attempting to join her

* In *Paris-Underground* Etta Shiber misspelled the name slightly, calling her "Mrs. Syms." Her full name was Rachel Symes, and in 1940 she was fifty-six years old; born and raised in Guernsey, she had been married for twenty-six years and had three children, ages sixteen through twenty-one.

† Among the Guernsey prisoners there was a difference of opinion about whether Louis Symes had actually committed suicide or whether a blow from a German guard had caused his death, with the suicide staged afterward. Rachel Symes herself always held the latter opinion, as she suggested in her 1964 claim for compensation for Nazi war crimes. The British Foreign Service office rejected her claim, as the cause of her husband's death remained unclear and Cherche-Midi prison "was not a concentration camp or comparable institution."

husband. "For once," Etta was to note, "I agreed with a German," and she spent the next several days doing what she could to comfort Mrs. Symes, holding her hand, sharing the fact that she herself was a widow from a long marriage and knew something of loss, and that while the pain of her husband's absence might never disappear, it did soften with time, especially if she could find a way to involve herself in other activities, and reminding her, most pointedly, that her children needed her now more than ever, that they had been deprived of one parent and must not be made to lose another.

As time went on Etta managed to get Mrs. Symes to talk of other subjects, especially of her beloved Guernsey, its cliffs aglow with golden furze and flowering gorse and tangles of heather and blackberry, lush meadows of timothy and clover grazed by the island's famous dairy cows. Along with the other main Channel Island, Jersey, Guernsey was a self-governing bailiwick that had been under the protection of the United Kingdom for the better part of a millennium, but in 1940, after the German conquest of France, Prime Minister Churchill had acknowledged that the islands were now indefensible. So in June of that year, Guernsey's children, some five thousand of them, had been evacuated to Great Britain, loaded by their heartsick parents onto the makeshift fleet that waited in the harbor to transport them to Glasgow and other ports of entry. It had made for a strange and disturbing scene, that seemingly endless line of children clutching gas masks and perhaps a favorite toy or stuffed animal with a few extra pieces of clothing in a feed sack or pillowcase, some crying, others bubbling with excitement, all of them marching together down to the sea as though under the power of a magic spell, as though Guernsey had turned into Hamelin.

On December 29, 1940, the prison authorities announced that the death sentences levied against James Symes and Hubert Nicolle had been commuted and that they would be sent to a prisoner-of-war camp instead; as for the rest of the Guernsey prisoners, they would be freed and returned to their homes. One of those prisoners, Ambrose Sherwill, would later recall in his diary: "Poor Mrs. Symes; in what a turmoil of mixed emotions she must have been. Widowed, released from prison, her son saved from probable death. She was wonderfully brave and even joked with us as we drove through the countryside. We were in a jocular mood and yet, conscious of what she was feeling beneath the brave face she was showing the world, again and again a ribald joke would be cut off halfway as the joker caught sight of her tense face."*

With Mrs. Symes gone Etta was moved to yet another cell. It was not quite like before, however; her time with Mrs. Symes had lifted Etta out of herself, caused her to think creatively and with purpose, and to set aside, if only momentarily, her own troubles. As the days passed, she began to feel less like an outsider in the prison, an aged interloper who didn't belong among the thieves and prostitutes and hard-core resisters who populated the women's corridor. She began to participate in the "prison grapevine" that was carried on surreptitiously while waiting for lunch in the corridor and in the cells at night when the guards were not around. So it was that the next month Etta learned that one of the female prisoners had been sentenced, as Louis Symes had been, to thirty days of solitary confinement in the punishment cell: Apparently some French laborers were working in a room that adjoined this prisoner's cell, and for days she had surreptitiously dug out a tiny hole in the wall with a nail file and a spoon, so that she could give messages to them. It was said that she was an Englishwoman married to a Frenchman, and that she had been arrested for aiding enemy soldiers, a crime for which the penalty was death.

---

* Rachel Symes would live for another thirty years; she died in 1971, in Guernsey, at the age of eighty-six.

18

KATE BONNEFOUS ARRIVED IN Marseille on November 27, 1940, rejoining Lt. Colin Hunter and Cpl. Gordon Hood-Cree—the first servicemen she had ever helped to escape. She had come to the city, Hunter would later attest, "to see how we were getting on and also to see if she could raise some money, as she had to use her own to provide railway fares and hotel accommodation for the British who were sent through." The two servicemen had been in Marseille for eight weeks, as they awaited an examination by a five-person international medical board at Fort Saint-Jean that would determine whether their injuries had rendered them unfit for future military service, thus permitting them to obtain exit visas to return to England. Gordon Hood-Cree was also recuperating from surgery that had recently been performed to remove the shrapnel that remained in his leg. (As an escaped prisoner of war, he had registered in the hospital under an assumed name, "Georges François," but his actual identity was something of an open secret among the French medical staff.) When Hood-Cree was released from the hospital, he and Hunter moved into the home of a local gangster they had befriended, who was, he said, "the most violently pro-British Frenchman I ever met. . . . Every night he and the whole family would sit around, their ears glued to the BBC news in French. He was so keen to hear it, he threatened to strangle anyone who made a noise while it was on."

After Kate arrived in Marseille, Colin Hunter brought her to Cannes to see a wealthy Englishman of his acquaintance, in hopes of obtaining a loan to support her work. The Englishman proved amenable, agreeing to provide 35,000 francs (about $15,000 in today's currency) the following day; Kate returned to Marseille, while Hunter remained in Cannes to collect the money.

That night, though, Henri Bonnefous arrived at the house in Marseille, bringing the awful news that the Gestapo had raided the apartment and arrested Etta.

Kate declared at once, "I am going back. I must get her out."

As Gordon Hood-Cree later observed to a newspaper reporter, "She was perfectly safe herself. She had done enough. All of us— [Hunter] and myself, three other officers, her husband, the maid, and our gangster friend—begged her not to go back. 'You can do nothing even if you go,' we told her. But she would not listen. Once she had made up her mind, nothing could stop her. 'She is my friend. She is alone in Paris. I must do what I can,' was all she would say."

That night Kate phoned Colin Hunter in Cannes to tell him that Mrs. Shiber had been arrested and their apartment seized by the Gestapo, and that she would be leaving right away to return to Paris.

"She was adamant in her wish to return immediately," Hunter recalled, "as she was this American's only friend in the world." What was more, Kate told him, Mrs. Shiber was "more or less innocent" and as a result she herself "felt the situation most keenly."

Despite Kate's insistence on leaving, Hunter was able to persuade her to wait until he had arrived back in Marseille with the Englishman's money, which he did the following evening. Her intention was to travel to the Pas-de-Calais before returning to Paris; while there she would see the two priests with whom she had been working, to give them 20,000 francs and warn them not to come to her apartment any longer—it was now Friday, November 29, and another delivery of escaped servicemen was due at rue Balny-d'Avricourt the following Monday. As the Gestapo was surely on the lookout for her, she donned a wig to alter her appearance* and set out northwest by train to meet up with Elie Teyssier near the town of La Réole.

What exactly Kate Bonnefous was planning to do once she had returned to Paris is not clear. By this point, of course, she was herself a fugitive and would not have dared to return to her own home, which had been seized by the Gestapo; likely she was planning to use a portion of her remaining funds for a hotel room while she remained in the city. It's possible that she intended to alert the American embassy of Etta's arrest, in the event that they did not yet know of it, and to arrange for Etta to obtain an attorney. She would also have been looking for a way to ascertain the status of their three dogs. Her automobile, like her apartment and the belongings in it, she must already have given up as lost.

In any event, she never made it to Paris. On November 30, near Castillon-sur-Dordogne, Kate Bonnefous and Elie Teyssier were arrested as they attempted to cross the line of demarcation back into occupied France. The two were transported to Fort du Hâ, a forbidding nineteenth-century stone prison constructed within the remains of a fifteenth-century castle in Bordeaux.

Since June 1940, one wing of Fort du Hâ had been reserved for political prisoners and was overseen by a German army major; this was known as the *quartier allemand,* or German section. In December 1940, when Kate Bonnefous arrived, the *quartier allemand* was not yet employing the more advanced forms of interrogation that would be introduced later on by a stern new prison warden, Lt. Friedrich-Wilhelm Dhose of the SS, described in one history as a "man most steeped in villainy"; the prison chapel, for instance, had not yet been converted into a torture chamber, its walls fitted with wooden planks from which hung giant hooks, shackles with multiple straps, and other instruments of suffering provided by Nazi ingenuity. Still, the prison's earlier interrogators had no shortage of techniques from which to draw, including threats, beatings, and plunging the victim's head into water until nearly drowned (a procedure known as *la baignoire,* "the bathtub"), alternated with false promises of im-

---

* Presumably she also carried a set of false identification papers.

munity or other special treatment: a regimen of pain and its allevia-
tion designed to extract desired names, dates, addresses—information
that only in the most distorted sense of the word could be termed a
"confession."

Despite all of this, Kate Bonnefous must not have given her interrogators the information they were seeking, because within a matter
of days she was removed from her cell and thrown into the dungeon.

No part of Fort du Hâ was as grim, nor as feared, as the dungeon—
referred to by prison officials more antiseptically as *le mitard,* or "solitary confinement." The dungeon was where prisoners were induced
to confess when more conventional means had proved unavailing. It
lay at the bottom of a stone staircase, ten feet below ground; there, a
hallway held a set of small, roughly carved wooden doors, such as
might have belonged to a quaint cottage in a German fairy tale, but
which here opened into something out of a horror story. A large
storage cellar had been walled off into separate compartments, each
one having a ceiling no more than four feet high, with a cement floor,
no electricity, no water, no heat, no windows, no light at all. A prisoner there received a single daily ration of two hundred grams of
bread, plus a bowl of soup every four days; a trapdoor was opened
and the food wordlessly handed down, along with an empty slop pail
that was exchanged for the filled one from the previous day. "The
smell that rises from this horrific lair," recalled one prisoner, "is beyond all imagination." Other than that brief moment, the dungeon
provided no human contact, no awareness of any life at all other than
the tiny, unseen creatures that crawled and swarmed and ate in that
fetid space.

Inside the dungeon, the prisoner was plunged into a vast and absolute darkness, unutterably alone, like an undersea explorer inside a
diving bell that has plunged to the bottom of the ocean. It was a
world without daylight, devoid of weather, removed from time, the
space less like a room than a coffin. For a while one could try to stave
off the isolation by training the mind, strengthening it as other prisoners strengthen the body with sit-ups or jumping jacks in their

cells; one could recite all the counties of Great Britain or all the American states and their capitals, could revisit every room in every house in which one had ever lived, the name of every schoolmate, make mental journeys to distant locations that cataloged all of the towns and cities through which one would pass. But exercise cannot last forever; eventually one begins to tire, and the lists and the maps fade away and then random images and memories come flooding in, detached from reason, looming in the mind as before one's eyes, dancing in the air like ghosts. More maddening still, the sustained loss of vision had the effect of sharpening the other senses, so that over time one could taste all the more acutely the mold that sprouted on the grains of the bread, smell more powerfully the putrefaction in the air, hear as loud as a drum the ceaseless and unnerving beat of one's own heart.

Relief was provided by the occasional torture sessions, for pain at least provided sensation, proof of life. Weak, starved, half-crazed with loneliness, a prisoner emerging from the dungeon would find it almost impossible to resist the interrogator any longer, to continue holding out when the only alternative was to be plunged once more into that malign and terrifying darkness, that death in life. Yet somehow Kate Bonnefous did resist, and so she was never freed from the dungeon, never returned to a cell with other prisoners. She remained there until January 3, 1941, when she was transported to Cherche-Midi prison in preparation for her trial.

Unlike Etta Shiber, Kate Bonnefous was interrogated regularly in Cherche-Midi—by her own account, every single day between January 10 and the first week of February. Daily she was brought to a dingy little office in the basement of the prison, the room warmed by powerful arc lights that shone down on the chair in which she sat. Sometimes her interrogators gave her cigarettes and spoke to her in normal tones; other times, seemingly without explanation, they brutalized her, demanding that she reveal the names of her associates, admit that she worked for the British intelligence services. They tied her to a chair, then ground lit cigarettes into the backs of her hands. Her fingernails were ripped out one by one with pliers. They poured gasoline on her hands and then ignited it; afterward they broke the blisters that formed on her skin. They kicked her, beat her with their fists, silently, coldly, with no more emotion than workmen digging a ditch.

Ultimately the Nazis of Cherche-Midi found Kate's point of weakness where the Nazis of Fort du Hâ had not: They tracked down her son, Len, who by this time had returned to France from North Africa, and they arrested him and placed him in Cherche-Midi prison as well. On February 3 they brought him to her cell, but only momentarily, long enough for her to see that he was now a prisoner. That was when Kate Bonnefous told her jailers at last that she would talk, but not until her son had been released from the prison. The next day he was brought to her cell before his release, and the two were permitted to speak to each other for five minutes.

By this time the Gestapo had already broken up the escape line that Kate Bonnefous had established out of her apartment in Paris; the life span of French escape lines, particularly those launched in the early, "artisanal" period, was usually measured in months rather than years.

They were all now in Cherche-Midi prison: Etta Shiber had been arrested first, on the afternoon of November 26, and then rearrested on December 22. Elie Teyssier had been arrested with Kate on November 30 and taken to Fort du Hâ before being sent to Cherche-Midi. Abbé Edouard Régniez had been arrested on December 24, Christmas Eve, after he finished saying mass in the church of Conchy-sur-Canche; Abbé Julien Berteloot was arrested two weeks later, as he was conducting a funeral in the village cemetery of Lattre-Saint-Quentin. Gustave Rackelboom, who ran the center for demilitarized soldiers, was arrested just a few hours after Etta Shiber on November 26, in front of the Gare Saint-Lazare train station as he was returning home from work. His colleague Jeanne Monier was arrested at almost the same time, in her office in the Hôtel de Ville.

In later years, Monier would reveal that the informant who broke up the escape line—the *mouchard* [snitch], as she called him—was a young Alsatian named Alfred Noëppel. He had come to the Office of Hygiene, Work, and Social Welfare on November 23, claiming to be a refugee from German oppression in Lorraine, and she provided him a transport pass as she had for so many others. On November 25, he appeared again, this time bringing with him two young Frenchmen, demobilized former soldiers, who told Monier that they hoped to cross the line of demarcation into the Unoccupied Zone and eventually to continue fighting against the Germans. It was, she attested after the war, "a very plausible motive," and she provided the additional transport passes. Presumably Monier sent the men on to Gustave Rackelboom at his reception center for demobilized soldiers, and he must have passed them on in turn, because later that day Alfred Noëppel and the other two arrived at Kate and Etta's apartment. Kate instantly took a disliking to him. "He didn't make a good impression on me," she was to say. "He held himself badly and seemed to have been drinking." Still, despite her reservations she began making preparations for the three to travel to Marseille; she was herself leaving for Marseille that very evening.

The following day, November 26, Jeanne Monier encountered Alfred Noëppel in her office once more—this time accompanied by plainclothes agents of the Geheime Feldpolizei, the secret police force of the German army. Her colleague in the Préfecture, Henri Grimal, was arrested in the same sweep.[*]

For his services to the Gestapo, Alfred Noëppel reportedly received a payment of 10,000 francs—about $4,000 in today's currency.

On January 7, 1941, Maynard Barnes, First Secretary of the American embassy in France at Vichy, once again wrote to Count Henri Thun, secretary of the German embassy in Paris, requesting information on the arrest and detention of Mrs. Etta Kahn Shiber. He added, "As it has, so far, been impossible for a member of my staff to obtain permission to visit her in order that legal counsel for her defense may be provided, if wanted, it is requested that this permission be procured."

Eight days later, he received this response:

In reply to the American Embassy's letters of December 6, 1940, and January 7, 1941, the German Embassy has the honor to in-

---

[*] The two young Frenchmen brought in by Alfred Noëppel appear to have been sincere: They were also arrested and held in Cherche-Midi until March 1941.

form the American Embassy that the American citizen Etta Kahn Shiber is involved in the case against Rackelboom and others for conveying prisoners of war over the line of demarcation which is now awaiting hearing by the Paris Military Tribunal.

Since the release of Mrs. Kahn Shiber after several weeks of preventive custody, the recent arrest of the principal offender has led to renewed examination and detention. It is, in particular, certain that Mrs. Kahn Shiber was a party to the conveyance of former prisoners of war over the line of demarcation. In view of the fact that the inquiry has not yet been completed, and in particular that the examination of the principal offender has yet to take place, permission to speak to Mrs. Kahn Shiber cannot as yet be given.

This response, while courteous and embellished with the customary diplomatic flourishes, raises as many questions as it answers. It does not, for instance, state who "the principal offender" is; presumably this refers to Kate Bonnefous, although Gustave Rackelboom is the only person mentioned by name, and by January 15, when the letter was sent, both of them had been in custody for more than a month—hardly a "recent arrest." The anodyne phrase "the examination of the principal offender has yet to take place" is also misleading at best, given the fact that Kate Bonnefous had been interrogated under extreme duress ever since her arrest; it seems to indicate, rather, that her interrogators had not yet received the information they were seeking.

Still, a few things are clear: Etta Shiber would continue to be denied contact with the outside world, including consultation with an attorney. She was now considered not merely a witness to the alleged crimes, but a participant in them. And for the first time there is mention of a trial, to take place before a military tribunal rather than in a civilian court. Other than Etta, the defendants were all French, and the trial was to be conducted in a French courtroom, on French soil—but the laws that would be applied, and those who would apply them, were German.

19

A GUARD ARRIVED AT ETTA's cell at eight o'clock on the morn-ing of March 7, 1941, ordering her to accompany him for trial. She still had on the navy-blue dress that she had been wearing at the time of her second arrest and that she had worn every day for nearly three months. Taking a moment to put on her fur coat, she walked with the guard through the long, dark prison corridors until they came to a cell near the top of a staircase; there the guard stopped, slid open the peephole to check inside, and unlocked the door. A mo-ment later Kate emerged.

She stood as straight and tall as ever, but her overcoat now draped more loosely on her slender frame; her face was even paler and thin-ner than before, the hollows of her cheeks more pronounced, cres-cent moons of worry and exhaustion waxing beneath her eyes. What was strikingly different was her hands: Whereas once they had been a creamy white, with slender, graceful fingers, now they were red and mottled, and they were pockmarked with grotesque-looking dark circles, deep and livid and jagged around the edges, like bomb craters on a battlefield.

For a moment Etta just gazed wordlessly at her friend, too stunned to speak, her heart thumping in her chest. In a low voice Kate said hello, and immediately the guard roared at them that no conversation was allowed between prisoners, and so they turned and walked silently together down the stairs and then out the front door, where they were met by other guards, who waited beside the green-painted transport van that would take them to court.

Four days earlier, Etta had finally been granted permission to meet with Jehan Burguburu, the attorney provided for her by the American embassy. The two spoke in a small office on the ground floor of Cherche-Midi, with a German civilian also present to monitor everything that was said; as Burguburu did not speak English, the conversation was conducted in French.

Jehan Burguburu—the family name is of Basque origin—had emigrated from Strasbourg with his wife and children during the mass evacuation of Alsace in 1939; he and his secretary, who was Jewish, went to work for the prestigious Paris law firm of Pierre Gide. According to Gide's biographer Michel Guénaire, Burguburu "displayed an impressive activity in the office," advising and representing "people from all milieus and backgrounds." Most important to the firm, however, was his work with German military tribunals.

In 1940 the German military authorities in occupied France established a system of military courts to handle the prosecution of crimes viewed as threatening to German security: attacks on German soldiers or property, espionage, aid to the enemy, and the like. These cases were overseen by a panel of three judges drawn from the German military, with another panel of six German soldiers who acted as a jury but, in point of fact, simply endorsed the judges' rulings. The procedures that were to be followed were those of German military law. As the tribunals were conducted entirely in German, it was necessary for the defense attorneys to be Germanophones; most of these attorneys were of Alsatian origin and had already been living in Paris or, like Burguburu, had taken refuge there after the war began.

Jehan Burguburu was thirty-five years old at the time he took on Etta Shiber's case; he stood five foot six and had a small, rather delicate frame (a childhood illness had left him with a weakened heart), and he wore horn-rimmed glasses and combed his black hair, gray-

ing slightly at the temples, straight back from his forehead. By every
account he was a man of high character, convivial in his private life,
sympathetic and loyal to friends and clients alike. Under other circumstances, Jehan Burguburu and Etta Shiber would have had much
that was pleasant to talk about: Burguburu was a great lover of music,
who himself played the piano; like Etta, he regularly attended the
symphony and the opera, often bringing along a copy of the musical
score, which he kept open on his lap so that he might follow along.

Now, however, Burguburu simply introduced himself, explaining
that he had been designated by Mr. Plitt of the American embassy to
represent her, and asking if she accepted him to serve as her defense
attorney. Once she agreed to this, he took out a pen and began to ask
her some preliminary questions. Neither he nor Etta ever indicated
the length of their meeting on March 3, but it could not have been
very long—Burguburu's notes for the session are contained on a single sheet from a stenographic pad, and they consist mainly of a few
basic details, written in French: her name, her age, married in 1909,
without children, husband dead in 1936, living in Paris since 1937.
Beyond that, he wrote only a few summary phrases, presumably derived from Etta's statements, in which he seems to be organizing a
line of defense: *Rien à faire directement—savait que cela marchait—
mais n'a rien fait par elle-même* [Nothing to do directly—knew that it
was going on—but did nothing by herself].

After the meeting had concluded he scribbled some notes on another page, this time in pencil, and in German, as he was now addressing himself rather than recording what Etta has said to him:
"Full transparency," he wrote—"she did not try to exonerate herself—
she followed and accepted what Bonnefous said." Under the heading
"Law" he noted that the penalty that applied to one would also apply
to the other, but that he wanted to find out where the real culpability
lay; then he noted simply, "To determine the facts I will have to continue to work."

At number 14 rue Saint-Dominique, the Hôtel de Brienne was an
eighteenth-century mansion that had housed the French Ministry
of War since 1817. Before then it had been the home of Letizia

Bonaparte, the mother of Napoleon, and was known as the Palace of the Mother of the Emperor. In a richly wallpapered upstairs office, Prime Minister Georges Clemenceau had surveyed German losses at the end of the First World War; twenty-three years later, in a ground-floor office overlooking the back garden, Gen. Charles de Gaulle had surveyed German victories at the beginning of the Second. It was upstairs at 14 rue Saint-Dominique, in the office of the chief of the general staff of the French army, that on October 15, 1894, Capt. Alfred Dreyfus had been arrested for espionage, the maximum penalty for which was death. Dreyfus was taken from the Hôtel de Brienne to Cherche-Midi prison; Etta Shiber had reversed the journey that morning, yet she too was to be charged with crimes against the state, for which the maximum penalty was death.

The grand entrance hall of the Hôtel de Brienne was filled with people, a sense of anticipation in the air, as before a theatrical opening or fashion show; the prisoners were taken quickly across the polished black-and-white checkerboard floor to a majestic circular staircase, its stone steps flared at the bottom like a ball gown. At the top of the staircase was a large, high-ceilinged room that must once have been used as a ballroom. The tall draped windows looked out over a charming enclosed garden; on the walls, intricate tapestries depicted medieval scenes; incongruously, a grand piano still stood in a corner of the room. Nearby, a Nazi flag hung from a golden standard, black swastika in a white circle against a field of red—as one French defendant would describe it, "the swastika swimming in blood." Several high-backed chairs had been placed behind a long table; thick bundles of papers lay on the table, tied with cords, which Etta presumed were the documents for the case. Two smaller tables faced the larger one, with seats for the court clerk and the interpreter (who would translate the proceedings into French for the defendants) and for the state prosecutor and the various defense attorneys. The attorneys would not be allowed to examine witnesses, nor even speak to their clients during the trial; they would each, however, be allowed a brief summation at the end.[*]

* The court had assigned Kate Bonnefous an attorney by the name of Alexandre Strelnikoff. In April 1941 the anti-Semitic, collaborationist newspaper *Je suis partout* included Strelnikoff in a list of several dozen Parisian attorneys with suspi-

Under the watchful gaze of a pair of helmeted German soldiers, observers began filing into the room, taking seats along a side wall. The immaculate uniforms they wore, the finely tailored suits, seemed to mock the shabbiness of the defendants' clothing. The eight defendants—Kate Bonnefous, Etta Shiber, Elie Teyssier, Edouard Régniez, Julien Berteloot, Gustave Rackelboom, Jeanne Monier, and Henri Grimal—sat together on a long bench, watched by soldiers on both sides. Several of them Etta was seeing for the first time. They were priests, civil servants, an agricultural worker, a retired shop owner: something of a cross-section of contemporary France. Two hours earlier they had woken up in prison cells with straw mattresses and slop pails; now they were in the Palace of the Mother of the Emperor, in a room with priceless tapestries and a chandelier of crystal and gold.

Shortly before ten o'clock, the defense attorneys arrived and took their seats, dressed in the traditional black legal robes with stiff white collars and jabots. The German officer who would be prosecuting the case, a Captain Schulz, wore a full-dress uniform. At exactly ten the three judges entered and with great solemnity took their seats behind the table; instantly the room grew silent. Like his colleagues, the head judge, Maj. Hans Dotzel, was in ceremonial dress, his uniform bedecked with medals and elaborate insignia and braid. At the age of forty, Dotzel was a model Nazi officer: disciplined, loyal, ambitious, and zealous in his service to army and party. He had served with distinction in the First World War and been awarded the Iron Cross, first class, at the age of only eighteen; in 1925 he received a law degree and went into private practice; in 1933, the year that Hitler came to power, he joined the Nazi Party and the following year became a squad leader with the Sturmabteilung (SA), the party's paramilitary wing, more commonly known as the Brownshirts. In 1938, as an army lieutenant, he participated in the occupations of Austria and the Sudetenland. In March 1939, Dotzel signed the certificate that attested to his membership in the Aryan race, and by the

---

ciously Jewish-sounding names. Two weeks later the newspaper printed a correction: "We have received affirmations that Monsieurs Henri Matouk, Jean Hug and Alexandre Strelnikoff, attorneys at the Court of Appeal of Paris, are not Jews. We gladly congratulate them."

following June he had been appointed to a military tribunal; in September, having been promoted to major, he began serving as a head judge in tribunals throughout occupied France.

The judges were followed into the room by the members of the jury, also in dress uniform; after a great show of heel-clicking and Heil Hitler salutes they also took their seats. With that Major Dotzel began to address the court, the interpreter relaying his words to the defendants. This was an official proceeding of the Court of the Commander of Greater Paris, he declared, on behalf of the German people; ordering the defendants to rise and face the tribunal, he administered an oath in which they all swore to tell the truth. Then, one by one, the defendants were asked to step forward to provide their personal details to the court. Of the eight defendants, Etta was the fifth to be called. She identified herself as Etta Shiber, an American widow, born in 1878, sixty-three years of age, no profession.

According to Jehan Burguburu's notes of the proceedings, Etta also described herself as being *"sans religion"*—without a religion. She further stated that she had *"un grand-père juif"*—one Jewish grandfather. This was not the truth, but it was highly advantageous, because it allowed her to fall outside the Nazi definition of a Jew, as had been promulgated in the Nuremberg Race Laws of 1935: anyone with three or more Jewish grandparents, regardless of one's own religious or cultural practice.

After the identification stage had been completed, each of the defendants stood once more, to hear the reading of the acts of accusation and, in turn, to respond to the charges and answer the questions put to them by the judges. The first defendant called to testify was Gustave Rackelboom. He was in charge of a center for demobilized French soldiers, he explained; in that capacity, Madame Bonnefous had come to his office on rue Guillaume Tell and "offered to pass men into the free zone." He had confined his activities, he said, to sending the men to Madame Bonnefous; he thought that he had sent perhaps fifteen in all. He had not received any money for his work—he had done it strictly out of a sense of *dévouement* [devotion].

Both Henri Grimal and Jeanne Monier testified only briefly; the judges seemed less interested in their role in the operation. Grimal, for his part, said that his goal was simply to help people leave Paris; he had given out free travel vouchers only for the Occupied Zone and had not known that these individuals were planning to cross the line of demarcation. Monier testified that she too had only issued travel vouchers; she admitted that she had suspected that some of these men were escaped prisoners of war, but she also did not know that they were intending to cross into the Unoccupied Zone.

Now Kate Bonnefous was called; a guard touched her elbow, and she rose and stepped toward the long table where the judges sat. Hers would be the longest and most extensive examination of any of the eight defendants. The confession that she presented under questioning was carefully measured, taking the bulk of the responsibility onto herself; unlike the testimony given by the previous three defendants, she did not attempt to downplay her activities, nor to deny full knowledge of what she had been doing. She explained that she had first encountered English prisoners through her work with the Foyer du Soldat. In her estimation, she had helped to pass fifteen to twenty English soldiers across the line of demarcation,* and about the same number of French soldiers; on certain occasions the Englishmen had stayed with her for two or three weeks before heading to Marseille. She had received some money from the American embassy, by way of Colonel Shaw, some 10,000 francs in all. (By this point Cecil Shaw had been arrested by the Gestapo and charged with a wide range of criminal activities; he would spend the remainder of the war in German prison camps.) The American embassy knew that she was handling evading and escaped soldiers; she mentioned one official by name—Edwin A. Plitt, the embassy consul, who had arranged for Jehan Burguburu to represent Etta and advised her to move to the Hôtel Bristol—but only in passing, to note that he would have forbidden her to return to Paris from Marseille if he had been aware that she planned to do so.

As for Madame Shiber, Kate said, *"Elle a tout fait avec moi"* ["She did everything with me"]. In every situation Madame Shiber had followed her instructions, had not taken any initiative, had simply rendered *aide et assistance* to her friend. It was apparent that Kate was

---

* A list of twenty British servicemen known to have been aided by Kate Bonnefous is provided at the end of the book.

taking responsibility not only for her own actions, but for Etta's as well; in the words of the age-old expression, she had chosen to fall on her sword. Her own activities might be judged as meriting a sentence of death, she seemed to be telling the tribunal, but Madame Shiber's did not.

"I listened to Kitty," Etta would say later, "with mingled admiration and pity."

Major Dotzel himself seemed deeply impressed with Kate, noting the candor of her admissions of guilt, her spirit of sacrifice, and the personal responsibility she took for her conduct. "Madame," he said at the conclusion of her testimony, "if I had a hat, I would tip it in salute to such courage and indifference to fate."

Etta was called next, and she also spoke only briefly, mostly to reiterate what Kate had said: Of that moment, she was to recall: "The judge began: Did you do thus and so? 'Yes, but I simply accompanied my friend.' I reiterated the fact that I had protested and had pleaded with her to cease our activities." Her activity, she maintained, had consisted entirely of aid and assistance. She did not know the route that was taken by the men to cross the line of demarcation, and she had never crossed the line herself. *"Si j'avais été seule,"* she said, *"je n'aurais rien fait":* "If I had been alone, I would have done nothing."

The testimony of the remaining three defendants was confined almost exclusively to a bare recitation of their activities: Elie Teyssier affirmed that he had charged 50 francs per person to cross the line of demarcation; he didn't know the exact number of soldiers that he had brought across, but there had been *"beaucoup de personnes."* Edouard Régniez testified that he had come to Madame Bonnefous's apartment on three occasions: once bringing two Englishmen with him, and twice bringing four. Julien Berteloot claimed even less than that for himself, stating that he had seen only a single Englishman ever sent to Madame Bonnefous.

The prosecutor's statement was delivered in German, without translation, as it was intended solely for the judges. At one point Etta understood the prosecutor to be saying that Frau Shiber had provided funds for the operation of the network—seemingly a reference to the $1,500 for which she had wired her bank in September, while they were sheltering Colin Hunter and Gordon Hood-Cree. When

Captain Schulz had finished his summary of the case, he took a sheet of paper from the table and read aloud the sentences that the state would be demanding from the tribunal: For Jeanne Monier, two years in prison; for Gustave Rackelboom and Henri Grimal, four years at hard labor; for Elie Teyssier, eight years at hard labor; for Edouard Régniez, Kate Bonnefous, and Etta Shiber, a sentence of death.*

The defense attorneys were each allotted fifteen minutes to speak on behalf of their clients. Jehan Burguburu, for his part, forcefully pleaded Etta's case, seeking to have his line of argument dovetail with Kate's: Frau Kahn-Shiber (as he called her) was not trying to escape her responsibilities, he argued, but at the same time it was evident that she had been acting under the influence of Frau Bonnefous; it was Frau Bonnefous, not Frau Kahn-Shiber, who had established the network, who had organized the escapes, who had made contact with the other defendants. Etta found that she could barely follow what he was saying, however, less for the language difficulties than for the prosecutor's sentencing request that still echoed in her ears. As she was later to recall: "It wasn't so much that I was frightened at the moment, or even surprised, for I had been more or less prepared; it was just that this thought monopolized my attention to the exclusion of everything else. I told myself that I would prefer death to years in such a prison as that which I had left. After all, I was no longer young. I had nothing to look forward to except death in prison, or perhaps being freed after my sentence, broken in health, and able to do nothing except await the release of death.

"But I had to adjust myself to this idea, which had suddenly become more real than ever before."

The trial had begun at ten o'clock; by one o'clock in the afternoon it was over, other than the deliberations and the reading of the verdicts.

* Unaccountably, the prosecutor asked for acquittal for Abbé Berteloot due to lack of evidence, and the court did not find him guilty of any crime. Still, after the war Berteloot was declared an *interné résistant* [resistant internee] for the months that he had spent in Cherche-Midi and Fresnes prisons, and Great Britain would award him the King's Medal for Courage in the Cause of Freedom, attesting that he had sheltered between thirty and forty prisoners.

At that time the court was dismissed for a lunch break while the judges deliberated.

The defendants were ordered to remain sitting on the bench; their attorneys arranged for them to receive sandwiches and glasses of wine, the first decent food or drink that any of them had been given in months. The tribunal had been carried on that morning with an almost operatic level of splendor and ceremony, but there was no missing the specter of death that hovered over the proceedings. Watching Major Dotzel and Captain Schulz perform their roles, Etta had been struck by how alike they seemed, this pair of officers from the same occupying army, too alike, she felt certain, to disagree. One had demanded the death sentence; the other would surely pronounce it.*

At two o'clock the judges returned to the courtroom. The room grew hushed as Major Dotzel rose from his seat and read from the sheet of paper he held before him.

The accused Rackelboom, he announced, had been found guilty of aiding the unauthorized crossing of the line of demarcation, and was sentenced to four years of penal servitude; for the accused Grimal, found guilty of aiding the unauthorized crossing of the line of demarcation, four years of penal servitude; for the accused Monier, found guilty of aiding the unauthorized crossing of the line of demarcation, two years of prison.

For the accused Bonnefous, found guilty of continued aid to the enemy—death.

The grim word seemed to linger in the air, tolling like a funeral bell: *Tode*. Kate Bonnefous's attorney would later note that she received the terrible news with "a calm and silent demeanor." Etta stood shocked, not believing that she had understood correctly, but at the same time knowing that she had. Her own judgment was to be pronounced next; thus far, as she had anticipated, the judges had given the prosecutor precisely the sentences he requested.

Dotzel proceeded: The accused Kahn-Shiber had been found

---

* By that point Nazi repression in the Occupied Zone of France was intensifying rapidly. In that month alone—March 1941—German military tribunals handed down sixty-two death sentences, and twenty-two executions were carried out by firing squads.

guilty of continued aid to the enemy and was sentenced to three years of penal servitude.

Hearing the pronouncement, Etta felt almost overcome with horror; she couldn't imagine spending three more years in the hell of a German prison. "I broke down completely," she would later tell a reporter.

Just one more sentence would diverge from the request made by the prosecutor: Elie Teyssier was found guilty of the unauthorized crossing of the line of demarcation, as well as aiding the unauthorized crossing of the line of demarcation, but he was sentenced to five years of penal servitude rather than eight. Like Kate Bonnefous, Abbé Edouard Régniez was found guilty of continued aid to the enemy, and he too received a sentence of death.

As a coda to the prison sentences, Major Dotzel announced that the assets belonging to the defendants Bonnefous and Kahn-Shiber were to be confiscated.

For a moment the room was completely still, as in the immediate aftermath of an explosion. Then the judges stood up and the tribunal was called to a close. The spectators began filing out of the room. Outside, a police van waited to take the prisoners back to Cherche-Midi. Silently a guard wrapped a chain around the wrists of Kate Bonnefous, the first woman in Paris to be condemned to death by the Nazis.

20

THE TRIBUNAL'S DECISION WAS affirmed by the military commander in France, Gen. Otto von Stülpnagel, who decreed that the sentences would be carried out as ordered. He did, however, defer the two death sentences until the appeals for clemency had been decided.

To that end, four days after the tribunal's decision had been handed down, attorneys for Kate Bonnefous submitted an urgent Recours en Grâce [Appeal for Pardon], asking for the sentence of death against her to be commuted to one of imprisonment. The appeal was directed to General von Stülpnagel, but it was understood that a matter such as this one would ultimately reach the desk of the führer himself.

The attorneys based their appeal on four arguments:

1. The condemned woman was past the age of fifty-five[*] and in poor health.
2. Madame Bonnefous did not personally benefit in any way from her participation in these activities—quite the opposite. Her actions were motivated by "a spirit of passionate sacrifice"; it had been well

[*] In fact Bonnefous was fifty-four. She would turn fifty-five on August 5 of that year.

established that "her life was entirely devoted to humanitarian works and to the relief of the suffering of others."

3. There was a too-great disproportionality between this condemnation to death and "the three years of imprisonment for the lady Schyber [*sic*], although the two women were inseparable." The disproportionality was all the more glaring, as the prosecutor had called for the death penalty against both women.

4. On a more practical note, the attorneys asked the military commander to consider whether the execution of Madame Bonnefous might not create "a halo of artificial glory" for her—in other words, whether her death by firing squad might not have the unfortunate effect of providing a heroic martyr for the French Resistance. "The generosity of the act of pardon," the attorneys asserted, "would not simply save the life of a weak and lost human being but would also be an act of opposition to any false mythologizing of the accused."

As they awaited a reply from General von Stülpnagel, Bonnefous's attorneys frantically reached out to others who might be able to intercede with Adolf Hitler, making representations on her behalf to the consulates of Sweden, Portugal, and Switzerland; to Otto Abetz, Germany's ambassador to Vichy; and to Emmanuel Cardinal Suhard, who had recently been appointed archbishop of Paris and was an important ally of Marshal Pétain.

Separately, Cardinal Suhard was also contacted by Achille Cardinal Liénart of Lille, urging him to request a commutation of the death sentence for Abbé Edouard Régniez. Cardinal Suhard complied with the urgent request, appealing to Comte Fernand de Brinon, Vichy's representative to the German High Command in Paris. That same day, March 9, 1941, he sent a letter to Pope Pius XII in Rome. "Your Excellency," he wrote:

Perhaps Your Excellency is already informed of this; but in the event that he is unaware, I want to let him know that one of his priests, the abbé Regniez, curé of Conchy-sur-Canche, was tried two days ago in a court martial, and that a sentence of death was pronounced.

Today I alerted Monsieur de Brinon, General Delegate of the French Government, and asked him to intervene if possible.

What can be done? I do not know: this case comes under military justice during wartime.

For the moment, the best thing is to wait and pray.

On Tuesday morning, March 25, the commandant of Cherche-Midi prison called Kate Bonnefous to his office to tell her that the führer had rejected her appeal: She would be shot at dawn the following Saturday.

Hearing the news, the condemned prisoner replied that she would like to be allowed to see her attorney, so that she might give him letters to her family that would not be read by the guards.

The next day she was visited by her attorney, who informed her that a pardon had once again been requested on her behalf by an intermediary of the pope; they had no assurances, of course, but they remained hopeful.

Saturday morning came and went, though, and no guards arrived at her prison cell to bring her to the execution grounds. No explanation was given for the delay, nor any indication of when the sentence was to be carried out. Her future was now being decided by immensely powerful men in far-off places; she could never have imagined, sending that note to Lieutenant Hunter in the hospital at Doullens, that one day her name would be known to Hitler and the pope.

There had been another woman in France condemned before her. On August 16, 1940, in Boulogne in northwest France, Blanche Paugan was arrested for having cut telephone lines;* one month later, the German tribunal at Arras sentenced her to death, but the ruling inflamed the local population and the sentence was commuted to life imprisonment. The first Frenchman to be executed for an act of resistance, Etienne Achavanne, was shot in Rouen on July 4, 1940, for

---

* At the time of the occupation, relatively few French people outside Paris owned telephones, and private calls between the zones were sharply restricted; as a result, telephone lines were primarily used by the German military and by the local police and civil authorities.

cutting a telephone line. On September 7, a young Communist named Pierre Roche, who had cut the telephone line between Royan and La Rochelle, was shot by a German firing squad after Gen. Otto von Stülpnagel—the same man who would now issue the ruling on Kate's fate—decided that the sentence handed down by a French court (two years at hard labor) was too lenient. Three days later, von Stülpnagel decreed that "all damage of means of transmission is forbidden under pain of death."

Many of the telephone poles stood right along the roadside, and their vulnerability and isolation made them tempting targets. The lines themselves consisted of copper wires no more than ten millimeters in diameter, sheathed only in black rubber; in some places a line had not been stretched tight enough and it hung down like a child's jump rope, at the lowest point barely the height of an upraised hand. A farmer carrying shears or a scythe to his fields—or anyone in a car with a large kitchen knife—could cut it with not much effort and disappear again without ever being seen.

In her cell awaiting judgment, Kate Bonnefous allowed herself a private consolation: On certain solo trips between Paris and Doullens she had cut telephone lines, and the Nazis had never found out.

Alone in cell 119 of Cherche-Midi prison, Abbé Edouard Régniez recited the rosary, sang *"Je suis chrétien," "Nous voulons Dieu," "J'irai la voir un jour,"* the hymns as simple and comforting as the children's songs he had learned as a boy. *Neige, neige blanche / Tombe sur mes manches* . . . Despite the countless privations of prison, his morale remained high. He was often visited in his cell by the newly appointed prison chaplain, Franz Stock. The chaplain was tall and blond and too delicate in his bearing to be a major in the German army, with a handsome face, full of compassion and charity, that recalled those of angels carved into northern cathedrals; by nature romantic and artistic, a pacifist at heart, he had shown himself willing to pass covert messages from one prisoner to another, or from a prisoner to his family—a mortal infraction in the eyes of his superiors. Abbé Stock was deeply pained by much of the work his assignment required of him, especially the last rites for the condemned; in four years serving the German prisons of Paris, he accompanied more than one thousand prisoners to the execution ground on Mont-Valérien.* Abbé Régniez could take comfort in the idea that in his last moments, this German would be by his side, reciting the prayers for the dying: *Adjutorium nostrum in nomine Domini,* our rescue is in the name of the Lord.

Edouard Régniez was now thirty-one years old—exactly the age his father had been when he was killed in the Great War. It was a strange and terrible coincidence. He could not bear to imagine his dear mother having to go into mourning once again, as she had after the death of her husband in 1915. Still, his most immediate concern was the three refugees, two Jews and an Englishman, whom he had been hiding in a village near Conchy-sur-Canche. He had placed them with a farm family, but they couldn't stay there forever—what was to become of them, now that he was imprisoned and likely never to get out?

How he had hated this prison when he was first brought there, hated its dark hallways and iron bars, the walls that cut him off from the men whose voices he heard in the corridors. Over time, though, as he grew familiar with the life of the prison, he found that his small and austere cell became a kind of cloister, a kingdom of silence, in which every hour felt like his last one. In that foul cell he could smell again the damp stone of the church of his youth; sitting on his hard straw mattress he felt the rattan seat of the wooden chairs in which the congregation made their devotions as the sun filtered through the stained-glass windows of Jesus and the saints, tinting the stone floor with streaks of violet and orange and red, like the sky at day's end. Everything seemed beautiful, everything had value; he loved it all from afar, as he had loved certain women in his past, admiring their beauty, charmed by their wit and intelligence, but always from behind walls put up by unkind circumstance.

Near the end of March he received a visitor in his cell—a fellow prisoner, a French captain by the name of Albert Girardon, who had been falsely accused of having killed a German soldier waving a white flag. Condemned to death, he had been saved on appeal by

---

* Abbé Franz Stock died in 1948, at the age of forty-four; his death was said to have been caused by "physical and emotional exhaustion."

Maître Burguburu, and now he was being released, but first Captain Girardon insisted on seeing the priest in the cell that faced his. For months they had found ways to communicate, through silent gestures, covertly passed messages, occasional snatches of conversation; now he could not bear to leave without saying farewell.

Girardon recounted the moment in his diary:

> [I] call out "Régniez!" and step toward him. The prisoner lights up, extending a friendly hand. Laughing, the abbé explains that he is going to be shot. "What bothers me the most," he says, "is my poor mother, for whom I am the only son and who lost my father in the war of '14. But this morning, she answered the letter I sent her, and she told me that she cannot regret my death, as it was due to an act of perfect charity. So life is beautiful!" And in pronouncing these extraordinary words, he rubs his hands together, raises a leg; it looks like he's sketching out a joyful dance step.

Despite her constant worrying about Kitty's fate, Etta found that her own situation inside the prison had begun to improve. In Cherche-Midi, prisoners were not permitted to receive food from the outside until after their trials were completed, as the Nazi military administration preferred that they be interrogated while in a weakened state. Now that she had been convicted and sentenced, though, Josiah P. Marvel of the American Friends Service Committee was able to visit her weekly, bringing with him a food package supplied by the U.S. consulate—tins of tuna, potato salad, bread, sugar, and the like—for which she was deeply grateful and which she always shared with her cellmates.[*]

In Cherche-Midi, the guards left the women's corridor routinely at six o'clock, making only occasional rounds afterward, and that was when the political prisoners began chatting with one another,

---

[*] Etta did not know that her brother in Syracuse had agreed to pay for the food, for which the consulate charged him two dollars per week. According to a State Department memorandum on the matter, "He [Chester] said that he was in very modest financial circumstances but would like to do what he could to help his sister."

through the overhead transoms or the spaces under their cell doors. If the sound of heavy boots was heard approaching on the stairs, someone would whistle *"Au clair de la lune"* as a warning, and everyone quieted down; when the guards had left, the conversations started up once more. Every night at seven o'clock the prisoners all chanted three times in unison *"Notre France vivra"* ["Our France shall live"], and on weekends, when the guards further reduced their rounds, the women organized group singing, most often children's songs that they had all learned as girls—*"Cadet Rousselle," "Brave marin," "Jean-François de Nantes"*—which gave the women's wing, with its airless cells and narrow, sinister hallways, something of the atmosphere of a boarding school; years later, one of the political prisoners would recall, "This festive manner of resisting gave us all the feeling of belonging to a community, a solid family."

One of the prisoners, Elisabeth de La Bourdonnaye, was a countess who had been arrested for sheltering a fleeing Jewish attorney in her home. Inside Cherche-Midi, she managed to get news from the outside world by having her children slip messages into the hems of her clean laundry, and one day she passed word among the prisoners that General de Gaulle had called for a national hour of silence that afternoon beginning at three o'clock. Agnès Humbert (an art historian and founding member of the Musée de l'Homme resistance group) was the only prisoner on the women's wing who still had a wristwatch—somehow the Nazi guards had allowed her to keep it. She said that she would announce the time for everyone, and proposed that another of the prisoners, Sylvette Leleu, who had an especially beautiful voice, begin the hour by singing *"Le chant du départ,"* the beloved battle hymn written two centuries earlier in honor of the French Revolution. From the cell next door, Renée Guitton (known among the women as the "switchboard operator") shouted the instructions at the top of her lungs; Humbert would note in her diary, "In the communal cells, on the ground floor, on the third floor, there can't be a soul who hasn't heard."

At three o'clock, Agnès Humbert loudly rapped a spoon against her enamel washbasin three times, and Sylvette Leleu began to sing: *"La victoire, en chantant nous ouvre la barrière . . ."* The final words of the chorus, in which the singer declares that a Frenchman must live, and die, for the Republic, reverberated through the narrow corridors, dwindling into a silence that lasted unbroken for one hour.

At four o'clock Agnès Humbert rapped four times on the wash-basin, and the prisoners stood as one and sang together the final verse of *"La Marseillaise."* "I hadn't realized there were so many of us," Humbert wrote in her diary. "This 'Marseillaise' seems to swell, becoming a tangible, palpable presence. Soon it will expand too far upwards, too far sideways to be contained by the prison walls; soon, it seems, the walls will burst apart and the roof will fly off. I know that the feelings that choke me are shared by us all. What beauty! What power of shared emotion! The guards . . . try in vain to shut us up. But where to start, who to blame? The din is ubiquitous! Then the sounds of boots kicking doors, shouts and oaths. The singing dies away, and all is silence."

On April 22, nearly one month after Kate Bonnefous was informed that her appeal had been denied and that she would be shot, her attorney received a letter from a clerk in the office of the Tribunal of Greater Paris. The message read briefly:

> We inform you that in the case against Rackelboom and others, the Commander in Chief of the Military has decided on April 7, 1941, that the sentence of death pronounced against Mme Cath-erine [*sic*] Bonnefous and Pastor Edouard Régniez is suspended.

Instead, the two would be given a sentence of life imprisonment at hard labor. Exactly where the sentences were to be served was not indicated in the ruling; for the moment, the two prisoners remained in Cherche-Midi.

When Etta learned to her great joy that Kitty's death sentence had been commuted, she reached out to her attorney with a request. On May 9, 1941, Jehan Burguburu sent a letter to the commandant of the Tribunal of Greater Paris, in which he asked that his client, Etta Shiber, be permitted "to rejoin her friend Madame Bonnefous in the cell where she is still detained in the prison of Cherche-Midi." He pointed out, "This should be possible given that, according to my knowledge, the two detainees are not locked in solitary cells." Maître Burguburu further noted that he believed the prison administration would agree to the request if the tribunal chose not to contest it.

Five days later, he received a written reply from a Dr. Bredfelt in the office of the military tribunal. The reply read in its entirety: "In the criminal proceedings against Mrs. Etta Shiber, you are informed that your request of May 9, 1941 cannot be granted."

Jehan Burguburu, however, was not yet dissuaded, and on May 20 he made a phone call to the military tribunal to continue to press his client's request. Eventually he was put in touch with a chief inspector there; as they spoke, Burguburu made handwritten notes on his copy of the request, recording the contents of the conversation:

"The inspector informs me that my request is rejected. Madame Bonnefous is a swine [*ein schwein*] and will be transferred to Germany."

21

I N MAY 1941, ETTA SHIBER was transferred out of Cherche-Midi to Fresnes prison, seven miles south of Paris, a vast multi-building complex with stone walls and red tile roofs and an arched front gate like that of a convent. At Fresnes, each small cell was equipped with a chair and a table, both of them chained to the wall, and a single hinged bed with a thin mattress, the metal frame also attached to the wall with hooks and a pair of chains. Etta shared the cell with two other women, and as she was significantly older, they allowed her the use of the bed and they slept on sacks of straw on the floor. According to the terms of her sentencing, Etta should have spent her time in Fresnes in solitary confinement (there was no "hard labor" that a woman of her age might perform there), but the prison was so crowded that the administration could not allow any individual prisoner to have a cell by herself. Instead, she was restricted to her cell at all times, not permitted to go out with the other prisoners for their two hours spent daily in one of the prison's three small courtyards.

Remarkably, the food at Fresnes was even worse than that of Cherche-Midi. Served at six A.M., the "coffee" was an evil-looking yellowish concoction brewed from barley; breakfast at ten thirty was a half loaf of dark bread with a small knob of margarine and a suspiciously firm slice of something referred to as "pâté"; both lunch and dinner consisted of a nauseating soup, just a thin broth with a few cabbage leaves or chunks of carrot or turnip floating in it. On Sundays, noodles were added to the soup and prisoners additionally received an inch-square block of cheese, all too often riddled with worms. Fortunately for Etta, Josiah Marvel of the AFSC had traced her to Fresnes, and he saw to it that she continued to receive weekly parcels of food. "I am sure that I owe my life to that aid," Etta later said. "It was malnutrition, certainly, which was responsible for the high death rate at Fresnes." Almost daily she heard the bell tolling from the prison chapel, which indicated that another death had occurred. Those most unfortunate ones were buried in unmarked graves in the prison cemetery, their names recorded for posterity only in the medical register, along with the causes of death, a kind of inventory of human abuse and misery: *hanging, heart attack, tuberculosis, embolism, suicide, fracture at the base of the skull, cerebral hemorrhage . . .* "Very often," Etta wrote, "in moments of depression, I heard that sound and told myself that one day it would sound for me, that I would never leave Fresnes alive."

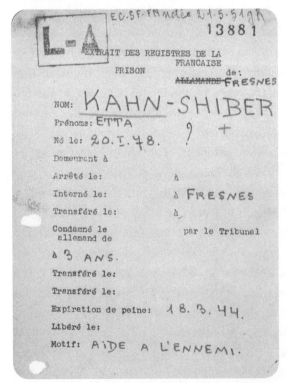

Etta Shiber's prisoner registration card from Fresnes prison

In May, Abbé Edouard Régniez was removed from his cell in Cherche-Midi and driven to the Gare de l'Est—known to the men of his and his father's generations as the *gare de la guerre*, the train station where soldiers on leave congregated before returning to the front to fight against Germany. Now he was traveling not as a soldier but as a prisoner, and not in a military convoy but aboard a regular passenger train, full of families, businessmen, tourists returning home after a lovely time in the City of Light. Unlike the others aboard the train, his final destination was a mystery to him, although he imagined it would be some sort of prison camp deep inside Germany, where he would serve out the remainder of the war, growing ever thinner, steadily weaker: It would be a race between the war's end and his own. Aboard the train, the soldiers who were escorting him removed his shackles so that he could eat, read a book, smoke a cigarette; perhaps it was simply deference to a man of God, but outside the walls of the prison, it seemed, sitting together on a train, the extreme hostility between captors and captive could ease slightly, evolve into some other sort of relation—not equals, to be sure, but a bit closer to fellow human beings.

In recent years he had come to see that he was really happiest, most at home with himself, when he was tinkering with machinery in a garage or workroom, or outside flying an airplane. He wasn't entirely comfortable anymore inside a church sanctuary; it felt confining now, a beautiful garment that no longer seemed to fit. For him, the best part of work as a curé was less the religious instruction than the sense of community it afforded him, the opportunity to form relationships of mutual service with his parishioners; the choice that he and certain of the parishioners had made, to resist the occupiers, was one that escaped the rules of logic, that existed outside any notion of self-interest. It had required a rupture with the ways of the past, a turn against the established order: throwing in his lot with the country rather than the state, with the church rather than the Church, following the dictates of his own conscience, wherever that path might lead. It had led him now to this beautiful countryside, the hills ablaze with spring flowers, remote villages tucked into valleys beneath them, houses gathered around the church as the ancients might once have gathered around a fire, seeking warmth and light against the cold night sky.

The train rolled steadily eastward, passing Reims, heading toward Verdun; so many of these names he recognized as battlefields from the previous war. It seemed they had been fighting forever, the French and the Germans. He had saved himself once before, as a prisoner of war eleven months earlier; he had discovered how an escape was like working the lock on a safe, waiting for just the right combination so that the tumblers fall and the door can open. He had done it once and believed he could do it again. Patiently he waited for the elements to line up for him: distracted guards, curved track, reduced speed, narrow gravel bed, embankment rolling down toward a field. It was May 7, 1941. He felt his mind empty out, like the sea before a tidal wave; he was running; he reached the railing of the train car and he leaped; he was in the air, all alone, and then the earth came rushing up to meet him.

In Fresnes, prisoners who had already been convicted and sentenced were permitted to receive one book per week from the outside; those prisoners could also write one letter per month, but the letter had to be brief and contain nothing specific about life inside the prison, or it would not pass the censor. At the end of August, Etta sent a letter to her defense attorney, Jehan Burguburu, who had visited her several times when she was in Cherche-Midi. It read in part:

> This letter is to let you know that I am well and as comfortable as one can be in prison. Time passes slowly, but still it does pass. On September 7 I shall have done six months of my sentence, although I have been in prison ten months! Not too gay. Here in Fresnes we are really very well treated. The personnel is French and everybody is very kind to me. I believe that they are all sorry for an old (?) lady. . . . I feel very lonely at times and, since the Embassy has left,[*] quite without friends, although I still feel that I may consider you as one. But I see nobody from the outside and I think I miss your friendly visits at Cherche-Midi. Well, some day we

---

* On June 10, 1941, the United States closed its embassy in Paris.

may meet again and in the meantime my thanks for past kind-
nesses and I hope this letter finds you and your family well. A
special embrace to that adorable little daughter.

As a postscript to the letter, Etta asked if Maître Burguburu might
be able to send some English-language books to the prison, as she had
none. Burguburu promptly replied, saying that he had no English-
language books but would try to obtain some for her by way of the
Quakers; despite the fact that he had not seen her in Fresnes—he
had still not received authorization to visit her there—he assured
Etta that she was not forgotten. "I rejoice in noting that your moral and
physical condition is rather good despite the circumstances," he wrote.

What Etta did not mention to her attorney was that in recent
months she had felt her health beginning to slip. Her blood pressure
had always been high, despite her lifelong attempts to control it, with
cardiac danger lurking in the background; now, though, after months
of bad food, insufficient sleep, enforced inactivity, and near-constant
tension and worry, she had noticed her heart beating in disconcert-
ingly irregular rhythms. Sometimes, unexpectedly, it skipped a beat,
as if to gather a bit of strength before proceeding; at other times, it
began to pound like a bass drum at the end of a symphony; and at
still other times it fluttered for a moment or two and then abruptly
lurched, as if trying to leap out of the cage of her chest. Irving had
died from a weak heart; so too had Bill; now she was sure she would
be betrayed by her heart as well. She felt herself caught in a down-
ward spiral: The worry and lack of sleep seemed to exacerbate the
erratic motions of her heart, which in turn caused her to stay awake
due to worry. Her heart felt like a ticking time bomb inside her. She
refused, however, to mention her condition to her jailers. In general,
her disposition was not to complain or call attention to herself in any
way, but more to the point, she had spent time in the Fresnes prison
hospital once before, when some particularly foul food had led to an
oral infection, and she found that the care she received there was no
better than the lack of attention she would have received in her cell;
she did not trust the German doctors with anything having to do
with her heart.

The cold that year seemed to arrive all at once, like a lock snapping shut. Cherche-Midi had been built with walls three feet thick, and the tiny windows that provided so little light did at least have the advantage of keeping in heat as well; Fresnes, though, was a modern prison, where the cells were hung from a multifloor steel grid, with large windows and cement floors that seemed to transmit the cold rather than prevent it. The prison had been designed with a central heating system, but this year no coal was available for the basement furnaces—even the warden's own office would be heated by a wood stove—and in the absence of heat Etta and her cellmates could do nothing but put on all the clothes they had and sit huddled in the cell, hands plunged deep inside their coat pockets. Etta's only consolation now was that she was not required to go outside every afternoon; her cellmates returned from the hours in the prison yard with blue lips and chattering teeth.

The Fresnes food regimen, designed to provide six hundred calories per day, was barely sufficient to keep a prisoner alive even during temperate weather; now the body had to burn extra calories to keep itself from freezing, and Etta and her cellmates were hungry almost all the time. Even under her fur coat and bulky layers of clothing she could tell that she was losing weight; the pounds that for years she had been desperate to lose she was now just as desperate to keep. One morning in the first week of November, the female prisoners were ordered to assemble in one of the prison courtyards, and to take all of their belongings with them. In the courtyard they were lined up in long columns four abreast and marched out of the prison gate toward a nearby train station. Etta could not help but think of what a sorry sight they made, several hundred tired, ill-clad women trudging through the streets carrying their belongings in bundles like hobos. At the station, the women were directed aboard a group of third-class carriages that had been attached to an ordinary passenger train. Coming aboard behind them, the guards warned the women not to try to escape—for if anyone did, they would be obliged to shoot her.

The train pulled out and began moving across the bleak November landscape, the hillsides a russet brown now, with only a few determined leaves still remaining on the trees. After nearly seven hours it finally stopped, at a town called Troyes, about one hundred miles southeast of Paris; there the women were ordered off the train, then lined up again and marched through the narrow, medieval-looking streets. Already famished and weakened by the privations of prison life, they were exhausted when at last they arrived at their destination—Hauts-Clos prison—and then they simply stood outside in the cold late-afternoon sun, staring up at the hulking structure in bewilderment and disbelief.

This building was clearly still under construction: Scaffolding covered whole sections of the exterior and heaps of bricks lay scattered about on the dirt. Located on the site of a former vineyard, Hauts-Clos was being built as a municipal hospital, but the war had halted progress midway. The Nazi administration in France initially used the unfinished structure as a prisoner-of-war camp, and then decided to adapt it into a prison for their steadily growing population of political prisoners. Eventually Hauts-Clos would be filled with more than three thousand inmates, but now, still nearly empty, it exuded the desolation of a construction site after hours.

Hauts-Clos prison at Troyes—with construction still unfinished—around the time of Etta Shiber's arrival there in November 1941

The women were ushered inside; their footsteps echoing in the quiet corridors, they climbed the narrow, winding staircase single file, gripping the walls for balance in lieu of a banister. The air inside the building was cold and damp, and through the bare windows the low sun made shadows on the rough cement floor. Etta could discern no heating system of any kind, nor any signs of plumbing other than a single unconnected pipe that jutted out from a brick wall. With four other women, she was pushed into a cell that had no furnishings at all, not even a bed—just five sacks of straw tossed into a corner. There was nothing to do but lay out one of the sacks on the floor, trying to make herself as comfortable as she could beneath her single thin blanket. In Fresnes prison, she had longed for the warmer air inside Cherche-Midi; now she longed for her bed in Fresnes. Despite her exhaustion she barely slept that night, her body aching from the cement that the straw seemed not to soften, chilled by the cold that seeped up from the floor.

Etta tried to assure herself that this lodging must be provisional—that even the Nazis could not expect anyone to survive in such conditions. But one day passed, and then another, and another, and it became clear that this bare, frigid cell was her new home. Even the window was useless, as it was covered with a layer of frost and so provided no view of the outside world, nothing that might distract in any way from the monotony of the gray walls and floor, the endless hours with nothing at all to do other than to lie under the covers trying to keep warm—and as the only available heat was that manufactured by the prisoners' own bodies, Etta and her cellmates pushed the straw sacks together on the floor, so that all five could lie side by side on three of the sacks, huddled together for warmth, while covering themselves with the remaining two sacks as well as the five thin blankets and whatever spare clothing they had beyond the layers they already had on, and wrapping shawls and towels and stockings around their necks and feet and hands. The women considered the heat they generated to be common property, which no one had the right to waste, and if one of them managed to dislodge a blanket or sack while changing position, thus letting in some of the cold air, she received an immediate scolding from the others. When a guard arrived with a meal, one of the women was chosen to get it, and she hastily sprang out from beneath the pile and brought it back for the others; then together they enjoyed the least luxurious form of a meal in bed that any of them could possibly imagine.

"Under these conditions," Etta was to write of that terrible winter in Hauts-Clos, "it can hardly be said that we lived individual lives. We were all units in one life, and that no very eventful one, like the microscopic animals which live in colonies, the smaller individuals constituting one larger one."

In December something unusual happened: One morning, rather than pause at the cell door to pour out tin cups of ersatz coffee before moving on to the next cell, the female guard actually came into the cell and filled the cups there; then, as Etta recalled, she said, "Which one of you is the American?"

Etta replied that she was.

The guard paused for a moment, as though considering whether to say more; then she said: "I've got news for you. America is in the war."

All of the women started with surprise—Etta too, though in reflecting on it later she realized that her reaction must have been more complicated than that of the others. For them, the entry of the United States into the war meant only one thing: the certain defeat of Germany. All of them knew the American entry into World War I had signaled the beginning of the end for Germany, and they were sure it would be that way once again. For Etta, though, the news meant something else as well: that she would no longer be protected by America's neutral status. Now she was an enemy combatant, just as the French and the English were, and none of her countrymen would be left to help her; that terrible aloneness she had dreaded was now a fact.

Perhaps it was the deepening sensation of vulnerability, perhaps it was just the endless hunger and cold, but that winter Etta once again began to experience, as she had in Cherche-Midi, long periods in which she lost track of what was going on around her. Her heart had begun to beat irregularly again; she could feel the occasional ripples that moved across her chest like shallow currents warning of a stronger, more dangerous undertow. Surely her blood pressure was too high again. At times she wondered about reporting herself sick, but she hardly imagined that the medical treatment she would receive in this unfinished facility would be any better than that of Fresnes. What she really needed, she knew, was a warm room, decent food, the means of keeping herself clean—the opportunity to relax her body. For her, having just turned sixty-four, the many privations of Hauts-Clos had led, among other things, to a growing apathy, which in turn meant that she was never able to come to a clear decision about whether to inform the prison authorities of her condition. Making things worse, the food parcels from the American Friends Service Committee had stopped arriving. Thus far she had survived thanks only to the benevolence of the Quakers and the reserve of strength that she had built up over years of comfortable living. That reserve was now gone, leaving her feeling broken down and useless, someone who had managed to outlive her own life.

So it seemed less surprising than inevitable, one day in February, when the general sensation of discomfort that she had been carrying in her chest burst without warning, like a worn-out fabric that abruptly tears apart. She felt as if a massive weight was pressed on top of her, pushing her down into the cement, while a powerful fist was gripping her heart and squeezing tight; her muscles went rigid and her nerves were frayed electrical wires and she struggled to breathe as if under water, until that fortunate moment when she lost consciousness and everything around her disappeared.

22

E TTA HAD THREE ATTACKS in all, over a span of twenty-four hours, losing consciousness each time; each time the prison doctor was summoned, and each time he checked her condition and decided not to send her to the prison hospital because, he explained, he could not guarantee that she would receive attention there, while in the cell she would at least have her fellow prisoners to watch over her and keep track of her condition. Finally the pain in her chest subsided and she felt her strength slowly returning, although she knew the attacks might recur at any time, just as suddenly and unexpectedly as before.

After some weeks the weather began to turn; March was warm enough for Etta and her cellmates to abandon their common bed. The large window in their cell lost its coating of frost and they could see the distant fields turning green, could smell the rich aroma of freshly turned soil. The official order that Etta not be allowed to go outside with the other prisoners seemed to have gotten lost somewhere between Fresnes and Hauts-Clos, because when the first exercise period was announced, she lined up with the others and no one said anything about it.

Outside, the promenade area was just a small yard behind the building that had been fenced off with barbed wire; even so, Etta couldn't remember the last time she had been able to walk in the sunshine, feeling the breeze warm on her face, with just a slight, refreshing trace of winter's chill. She walked as briskly as she was able, her legs unsteady at first beneath her, heart pounding from the exertion; little by little she felt that persistent sense of lethargy beginning to ease, the apathy that had overtaken her cracking like a frozen pond at the first thaw. Even in prison, it seemed, spring brought a sense of rebirth. Still, Etta knew that another two years remained on her sentence—two more frigid winters—and she didn't see how she could possibly survive them, especially given the damage that had already been done to her heart. One day Etta asked a guard to take her to the warden's office, where she filled out a form requesting a term of clemency, on the basis of poor health.

In September 1938, a senior U.S. Foreign Service officer named Nathaniel P. Davis wrote a memorandum urging the creation of an agency to oversee the relief and repatriation of Americans living overseas in the event of a major war. One year later the Roosevelt administration issued Departmental Order 810, establishing a new agency inside the Department of State very much along the lines that Davis had proposed. The Special Division, as it was called, was charged with identifying American civilians in Europe and the Far East who would be in danger in the event that the United States joined the war. Before long, President Roosevelt had expanded the agency's mandate to identify German, Italian, and Japanese citizens living in the United States and Latin America. In the event of war, he believed, at least some of those citizens would serve the Axis powers as agents of propaganda and espionage in the Western Hemisphere; if they were rounded up and interned inside the United States, on the other hand, they could be used as hostages to be exchanged for American prisoners of war. With the assistance of FBI director J. Edgar Hoover, who stationed agents (under the more opaque title of "legal attachés") at U.S. embassies throughout the region, Roosevelt undertook a campaign to persuade Latin American governments to intern and deport Axis nationals living within their borders, once the United States had declared war; by October 1941, the State Department had reached confidential agreements with nearly all the nations of Latin America.

On December 8, within hours of the Japanese attack on Pearl Harbor, a vast, continent-wide machine of secret internment and deportation was set into motion. In Peru, for instance, 702 Germans, 49 Italians, and 1,799 Japanese were arrested; subsequently they were placed aboard American troop ships to be transferred to the United States, at which point the Peruvian government froze their bank accounts and seized their homes and businesses. (Indeed, for Latin American governments the inducement was primarily economic in nature: They would assist in deporting Axis nationals to the United States, and in return would be rewarded with the assets of those who had been deported.) Ultimately, fifteen Latin American countries handed over some six thousand civilians; only three—Argentina, Brazil, and Mexico—refused to do so. In the United States, the deportees were classified as "dangerous enemy aliens" and housed in internment camps in Texas, Oklahoma, Louisiana, Florida, and Tennessee to await possible exchange for American prisoners. Among the German internees, some were indeed Nazi Party members, and a few were spies; others, though, were descendants of German immigrants who spoke only Spanish, or children of mixed marriages who knew nothing of Germany, or, most disturbingly, German Jewish victims of Nazi persecution who were desperate not to be returned to the very country from which they had fled.

Almost immediately upon American entry into the war, back-channel negotiations were begun between the Allied and Axis powers, conducted via neutral intermediaries, which culminated in a series of agreements to oversee the repatriation of medical personnel, chaplains, diplomats, and civilian internees, under rules derived from the Geneva Convention of 1929. The organization of these so-called mercy missions was a colossal undertaking: Thirty of these voyages would take place over the course of the war, involving the exchange of several thousand prisoners on each side. According to *Lifeline Across the Sea,* a history of the mercy missions, "The numbers of persons for exchange were intended to be equal, i.e. on a head-for-head basis, although that was not always the case."

In the course of the negotiations, discussion arose about the possibility of a head-for-head exchange of two civilian women—one
German, the other American—each of whom had been imprisoned
on charges of conspiracy. On January 14, 1942, the Swiss legation in
Washington, D.C., (which was representing the interests of the German government in the United States), contacted the State Department to request that a thirty-year-old woman named Johanna
Hofmann be placed on the list of German nationals to be exchanged
for American prisoners. Hofmann, a hairdresser and manicurist on
the ocean liner *Europa,* had been arrested by FBI agents in 1938 for
her part in a massive German conspiracy to violate American espionage laws, by serving as a courier of stolen military intelligence. Convicted and sentenced to four years' imprisonment in the Federal
Industrial Institution at Alderson, West Virginia, Hofmann was released on parole in December 1941 and taken to Ellis Island in New
York to be interned there as an enemy alien.

Two days after receiving the Swiss legation's request, Joseph C.
Green, a career Foreign Service officer now with the Special Division, sent a memorandum to Breckinridge Long, a former ambassador to Italy who had been appointed the division's first chief. "There
is a somewhat parallel case of an American, Mrs. Etta Kahn Shiber,"
Green pointed out in his memo. "Mrs. Shiber was arrested by the
German military authorities in December 1940 and in March 1941
was sentenced to three years penal servitude and confiscation of her
property for continued activity and aid in favor of the enemy." He
suggested to Long that the United States government might consent
to the inclusion of Johanna Hofmann in an exchange of nationals, if
the German government would agree to release Mrs. Shiber and
permit her to leave occupied France for the United States.

Green sent a copy of the memo to a State Department official
named Sidney K. Lafoon, who replied on January 27. "This Government," he wrote, "is disposed to permit Miss Hofmann to return to
Germany at such time as the mutual exchange of German and
American nationals takes place, provided the German government is
agreeable to the release of Mrs. Etta Kahn Shiber." However, he indicated, a final determination had not yet been made on the matter,

and the State Department would communicate further with the Swiss legation once a decision had been reached.

On February 4, Breckinridge Long moved the question further along bureaucratic channels, with a memo to United States attorney Francis Biddle requesting that the Department of Justice "furnish the Department of State with an indication of the reply which it should make to the inquiry of the Swiss Legation."

There the matter remained for many weeks. Finally, on April 20, 1942, Joseph Green sent another memo to Breckinridge Long, noting in frustration that the department's files "do not contain any record of a memorandum of conversation or other document regarding Justice's consent to Miss Hofmann's departure." He pointed out that on March 17, the Swiss legation had sent a letter to the Special Division indicating that Mrs. Shiber would be permitted to leave France upon confirmation that Miss Hofmann was to be released from the United States; this was the very proposal that had been suggested by the State Department, but the Special Division had not yet replied to the Swiss legation. "In view of the fact that the Department has definitely committed itself to the release of Miss Hofmann on the condition that Mrs. Shiber would be released by the German authorities," Green added tartly, "it would seem highly inadvisable at this time for this Government to withdraw its consent or to refuse to permit her to leave this country."

Still no official response was forthcoming from the United States government. On April 30—three and a half months since the Swiss legation asked that Hofmann's name be placed on the exchange list—an internal State Department memorandum reported, "The German Government through the Swiss Legation is pressing for a decision in regard to the release of Miss Johanna Hofmann and her return to Germany with the diplomatic group."

By that point, time had grown very short. The first stage of a long-planned, carefully negotiated prisoner exchange—a round-trip ocean voyage transporting Axis nationals east across the Atlantic and then Allied nationals back west—would commence in only one week: On May 7, a Swedish ocean liner called the *Drottningholm* was scheduled to sail from New York, bound for Lisbon. The ship would be carrying nearly one thousand passengers; it was not yet clear whether Johanna Hofmann would be among them.

In the first week of May, almost miraculously, Etta's request for clemency was accepted out of the blue by prison authorities. She would be given six months' leave from the prison, the warden informed her, so that she might regain her health; the only condition was that she report in person each week to the local German military authority, the Kommandantur, to have her release certificate stamped and to report any change of address. With that, the gates of Hauts-Clos swung open for her.

In Troyes she boarded a train for Paris; there she found lodging with a friend of hers, Marguerite Boë, in a charming Art Deco building on avenue de Ségur in the seventh arrondissement. In Mademoiselle Boë's apartment, Etta was shocked to see the woman who gazed back at her in the mirror. New lines had appeared in her face, which was as gray and stained as an old teacup, and her hair, which she had always kept neatly permed, was long and unkempt and almost entirely white; she looked like a photographic negative of her earlier self. Her navy-blue wool dress was wrinkled and shapeless and hung on her frame like a shroud. But it was thrilling to be able to close the bathroom door and fill the tub with steaming-hot water, and then bathe for as long as she wished, all alone, and come out actually clean, while knowing that a soft bed awaited her when she was done.

On May 11, during her visit to the Kommandantur, the military desk officer informed Etta that in accordance with an agreement between Germany and the United States, she was to be sent home as part of a prisoner exchange; the train to Lisbon would arrive in a matter of days. "It is almost too good to be true, and of course I am very happy," she wrote to Jehan Burguburu.* "I thought that this piece of good news would interest you, and so I took the liberty of writing. I am sorry that I shall not have time to see you before I leave Paris, but, as you know, one has a great many things to do, and a very

---

* "I am writing these lines in English," she noted parenthetically, "because I am too excited to write in either French or German."

short time in which to do them. My very best thoughts to you always and warm greetings."

Jehan Burguburu replied the very next day. "Dear Madame," he wrote, "I thank you most strongly for your communication of yesterday, and I am very happy to learn of your impending repatriation.

"All my wishes for health and well-being accompany you, dear Madame, and I express the wish to see you soon once more in Paris, in a peaceful Europe."

Paris had changed shockingly since Etta saw it last. Even in the spring sunshine the city felt dark and gloomy, its buildings coated with the residue of coal smoke. Walls everywhere were plastered with notices from the MBF, the German military command in France, listing names of "terrorists" who had been arrested or executed. The streets were almost entirely empty of vehicles other than German staff cars or supply trucks, or an occasional bus or private automobile with a bulky *gazogène* unit strapped to its roof or trunk, a tank that burned charcoal or wood chips rather than gasoline. The Nazis had ordered that metal statues be removed from public squares and melted down for the German war industry; thousands of figures of French philosophers and statesmen and physicians and mathematicians, along with a menagerie of fantastic creatures and an assembly of demigods, had been dismantled and shipped off to scrap yards, with only their stone pedestals left behind like decapitated tree stumps. To walk through Paris these days was like walking through a Roman ruin, a landscape haunted by glories of the past.

Anti-Semitism had long been an undercurrent in French society, a low, disquieting hum that rose and fell but never entirely died out; now, though, it had been joined with political power, and the animus that had been at least partially constrained by social convention could be unleashed. Attacks on Jews and Jewish property had become almost commonplace; in October 1941, seven synagogues were bombed in a single night. The Institut d'Étude des Questions Juives [Institute for the Study of Jewish Questions] put on a major exhibition at the Palais Berlitz called *Le Juif et la France*, purporting to reveal the malign influence that Jews exerted on all aspects of French life; posters promoting the exhibition, displayed on billboards and in Métro stations throughout Paris, depicted a horrific caricature of a bearded, hook-nosed Jew, dressed in a prayer shawl, grasping a globe in his taloned fingers. An anti-Semitic newspaper called *Au Pilori* ran a contest offering a prize for the best proposal for "what should be done with the Jews." In one of the published responses, a reader suggested that they be dumped in the jungle, to be set upon by wild animals; another imagined that, amid a leather shortage, the skin of Jews could be used to make shoes and handbags. Another reader asserted that the only proper destination was the crematorium—"and for all of them, from the oldest to the newborn." As the historian David Drake has noted, this was eighteen months before the Nazis devised their own "Final Solution of the Jewish Problem" at the Wannsee Conference outside Berlin.

Most ominously, the first mass roundups of Jews began in May 1941, when French gendarmes arrested 3,710 Jews of foreign birth and sent them to internment camps outside Orléans. In August, the eleventh arrondissement was cordoned off and 4,230 Jewish men, both native and foreign-born, were arrested and sent to Drancy, a half-finished apartment complex in the suburbs of Paris that had been converted into an internment camp; in December, nearly one thousand more Jews were arrested, including physicians, attorneys, writers, academics, scientists, and other leading figures—those whose careers had so dramatically illustrated the tolerance and openness of French society.

On May 29, 1942, the German military commander in France signed a new decree, to be enforced starting the following week. Hastily the Vichy government submitted an order for five thousand meters of yellow cloth from a Paris company called Barbet-Massin, Popelin & Cie, which offered a special rate of 21 francs per meter. Another company began working around the clock to fashion the cloth into insignia according to the specifications of the decree ("having the dimensions of the palm of a hand," read one of them, "and outlined in black"), while still another organized the plans for distribution. Within days some four hundred thousand pieces had been produced—that was considered enough for a start—and a price had been decided upon: Each recipient would be charged one month's worth of clothing rations.

On June 7, the Eighth Ordinance was put into effect in occupied France: "Jews over the age of six are prohibited from appearing in public without wearing the yellow star."

A slim, elegant triple-screw steamship, the *Drottningholm* was one of the "floating palaces" beloved by transatlantic travelers of the early decades of the twentieth century; its interior had been designed by Swedish artisans and featured a glass-enclosed veranda, a dining room with a skylight and wood-burning fireplace, a library, a music room, and a smoking room of carved oak and polished birch that created "an atmosphere," one passenger recalled, "of a mellow country inn." Originally built for a Scottish passenger line, the ship was launched from a Glasgow yard in 1904 as the *Virginian*. In one of her earlier voyages, crossing the North Atlantic in 1912, the *Virginian* had delivered iceberg warnings to the RMS *Titanic;* during the First World War she had been used as a transport ship and had once been torpedoed and beached off the Irish coast. After the war, the ship was refurbished and, rechristened the *Drottningholm,* converted into an ocean liner on the Swedish American Line, sailing between New York and Scandinavia. In March 1942, the *Drottningholm* was chartered by the U.S. State Department, via the Swedish and Swiss consulates, to conduct repatriation voyages; specially illuminated and painted a stark white with the legend DIPLOMAT—DROTTNINGHOLM—SVERIGE in large black letters along the hull, she sailed as a protected cartel ship under the auspices of the International Red Cross.

The *Drottningholm*'s first repatriation voyage, which set out on May 7, 1942, had transported 948 Axis deportees from New York to Lisbon. "As usual," remarked a State Department official who accompanied the voyage, "the Germans were super-organized." By the end of the first day they had established nightly sing-alongs and lectures on Nazi ideology and had appointed a ship's group leader and several section leaders, as well as fire marshals for every gangway on the ship; they also laid claim to the typewriters of the C Deck writing room, where the group leader typed out instructions for every German passenger on various matters, closing each one with the salutation *Heil Hitler.*

Now, on the return voyage, the *Drottningholm* was carrying 908 passengers, the majority American-born but comprising thirty-three nationalities and speaking sixteen languages among them. In the words of an Associated Press story, the ship was "a floating cross-section of melting-pot America," including diplomats, government workers, businesspeople, aid workers, clergymen, teachers, students, and foreign correspondents for American newspapers and wire services, many with their families. Only one passenger aboard the ship, however, had been tried and convicted and sentenced by a German military tribunal, and that was Etta Shiber.

The ten-day crossing took place amid an atmosphere of barely restrained jubilation, of laughter and music and hungry people gorging themselves on milk, butter, sausages, fruit, and other luxuries denied them for so long. Ninety-one of the passengers were Polish Americans who had been held in a German internment camp at Laufen, near the Austrian border; in the evenings the Laufen internees, having gone through the regular dinner menu followed by the entire à la carte service, sang "wild Polish songs" on the forward hatch. A two-year-old American girl named Margaret, the daughter of an employee of the American embassy in Berlin, mortified her parents by marching up and down the deck giving the Hitler salute to everyone she passed. "She had a German nurse and she saw everybody heiling in Berlin, so she formed that habit," her mother explained to a reporter, adding, "I hope she'll get over it soon now."

All through the journey the white-uniformed Swedish crew maintained steadfast good humor while giving advice on seasickness to passengers unused to such rich foods (especially when combined with the roll of the ocean); and busily preventing the fifty-two children aboard the ship from climbing onto the captain's bridge or hiding in lifeboats or pushing deck chairs overboard; and arranging and rearranging table seating; and organizing meals for the several dogs and the two turtles that had been brought aboard, as well as one child's pair of pet crickets, which had quickly made themselves known to the occupants of the next-door cabin. When they weren't at meals the passengers read magazines, or played bridge, or clustered around the radiogram in the ship's library to get the latest news from home, or just sat in the sun on the top deck gazing out at the endless sea. In the evenings, some danced to phonograph records in the music room, while several of the better-dressed passengers gathered in the ship's bar to drink and smoke and sing uproariously. One of them, Teddy Getty (wife of the industrialist J. Paul Getty), was a former nightclub singer, and she regaled her fellow passengers with a ditty she had composed to the tune of "Home on the Range":

Oh, please take me home on the old Drottningholm,
Where the unemployed diplomats play,
Where seldom is heard an intelligent word,
And the bar remains open all day.

Etta, for her part, did not feel especially festive, and she spent much of the crossing by herself, sitting in the ship's promenade lounge. The tunes that played in her head were more apt to be *"La chanson de Solveig,"* or *"La petite Tonkinoise,"* or one of the other songs the political women would sing in Cherche-Midi, or the *"Ave Maria"* that had reverberated through the silent prison on Christmas Eve 1940. She thought of Genevieve, Mary Bird, Mrs. Symes, of all those poor women—some barely more than girls—caught in the enormous vortex that was steadily engulfing Europe. Somehow, almost miraculously, she had been allowed to escape, for reasons that weren't entirely clear to her. While she was waiting to board the *Drottningholm* in Lisbon, John C. Wiley, the United States ambassador to Portugal, had come over and introduced himself; he was surprised to discover that she had been kept in complete ignorance of her own case.

The ambassador explained that Etta had been exchanged for a young woman named Johanna Hofmann, who had been part of a major German spy ring that the FBI had broken up in 1938. The name, he said, was probably familiar to her—it had been in all the papers a few years before.

Etta had indeed heard of Johanna Hofmann. On holiday in Nice in 1939, she and Kitty had seen an Edward G. Robinson picture called *Confessions of a Nazi Spy;* she recalled that one of the featured roles, a young hairdresser on a German ocean liner, was based on the real-life Johanna Hofmann.* Later, thinking back on the conversation with Ambassador Wiley, Etta felt somewhat embarrassed; it hardly seemed like a fair trade. She wasn't some international spy, after all, transmitting top-secret military intelligence—she couldn't imagine that any movie would ever be made about her wartime activities. As she stated in her testimony to the military tribunal, if she had been alone, she would have done nothing; it was only because of Kitty that she had been able, say, to divert the attention of a German hospital guard, or to remain silent while being interrogated by a Gestapo agent, or even just to keep her body from shaking, with two Nazi officers sitting in the back seat and an escaped British prisoner in the luggage compartment of their car. "Whatever merit there was in what we did belongs to her," Etta would later maintain. "I only followed where she led." All of it, from her arrival in Paris in 1937 to her departure in 1942, had been due to Kitty. It was Kitty's friendship that had allowed her to regain some sense of normalcy when she was at her lowest ebb; later, it was Kitty's quiet, firm command of a situation that had calmed her nerves and emboldened her to act, Kitty's own example that had inspired her to do things she hadn't imagined she could do—Kitty who had maintained a confidence in her that Etta herself had never been able to muster.

During the voyage, Etta sometimes went up on deck, where she leaned against the railing and watched the water disappear into the distance. Every moment aboard ship brought her nearer to safety, if not exactly to home. After five years, she was returning to America with only a few pieces of clothing—most of those donated by Marguerite and some of her friends. Her nephew John would be at the pier in Jersey City to meet her and put her on a train for Syracuse.

---

* *Confessions of a Nazi Spy* is considered to be the first anti-Nazi movie ever made by a major American studio. Several of the actors portraying Germans in the film were refugees from Hitler and performed under false names for fear of reprisals against relatives who were still living in Germany. The Brooklyn-born actress who played the Johanna Hofmann role, Dorothy Tree (née Triebitz), was the daughter of Jewish immigrants from Austria. In 1952 she was denounced as a Communist by a Hollywood screenwriter called to testify before the House Un-American Activities Committee and was subsequently blacklisted; she never acted again.

She figured that she would stay for a while with Chet and Helen and their family, let them fuss over her, bring her back to health; eventually, though, she knew she would return to New York, the city of her birth and, other than Paris, the only place she had ever really known. Even now, still weak and exhausted and overwhelmed by all she had been through, she recognized that there was much to look forward to in the years remaining to her: going to the theater and the movies, listening to symphony programs or the opera on the radio, eating whatever she wanted, drinking glasses of wine. From now on any comfort, however modest, would be a kind of luxury. She had no desire greater than to forget all that had happened to her, nor one more impossible. Kitty's face—with its sad, dark, half-lidded eyes—returned again and again to her memory, like a motif in music, pulling her back to the central theme.

From the railing of the great mercy ship, Etta could see for miles in any direction, all the way to the horizon. She felt herself moving in an immensity of water, an expanse measureless and vast. The water around the ship was a brilliant blue; receding into the distance it slowly, almost imperceptibly, changed to gray.

PART TWO

A Matter of Record

And whoever saves one life, is considered as one who has
saved the entire world.

—JERUSALEM TALMUD, Sanhedrin 4:1

23

On September 20, 1943, the prestigious New York publishing house Charles Scribner's Sons published a memoir entitled *Paris-Underground*. The author of the book was said to be Etta Shiber "in collaboration with Anne and Paul Dupre," but in fact there was no Anne and Paul Dupre; these were the noms de plume of a married couple by the name of Betty and Paul Winkler, French émigrés who had moved to New York at the beginning of the Second World War. In Paris, Paul Winkler had owned a successful newspaper wire service called Opera Mundi, and after settling in New York, he founded a literary agency, the Press Alliance, which translated and distributed news articles from around the world and produced books that were written by employees of the agency and published under the Dupre name. The copyright for *Paris-Underground* was held not by Etta Shiber, but by an entity called Press Alliance, Inc.

Narrated by Etta Shiber, *Paris-Underground* tells the dramatic and moving story of how she and her close friend Kitty, aided by a young French priest, establish an escape line that manages to transport scores of British servicemen out of occupied France; the women rescue some of the servicemen themselves, smuggling them past German checkpoints in the luggage compartment of their car. After only a few months, though, the line is discovered, and the two women are arrested by the Gestapo and imprisoned. Convicted by a German military tribunal, Etta is sentenced to three years' imprisonment and Kitty to death, a sentence that is later commuted to life imprisonment. The book concludes where it begins, with Etta returning to New York on the mercy ship *Drottningholm,* having been exchanged for the German spy Johanna Hofmann, while Kitty's ultimate fate remains unclear. The final pages contain a ringing call to Americans to support the war effort, on behalf of those courageous members of the French Resistance whose struggles had been chronicled in the book, as well as the millions of others whose lives had been changed— or ended—by Nazi aggression.

Published in the midst of World War II, when many of the characters were still living in occupied Europe, *Paris-Underground* gave pseudonyms to all of the book's central characters, other than Etta Shiber herself. An author's note at the front of the book stated:

> The basic facts of this book are a matter of record. Most of the names of the persons whose activities are described in this book have been changed, for obvious reasons. A few details, not already matters of record known to the Gestapo, have been recast, a few omitted, and the roles of various persons interchanged, in order to make it impossible for any use to be made of this book by the German authorities against anyone described in it.

At Charles Scribner's Sons, the publication of *Paris-Underground* was overseen by the legendary editor Maxwell Perkins, then the firm's editorial director and vice president, whose authors included literary titans such as F. Scott Fitzgerald, Ernest Hemingway, and Thomas Wolfe, and who was himself one of the most revered figures in the history of American publishing. With a first printing of 298,000 copies, *Paris-Underground* was the lead title of Scribner's fall 1943 catalog, and the house allocated $10,000 to an advertising campaign in support of the book—a sum large enough to merit mention in the industry's trade publication, *Publishers Weekly.*

The reviews for *Paris-Underground* were rapturous. On the front page of *The New York Times Book Review,* the British author Hilary St. George Saunders called the book "poignant," "remarkable," and "moving and wonderful," while noting that it had "all the ingredients of the most exciting thriller." In the daily edition of *The New York Times,* the reviewer Orville Prescott echoed Saunders in observing, "No spy story could be half as exciting as this modest, unassuming, factual narrative of harrowing risks and ingenious ruses that fooled the Gestapo time and time again, and the ultimate failure with capture, imprisonment and a mockery of a trial."

The Saturday Review of Literature called *Paris-Underground* "a strange and inordinately thrilling story. . . . It is authentic, probably the best picture we have yet had of France under the occupation. And it is a book which should make every American feel proud." "So exciting and brave that it is painful," said *Newsweek;* "as patriotic and stirring a book as anyone would want to read," said *The Boston Globe;* "a remarkable story," said *The New Yorker;* "bitterly convincing," said the *New York Herald Tribune.*

No less an intellectual luminary than Diana Trilling, in a *Harper's Magazine* essay entitled "What Has Happened to Our Novels?," after bemoaning the lack of excitement, adventure, and drama in present-day fiction, remarked that these admirable qualities "are present in full measure in the books of our war correspondents and in the personal reminiscences of people whose lives have been intimately touched by modern history." As evidence of this, she noted that *Paris-Underground* "holds our interest with an intensity that few modern novels can equal."

On October 10, 1943, *Paris-Underground* appeared for the first time on the *New York Times* bestseller list, twelfth in the "General" (meaning nonfiction) category. By the following week it was up to number six; the next week it was number four; and by the first week of November it was the third-bestselling nonfiction book in America. *Paris-Underground* would remain on the *Times* list for eighteen weeks, until February 13, 1944. By that time the book had gone into eight printings and had sold nearly half a million copies.

In 1943 the Charles Scribner's Sons publishing house had seven bestsellers, with combined sales of over two million. Six of the books were novels; the other was *Paris-Underground.*

For a period of time, *Paris-Underground* was virtually inescapable anywhere in America. The book was adapted into an illustrated format, along the lines of action comic strips like *Steve Canyon* and *Terry and the Pirates,* and serialized by the King Features Syndicate, running daily in newspapers around the country for five weeks. *Paris-Underground* was named a Book-of-the-Month Club main selection for October 1943; a condensed excerpt of the book appeared in *Reader's Digest,* which had a circulation of over seven million. That month Leonard Lyons's syndicated showbiz column, "The Lyons Den," brought word that an unnamed Hollywood studio had offered $100,000 for the film rights to *Paris-Underground*—more than $1.7 million in today's currency, and as much as had ever been paid for a work of nonfiction; a deal had not yet been struck, though, as Etta Shiber's agent was reportedly asking twice that price.

On Tuesday evening, October 12, 1943, a radio play adapted from the book was presented on the NBC radio show *Words at War,* a weekly anthology that featured dramatizations of the most significant books to emerge from World War II; the scripts were adapted for radio by some of the country's leading playwrights, with top-flight directors and prominent radio actors in the leading roles, accompanied by a full symphonic orchestra. The *Paris-Underground* episode concluded with a brief appearance by Etta Shiber herself, in which she related to the listening audience how an American government official had once compared her to Edith Cavell, and then stated firmly:

"Well, he was wrong there. I am certainly no Edith Cavell. But my friend Kitty is. I only followed where she led, and she is paying very dearly for all she did." As dramatic orchestral music began to swell in the background, she continued, "I do not know whether or not the Germans have put her to death, but I shall go on hoping that the God of justice will continue to remain at her side, and whenever my heart begins to ache with loneliness for her, I have her last words to sustain me, the words we spoke before they separated us." Here Joan Alexander, the actress who portrayed Kate Bonnefous, recited the drama's final lines:

> Don't worry about me. I am not sad. I did what I had to do. I knew the price and I was willing to pay it. I have given England one hundred fifty lives for the one she is losing now. Think of that

when you think of me. And when the war is over, go to England, and walk along the embankment of the Thames in the spring, where I always used to walk. I will be with you. See if you can find some of the boys we sent to England. Tell them as I once helped them, now they must help me. They must carry on the work I can no longer do, by continuing to be what they have always been—enemies to tyranny, unwavering defenders of freedom.

And with that, the music crescendoed, and the announcer returned to the microphone to narrate the closing credits.

As someone who was constitutionally shy, diffident, and anxious, Etta Shiber enjoyed nothing less than public speaking. Upon her return from France she had turned down all interview requests, including an invitation to appear on the *We, the People* radio show, a CBS network program with an audience of millions, which featured "average" Americans telling about extraordinary experiences in their lives. After the publication of *Paris-Underground,* however, feeling a deep responsibility to promote the book and to publicize the heroism of the characters depicted in it, particularly Kitty (to whom the book was dedicated), Etta managed to set her nervousness aside to appear on numerous radio shows. Among these was NBC's *The Author Meets the Critics,* in which she conversed with book critic Harry Hansen, Random House editor in chief Bennett Cerf, and *The New Yorker*'s European correspondent, Janet Flanner. "Her appearance, her composure, her matter-of-fact attitude toward the dangers through which she passed explain better than anything else why she was able to accomplish such remarkable feats," Hansen would recall of the episode. "I asked her whether she was afraid when the Nazi Gestapo interviewed her, and she said, 'Of course I was afraid.' But she is too calm and self-possessed to give herself away." Cerf was sufficiently taken with Etta's performance that he invited her to appear on his own radio program, *Books Are Bullets,* in which he interviewed authors who had written outstanding books on the war. Perhaps most impressively, she was one of three featured speakers for the prestigious Book and Author Luncheon, sponsored by the American Booksellers Association, at which she addressed an audience of more than fourteen hundred in the Grand Ballroom of the Hotel Astor;

according to a news report, she "urged that lend-lease arms be smuggled to the French underground."

In subsequent weeks Etta was also at the Plaza Hotel, speaking to the Coordinating Council of French Relief Societies; at the New York Times Hall, alongside the author Pearl S. Buck for a panel discussion titled "The French People"; and at the Bellevue-Stratford Hotel in Philadelphia, participating in the Philadelphia Booksellers' Association's Famous Authors Luncheon, at which the featured authors also included Betty Smith, promoting her newly published novel *A Tree Grows in Brooklyn,* and at which the audience once again numbered more than a thousand. Etta was the guest of honor at the fundraising breakfast for the Hunter College Alumnae; she could hardly imagine how she, the shy girl at the edge of the 1901 class photo, was now addressing an audience of more than five hundred alumnae, helping them to meet their goal of selling $110,000 in war bonds.

Etta Shiber being greeted at the Philadelphia
Booksellers' Association's Famous Authors
Luncheon, held at the Bellevue-Stratford
Hotel on January 17, 1944

On all of the radio shows, as in all of the feature stories written about her, Etta's unprepossessing appearance was much remarked upon, observers inevitably drawing on the trope of the improbable heroine—one reminiscent of an older, decidedly unglamorous female relation. "I never saw a plainer, more maternal looking woman,"

Harry Hansen declared in his newspaper column. Bennett Cerf remarked wonderingly, "I expected to see a young girl, and I find Mrs. Shiber looking more like somebody's aunt." "Etta Shiber is a motherly woman in her sixties," began Orville Prescott's review in *The New York Times*. An Associated Press wire story noted that "Mrs. Shiber is the perfect housewife, middle-aged, quiet, with the face and figure of the typical American mother." The wire story sent out by the Central Press referred to her more bluntly as "a chubby little old lady." The success of *Paris-Underground* earned Etta Shiber an entry in the 1943 volume of *Current Biography,* in which she is described as "a soft-spoken, modest, grandmotherly woman."

The *Current Biography* entry additionally characterized Etta as "a heroine of the Second World War" while noting, "Her story, told simply and honestly, needs no fictional embellishments to become exciting and dramatic." Along with Etta's age and appearance, the truthfulness of her story was a mainstay of public commentary about *Paris-Underground,* the critics marveling at how the book had achieved a novelistic quality without needing to resort to fictionalization. "It is a thriller," pronounced *The Saturday Review of Literature,* "better than any spy fiction because it is true."

No one has ever been able to determine exactly how many men Kate Bonnefous and Etta Shiber rescued. An examination of the historical record, including escaper reports compiled by British military intelligence during the war, suggests a total of perhaps twenty British soldiers, plus an equal number of French escapees. Trial notes made by Jehan Burguburu indicate that Kate Bonnefous acknowledged having aided "*15–20 anglais*" and "*15–20 français.*" Her estimate is consistent with the admissions made by the other defendants: Gustave Rackelboom claimed that he had sent fifteen Frenchmen to Bonnefous's apartment, and Edouard Régniez that he had delivered ten Englishmen. These figures themselves comport with the workings of an escape line that ran through a single apartment and was in existence for only three months (Colin Hunter was rescued on August 28, and Kate Bonnefous was arrested on November 30) and fully operational for only two; deliveries of soldiers were made irregularly over a period of eight weeks, no more than twice weekly, each time with the arrival of between two and four men.

Yet *Paris-Underground* includes a scene in which Kate and Etta's housemaid, Margot, prepares a special luncheon to celebrate the safe delivery of the line's *150th* British soldier. Kate herself refers to that figure in her heroic farewell speech to Etta, when she observes that she has "given England 150 lives" in exchange for her own. The figure 150 was cited again and again in advertisements, reviews, and feature stories, although it was occasionally embellished—at least once by Etta Shiber herself, in a profile of her in *Family Circle* magazine, when she was asked how many soldiers she and Kitty had passed on to safety, and she "almost bashfully" replied, "More than 150."

Even that figure, however, proved subject to inflation. The *Book-of-the-Month Club News* article announcing the selection of *Paris-Underground* reported that Mrs. Etta Shiber had smuggled "nearly 200 British soldiers out of occupied France under the very noses of the Germans."* The estimate of "nearly 200" was repeated in a feature story in *The Christian Science Monitor,* and was in turn rounded up to an even two hundred in stories in the *New York Post, The Pittsburgh Press,* and the *Washington Star.* In one syndicated column distributed nationwide, the claim was made that Etta Shiber had helped transport "over 250 British soldiers through the lines to safety."

Was the number of servicemen saved, then, one hundred fifty? Two hundred? Two hundred fifty or more? No one seemed to know for certain—including the author herself—nor did anyone appear to notice that the number being bandied about was not only highly elastic, but implausible on its face. Exactly where all these British soldiers were coming from, or by what means they arrived at Kate and Etta's apartment in Paris—or how these two women, over a span of just a few weeks, managed to safely shelter so many English-speaking men of service age, and feed them during a time of severe rationing, and arrange to have that many photographs taken and false identification cards prepared, and pay transportation costs for all of them (not to mention for an untold number of additional

---

* That article was written by Paul Winkler, Etta Shiber's agent and himself one of the book's pseudonymous co-authors.

French escapees)—is nowhere ever considered, much less scrutinized.

Clearly, somewhere in the process of writing, editing, and publicizing *Paris-Underground,* a decision was made that the rescue of twenty British servicemen and an equal number of French resisters was somehow *not enough*—not enough, at least, to gain the attention of the book-buying public. (No fewer than fifty-seven personal war narratives were published in 1943 alone, by authors such as John Hersey, Ernie Pyle, and Eddie Rickenbacker; every major publishing house included at least one such memoir on its list.) The fundamental appeal of *Paris-Underground* lay in the seeming incongruity between the nature of the two protagonists—mild, comfortable women of a certain age—and the daring and courage of the acts they performed. "Two women less likely to get involved in the murderous melodrama that will make our times an object of pity and horror to future ages would be hard to find," *The New York Times* observed, neatly stating the central dichotomy. "Yet the chances are that no two women have played a more gallant and dangerous part in the Second World War." As the consequence of the acts was exaggerated, the incongruity was heightened—and so too, it must have been felt, would be the popular appeal.

Nor did the imprecision of this foundational detail seem to cast any doubt on the veracity of other details presented in the book. Even the reviewers who wondered about the possibility of authorial embellishment almost immediately backed away from the suggestion, adverting to the time-honored notion that truth is stranger than fiction, especially in a time of war. In *The New York Times,* Hilary St. George Saunders observed of *Paris-Underground* that "no author of fiction would dare to foist upon a sophisticated public such a tale of chance, coincidence, improvisations, and simple ruses. These belong to life itself, as it is lived in occupied Europe today, in the tortured lands where the Gestapo once thought it held all the cards." "The tone of some of the incidents recorded may, in the author's recollection, have become heightened," *The Sunday Times* of London acknowledged, "but it is probable that her narrative represents what really happened. The book has the quality of a first-rate 'thriller.' If, in parts, it is melodramatic, so, almost certainly, must life in occupied

France too often be." (The reviewer added courteously, "We have, and there is no reason to doubt, her word for it that the story is substantially true.") Similarly, the *Chicago Tribune* declared that *Paris-Underground* "has the unfinished quality of an episode from life. The simple, strong way in which it is written adds to the impression of sober truth. Even when a French peasant gives Mrs. Shiber a somewhat grandiloquent message for the people of America from the people of France, the reader only gulps a little and does not accuse the author of having made this up."*

The near-universal confidence in the authenticity of *Paris-Underground* must have stemmed, at least in part, from the conviction with which the book's promoters asserted it. Print advertisements trumpeted *Paris-Underground* as "the most amazing true story to come out of the War." One of the judges who selected *Paris-Underground* for the Book-of-the-Month Club, the author and educational reformer Dorothy Canfield Fisher, wrote in her introduction to the *Reader's Digest* excerpt: "This absorbing record of the experiences of two women vs. the Gestapo, and of the moving heroism of millions of little people in France, is not only literally, factually true, it sounds true. The author just sets down what happened, with a singularly honest absence of any effort to dramatize the facts or to make herself out a heroine. But she is a heroine—of hair-raising adventures. No American should miss this astonishing story of bravery, daring, and self-sacrifice. No American can forget it."

The lengthy condensation of *Paris-Underground* that ran in *Reader's Digest* begins with the most famous scene in the book. Kitty and Etta have fled Paris by car in advance of the Nazi occupation. That evening they stop at an inn near Orléans to get some food for their dogs; there they meet an innkeeper, in a state of distress, who reveals that he has someone in the back room who speaks only English and

---

* Only the anonymous reviewer at *Time* magazine suggested the possibility of fictionalization without immediately backtracking: "Names and places have been changed and shuffled to confuse the Gestapo. Mrs. Shiber valiantly insists that otherwise it all happened that way. But some readers may suspect that 'Paris-Underground' has been somewhat influenced by Alfred Hitchcock."

must be made to leave. With that, he brings out a tall young man wearing an RAF uniform. It turns out that he is an English pilot named William Gray, who was unable to evacuate with the other servicemen at Dunkirk; he is now on the run, and with the Germans bearing down fast on Orléans he will surely be captured before long. Something about his appearance reminds Etta of Irving—the text indicates nothing more specific than "the same nose, the same chin"—and in a burst of empathy she persuades Kitty that they should hide William in the luggage compartment of their car and smuggle him back to Paris.

The rest of the action flows directly from that crucible of a moment at Orléans: The two women shelter William Gray in their apartment as they try to figure out how to get him out of the Occupied Zone. Before long they receive a surprise visit from a pair of Gestapo agents, part of a sweep of the neighborhood in search of British servicemen. Kitty waylays the Gestapo in the sitting room while Etta tries to conceal William Gray in her bedroom. As her eyes frantically search the room for a hiding place, her attention comes to rest on a photo of Irving on her dresser. In a moment of inspiration, she instructs William to take off his clothes, get into bed, and pretend he is very ill; having tied a towel around William's head to partially conceal him, Etta successfully passes him off to the Gestapo officials as her ailing brother Irving,[*] using Irving's old American passport and identification card to deceive the Germans.

Eventually Etta and Kate manage to procure a fake travel pass for William Gray through an acquaintance of theirs who is working with an underground group; once again hiding the Englishman in their luggage compartment, they bring him to a small town along the demarcation line, where they deliver him to members of the group for transport into the Unoccupied Zone. Sometime later, they are overjoyed to receive a postcard message from William that indicates he will soon be back in England.

An especially exacting reader, having finished these scenes, might wonder why Etta bemoans the difficulty of feeding William Gray without having an extra ration card for him, when ration cards were

[*] Irving Weil was of course Etta Shiber's cousin, but the book identifies him as her brother.

not introduced in Paris until September; or how they delivered William Gray to "a small town on the demarcation line," when the Germans did not establish the line until after the time he was said to have departed. These are small details, though, chronological in nature, and might be explained by the author's note indicating that some of the incidents in the book had been "recast" to prevent the German authorities from making use of them. Certain other concerns, however, can't be explained away quite so easily.

The real-life British soldiers rescued by Kate and Etta from the military hospital at Doullens, Lt. Colin Hunter and Cpl. Gordon Hood-Cree (called in the book "Jonathan Burke" and "Lawrence Meehan," respectively), publicly identified themselves after the war, paying special tribute to the courage of Kate Bonnefous. So too did Capt. Derek Lang and 2nd Lt. John Buckingham, the two British servicemen whom Kate encountered with their companion Georges Siauve-Evausy at the American embassy and whom she invited back to her apartment to develop an escape plan.* The English pilot "William Gray," however, never came forward, and no claims have ever been made for his actual identity.

The definitive work on the escape lines of the Second World War, Oliver Clutton-Brock's magisterial *RAF Evaders: The Comprehensive Story of Thousands of Escapers and Their Escape Lines,* includes a sixty-five-page-long appendix, "List of RAF Evaders: 1940–1945," with the names of 2,198 such evaders; none of the details given for these evasions—dates, geography, etc.—comports in any way with those presented in *Paris-Underground.* (The vast majority of the British left behind after Dunkirk were soldiers rather than airmen; as a general rule, pilots—British and American alike—did not begin appearing in escape lines until later in the war.) The website Conscript Heroes, which is devoted to World War II escape lines and contains an annotated list of more than three thousand British escapers and evaders across all branches of the military, likewise offers no possible real-life counterpart for the pseudonymous William Gray. In 2020 the founder of Conscript Heroes, Keith Janes, published an article entitled "Catherine Bonnefous, Etta Shiber, and Some of the Men

* Oddly enough, *Paris-Underground* makes no mention of this incident.

They Helped"; in it, he noted that the two women "first helped a pilot that she [Shiber] calls William Gray," but added, "I have not been able to put a real name to the evader."

After the scenes of the English pilot's rescue and transport to safety, *Paris-Underground* describes how Kate hits on the ingenious idea of placing a classified advertisement in *Paris-Soir* in the name of William Gray, "seeking friends and relatives." The idea is to attract the attention of other British soldiers in hiding without drawing the suspicion of the Gestapo—but instead they receive a reply from a priest, "Father Christian Ravier" of the northern village of Conchy-sur-Canche. They drive into the *zone interdite* to meet Father Ravier, and thus begins their arrangement with the priest, in which he delivers to them, a few at a time, the British servicemen under his care.

A classified ad such as this one, then, would not only locate in time the early escape-line activities of Kate and Etta, it would also disclose the real name of the pilot later dubbed "William Gray." Yet a search of the two major daily newspapers of the period—*Paris-Soir* and *Le Matin*—from June through November 1940 reveals no advertisement along the lines of the one described in *Paris-Underground*.

On the question of the elusive William Gray, another important source of relevant information has never before been made public. Etta Shiber was a faithful letter writer, and in the months preceding and following the Nazi occupation of Paris she wrote long letters to both her brother, Chester, and her sister-in-law, Helen, in Syracuse, providing a wealth of quotidian details about her life with Kitty and the dogs—shopping, meals, the weather, their work for the Foyer du Soldat, the growing privations of the war. In her final letter, dated August 10, she described in close detail her flight from Paris with Kate and the three dogs. In fact the trip lasted not three days but three weeks, and the actual itinerary was very different from the one described in *Paris-Underground:* departing from Paris on June 13; then south to Orléans (where they spent the night in the car); farther south to Vierzon and Châteauroux (where they worked for several days with the local American Hospital of Paris outpost); west to Poitiers; and then, in quick succession, the western towns of Bressuire, La Baule, and finally Guérande, where they remained until July 4, at which time they returned to Paris. They did not meet a frantic innkeeper in Orléans; they did not pick up an escaped pilot there; they did not return to Paris that night, but instead continued on their exodus, toward a distant region of France, for another twenty days.

This is why Keith Janes of Conscript Heroes was unable to place a real name to the evading RAF pilot: There was, in fact, no "William Gray." His existence was not just an exaggeration, or a "fictional embellishment," but an out-and-out fiction. Which means, in turn, that the search of their apartment by the Gestapo—the ruse of the ill brother in the bed, et cetera—didn't happen either. Nor was a classified advertisement ever placed by Kate Bonnefous in the pages of a daily newspaper, in William Gray's name or any other. And because there was no advertisement, there was likewise no letter of reply from a priest in Conchy-sur-Canche.

As with the imaginary RAF pilot and the phantom innkeeper, so too—it turns out—with the Nazi prosecutor who flirts with Kate Bonnefous and then moves into her vacated apartment; and the sympathetic café owner and his nephew who bring the ladies their clandestine mail; and the German officer with a face scarred by a duel who conducts the first interrogation; and the spy who trails Etta after her first release from Cherche-Midi; and the prostitute from Montmartre who passes a message from Etta to Kate in prison; and so many of the other memorable characters who populate the pages of *Paris-Underground*.

There are notable omissions as well. The co-defendants Jeanne Monier and Henri Grimal, for instance, have no counterparts in the book; nor does Abbé Julien Berteloot, the priest who was acquitted by the military tribunal; nor does July Boulanger, the colleague of the two priests, who delivered British soldiers to Kate and Etta's apartment on a weekly basis.

Reading *Paris-Underground* from this perspective, one feels a creative mind at work throughout, shaping the story for maximum impact, adding cloak-and-dagger elements ("chance, coincidence, improvisations, and simple ruses") when necessary to build suspense, trimming characters and events that slow the forward momentum of the narrative. Etta is being transformed as well, turned from a *protagonist* into a *heroine:* presented as less passive than she actually was, making the evolution in Etta's character under the pressure of the German occupation even more striking and dramatic than the one offered by life itself. In *Paris-Underground,* for instance, when the women are unexpectedly confronted with the trapped RAF pilot in Orléans, it is *Etta* who suggests that they hide him in the luggage compartment of their car. ("He'll have a better chance of giving the Germans the slip in the big city than here," she tells a dubious Kitty. "We'll get him to Paris, and then figure out what to do with him there.") Similarly, when the Gestapo agents ring their doorbell, it is Etta who quick-wittedly contrives the scheme to disguise him as her brother, in essence rescuing him for a second time.

Of course, all memoirists have to make choices about which details to include, and all memoirs inevitably contain inaccuracies—be they misremembered events, re-created dialogue, or just the unavoidable colorations of memory. Some less fastidious examples of the form, in an effort to simplify an unwieldy storyline, might compress incidents or rearrange chronologies. Memoir writing allows for gradations of inaccuracy, which ideally the author acknowledges and the reader can then take into consideration in judging the overall reliability of the account. Inventing characters, however, and concocting scenes that never happened, is deceptive and manipulative of the reader, while also having the unfortunate effect of introducing factual inaccuracies into the historical record. To take but one example: In her 2007 book *Paris, les lieux de la Résistance* [*Paris, the Sites of the Resistance*], the French author Anne Thoraval correctly identifies 2 rue Balny-d'Avricourt as the address from which Etta Shiber and Kate Bonnefous operated their escape line in 1940. The first sentence of the entry, though, reads: "Etta Shiber, American, and Kitty Beaurepos, French-English, sheltered in their Parisian apartment on the rue Balny-d'Avricourt the British aviator William Gray after the days of Dunkirk."

How did this happen? How did a book that was hailed as one of the most important memoirs of the Second World War, that was excerpted in leading magazines and newspapers and spent months on the nonfiction bestseller lists—how did such a book turn out to contain so much fiction?

24

THE HUNGARIAN AUTHOR Aladar Anton Farkas emigrated to New York from France in November 1941, arriving in the city seven months before Etta Shiber. He had sailed from Marseille on the steamship *Exeter*, accompanied by his wife, Siv, and two older brothers. Aladar Farkas was forty-five years old; he had brown hair and brown eyes and was physically striking, very thin and six feet five inches tall. In Paris he had supported himself as a writer, publishing numerous articles as well as several novels and a variety of nonfiction books under a pen name that he had adopted, Oscar Ray. His most recent manuscript, as yet unpublished, was a nonfiction account of Adolf Hitler's secret machinations to attain power (the book's proposed title was *Le dossier sanglant d'Adolf Hitler*, or *The Bloody Case of Adolf Hitler*), co-written with Otto Strasser, a German politician who had broken with the Nazis early on and was now living in exile in France. Farkas was Jewish, and his anti-Nazi beliefs were well known, and as the Germans descended on Paris, he and Siv fled to the village of Issac in the Dordogne, finding shelter in an abandoned mill there.

Sometime before his flight from Paris, Aladar Farkas gave the manuscript of his latest book to his literary agent, Paul Winkler, the founder of the Paris-based agency Opera Mundi. A multifaceted operation founded in 1928, Opera Mundi served as a literary agency, a magazine publisher, and a translator and syndicator of newspaper columns and comic strips. Like Farkas, Winkler was a Jew of Hungarian descent, but he was the child of an affluent family (his father was a bank director in Budapest) and had come to Paris as a young man, where through much of the 1920s he served as a local correspondent for *The Washington Post* and the *Toronto Star.*

Paul Winkler had arched eyebrows and a slightly lupine smile; he was a polyglot, a horseman, a shrewd businessman, a small-statured man of large appetites and enormous contradictions, described by someone who knew him as "at once naïve, cynical, fun-loving, full of culture, ruthless, with a great generosity." He also had an apparently unerring understanding of popular taste—knowing what consumers wanted, sometimes even before they knew it themselves. A voracious reader of international newspapers, he noticed early on the popularity of comic strips in the United States, and he predicted correctly that in France *la bande dessinée* would likewise become the latest form of popular expression. At a time when the newly formed Opera Mundi agency had only "an office, a telephone, and an assistant," Winkler negotiated a deal with the world's largest distributor of comics, King Features Syndicate of the mighty Hearst publishing company, to become the exclusive French agent for translated comic strips including *Mandrake the Magician, Flash Gordon* (or *Guy l'Éclair,* as he was known in France), *Prince Valiant,* and *Popeye.* In 1930, Winkler traveled from Paris to California, by ship and railroad, to meet with Walt and Roy Disney personally; the Disney brothers were so impressed with the young man's intelligence and ambition that they named him the sole European distributor for Mickey Mouse cartoons.

Shortly after the German occupation of France, Winkler learned that as a prominent Jewish businessman, he was a target of the Vichy government's newly established Commission for the Revision of Naturalizations. Availing himself of his connections with the Disney and Hearst corporations, he managed to obtain travel visas from the U.S. State Department for himself, his wife, and their three children. In October 1940, he and the children arrived in New York on Pan American Airways' Dixie Clipper "flying boat," and his wife, Betty, followed shortly afterward. In New York, Winkler started a new literary agency that he called the Press Alliance, which represented authors and journalists, translated foreign language works, and produced books of its own using a staff of in-house writers.

By 1941, Aladar Farkas, like many European intellectuals, was desperately trying to escape from Vichy France. His sister, Roza (Ray) Farkas Paioff, who had married an American and lived in Brooklyn Heights, had been waging a campaign to persuade the State Department to issue travel visas to Aladar and her two other brothers. In November 1940, Hugh Fullerton, the American consul in Marseille, denied the request for temporary visas, as the Farkases were "not in a position to show that they will be able to return to a residence abroad at the termination of their visit." In other words, the very insecurity and impermanence of their condition—the fact that they, as Jews of strong antifascist convictions, could never find a home in Nazi-occupied Europe—itself disqualified them from finding sanctuary in the United States. In case his point was not clear enough, Fullerton closed his letter by noting: "It does not appear that they will be able to obtain immigration visas for a long time to come."

With that avenue blocked to her, Ray Farkas Paioff appealed to a nongovernmental organization called the Emergency Rescue Committee. Based in New York and supported by private donations, the ERC had been founded after the German invasion of France to aid the flight of anti-Nazi refugees from occupied Europe, particularly those working in creative and intellectual fields. The committee's representative in Marseille was a young journalist named Varian Fry, who worked ceaselessly and under the most trying conditions to obtain emergency visas, manufacture fake passports, and secure safe passage on ships and with guides for overland treks through the Pyrenees into Spain. Though it was in operation only between 1940 and 1942 (when it was dissolved by the Vichy government), the ERC helped nearly two thousand refugees to escape, including the artists Marc Chagall and Marcel Duchamp, the writer Franz Werfel, the director Max Ophüls, the anthropologist Claude Lévi-Strauss, and the political philosopher Hannah Arendt.

Among those from whom Ray Farkas Paioff sought letters of support on behalf of Aladar Farkas was his literary agent, Paul Winkler. In May 1941, Winkler sent a letter to the Emergency Rescue Committee explaining that Farkas had written for Opera Mundi for several years and that "almost all his articles had a political and most definite anti-Nazi character." He wrote:

> Farkas has a unique documentation about the history of the Nazi movement and the different intrigues behind the curtains in Germany, and all his articles emphasized the corrupt character of Nazi activities. Although they were signed under a pen name, I am certain that the identity of this pen name was well known to Berlin and that the German authorities consider Farkas as one of their most dangerous enemies. . . . If Aladar Farkas should fall into the hands of the Germans his life would be in serious danger and I also believe that his family risks at least being put into concentration camps in view of their connection with him.

The Emergency Rescue Committee agreed to take on the case, and on August 25, Ray Farkas Paioff received a phone call informing her that visas had been obtained for the Farkas family; on November 10, 1941, Elsiv Holme Farkas and the three Farkas brothers sailed into New York Harbor.

In New York, Aladar Farkas lost no time in looking up Paul Winkler, and the two had a joyful reunion; in the course of their conversation, Farkas asked about the status of his manuscript on Hitler. Winkler told him that, regrettably, he had been forced to burn it before he fled, as he feared having such material in his possession when he passed through Nazi checkpoints. Winkler suggested that Farkas could try to reconstitute the destroyed manuscript, but in the meantime, the unusual agreement that the two had used in Paris would continue in New York: Winkler would give Aladar Farkas a weekly retainer, in this case $25 per week (Farkas protested that this amount was insufficient to meet his living expenses but finally acceded to the deal), against the 50 percent that he took as an agent's fee from the monies Farkas earned as a writer.* In the coming months

---

* Farkas and his wife had arrived in the United States with little money and would now be living essentially hand to mouth. By contrast, Paul Winkler's rental the year before of a large furnished apartment at 131–35 East Sixty-sixth Street was considered significant enough that it was the lead item in the weekly roundup of recent transactions in the *New York Times* real estate section: "Head of Syndicate Leases Suite Here."

Farkas wrote several articles, two of which Winkler placed in *Life* magazine and one in the Sunday magazine of the *New York Journal American*. Farkas also spent, as he put it, "many heartbreaking months" trying to re-create his lost manuscript; finally he gave up on that and began to think about a new book project.

For some time before his arrival in the United States, Aladar Farkas had been considering the possibility of writing a novel about the French underground. Now he set to work on it in earnest, and by June 1942 he had completed an outline of the projected book and had begun writing it. That month he read a newspaper article that mentioned an American woman, Mrs. Etta Shiber, who had returned to the United States after having been imprisoned by the Gestapo in Paris. Farkas knew nothing about Etta Shiber beyond the few details that appeared in the article, but it occurred to him that her experiences with the Gestapo could provide some interesting factual incidents and give a stronger sense of verisimilitude to his novel. Farkas wanted to interview Etta Shiber but felt incapable of doing so because he didn't speak English; he asked Paul Winkler if he might arrange for someone to interview Shiber for him, and Winkler, who was enthusiastic about Farkas's book idea, said that he would do so as soon as possible.

Soon afterward, Winkler told Farkas that he had managed to obtain an interview—but that Mrs. Shiber's story was in fact so sensational that Farkas should write an additional book, this one about Mrs. Shiber's experiences, rather than simply try to incorporate the material into his book; America, Winkler said, had room for more than one underground story. "I declined this suggestion," Aladar Farkas would later attest, "and told Paul Winkler that I had no objection to somebody else using the material secured from Mrs. Shiber, if it was desired to have a book devoted entirely to it. My purpose was merely to supplement my story with some factual data to give it reality."

Paul Winkler went ahead with the idea of a book focused on Etta Shiber, and in short order one of his employees at the Press Alliance had produced a synopsis of the proposed book, as well as a sample first chapter. Winkler, though, found this effort "highly unsatisfactory"—it didn't hold the reader's interest, it lacked all sense of suspense—and this opinion was shared by several publishers with whom he shared the work. Realizing that he would have to abandon his original plan for the Shiber book, he went back to Aladar Farkas. As Farkas subsequently recalled, "He asked me whether I was ready to adopt my first suggestion that Mrs. Shiber's material merely be utilized in my fictional work to lend reality to it. However, he urged that I change the form of the novel to a first-person recital. This, he insisted, would make it easier for him to secure the publication of my book. I assented to this—never intending, of course, despite the new form, to claim that this was not a fictional work."

At this point Paul Winkler turned over to Aladar Farkas a fifty-four-page typewritten statement by Etta Shiber about her experiences in France (Farkas described it as "a disconnected narrative of various incidents, unskillfully written by a person who obviously has had no previous literary experience"), as well as the sample chapter written by one of his employees. Farkas went to work, adapting his story to Etta Shiber's experiences, while rewriting it as a first-person narrative along the lines suggested by Paul Winkler.

The imaginative transformation wrought by Aladar Farkas on the materials he had been provided is evident from the very first sentences. The first two paragraphs of Etta Shiber's memoir, as composed by Winkler's original writer, read as follows:

I am writing these lines on the deck of the SS "Drottningholm," sailing back from Europe. The United States exchanged me for Johanna Hoffman, the famous German master-spy, who had been captured on the "Bremen" by the FBI. Her trial made public an international scandal and disclosed the activities of the German spies in the United States.

Johanna Hoffman was a member of a dangerous organization of spies. She was considered the most able woman agent of the German Intelligence Service. And what had I done that my country should release this dangerous woman in exchange for my life? That is what I am going to tell.

It's not hard to understand why publishing houses would reject such a work. The writing here sounds less like a personal memoir than a school composition—labored, perfunctory, disengaged. In the hands of a talented writer, however, the book's opening paragraphs take on an immediate sense of suspense, the world of the story brought vividly to life through a wealth of specific details, the sentences rhythmic and authoritative and imbued with a genuine narrative voice:

> I said no good-bye to Europe. I was below decks when the ship began to move. Her engines were so smooth and noiseless that they must have been running for some time before I became conscious of their muffled pulsing. I hurried up on deck, expecting to find the ship coursing down the broad Tagus River, with the many-colored buildings of Lisbon piled in confusion on its shore.
>
> But from the deck, there was already no sight of land. Behind us, I knew, was the coast of Portugal, but it was lost in the evening haze. The sea was a dirty gray. The engines of the great ship hummed soothingly, monotonously, as she plowed smoothly through the waves, America-bound at last.

Winkler showed Farkas's proposed outline and sample chapter to some New York publishing houses, reporting back that this time the responses were very encouraging; no time should be lost, he said, in completing the manuscript. It was agreed that they should now engage the services of a translator—Farkas wrote only in Hungarian—and they posted a classified advertisement in *Az Ember*, a Hungarian-language newspaper published in New York City. In November they hired an émigré writer named Joseph Szebenyei, and over the course of the next several months Szebenyei translated chapters as they were delivered to him by Farkas, transmitting them in turn to Paul Winkler. By the beginning of 1943, Farkas had completed a manuscript of some eight hundred typewritten pages, under the title *Lest They Die*.

Over the coming months, Farkas inquired from time to time about the status of the manuscript. Winkler told him that editors at the Charles Scribner's Sons publishing house were especially enthusiastic about the book; as soon as an agreement had been reached, he said, he would submit the contract to Farkas for approval and a signature. "In view of my close professional relationship and friendship of many years with Paul Winkler," Farkas was to say, "I relied on his promises."

It was around this time that Farkas noticed that the weekly stipend checks he was receiving from the Press Alliance now bore the memo "Salary." Farkas had never been a salaried employee of the Press Alliance, but Winkler dismissed his concerns when he asked about it, explaining that this was simply a matter of bookkeeping. In July 1943, however, Farkas's brother Nicholas, who had been a noted director in Europe, went to the offices of the Press Alliance to discuss the possible sale of film rights to the book. While he was there, he saw on Paul Winkler's desk the printed proof of the book's title page; Nicholas was astonished to see that the book's title had been changed to *Paris-Underground,* and that the authorship was credited to "Etta Shiber in collaboration with Anne and Paul Dupre." After hearing this from his brother, Farkas stormed over to Winkler's office to demand an explanation.

Winkler admitted that he had signed a contract for the book with Charles Scribner's Sons;* he explained that "Anne and Paul Dupre" stood for his wife and himself, and that it was the trademark byline used on all books prepared by the ghostwriters of the Press Alliance. He further assured Farkas that he would receive 25 percent of all the royalties received from the book—a lower figure than usual, as in this case the credited author needed to receive a percentage as well.

Indignant, Farkas protested that those terms were unacceptable. This book, he insisted, was his literary work and must be published under his own name, and only in accordance with the terms of the financial agreement that had been in place between them since 1934, in which he received half of all the royalties earned by the work, against the advances laid out by Paul Winkler as stipends.

On July 23, 1943, Farkas received a letter from Paul Winkler on

* In fact, the contract had been signed many months earlier. Charles Scribner's Sons sent the letter of acceptance on October 15, 1942, setting out the terms of the agreement: an advance of $2,000, with $600 to be paid on the signing of the contract and the remaining $1,400 on delivery of the manuscript, and 10 percent of earnings on the first three thousand copies sold and 15 percent thereafter. Paul Winkler had spoken with Etta Shiber and agreed to those terms in writing the very next day.

Press Alliance letterhead in which Winkler stated for the record that Aladar Farkas was a salaried employee of the Press Alliance, Inc. Farkas sent a long, anguished letter of reply on the very same day. "Paul," the letter read in part (in translation), "I had no idea that you could stoop to such a monstrous scheme for the mere gain of a few lousy dollars. To think that in this new country, you, in whom I had such implicit faith and confidence, should be guilty of foxing me out of the credit and recognition due me as an author!" He informed Winkler that he was returning the two most recent stipend checks, as yet undeposited, which bore the memo "Salary." "Had I known the true meaning of the word at the time I received the previous checks," he wrote, "I can assure you I would have torn them up and flung them in your face." Farkas closed the letter by demanding that Paul Winkler send him a written contract setting forth a fifty-fifty split of all future royalties earned by his writings, as had always been the arrangement between them; if not, he said, he would seek legal counsel and do all that was necessary "to see that justice is done."

No such contract was forthcoming, and so Aladar Farkas obtained the services of an attorney from the Authors Guild; in October he filed suit in the Supreme Court of the State of New York against Paul Winkler, Betty Winkler, the Press Alliance, Inc., Etta Shiber, and Charles Scribner's Sons, demanding $30,000 as well as authorial credit on all future editions of *Paris-Underground*. In filing his suit, Farkas submitted a lengthy affidavit in which he recounted his writing process on the book, including a list of eighteen characters he had created to supplement "the few persons referred to by Mrs. Shiber." The first two of these fictional characters were:

A French innkeeper, who helps Mrs. Shiber and her friend Kitty
to save an English prisoner who was hiding in his inn;
    Said English prisoner, by the name of William Gray.

Aladar Farkas additionally submitted a notarized affidavit from translator Joseph Szebenyei that described how Farkas had conveyed chapters to him one by one, sometimes typing the final pages even while Szebenyei waited in his apartment; Farkas, he said, would often discuss his plans for the upcoming chapter and ask Szebenyei, a fellow writer, for his reaction. Szebenyei attested that he had read *Paris-Underground* as published by Charles Scribner's Sons, and that it was "a literal reproduction, with only a few insignificant changes of style, of my English translation of the Hungarian manuscript written by plaintiff herein."

Paul Winkler, in his own affidavit, reiterated his contention that Aladar Farkas was a salaried employee of the Press Alliance, Inc.; that no fewer than five people had worked on the final version of the manuscript; and that *Paris-Underground* had been produced "according to the time-honored system known as ghost writing." Farkas, he claimed, "was assigned to do some of the work of collating Mrs. Shiber's experiences because he was on the Press Alliance payroll and it was not always easy to find work he could do, since he had to work in Hungarian."

On October 19, 1943—nine days after *Paris-Underground* first appeared on the *New York Times* bestseller list—the case was settled out of court. It was agreed that the Press Alliance would pay Aladar Farkas the sum of $15,000 ($2,500 of which was against the possible sale of film rights) and that future editions of the book would contain the amended credit line "By Etta Shiber in collaboration with Anne and Paul Dupre and Oscar Ray." In return, Aladar Farkas agreed that he would not "at any time hereafter circulate, advertise or publicly announce or mention in interviews with the press, statements to the press, or for public consumption, the claim that he is the sole author of the said book, *Paris-Underground.*"

After the settlement was announced, Charles Scribner himself issued a statement in which he pointed out that the agreement did not affect the royalties payable by his publishing house, nor any other of its contractual obligations. "Despite the efforts by Mr. Farkas to make sensational claims," he said, "the book *Paris-Underground* remains what Scribner's has always stated it to be—an account of the personal experiences of Etta Shiber."

That assertion—the factual basis of Etta Shiber's book—was left untouched by the terms of the settlement, which turned entirely on questions of financial compensation and authorial credit. The case received little attention in the press (as did an appeal filed by Farkas the following year, claiming that the authorial credit had not been adequately provided), and what there was focused likewise on compensation and credit. The only two substantial articles that ever appeared regarding Farkas's claims, one in the trade magazine *Publishers Weekly* and one in the *New York World-Telegram,* each devoted only a single sentence to the issue of the fictionalization of the memoir.

Yet a substantial portion of Farkas's affidavit is a passionate, forceful exposition of how his book was, at its heart, a work of the creative imagination: "I always intended that my work be published as a work of fiction," he wrote. "The book as published contains a statement that the basic facts in the book are a matter of record, and on the cover of said book appears the statement that it is 'a true story of the war.' Thus, the defendants have defrauded both myself and the general public."

Inside the Charles Scribner's Sons publishing house, there seems to have been at least some concern about the truthfulness of the book, because on July 13, 1943—just as the advance edition of what was still called *Lest They Die* was going to press—Paul Winkler wrote a letter of assurance to Maxwell Perkins. "There cannot be the slightest doubt as regards the authenticity of the material contained in the Shiber book," he affirmed (somewhat astonishingly, in retrospect). According to his account, he had first become interested in the case when he read a newspaper report of Etta Shiber's arrest. He dispatched his wife (who had not yet left Paris for New York) to see if she could make contact with Mrs. Shiber and obtain her story, but that proved impossible; later, when he read that Mrs. Shiber had arrived in New York after being exchanged for Johanna Hofmann, he immediately got in touch with her. "Like many people who come from occupied territories," he wrote, "she was at first very reluctant to talk," but he persisted, and finally "she agreed to tell us her experiences." For two months, Winkler went on, employees of the Press Alliance sat with Etta Shiber every day, faithfully making notes of her recollections, "piece by piece, as she remembered them."

Paul Winkler's explanation seems to have assuaged any doubts that Maxwell Perkins might have had; in a statement issued on behalf of Scribner's, Perkins asserted, "Everything that could be done to be certain that it was the accurate story was done. . . . Mrs. Shiber was consulted almost daily for a period of five months* by members of the Press Alliance staff who took careful notes by shorthand and otherwise, and the extent of what she said covered the entire length of the book." This latter claim is difficult to credit, however, given the fact that a substantial portion of the book consists of events that never took place; Perkins himself was merely relying on affirmations that had been made to him by Paul Winkler. Still, several months later—long after Aladar Farkas's suit had been settled—Maxwell Perkins reiterated these points in a letter to Harry Hansen, who wrote a daily column about books for the *New York World-Telegram;* he further noted that Shiber's recollections were "disjointed, and inconsecutive, and needed to be fitted together and completely rewritten. And then she was consulted over a period of several more months with regard to the accuracy of the rewriting."

In his letter to Hansen, Perkins additionally pointed out that the house's attorney had questioned Etta Shiber before publication, as did representatives of the Book-of-the-Month Club, and that editors at *Reader's Digest* had spoken with individuals who knew Etta Shiber's story at first hand. Perkins did not identify these individuals by name, but the only persons known to have been contacted before publication are Josiah P. Marvel of the American Friends Service Committee and Edwin A. Plitt, formerly of the American consulate in Paris. Each man, however, commented only on the sections of the book in which he appeared, which he would have had no reason to dispute—those particular sections, after all, were not among the ones that Aladar Farkas attested to having made up.

On July 23, 1943, Edwin Plitt sent a letter to the founder and president of the Book-of-the-Month Club, Harry Scherman, in which he noted that Scherman had given him an advance copy of the book and then called him to ask for his "confidential criticism" of it. "As I told you over the telephone," Plitt wrote, "I am not in a position

---

* As with the number of servicemen rescued, the length of time spent with Etta Shiber seems to have been subject to inflation.

to offer any specific suggestions as to whether the story as written agrees with the official records concerning the case. In my opinion, the story is well written. My recollection of the American Embassy's role in her adventure, as related by Mrs. Shiber, appears to be correct."

That, however, was not Edwin Plitt's primary motivation for writing to Scherman; he was writing for a different reason, and one that he considered far more urgent:

> While I am fully aware of the praiseworthy motive of acquainting an interested American public with first-hand accounts of actual experiences with the Gestapo, I cannot overlook the fact that there is no assurance that the principals who are mentioned in the book, either by their correct names or otherwise identified, may no longer be alive or within reach of the Gestapo. This book, if it should fall into the hands of the Gestapo, would therefore, in my opinion, lead to the re-arrest and possible execution of those who may have been freed or lightly sentenced during the trial, and most certainly to the retrial and execution of those still under detention. I would urgently recommend, therefore, in order to protect the lives and liberty of the people concerned in Mrs. Shiber's narrative, that its publication be withheld until after the war is won, or that the book be submitted first to the Department of State for an expression of official opinion as to the advisability of disclosing such information now.

The stakes involved in publishing this book, as Edwin Plitt understood them, were very high indeed, and when Paul Winkler heard about Plitt's concerns he wrote immediately to Harry Scherman to reassure him, as he had earlier with Maxwell Perkins. "I understand perfectly Mr. Plitt's reaction to Mrs. Shiber's book," Winkler wrote. However, he went on, Plitt was not familiar with the meticulous precautions that had been taken with it:

> We did not have to be concerned with details which were fully known to the Germans, but we did a thorough job of recasting

characters and descriptive details wherever we were afraid that indiscretions might arise. I am glad to say that this editorial work
which we have accomplished does not affect the authenticity of
the book in the eyes of people like Mr. Plitt and Mr. Marvel, but I
can assure you, and Mrs. Shiber agrees with me on this, that if any
Gestapo investigator took the book and tried to check up on
things which are not already in his files, he would find himself up
against a stone wall.

Winkler is playing a bit fast and loose here—Edwin Plitt and
Josiah Marvel specifically did *not* attest to the authenticity of the
book as a whole—but he was confident and sweeping in his asser-
tions, and, importantly, Maxwell Perkins trusted him. Perkins himself wrote a letter of reply to Plitt, noting first about Winkler,
"[I] have every reason to feel complete confidence in his abilities
and in his judgment, as well as in his motives." He then addressed
Plitt's concerns directly: "From the very start, when we discussed
this book with Mr. Dupre [Winkler], who with his wife prepared
it with Mrs. Shiber, we emphasized the very great importance of
taking every precaution against endangering anyone who might be
mentioned in it. And this was done by changing names, descriptions, locations, etc. And in a conference today with Mr. Scherman, Mr. Meredith Wood of the Book-of-the-Month Club, and
Mr. Dupre, further changes were decided upon, and are in process
of being made."

Until that point, remarkably enough, Kate Bonnefous, Henri
Bonnefous, and Edouard Régniez had been identified by name in
the book. Now it was decided to shield their identities with pseudonyms, as had been done with the real-life servicemen and with
some of Kate and Etta's co-defendants; it was further decided to
withdraw and destroy the advance editions of the book that provided
their real names. Still, the alterations were essentially cosmetic—
only surnames were changed, and those just slightly, each one maintaining the same first letter and number of characters: Bonnefous
became "Beaurepos" and Renier (as Etta thought the name Régniez
was spelled) became "Ravier." Moreover, Kate and Etta's actual ad-

dress at 2 rue Balny-d'Avricourt was left untouched, as were the village of Conchy-sur-Canche and the military hospital at Doullens. And while *Paris-Underground* describes their *passeur*, Elie Teyssier, as a vineyard owner rather than a *métayer*, the name that was given to him—Tissier—is virtually identical to his real one.

Edouard Régniez had escaped from German captivity, and his whereabouts were now unknown; Henri Bonnefous was thought to be living somewhere in North Africa, but might have returned to France; and Kate Bonnefous and Elie Teyssier were still in prison (if indeed they were still alive), though no one knew where or under what circumstances. Whether they were in German hands or not, the Gestapo would have had no problem identifying these individuals as they were presented in the book, given the thinness of the chosen pseudonyms, the correct addresses, and especially the fact that Etta Shiber had been tried in a German military tribunal alongside Kate Bonnefous, Edouard Régniez, and Elie Teyssier, and the Nazis already knew her name and that of her co-defendants.

Paul Winkler spoke to Etta soon after he heard about Edwin Plitt's letter of concern; he reported back to Maxwell Perkins, "I just mentioned vaguely that some suggestion was received from Mr. Plitt that the book might harm the people mentioned in it. Even this was sufficient to arouse anxiety in her."

By this time, Etta Shiber had been back in the United States for more than a year. She was still living in upstate New York, in the home of her brother and his wife and their two sons. Though Chester and Helen were by no means well off (Chet worked as a salesman in dry goods), Etta was scarcely able to help out with the household expenses. As Winkler noted to Perkins in his letter, "Helping the British soldiers, she spent all her personal funds. She has lived for a year on what the book has brought her so far, in extremely modest circumstances, but always very trustful that the book would be a success and would not only permit her to say the things she wanted to say, but would also make some money to enable her to live without worries during the years which remained for her."

When William Shiber died in 1936, he left Etta an estate valued at $7,830—a reasonable enough sum for the time, but hardly a fortune. (He did not hold a life insurance policy.) By the time she sailed

Etta Shiber in her brother Chester Kahn's home in
Syracuse, New York, in an undated family photograph

back from France in 1942, she had only a few hundred dollars
remaining—whatever had been returned to her by the Germans
after her release from Hauts-Clos prison.* She was now sixty-four
years old, widowed, in ill health, and with no job prospects, and the
savings that she had thought would last her the rest of her life were
gone. Barring a miraculous change in fortune, she faced the prospect
of living out the rest of her life either destitute or dependent on the
goodwill of her brother and his family.

And so, when Paul Winkler unexpectedly approached her with
the idea of turning her experiences into a book, it must have seemed
something of a godsend. Still, Etta resisted Winkler's initial advances. Ever diffident, she was not at all convinced that her experiences were worthy of a book-length treatment: She and Kitty had
saved British prisoners, she told him, and then they had been caught
and had gone to prison—was that enough for a book? Paul Winkler

---

* An additional $485.18 remained in the account that the American embassy in
Paris maintained for Etta while she was in prison, some money having been with-
drawn by the State Department to cover the cost of her return voyage on the
Drottningholm. When the American embassy departed occupied France in November 1942, that sum was transferred to the embassy in Berlin; Etta wrote to
Edwin Plitt from her brother's house in hopes of getting the money back, but it's
not clear whether she was ever able to reclaim it.

assured her that it was; and moreover, he believed that it was an eminently useful book, because it would inform Americans about the nature of the enemy they were facing, and bolster public morale at a time when the outcome of the war was still very much in doubt.

For Etta, Winkler's words could not help but be strengthened by the knowledge of what he too had experienced in Europe: Like her, he was a Jewish refugee from war-torn France; he too had been targeted by the Nazis. Temperamentally, though, Winkler was virtually her opposite: He was gregarious where she was reserved; he was worldly where she was insular; he was shrewd where she was guileless; he was self-assured where she was anxious. And of course, he had money and she had none. Paul Winkler was an exceptionally persuasive individual—he hadn't become Walt Disney's man in Europe without being so—and eventually, after enough talking, Etta agreed to give him her story.

Of course, Etta had never written a book before, whereas Winkler had written many—or at least, many had been written for him. He understood the ins and outs of the publishing business, he had learned the ingredients of a bestseller, and when the facts of a story were not in themselves sufficient to the task, he knew enough to put them in the hands of a talented novelist who could craft an exciting plot that would adhere to the facts when possible and depart from them when necessary. Any such writer would recognize the need to create a precipitating incident early in the narrative, a dramatic event that sets the plot into motion by forcing the main characters to act; ideally, that action would be initiated by the point-of-view character. In this case, the precipitating incident is the encounter with the trapped pilot "William Gray," and the action is the decision to hide him in the luggage compartment of their car, as suggested not by Kitty but by Etta.

If Etta ever questioned the use of fictionalization, Winkler would have had little difficulty in impressing on her the necessity of getting the book in front of as many readers as possible, while also pointing out that nothing in it violated what might be called the essential truth of her story: that two women of a certain age, of their own volition, had risked their safety and their freedom to transport Allied servicemen out of occupied France. From her very first conversation with Paul Winkler, Etta had doubted that her story was sufficient for a book, and any argument that Winkler might have put forward about the need to augment certain details—to make the story more interesting, more readable, more important—would undoubtedly have resonated with Etta, given her own lack of self-confidence, her almost reflexive tendency to diminish herself, her longtime willingness to let others make decisions for her.*

Etta desperately needed the money as well. By the time she finished her initial consultations with the Press Alliance, Etta was living entirely on the payments that Winkler extended to her as an advance against royalties. If she was going to move back to New York City, she needed those royalties to be substantial, and as time went on, her dependence on the eventual success of the book grew ever stronger. Knowing Etta's nervousness and vulnerability, Winkler had delayed telling her about the selection by the Book-of-the-Month Club—that was something of a winning lottery ticket for a book of the time—until he was sure it was definite. When he did finally deliver the good news, he reported to Maxwell Perkins, Etta was "overjoyed," but later, after Edwin Plitt wrote of his concerns and she heard from Winkler that Harry Scherman was expressing some hesitation about the selection, her sense of despair was profound:

"I suddenly realized," Winkler told Perkins, "that perhaps I should not have spoken at all because the nervousness which our conversation provoked in her may be very harmful for a woman with her heart condition and blood pressure. . . . She spoke about committing suicide if there were any difficulties now."

---

* It should also be noted that in 1942 the standards for veracity in nonfiction writing such as memoir and reportage were less strict than those of the present day, with some writers taking liberties with their material that now would not be considered acceptable. Perhaps most famously, the acclaimed *New Yorker* reporter Joseph Mitchell often resorted to composite characters in his work. One of his frequent and most memorable subjects, for instance, "Old Mr. Flood"—a dapper, ninetyish habitué of the Fulton Fish Market in lower Manhattan with "icy-blue eyes" and a "red, bony, and clean-shaven" face—turns out never to have existed. *The New Yorker* did not discipline Joseph Mitchell for journalistic indiscretions; indeed, when Mitchell was having trouble finding a central character for his Fish Market story, it had been the magazine's founding editor himself, Harold Ross, who suggested using a composite character, pointing out that *The New Yorker* had already done so on several occasions.

Winkler hastened to add, "I do not want to take this seriously." Yet this did not prevent him from mentioning the possibility to Maxwell Perkins—in hopes, he intimated, that Perkins might decide to pass along the information to Harry Scherman: "The hesitation of the Book-of-the-Month Club is based purely on human considerations," he wrote, "though in reality no risk is involved, all precautions having been taken; on the contrary, the human consideration which I refer to should be an argument, if any is needed, in the opposite direction."

The Book-of-the-Month Club didn't face much risk if they selected the book, Paul Winkler seemed to be suggesting, but there was at least a possibility that Etta Shiber would kill herself if they didn't. He personally was "very hesitant about mentioning this matter to the Book-of-the-Month Club," as he didn't want "to give them the impression that I want to influence them with sentimental considerations." Still, Winkler thought it best that Perkins knew about the situation—in the event that he might decide to say something.

There is no record of Maxwell Perkins ever delivering this lurid piece of information to Harry Scherman, or to anyone else at the Book-of-the-Month Club. In any event, the assurances offered by Winkler and Perkins seem to have carried the day: In October 1943, *Paris-Underground* was offered as a dual main selection of the Book-of-the-Month Club, at which point the book began moving up the nation's nonfiction bestseller lists.

25

THE BACKSTORY PRESENTED FOR Kate Bonnefous in *Paris-Underground* is brief but essentially accurate, making note of her privileged London upbringing, her society-girl education, her early marriage and relocation to Italy, the birth of her son there and the subsequent move to Paris, the remarriage to a French wine merchant and the amicable separation from him. For Etta Shiber, though, there is no backstory whatsoever. It is as if her life began in 1925, at the age of forty-seven, when she met Kate Bonnefous for the first time in that dress shop on rue Rodier. Nothing is said of her family ancestry (including her birth name, Kahn, or that of her cousin Irving Weil), her birthplace of New York City, her work as a public-school teacher, nothing of her marriage to William Shiber as officiated by Felix Adler of the Society for Ethical Culture. For this total absence there can be only one reasonable explanation, which is that it was intended to obscure the fact that Etta Shiber was Jewish.

Though the specter of Nazism haunts the pages of *Paris-Underground*, Jewishness is mentioned only four times, always in the form of anecdotes about individual Parisian Jews' encounters with Nazi officers, and never in relation to Etta. At one point early in *Paris-Underground*, for instance, Kate Bonnefous pleads with Etta to return to the United States. Yet the narrative presents Kate as resorting to the rather specious claim that Etta should leave because she is an American and doesn't have a direct stake in the war, rather than to the self-evident and far stronger argument of Etta's vulnerability as a Jew living under Nazi occupation. Etta herself does make reference to God on several occasions, but He seems to function as a kind of all-purpose benevolent deity, divorced from any specific faith or particular holy book; the reader is left with a vague, generalized notion of belief, a religiousness devoid of religion.

Not only was the book's purported author Jewish, though—so were its primary author, Aladar Farkas, and one of its pseudonymous co-authors, Paul Winkler. Both of those men had been forced into exile in large part because of their religion; both had written extensively about the Nazi threat and were under no illusions about the fragile and imperiled condition of the Jewish people still trapped in occupied Europe.* It's impossible that either of them could have believed that Etta Shiber's Jewishness was a detail not worth mentioning. As with the number of British servicemen rescued by Kate and Etta, a conscious decision seems to have been made here to alter the factual record—this time not by addition but by subtraction. To do so entailed a significant narrative loss (after all, the notion that Etta Shiber, a Jew, was conducting illegal operations under the eyes of the Nazis could only serve to build dramatic tension), but at the same time, one can understand why the decision might have been made, given the historical context in which *Paris-Underground* was published.

The historian Doris Kearns Goodwin has written of "the xenophobic, anti-Semitic mood of [the] country in the late 1930s and early '40s," and indeed, in the years leading up to World War II, national polling on the subject revealed a widespread American discomfort with Jews, at home as well as overseas. In 1938, for instance, an Elmo Roper poll asked, "What kinds of people do you object to?" Twenty-seven percent of respondents answered with "noisy, cheap, boisterous and loud people," while another 14 percent chose "uncul-

* In addition to his newspaper journalism, Paul Winkler was the author of *The Thousand-Year Conspiracy: Secret Germany Behind the Mask,* the only book to appear under his own name; it came out in 1943, the same year as *Paris-Underground,* and was likewise published by Charles Scribner's Sons.

tured, unrefined, dumb people"; the most popular answer, though, at 35 percent, was simply "Jews." The following year, another Roper poll found that only 39 percent of respondents believed that Jews "should be treated like everyone else," while 53 percent believed that Jews were "different" from other people and should be subjected to "restrictions" in their social and business lives; 10 percent of those polled favored deportation of Jews. Even that was mild when compared to a different poll that found that fully one-fifth of respondents wanted to "drive Jews out of the United States."

In November 1938, in the wake of the terrifying Kristallnacht pogrom unleashed against Jews in Nazi Germany, Gallup pollsters asked Americans, "Should we allow a larger number of Jewish exiles to come to the United States to live?" Nearly three out of every four respondents said no. According to another 1938 poll, this one conducted by the American Institute for Public Opinion, 48 percent of respondents believed that the persecution of the Jews in Europe was partly their own fault; 11 percent believed it was "entirely" their own fault. (One wonders about the additional percentage of respondents who might have believed such things but did not want to admit them to a pollster.)

For the better part of a decade, the Roosevelt administration had been unsuccessful in its efforts to expand long-standing immigration quotas to allow a greater number of Jewish refugees to enter the United States,* and eventually the president's advisers persuaded him not to reopen the question of quotas or the powerful isolationist wing in Congress would eliminate immigration entirely. It was a period when a Democratic congressman felt free to rail against "warmongering international Jewry" on the floor of the House of

---

* In her book *Rescue Board: The Untold Story of America's Efforts to Save the Jews of Europe,* the historian Rebecca Erbelding noted that the Johnson-Reed Act of 1924 "capped the number of immigrants from outside the Western Hemisphere at about 154,000 people per year, a far cry from the more than 10 million who had arrived in the United States in the decade prior to World War I. . . . The quotas severely restricted persons from southern and eastern Europe, who had formed the majority of the immigrant population in recent decades, and kept most Asian and African people out entirely. Countries with large populations of Jews, Slavs, and people thought to be racially undesirable, poorer, and harder to assimilate were specifically targeted."

Representatives, when a Republican senator could write an article in which he proclaimed his opposition to the idea that the United States should "go to war for the sake of protecting Jews of any country whatever," and then publish that article in the pages of a German newspaper. At all levels of society, American political life was dogged by the suggestion—sometimes whispered, sometimes proclaimed—that a "Jewish lobby" was pushing the country into an unnecessary war, one primarily intended to rescue foreign Jews rather than to preserve democracy or safeguard the United States or any other such lofty goals.

When the United States did enter the war, many American Jewish organizations chose to refrain from public demonstrations, for fear of undermining support for the war by linking it too closely with the plight of the Jewish people. As the war went on, they lobbied privately for a range of measures that might help save some Jews overseas—from easing restrictions on refugees to bombing the rail lines to the death camps—but Roosevelt administration officials refused, insisting that such measures distracted from the war effort and that the only way to save the Jews of Europe was to win the war. "Ever since 1933," observed the historian Joseph W. Bendersky, "the Roosevelt administration had to dispel notions that it placed the needs of foreign Jews over those of Americans. In wartime, such undercurrents took on additional gravity. Thus, the president and other governmental agencies were ever careful to avoid creating the impression at home or abroad that American boys were dying for Jews."

Paul Winkler—worldly, sophisticated, politically minded, and himself a European Jewish refugee—would have been acutely aware of the isolationist currents in American political life, the tenacious anti-Semitism, the suspicion that the war was being fought on behalf of "Jewish" interests rather than "American" ones. If he wanted the book to be a commercial success, while helping to build public support for the Allied cause, it was far preferable to present Etta Shiber as a representative middle-aged housewife with whom Americans across the country could readily identify, rather than as what she actually was—a college-educated New Yorker from a German Jewish background, who had cosmopolitan tastes in music and literature, who lived with a highly cultivated unmarried male cousin, and who had been trained as a teacher at the Ethical Culture School, originally called "The Workingman's School," which provided a free education to the children of the poor. Though Etta Shiber was the subject of numerous feature articles in newspapers and magazines, none of the journalists who wrote these stories seem to have asked the background questions that are typically asked of a bestselling memoirist. Instead, they chose to reinforce the conventional trope presented of Etta in the book, of a kindly, unassuming, somewhat bewildered elderly lady—the type of woman, one such article suggested, who might be found "on some country hotel porch, rocking back and forth, gossiping, playing bridge and vowing to go on a diet."

Early sales of *Paris-Underground* were so strong that Charles Scribner's Sons ordered a second printing on September 20, 1943, the very day the first edition went on sale; a third printing followed one month later, and a fourth only two weeks after that. By that time more than half a million copies of the book were in circulation. The film option was being handled by Myron Selznick, brother of the powerful producer David O. Selznick and himself one of the leading agents in Hollywood; the names being bandied about to play Kitty in the movie included Claudette Colbert, Irene Dunne, Rosalind Russell, and Olivia de Havilland.[*]

Perhaps most important, *Paris-Underground* also seemed to have accomplished the task of bolstering American support for the war effort. In addition to everything else, it was an October 1943 selection of the Council on Books in Wartime, which promoted certain books in the interest of "building up an informed public opinion which will aid in winning the war and winning the peace which will follow the victory." Shortly after its publication, Claudine Gray, a professor emeritus at Hunter College in New York, sent a letter to Charles Scribner to congratulate him for the great public service he had rendered by publishing *Paris-Underground*. "In discussing the book with friends and colleagues," she wrote, "I find everywhere the same

[*] Ultimately the part went to the actress Constance Bennett, who also co-produced the film; in the screen version, the character's name was changed to Kitty de Mornay—a pseudonym of a pseudonym.

reaction, which may be expressed by the simple sentence: 'Now I know why we are in this war.' I think the story will do a better propaganda job than many books of argumentation and discussion, simply because it has no such aim, but merely tells in plain and simple language what is happening in the occupied countries of Europe." The writer Adela Rogers St. Johns sent a letter inviting Etta for tea in her townhouse overlooking the East River. "I think no other American woman could at this time do our country so magnificent a service," she wrote. "Beside it, even the saving of the lives of young soldiers in spite of the danger is a small thing. I honestly believe that your book will help to save not only many, many more lives than that, but that it will save many in this country from spiritual death itself."

Letters about *Paris-Underground* poured into the New York offices of Charles Scribner's Sons, mostly from readers praising the book and asking for further news of Kitty's fate. To each one the house's secretaries typed out the same response: "We do not yet know what became of Mrs. Kitty Beaurepos, but we hope to eventually, and shall inform you."

Etta herself had no information on the matter, although whenever she was asked, she said that she believed Kitty was still alive. Before 1944 was out, Etta had moved back to New York City, renting an apartment on West Seventy-third Street; later on, she took up residence in a furnished suite in the Hotel Beacon on Broadway and West Seventy-fifth Street, where the amenities included maid service, a restaurant and a café, a gymnasium, a beauty salon, a roof terrace, and "Ladies' and Gentlemen's Solaria" equipped with massage tables and sun chairs. She had never lived on the Upper West Side before; it was a pleasant, if slightly run-down, neighborhood full of small family-run shops and inexpensive restaurants, the side streets lined with nineteenth-century brownstones and taller brick apartment houses. Some of the windows displayed banners that indicated the number of family members serving in the armed forces, a blue star for each; if a son or daughter was killed in the war, the blue star was replaced with a gold one, and the mother of the family became known, in sorrow and reverence, as a Gold Star mother.

Even so, it was easy to walk around the neighborhood and forget for a while that the country was at war: The shelves at the A&P were well stocked, the movie houses were full, and all around her people laughed and hurried to appointments and made plans to meet for dinner. More and more she felt the distance between this life and the one she had left behind. She had not regained her health since returning to America, not really; as she had anticipated, the weight she lost in prison had come back with no trouble, but she tired more quickly now, her body ached unaccountably, and her heart seemed to have lost its spring, like a rubber band that has been stretched too far.

When the weather was good she could sit in nearby Verdi Square, beneath the heroic marble statue of opera's greatest composer. She still remembered seeing *Aïda* with Irving at the Metropolitan Opera House in 1908; that had been Toscanini's first New York appearance, and Etta considered the evening one of the highlights of her life. Over the years they had attended so many performances together: They had seen Jascha Heifetz's Carnegie Hall debut at the age of sixteen, had seen Yehudi Menuhin's debut at only eleven, when after the final encore the audience pressed as one toward the footlights, cheering and applauding, until finally he appeared once more on stage, already dressed in his overcoat, cap in his hand; in his review, Irving had called the boy's rendition of Beethoven's concerto for violin and orchestra "a kind of miracle." She felt herself living increasingly in the past now, her mind populated with those she had loved, most of whom were dead or, like Kitty, might be. Kitty was never far from her thoughts, and Etta believed that her friend must be thinking of her too. In her last published interview, with *Family Circle* magazine, she reiterated her conviction that Kitty was still alive, before adding, "and I will go back to live with her in Paris or in England if she wants me to."

Etta had been disturbed to learn that Kitty's brother, Leonard, had complained to the British Foreign Office after the *Daily Mail*, one of England's most widely read newspapers, presented a five-part series of excerpts from *Paris-Underground*, the book "which is sweeping America." He said that he couldn't fathom how Kate's American friend could write a book about her anti-Nazi activities while Kate's present status with the Nazis was still unknown; particularly distressing was the headline that referred to her in large block letters as "THIS WAR'S NURSE CAVELL"—when Edith Cavell famously had been executed by the Germans during the First World War for her aid to escaped Allied prisoners. Etta had sent Leonard a reply by way of the British consulate in New York. She wrote, "I felt I had no right to refuse any important English paper which was interested in speaking about the book, which to me is simply an homage to an Englishwoman who is the finest person I ever met." She sent him a copy of *Paris-Underground* as well, along with several newspaper reviews that extolled Kitty's heroism, including one from the *Philadelphia Bulletin* that read in part, "Kitty emerges as the great heroine of the war and the reader should be grateful to Mrs. Shiber for the superb portrait of this brave, selfless Englishwoman."

Leonard and Kitty, Etta knew, had always been close; Kitty had named her son after him, and the Robins family took Len in after France fell to the Nazis. As a young man, Leonard had fought in the Battle of the Somme in World War I, and now he worked as an engineer in the British armaments industry; he was an intelligent, serious man, and Etta hated the idea that he considered her book a threat to Kitty's safety. What was worse, his complaint echoed the prepublication concerns expressed by Edwin Plitt: "This book, if it should fall into the hands of the Gestapo, would therefore, in my opinion, lead to the re-arrest and possible execution of those who may have been freed or lightly sentenced during the trial, and most certainly to the retrial and execution of those still under detention."

Etta had been uneasy from the very outset about the possibility that the Germans might be able to make use of information contained in the book; indeed, she had agreed to speak to the Press Alliance only on the condition that neither she nor anyone else would be harmed by its publication. Still, she worried: Might she, in fact, have endangered Kitty? Just the thought of it was unbearable. "Such an infinitely important thing it is to do the right!" Felix Adler had exhorted the teachers of the Ethical Culture School, so long ago now. "Our worth as human beings, the success or failure of our life, so utterly depends upon this, that we want to use every possible diligence that we may not miss our aim."

For another year there was nothing but silence on Kitty's fate. Meanwhile the world spun heedlessly on, lavish in its provision of calamity and horror. In April 1945, Etta suffered yet another loss: Her brother, Chester, died in Syracuse at the age of sixty-five. These days, she supposed, it was something of a luxury to be able to die of natural causes, in one's own home; still, that was scant comfort for those who remained behind to grieve. That summer, Etta rented a room in a little Catskills hotel called the Riverview, in a village highly regarded for the abundance of its trout. The fresh air and pine woods and star-filled night skies were a welcome relief from the city, from radio programs and newspaper headlines and grainy, shocking newsreel footage. She had become the type of woman who could be found rocking on a country porch and vowing to go on a diet, as had once been imagined of her.

It was there, in that secluded mountain hamlet, that Etta learned that the Second World War was over. And there that she received word that Kitty had survived it.

She had no additional details, nothing beyond that single, all-important fact. She wondered about Kitty's condition, wondered whether she would stay in Paris or return to England, whether she might want Etta to come live with her again. Immediately, as she had always done, Etta took pen to paper. "My dearest Kitty," she wrote,

> What a thrill I had when I received word that you have come
> through the frightful ordeal. I don't know what you went
> through, but having spent eighteen months in prison myself, I
> can imagine. At the end of this period, I had developed such a
> severe heart condition that I was given six months parole, to go
> to Paris and be made well! The condition was very high blood
> pressure, which is greatly relieved and though it can never be en-
> tirely cured, I am not dying of it as yet. As you see, I am in the
> country and shall be for some time to come. That you were able
> to survive is a miracle, but I was always sure that you would until
> I heard of the dreadful atrocities that the Germans were inflict-
> ing on prisoners. I confess that I had my doubts, for the human
> being can stand just so much. But I consoled myself with the

idea that in the concentration camps it was, perhaps, worse than in prison. I am wondering what it has done to you. I too lost everything—it was all confiscated after our trial and I came back with almost no money and no clothes, except a few rags that were given to me. There is much that I would like to talk to you about but which I am not able to write about at length. The long term of imprisonment, with all the hardships both physical and mental, did something to me and has made it almost impossible to write a long letter. I was exchanged for that Nazi spy Johanna Hofmann who was coiffeuse on the Bremen. If you recall, we saw a movie of her story in Nice called "The Confessions of a Nazi Spy." I sailed for home from Lisbon and the first moment of security I felt was when I stepped on American soil. . . .

I was so happy to hear that you are alive, and I hope to hear that you are well. So, do write and tell me how things are going and whether you have read my book "Paris-Underground." It has been made into a movie which is to be released on September 14—your part is taken by Constance Bennett, mine by Gracie Fields. But it has been so changed that all you will recognize is the title.

So much for now. My love and I am so grateful that you have come through.

Always lovingly,
Etta

By the time Etta wrote that letter, Kate Bonnefous had already been free for six months. She had written to her brother, Leonard, to let him know that she was alive, and to her son, Len, as well, and to her husband, Henri, and to her attorney, and to at least one of the soldiers whom she had helped free, Colin Hunter. By that time, too, she had read *Paris-Underground,* although she had not written to Etta about it, nor about anything else.

Before long, the secretaries at Charles Scribner's Sons were typing a new response to the letters they received asking after Kitty's status: "We are glad to be able to tell you that we have had word that Kitty

Beaurepos is alive and well, after numerous adventures both in and out of prison."

Seven years later, in 1953, when the pace of letters had slowed, a member of the editorial staff at Scribner's took the time to write a more personal letter in reply to an inquiry that the house had received: "I am so sorry to have to tell you that Mrs. Shiber died in 1949. She had been living here in New York after her return from Europe. You may be interested to know too that a year or so ago we heard indirectly that Mrs. Shiber's friend, Kitty, had died in France where she had been living after her liberation from the German prison camp."

Etta Shiber had actually died in 1948, not 1949, on the afternoon of December 23, just a few weeks shy of her seventy-first birthday; she had suffered a fall during the summer and had broken a hip and never recovered. She died in her room at the Hotel Beacon, where she was under regular nursing care. The few personal effects that she left behind—an empty steamer trunk and suitcases, some articles of clothing, a table radio, a purse with eight dollars in it—were assessed at a value of $95. She owed the hotel $560 for that month's rent, as well as $566 to her three nurses; another $311 would go to Riverside Memorial Chapel, a nearby Jewish funeral home. The bulk of her estate—which amounted to $6,408 in all—she left to her sister-in-law, Helen T. Kahn.

Etta died with an outstanding claim for $25,000 against the actress and producer Constance Bennett, who had purchased the film option for *Paris-Underground.* The option money had never come in, and after Etta's death, Helen Kahn hired an attorney to investigate the claim. The attorney's final report stated: "My investigation disclosed that the picture produced was a failure and that Miss Bennett sustained substantial losses from the production, the payments made by her in relation to the production having left her seriously embarrassed. It was hoped that this condition might improve, and the representative of Press Alliance, Inc., which represented the decedent in connection with this venture, has expressed an opinion, in which I concur, that the claim against Miss Bennett is now worthless."

The 1953 letter from Scribner's also mentioned that Kitty "had died in France." In fact, Kate Bonnefous was still very much alive, living in a seaside town on the French Riviera, in a house that had been provided to her by the British government.

By that time, both Great Britain and France had decorated her with medals to honor her service, but Kate—who was modest and reticent in the typical British manner—preferred to say little about that.* She said even less about the period of her imprisonment. But she remembered it all—including how the Nazis had sentenced her to death for a second time. That was something that Kate Bonnefous spoke of only once, not long after her return to France. Many years later, though, when she filed a claim under the newly established Anglo-German Agreement for Compensation to Victims of Nazism, she included the second death sentence among a list of atrocities that the Nazis had perpetrated against her. Over time, some of the people she had known in those years seemed to have cauterized their memories like wounds, burying them beneath layers of scar tissue, but she had never been able to do that. She remembered everything, much more than she cared to. The French doctor who had examined her as part of the claim against Germany recorded a grim list of her ailments, most of them brought on by trauma: among others, photophobia (sensitivity to light), spinal arthritis, edema, spastic colon, ulcers, edentulism (loss of teeth), cardiac arrhythmia, insomnia, anxiety, and, perhaps most terrifying of all, hypermnesia—the condition of having too vivid a memory.

---

* Though she did once tell a Scottish newspaper that her rescue activities had begun when "I saw a notice in the evening paper stating that Major Colin Hunter of the Cameron Highlanders and a number of other officers were in a German military hospital in Doullens wounded"—that is to say, *not* with a fleeing RAF pilot encountered in Orléans.

PART THREE

Into the Night and Fog

You can squeeze a bee in your hand until it suffocates, but it will not suffocate without having stung you. You may say that is a small matter, and, indeed, it is a small matter. But if the bee had not stung you, bees would long ago have ceased to exist.

—JEAN PAULHAN, writer and early member
of the French Resistance

26

S HE IS TRANSPORTED TO Ziegenhain Prison on July 8, 1941, the hottest day of that year. By afternoon the thermometer will register 35 degrees Celsius—95 on the Fahrenheit scale—and in the third-class carriage where Kate Bonnefous sits beside a German guard on a bare wooden seat, the windows remain closed and the door has been locked from the outside. Because she tried to escape from Cherche-Midi, she has been taken aboard in handcuffs, as she will be whenever she is moved from one prison to another. Her hands, blistered and cracking and mottled with dark circles, resemble a burned landscape. Inside the other compartments, the passengers do not know that the train is carrying an enemy of the state. She herself does not know what fate awaits her in Germany, be it continued imprisonment, or a slow death by forced labor, or execution via rifle shot or guillotine. It has been only three months since the führer commuted her death sentence; one who grants life, though, may also take it away, and she can have no confidence that he will never change his mind.

The train tracks run along the right bank of the Moselle River, little more than a stream here, fringed with rushes and watched over by stands of willows. Farther north the landscape grows wilder, with thickets of gnarled pines and sheer cliffs rising over mountain lakes;

large black birds swoop and soar, the sun inscribing the path of their flight on the water below. Ruined castles, monasteries, and fortresses gaze blindly from atop sandstone hills; the train seems to be moving backward through the centuries, to a time when knights battled for this land in the service of barons and lieges. Black-and-white station signs flash by, revealing strange, primordial-seeming names: ÜRZEN, KÜHR, GONDORF, ALF. At one of the stations the carriage is unlocked and she is led down to the train platform. Outside, the air is dry and still and very hot. On the platform Kate is handed over to a local policeman, who replaces the guard's handcuffs with a set of his own; together they set out on foot through the town of Ziegenhain, the fabled home of the Grimms' Little Red Riding Hood.

It's strange how so many of the towns she will pass through on her long journey to the east look like a fairy tale come to life, with tidily kept cobblestone squares ringed by Gothic churches, clock towers, and rows of little wedding-cake houses, delicate confections of pink and blue and yellow and green. Many of the streets here are lined with fruit trees; in the fall they will be perfumed by the winy scent of fallen apples. Above the tree line the prison looms dark and sinister, like a dreadnought in wait on the horizon. A hulking structure with rows of pointed gables and a circular watchtower, built in the twelfth century as a royal hunting retreat, it is one of the many castles that the Nazis have converted into prisons. One section of the castle has been reserved for female prisoners; eventually some 140 will be incarcerated there, from France, Belgium, Luxembourg, Czechoslovakia, Poland. Kate Bonnefous is among the first women to be sent to Ziegenhain; she is the only one originally from England.

Inside the prison, she is directed to a large room that contains both male and female guards, one of whom commands her to undress. For some time she stands naked under their gaze; the female political prisoners have an apothegm for moments such as that: "Drape yourself in dignity." Her clothing is placed inside a canvas bag with her name on it and sent off to be sterilized in an autoclave; she will have no use for it here. She is handed a rough, crumbly bar of sand soap and placed under a cold shower to wash herself. When she is finished, a doctor comes to examine her, inspecting every orifice of her body for disease or hidden objects. As long as she is in

Ziegenhain Castle, as it appeared on a postcard from
the early years of the twentieth century

prison, she understands, her body will be a source only of hunger and
pain and humiliation, an obstacle that needs to be overcome. She is
given a bundle containing a gray sleeved undershirt (female prisoners are not provided underpants), gray stockings with red stripes at
the ankles, a blue striped chemise, a black cotton dress, and a heavy
pair of wooden clogs; her hair is to be hidden beneath a checked blue
scarf. The overall effect, of conformity and submission, is something
like that of a religious sect from an earlier time; the effect is magnified when she joins the general population, rows of women sitting at
long tables, all dressed alike, bent silently over their work.

In Ziegenhain, as in the other castle prisons, the Nazis take advantage of the captive population to assist in the war effort. Sometimes female prisoners are loaned out to nearby factories owned by
German companies; more often, sections of the prisons are converted
into vast workrooms. Work begins at seven o'clock in the morning
and continues until seven o'clock at night, with a break only for lunch
and a brief promenade in the prison yard. The work itself is mindless
but wearying: untying knots from ropes, for example, or stuffing
feathers into down comforters, or sewing buttons onto the thick, stiff
camouflage jackets worn by motorcycle units. Among the female po-

litical prisoners, organized resistance to this forced labor will not develop until later in the war; still, even now the work proceeds more slowly than it otherwise might, as some of the women surreptitiously tie new knots before untying them, and find other ways of impeding, even if only imperceptibly, the smooth functioning of the workroom.

Because she is the only Englishwoman in the prison, Kate is constantly mocked and insulted by the German guards. One afternoon, during a promenade, she slips away; just as she has made her way out of the prison yard, there is a torrent of shouting and barking and she is set upon by guard dogs, who knock her down and sink their teeth into her legs. She spends the day in the infirmary. Later, after she has been brought back to her cell, she is visited by the prison commandant; Kate tells him that she had "had enough of being insulted by the Germans and indeed I tried to escape."

As punishment for attempting to escape, the commandant says, she will be sent to the dungeon for fifteen days.

The dungeon is a large underground room, dark and damp even in the summertime; it exudes the stink of a slop bucket, and in place of a mattress it contains only a concrete slab shaped like a gravestone. The guards there order her to strip naked and to begin marching; she does what she can to drape herself in dignity. All day long she is forced to march on the cement floor; so too the next day, and the next. The cement wears away at the bare soles of her feet, each step becoming a sort of blow, the pain shooting upward from her feet through her body. Prisoners in the dungeon are given only small portions of bread and water to subsist on, once in the morning and once at night, and over time her hunger turns to nausea and then to cramps, a kind of writhing like a small, furious animal attacking her from the inside. If she stops walking, the guards whip her legs with leather straps. At the end of five days, she is too exhausted even to eat the morsels of bread that she is given. Finally the marching is brought to an end, and she spends the rest of her detention sprawled naked on the floor in a kind of dreamless half sleep.

At long last she is ordered back upstairs—she must crawl up the stairs because she is too weak to walk—where she is placed in a solitary-confinement cell. "From that moment," she will say later, "they must have seen that I had a lot of grit and courage, because I was no longer insulted."

She remains in solitary confinement for fifteen months, her only companions the lice, fleas, and bedbugs that infest the straw sack on which she must sleep. Her diet consists primarily of dark bread, sometimes moldy, and soup made from turnips or beets or potato peels; on Sundays she also receives two small boiled potatoes and a thin slice of blood sausage. Whistling provides one of her few diversions; she finds that it helps keep her mind focused and her spirits up. Her cell has a small window that overlooks the prison yard, and in the afternoons she whistles while the other female prisoners take their promenade. The song she likes best is *"La Madelon,"* a World War I song that has become synonymous with November 11, Armistice Day, a holiday the Nazis have banned in France. It amuses her to be whistling a patriotic French song under the noses of the German guards. One day as she is whistling *"La Madelon,"* she notices that one of the prisoners has lifted her head at the sound of the melody, so she knows that she is being heard.

At night she is often awoken by hunger or, worse, the screams of some unknown woman. Still, nighttime is better: In the darkness of her cell the walls are erased, and she can imagine herself elsewhere, once more in places she has known and loved, like her brother's house in Hendon, that big, odd, wonderful family house where Leonard built furniture and grew and dried his own pipe tobacco and kept bees in backyard hives. In the darkness she can almost sense him sitting beside her once more, tooling around the British countryside in his open-top MG roadster. She doesn't know if she will see her loved ones again. She wonders whether Henri has finally made it to North Africa, whether Sonny, discharged from the Navy, might regain his position as a salesman for Peugeot. She remembers his wedding so well, that elegant June ceremony in a church not far from her apartment, how happy Sonny had looked, Mireille with her long satin train and the delicate white flowers pinned in her hair. All of that seems so far away now. By this time she has not seen her son in well over a year; it is possible that she has become a grandmother without knowing it.

Kate Bonnefous was condemned to death by the Military Tribunal of Greater Paris in March 1941; one month later, Adolf Hitler commuted her death sentence to one of life imprisonment. That very same month—April 1941—another French *résistante*, Louise Woirgny of Orléans, was arrested by the Gestapo; like Kate Bonnefous, she had founded an escape line that passed Allied servicemen to the Unoccupied Zone, and the Military Tribunal of Greater Paris likewise sentenced her to death in July. Again Hitler refused to confirm this judgment, believing that her sudden disappearance would be more intimidating than her execution; it would also have the advantage of not allowing the French Resistance to turn her into a martyr. He told an aide, "This woman must be transported to Germany, and there be isolated from the outside world."

In the fall of 1941, as resistance to the Nazis grew in the occupied nations of Western Europe, Hitler further decided that lengthy trials and prison sentences for so-called political crimes—even life sentences at hard labor—were regarded by the local populations as signs of weakness and thus encouraged future resistance. Executions were much to be preferred, but only if they could be carried out quickly, without the possibility of inflaming local public opinion. In December he instructed Field Marshal Wilhelm Keitel, chief of the Nazi military high command, to issue a decree stating that the only adequate punishment for crimes committed against the occupying power was death; however, if the trial and execution could not be completed in a very short time, the accused person should instead be transported to Germany and forbidden all contact with the outside world: made to disappear—in the expression used by Hitler himself—"into the night and fog."

The phrase "night and fog" had been taken from the opera *Das Rheingold,* by Hitler's favorite composer, Richard Wagner. Early in the opera, Alberich, the dwarf king who dreams of conquering the world, recites a mystical incantation to render himself invisible to the slaves who work to amass his piles of gold: *"Nacht und Nebel—*

niemand gleich!" ["Night and fog—as if no one were there!"] With that, he vanishes into a column of smoke.

In the world of the Nazis, though, it was the slaves themselves who vanished. Transported out of their home countries, hidden away inside German prison camps and fortresses, the NN prisoners, as they were called—for *Nacht und Nebel*—were entirely cut off from the outside world. They were not allowed to send or receive mail; all outside requests for information about them were summarily denied. In Germany, NN prisoners could be tortured, starved, exploited, terrorized, deprived of all rights; as far as the rest of the world knew, they had simply been erased.

The Nazi military high command issued three "Night and Fog" decrees, the second of which made clear that female political prisoners were not to be executed, other than those who had been convicted of assassination or of membership in an armed organization: "The Führer desires (certainly in recalling the Edith Cavell affair of the First World War) that in principle death sentences against women in the occupied territories of the West do not take place. These women are not expressly pardoned, but the decision specifies that the execution order remains suspended until further notice."

One of those female prisoners, a young Parisienne named Monique Sisich, later wrote in her memoir *A Nightingale in the Storm:* "The decree meant that we no longer had an identity, no name, no sex, no number, only the label *NN.* No one could trace whether we were alive or dead. No information was allowed to be transmitted. We did not belong any longer to the world of the living—we were entering the world of Night and Fog."

Writing in *Nuit et brouillard à Hinzert* [*Night and Fog at Hinzert*], the historian and priest Joseph de La Martinière (who had himself been an NN prisoner during the war) noted: "In September 1942 a new category of NN transports began, to Lübeck for women and Sonnenburg for men. This time it didn't involve persons sent to Germany to be tried there, but persons already condemned by military tribunals before their departure." One of these persons was Kate Bonnefous.

On October 14, 1942, her civilian clothing is returned to her, and she is given the order to get dressed and be ready: She will be leaving Ziegenhain for the women's prison of Lübeck-Lauerhof. At the train station, the prisoners board a third-class carriage that has been converted into a *wagon cellulaire*, with two rows of cramped, cell-like cages divided by a narrow center aisle, the windows covered with wire mesh. Though Lübeck is scarcely three hundred miles from Ziegenhain, the trip takes more than two weeks; along the way, the train makes stopovers at prisons in Kassel, Hamburg, and Hanover. In each one the women are stripped naked to have their bodies examined not by guards or doctors but by common-law (that is to say, nonpolitical) prisoners; they are herded together with many other prisoners into a single large cell with no sleeping accommodations, and fed from bowls also used for washing up and doing laundry. Finally, on October 30, they arrive in Lübeck, a port city on the northern coast of Germany, fourteen miles upriver from the Baltic Sea.

Lübeck had long been regarded as the most beautiful city in northern Germany, its narrow streets lined with half-timbered medieval buildings, its town hall a jewel of Gothic brickwork, with ornate arcades and arches and the soaring copper spires of a great civic cathedral. Seven months earlier, on the night of March 28, 234 Royal Air Force bombers had unleashed a devastating raid on the city; twenty-five thousand incendiary devices fell on Lübeck that night. "A fiery parasite upon the body of a city began to writhe terribly into life," one of the pilots would note. "I saw the first flares, the target markers going down, the incendiaries budding, flowering, the short bright blossoming of the bombs."

The grim traces of burning are still vivid in Lübeck as Kate Bonnefous and the other NN prisoners view it through the windows of their train car. Though restoration work has begun, the city remains charred and broken, whole blocks gutted, walls sheared away from houses, buildings reduced to wood and stones; the windows of churches and medieval brick arcades are vacant and dark, staring out like empty eye sockets.

On the outskirts of the city, the prison of Lübeck-Lauerhof turns out to be a more modern facility than Ziegenhain, the cells fitted with a toilet and sink and narrow iron beds with thin pallets covered by sheets; there is even a small mirror and a bucket and mop. Though most of the women share cells with other prisoners, Kate Bonnefous is once again placed in solitary confinement and forbidden the daily half-hour promenade. The prisoners are made to work ten to twelve hours a day; the work is generally done inside the cell rather than in a large workroom, although the prison does have a room equipped with sewing machines for more complicated jobs. In their cells, the women learn to communicate by "writing" on the walls—that is to say, by tapping on the walls with a hard object, the number of beats corresponding to a letter of the alphabet. While functional, this method is slow and laborious, and during the promenades the newly arrived deportees learn that it is also possible to speak to one another through the toilets. To do so, one must first use the mop to remove the water in the toilet bowl; three knocks on the drainpipe alerts others along the same line to do likewise. In this way a crude but effective type of telephone can be created, with the reverberant porcelain bowls acting as receivers. The women talk to one another in voices that they can never attach to faces, but still, the news, rumors, stories that they pass along (they refer to it by the French colloquialism *"le téléphone arabe,"* something like the English "grapevine") help to make the solitude a bit more bearable.

On Christmas Day 1942, a guard comes to Kate Bonnefous's cell to inform her that she has been granted the privilege of receiving a visitor in her cell that day. She requests the young blond prisoner at the other end of the hallway.

That afternoon the young woman arrives at the cell. *"Mais, Madame,"* she asks in some confusion, *"je ne vous connais pas?"* ["But, Madame, do I know you?"]

"Yes," Kate replies. "I'm the one who whistled *'La Madelon'* at Ziegenhain."

In Lübeck, Kate had seen this young woman on a promenade and recognized her as the one she had earlier noticed at Ziegenhain; through *le téléphone arabe,* she has figured out in which cell this woman is being held.

Her name, it turns out, is Simone Harrand, and as Kate suspected, she is French (only a Frenchwoman would recognize *"La Madelon"*); she is tall and pretty, with a high forehead, striking blue eyes, and a button nose. The two women spend the afternoon talking in Kate's cell. The words come tumbling out; it is exhilarating to find a friend in such unlikely circumstances. "Lacking Champagne," Simone would recall, "we got drunk on words."

Simone is twenty-three years old, a former Catholic schoolgirl from Dijon. Before the war, she had been an activist in a left-wing Catholic organization for working-class youth, and in 1941 had joined a local underground group that aided escaped British service-men. Arrested by the Gestapo in July 1942, she went before a mili-tary tribunal and was sentenced to death and deported to Ziegenhain; she, too, has now been brought to Lübeck as an NN prisoner. De-spite her dreadful situation, Simone retains a spirited demeanor: She says that she can always sense when a guard is spying on her through the peephole of her cell; depending on her mood, she smiles or thumbs her nose or sticks her tongue out, just to show she hasn't been fooled, and afterward she feels pleased with herself, although she understands that it's a small consolation. She believes that war accomplishes nothing, other than to enrich a handful of arms manu-facturers. Her private dream is that one day all schools, everywhere, will teach the same second language—Esperanto, perhaps, or even better, sign language like that used by the deaf—so that humanity might learn how to understand itself.

More than half a century later, Simone Harrand could still recall that afternoon with Kate Bonnefous (whom she referred to as "Cath-erine," perhaps in deference to her age). She wrote: "Catherine had certainly been the first Parisian woman condemned to death. She had lived for many years in England. She spoke with a light English accent which, mixed with her Parisian accent, gave her a lot of charm. . . . We got to know each other very quickly. Very, very nice, this Catherine. On that Christmas, I was so happy to unexpectedly make the acquaintance of this intelligent woman with a strong per-sonality."

Kate can feel her body degrading from one day to the next, her hair and skin growing dull, ankles swelling from starvation and lack of circulation. Hunger is a constant torment, a powerful ache at her center that radiates outward into her muscles, causing her limbs to tremble as though she is in the grip of a wasting disease. She has developed a constant headache; her eyesight is weakening and her hands have grown numb from innumerable hours of fiddly work in insufficient lighting.

One day that fall, guards pull Kate again from her cell, but this time they bring her to a different room, where Gestapo agents are waiting for her. There she is placed in a chair, her arms and legs tied down with straps. She is familiar with the routine of interrogation, but here in Lübeck-Lauerhof, as opposed to Fort du Hâ and Cherche-Midi, she doesn't know what she has done to warrant it. One of the agents asks her to provide them with the names and addresses of all her associates. This is confusing, as the Gestapo already knows who they are—Régniez and Teyssier and Cecil Shaw and the rest—and in any case by this time they have all been arrested, one arrest following upon the last, like pearls dropping from a broken string.

The men maintain a polite tone with her, but it is a Gestapo politesse, icy, tinged with hauteur and menace. They indicate that they had not previously been aware of the impressive scale of her achievements. Apparently she and her American friend saved not twenty English soldiers, but one hundred fifty. There have been stories about it in the English papers. She is even being referred to there as "the new Nurse Cavell." The agents' voices take on a harder edge. These are serious crimes for which she has not yet assumed responsibility; the confession she gave to the Tribunal of Greater Paris turns out to have been far from complete. They are demanding information about events that she doesn't understand, people she has never met; they seem to know things about her past that she herself doesn't know. All she can do is insist on her own ignorance, which happens, in this case, to be the truth. The Gestapo men seem profoundly disappointed by her unwillingness to help. One of them approaches her; then, leaning closer, as if to confide a secret or brush away a loose hair, he punches her in the stomach. All at once she cannot breathe. He punches her again, and then again; she can feel something coming loose inside her. Instinctively she tries to ward off the blows, but her arms are tied tight. She must have been sold out by someone; someone has been making up stories about her. That sort of thing happens all the time: for money, to protect someone else, often just to avert further torture. She cannot imagine who it might be; she has been inactive for so long that she seems hardly worth the effort. What did they mean about the English papers?

After a while she realizes that the blows have stopped. She is gasping for breath. The Gestapo agents continue to ply her with questions. Once again they claim that she is an agent of British intelligence; a woman like her, she must have been in league with them, she could never have done all this on her own. She wills herself to stay silent. The men light cigarettes and sit for a moment thoughtfully smoking. The rich scent of the tobacco is agonizing; it has been so long since she had a cigarette. The rough one approaches her again, then slowly presses the lit end of his cigarette onto the back of her hand. For just an instant she feels nothing at all; then the pain arrives, excruciating at first before receding into a dull burning throb. He moves the cigarette to the other hand and presses down firmly, then returns to the first, pausing each time, examining her like a specimen on a slide. Her hands are clenched tight, nerves screaming. Still she doesn't speak. The room takes on the putrid smell of burning flesh. Then the Gestapo agent seems to make up his mind about something, and he leaves the room; when he returns he is holding a heavy iron key ring, like the kind the guards carry on their belts. He stands before her, and then, without warning, he smashes her in the face with it. Instantly the world explodes. Her mouth fills with blood, warm and thick and tasting of metal; she feels something sharp like gravel in her mouth and she knows that her front teeth have been knocked out. She struggles to hold her head up, fearing that she might drown in her own blood. The room is ringing all around her; the edges of things have grown blurry, her eyes have filled with tears.

Eventually the Gestapo agents call the guards to take her back to her cell. Before she leaves, they tell her that because she still refuses to talk, she will again receive a sentence of death. And this time she will be executed, without first being given the courtesy of a trial: She has vanished, she is a ghost, and ghosts have no need of the law.

The weeks pass, though, and still she is not taken. There are no pre-dawn footsteps in the corridor outside, no Angel of Death in hobnail boots stopping at the door of her cell. It is not possible, it turns out, to really imagine one's own death. In this case she cannot even imag-ine the lead-up to it: The Gestapo men had told her that she would be shot, but she also heard that one of the other NN prisoners at Lübeck had been sent back to Hamburg and decapitated by guillo-tine in the prison courtyard, so there is no way to know for sure. Each sunrise she is granted another twenty-four hours. It is more time in which to lose herself while knitting gloves or repairing socks, casting her mind back to childhood neighborhoods of tidy, two-story brick townhouses with flower boxes and lace curtains in the windows, and at the bottom of the hill a row of little stores—the tobacconist, the milliner, the dairy, the druggist, and, best of all, the confectioner with his displays of nougats and sugar almonds and Turkish delight, everything dressed up in silver foil and frilly colored paper: memo-ries of a sort to carry one across time and distance, back to a place that seemed manifestly worth fighting for.

The high window of her cell allows a glimpse of sky; from her cot she can watch the changing of the light. She is not the same as be-fore, will no longer be the same. Her mouth aches all the time now; there are wide gaps between her teeth, ugly and irregular and indica-tive of violence, like vacant lots on a bombed-out block. It's difficult to eat even the soup they serve in the prison, with its undercooked chunks of potato or turnip. Her stomach hurts as well, sometimes with sharp pangs, but always irritated and sour, as though a bag of foul liquid has burst inside her.

By the end of 1943, the NN prisoners can sense that the guards believe the war is turning against them. Just forty miles away, in Hamburg, tens of thousands of civilians have been killed in a single night. British and American bombers drop thousands of tons of high-explosive and incendiary bombs on the city, the ratio precisely calculated for maximum damage; a tornado of fire rises a quarter of a mile into the night sky, an apocalyptic vision worthy of the mis-sion's code name: Operation Gomorrah. New prisoners are arriving constantly; the overcrowding is such that for the first time Kate is made to share her cell with several other women. One of the more recently arrived NN prisoners, a young poet and music-hall artist named Maria Pinson, had been imprisoned in Hamburg during the bombing there; she vividly describes the shuddering walls, the trees turned into torches, the terrified cries of the women who think they will be burned alive inside their cells. Soon the Allied bombardments reach the vicinity of Lübeck. The prisoners can hear the explosions, sometimes once a week, sometimes several nights in a row, especially during times of a full moon; through their cell windows they see the orange glow of distant fires, watch with horror as pulsating streams of antiaircraft fire burst into white carnations in the night sky.

In March 1944, it is announced that the NN prisoners will be transported farther east. Some of the prisoners will be sent to the prison at Cottbus, southeast of Berlin; some will be sent to the prison at Jauer, in the Lower Silesia region of western Poland. In April the convoys out of Lübeck begin.

On April 28, 1944, Kate Bonnefous is officially declared an NN prisoner, in a secret decision handed down by the Military Tribunal of Kiel, one of five special courts overseen by the Gestapo to handle Nacht und Nebel cases. Less than two weeks later she is selected for removal to Jauer. The women who are to be transported have their valises, money, and other possessions returned to them, and in the early morning of May 9, they are assembled in the shower room and divided into groups for the two destinations. It is strange to see all of the women in their civilian clothing, wearing whatever they happened to have on at the time of their arrest, colorful dresses, cardigans, slingback shoes, handbags, jewelry; some have even applied lipstick for the journey. Thirty women—eighteen Frenchwomen, ten Belgians, a Norwegian, and a Polish Jew—are being sent to Jauer. They are each given a food packet containing a few slices of bread, and then they climb into the back of farm wagons and try to make themselves comfortable for the first leg of the trip, some 250 miles to the city of Stettin, on the Oder River near the border with Poland.

In Stettin the women are taken off the wagons, to board a train heading south toward Jauer. By this time Kate has been held incommunicado for nearly three years, and she is desperate to find a way to contact her loved ones, to let them know that she is still alive. In the train station at Stettin, she notices a railroad worker who appears to be French. When the guards are not looking, she manages to attract his attention; then, quickly and quietly, she entreats him to send a message to her attorney in Paris. The workman is named Jean Favre, and he is a demobilized soldier who has been deported to Germany as one of thousands of forced laborers. That same day, May 9, he sends a postal card—affixed with two Adolf Hitler postage stamps—to Maître Georges Herr at 20 avenue de l'Opéra, with a message in French on the back. "Monsieur," he writes,

> Working today at the train station of Stettin, I had the occasion to make the acquaintance of Mme. Bonnefous, transferred from Lübeck to Jauer, near Breslau in Silesia, to work in a camp. She was part of a convoy of Frenchwomen. Not having been able to speak freely and at length, she nonetheless asked me to reassure you. Her health and morale are excellent and she hopes to see you again soon. Being myself an exile I am happy to have been able to render her this little service.

27

MORE THAN FIVE HUNDRED years old, the castle of Jauer is a grim, massive structure with crenellated stone walls dotted with shooting holes, and high iron gates, and even the remains of a moat; embellished with turrets and corner bastions and a brick clock tower, it is almost perfectly triangular in shape, surrounding a cobblestoned interior courtyard graced by a single large chestnut tree. In the early days of World War II, the Nazi prison administration had estimated that the castle could hold 471 prisoners, but as the war goes on, and resistance grows, so too does the prison population, and by the time of Kate Bonnefous's arrival in May, more than fifteen hundred women are being held there, both NN and common-law prisoners; an additional one hundred prisoners assigned to the castle live elsewhere, in a factory in the nearby city of Schweidnitz, where they perform forced labor for the German electrical firm Siemens. Several storerooms in the attic of the castle have been turned into communal dormitories, and the cellar and first and second floors contain large workrooms.

Each of the workrooms holds from one hundred to two hundred prisoners, all dressed in the same long black cotton dress with vertical orange stripes, on their feet a pair of almost comically large, bulky wooden clogs. They sit on backless benches at tables of twelve, six on a side, forbidden to get up or to speak, working from seven in the morning until seven at night. The only break comes at noon, when they are sent out in shifts for a half-hour promenade in the interior courtyard; the women are required to walk single file and in total silence, keeping two yards' distance from each other and holding their hands behind their backs. When the promenade is over, they return to the workroom for a lunch of soup and bread; as the prison is a Christian facility, the meal is followed by a prayer, one of four mandated for the day.

The rooms are overseen by a staff of professional female guards, each one fearsome and grotesque in her own manner, and each known among the prisoners by her own unflattering nickname. One of them, "*la Naine*" [the Dwarf], originally from the Transylvania region of Romania, stands four feet ten inches tall and has hair dyed jet black pulled back into a tight bun. Renate Lasker, a German writer and one of Jauer's few Jewish prisoners, would recall of her after the war: "That woman, whose German was no more than rudimentary, and who had inherited the virulent anti-Semitism that has always been a feature of certain sections of the population of Romania, concentrated her venom on me. She never missed an opportunity to taunt me with my imminent death in a gas chamber." Most brutal of all is Frau Hartmann, known simply as "*la Terreur.*" More than sixty years old, perpetually red-faced and seemingly fueled by pure rage, she screams at the prisoners from morning until night and takes every opportunity to beat them for even the smallest infraction of the rules. One Belgian inmate described her as "especially distinguished by her sadism, her wickedness. . . . [She] took a malign pleasure in withholding food, making us eat in five minutes, prolonging the promenades whenever it rained. She attacked especially the ill and the aged."

As in Ziegenhain, a prisoner is only permitted to go to the bathroom when her table is selected to do so. "Numerous women are suffering from dysentery," one prisoner reports, "and a too-long delay provokes dramas. The guards curse, the unfortunates are humiliated, but no care is provided to them." Another will observe later, "We had to adjust our intestines to the caprices of the guards." The prisoners knit string bags, weave camouflage netting, sew pieces of felt into slippers; the air in the windowless room is filled with dust and particles that sting the eyes and nose and work their way into the lungs. In the evening, after soup and prayer, the women stand and walk silently in double lines to their dormitories. Well into springtime the rooms beneath the eaves of the castle are cold and damp, and most of the women sleep fully clothed, beneath blankets that seem to provide no warmth. "After a few days of this regime," one of the prisoners will recall, "several are coughing and end up with tuberculosis. The others will have rheumatism long before they get old."

By 1944 more than four hundred Nacht und Nebel prisoners are being held in Jauer, most of them French and Belgian, with a scattering of other nationalities. They are teachers, nurses, scientists, factory workers, artists, poets, nuns. Like Kate, many entered the Resistance by sheltering escaped British and French soldiers; later they produced false identification papers, wrote and distributed clandestine newspapers, transported money and arms, passed military intelligence to London. As political people, they understand the importance of maintaining group morale, and on Sunday evenings, when prisoners are permitted to return to their dormitories at five o'clock, they conduct talks on issues of politics and history and perform comic playlets that the writers among them have jotted down on sheets of toilet paper (the paper, a precious resource at Jauer, is returned to the bathroom after the play has been performed). Sometimes they act out *tableaux vivants* based on famous paintings; once, to commemorate the July Revolution of 1830, they choose *Liberty Leading the People,* by Eugène Delacroix, with the young French communist Léone Bourgineau playing the role of Liberty, nude but for a carefully draped sheet. "There was a real spirit of camaraderie," Bourgineau will recall years later, "not only between those from different countries, but between groups with different beliefs. The guards were always surprised, when they undertook a search, to find all the things we had fabricated. We even made hair curlers."

On occasion a sympathetic guard passes a newspaper to a prisoner, and at night someone will translate it aloud for the others, with commentary on the meaning of the recent events. Lying hungry on their straw pallets, the women share recipes for *canard à l'orange,* fruit tarts, stews as made by various mothers and grandmothers. On

Christmas Eve, huddled in their blankets, they sing canticles before a crèche molded out of old newspapers and populated by the Holy Family and the animals of the manger, woven from pieces of string and fabric that the women smuggled out of the workrooms.

The winter of 1944–45 arrives unusually early, bringing with it an especially intense cold: For the NN prisoners, the only consolation is the deepening conviction that this will be their last winter in captivity. In their unheated attic dormitories, they often snuggle together on a single straw pallet, taking turns rubbing one another's backs to keep warm; the rooms are so cold that the water in their metal jugs freezes overnight, and the layer of ice must be broken before the women can wash themselves. They are provided no additional clothing for the winter, and the outdoor promenades proceed as always, the prisoners making their half-hour turns of the courtyard dressed only in their thin cotton dresses and wooden clogs. The cobblestones are icy and slick, difficult to walk on with hands clasped behind backs; if one of the women is deemed to be walking too slowly, the guards beat her on the legs and feet with their steel truncheons. If, as sometimes happens, a prisoner succumbs to hunger or illness or exhaustion and collapses, the guards forbid the others to give her any assistance: She must remain lying on the ground until she regains consciousness and can pick herself up. Only on the rarest of occasions is an NN prisoner admitted to the hospital infirmary. Fever alone is not sufficient grounds for admittance, and often a prisoner who is examined and deemed to be in good health is deprived of food and sent to the cellar dungeon for "having bothered the doctor."

That winter Kate Bonnefous develops bronchitis, which she attributes to the forced promenades in freezing weather and which will trouble her for the rest of her life. The guards, she says later, "looked for every opportunity to push us or beat us." By this time Kate is both ill and aged, and as such she has become one of Frau Hartmann's favorite victims. Once, after she has been reprimanded for walking too slowly, the guards throw her to the ground, dislocating one of her hips, and then punch and kick her unmercifully; at war's end, doctors examining her will diagnose a displaced kidney, damaged lumbar vertebrae, and a bruised colon. On a second occasion, the guards beat her so badly that she is left with a broken instep in one foot.

Because of that injury, Kate is not among the more than one thousand prisoners who are evacuated from Jauer on January 28, 1945. Earlier that month, Soviet troops had launched a massive offensive, and by the third week of January units of the 1st Ukrainian Front have reached Upper Silesia. The prison is now in a state of uproar. Many of the German common-law prisoners are abruptly released. The prisoners working at the Siemens factory in nearby Schweidnitz are recalled to Jauer; they bring news that the German population of Breslau is fleeing at the approach of the Russians. The women begin to hope that the Germans will not have time to evacuate the prison. It is an inviolable principle of the Nazi regime that Nacht und Nebel prisoners must never be allowed to fall into the hands of the enemy; Heinrich Himmler himself has ordered prison evacuations in the face of the advancing Red Army. Soon officers of the SS, the Nazi paramilitary force, have arrived at the castle to oversee the imminent departure. On January 22, the prison's chief of work reads aloud a list of 121 French and Belgian prisoners who will be sent on a hastily improvised rail trip to the Ravensbrück concentration camp; smaller convoys depart for other prison camps to the north and west. One week later, nearly all of the remaining prisoners are made ready to march: The prison is emptying out.

All through the day and well into the evening, groups of women are sent to the basement storeroom to recover their civilian clothing. Upon returning, some report that they have seen German guards in the courtyard, tossing papers into a bonfire. Somehow the rumor spreads that the prisoners will have to walk fifteen kilometers, perhaps even twenty, to get to the railroad station where a train is waiting for them. The very idea seems preposterous—most of the women are weak and undernourished and have trouble enough with just a half-hour promenade. Outside, snow has begun to fall; that night, the thermometer in the courtyard will register a Celsius temperature of 25 degrees below zero, 13 below on the Fahrenheit scale.

In the attic dormitories, the women prepare for the journey. Many of them—those arrested during the warmer months—have only lightweight clothing, hardly adequate for a long trek in snowy, subzero weather. A young prisoner named Agnès Leroy, who comes from a farm family near Reims, has a valise full of warm clothing that her mother brought her when she was in La Santé prison in Paris. She distributes extra sweaters and socks to those who need them, as well as pairs of knitted wool gloves, intended for the German army, that over time she has smuggled out of the workrooms. Dinner that night consists of a soup that is noticeably thicker than usual; later, guards arrive with the news that those who will be making the journey the next morning have been authorized to receive an extra blanket from the storeroom. A Norwegian prisoner shows the others how to slice the blankets up into strips, which are then wrapped from foot to calf like a large bandage; these booties, she promises, will keep their feet from developing frostbite during the march.

Sleep that night is almost impossible. The brick clock tower sounds the reveille at five A.M. Silently, shivering in the unheated rooms, the women emerge from beneath their blankets and prepare themselves for the day ahead. Down the hall, they each receive a half loaf of bread, a slice of sausage, and two tablespoons' worth of margarine; despite their hunger, they know that they must save some of the food for later on, when they will need it. Before long they have said their goodbyes to the women who will be left behind. "It is heartbreaking to abandon them," notes one of the Belgian prisoners.

By six o'clock, just before departure, hundreds of women have gathered in the communal hall of the castle; many of them are on their knees, heads bowed in silent prayer. The prison chaplain addresses them, his words echoing in the large, silent room. "You are setting out into very great peril," he says gravely. "For some of you, this will be the end of your sufferings. Have courage. Be strong. Your life will be in danger, and so I treat you as I do soldiers leaving for combat. I grant you all a general absolution."

Kate Bonnefous is still upstairs, with some two dozen other French and Belgian NN prisoners who have difficulty walking; eventually guards arrive to lead them to the infirmary, where the most seriously ill prisoners are held. Among them is a Catholic nun, Joséphine Krebs, known as Soeur Élisabeth; part of an escape network in Lorraine, she had been one of the very first female prisoners deported to Germany, like Kate Bonnefous, in 1941. The forty-nine-year-old prisoner Osithe Docquier is there with her daughter, twenty-five-year-old Henriette, with whom she had worked on the Pat O'Leary escape line; once lively and vivacious, now Henriette has contracted tuberculosis and is feverish and coughing up blood.

Locked inside the infirmary, the prisoners cannot help but feel a sense of shame in having been left behind, in having been judged, even by the Nazis, as too weak to join their comrades. It has been a very long time since any of them had use of a mirror, but they can see themselves reflected in one another's ghastly appearances. Their bodies look shrunken inside their clothing; the glow of the lamplight finds new shadows in their gaunt faces. Unexpectedly, two young prisoners—one of them the farm girl from Reims, Agnès Leroy—suddenly appear in the infirmary; having taken pity on "this poor cohort," they have decided that they will stay and help care for Soeur Élisabeth and the others. Two guards in the communal hall have agreed to this, but the guard on duty in the infirmary chases them away and the two take their places at the end of the line of march. Inside the infirmary, the prisoners are in a state approaching despair: They do not know what is to become of them. "We were twenty or so women truly in the hands of the Germans," Madeline Dubois, a teacher and union activist, will recall. "We were as good as dead there! What discouragement—we remained, while our companions had departed. They were doubtlessly on their way to deliverance."

A ragged line of more than one thousand women moves slowly through the darkened streets of Jauer; many have blankets wrapped around their heads like monks' cowls. Some of the Frenchwomen among them had been humming *"La Marseillaise"* as they passed through the gates of the prison, but soon that melody died away and the early morning was almost silent but for the soft crunch of feet on frozen snow.

The cold is so intense that it seems to have weight, force; it penetrates their meager clothing and burrows deep into their bones. After just a few moments their lungs are burning; their breath steams and rises in the frigid air. Before long day has broken, but the sun on the horizon seems no longer able to generate warmth, nor reveal color.

Dark clothing, white snow, gray sky: It is like living inside the world of a black-and-white movie. They leave the town behind and begin making their way through the winter countryside. Some of the women have looped belts onto the handles of their valises and are pulling them like children's sleds through the snow. Those who are not wearing gloves find that the skin on their hands is already beginning to freeze; a few of the women have little bottles of oil among their possessions, and they give the oil to their comrades to rub on their hands. A frigid wind sweeps across the fields, stinging their cheeks and filling their eyes with tears. Snowflakes freeze on eyebrows and lashes; dripping noses create tiny icicles. Their feet begin to tingle, then ache, then seem to petrify. Some of the women walk in pairs, holding each other up: To fall in the snow under these conditions, they know, would be catastrophic. Alongside the line of march, trucks carry German soldiers; now and again one of the trucks dispenses a new squad of SS guards, male and female, as well as rifle-carrying members of the Hitler Youth, some of whom appear to be no older than children. The guards walk up and down the line, shouting constantly at the women to keep moving; a single word of response brings a slap to the head, a revolver pulled from a holster.

Occasionally the column is forced to halt, due to an obstruction up ahead. At each stopping point, some of the women take the opportunity to abandon their suitcases, unable to carry them any farther. Pockets can be filled, though, or an apron turned into a cloth bag, and while the line remains stationary they must perform a hurried triage, deciding which objects—photographs, letters, medicine, a prayer book, a hairbrush—they might still bring with them. The roadside comes to resemble the scene of a shipwreck. German soldiers rummage through the belongings like jackals at a kill, looking for anything that might be of value.

One of the women had been operated on only a few days earlier and has not yet fully recovered. She is helped along by other prisoners, but eventually the walking causes her wound to reopen; weak and bleeding, she finally collapses. *"Partez,"* she tells her companions, *"laissez-moi"* ["Go, leave me"]. They have no choice but to leave her on the frozen ground, where they are sure she will die. The marchers who fall are kicked and beaten by the SS guards; those who are still unable to rise are left by the side of the road like bundles of old clothing, until they are picked up by a dump truck, driven by German civilians, that follows along at the end of the line.

After ten kilometers of walking, or just over six miles, the women are allowed to stop at a farm for half an hour. They use the opportunity to eat some of the bread they received that morning. Many have carried the bread inside their blouse, where it is warmed by their body; those who put the bread in their bags discover to their horror that it is frozen and cannot be eaten.

By afternoon it is apparent that they have already covered more than fifteen kilometers, more even than twenty; no longer can they hold to the reassuring notion that this is simply a walk to a train station. Now there is no destination in sight; now they are just marching, trapped in a ceaseless, infernal rhythm, prisoners on a road where the only end point is death.

When, long after dark, the women are finally herded into an abandoned brick factory, they have walked for thirty kilometers—nearly twenty miles. Inside the factory they are given only a bit of water, no soup, no warming drink of any kind. Those whose bread had frozen earlier in the day find that it has still not thawed; they have no choice but to lie on the bread that night to defrost it. The women huddle together on the cold factory floor, hugging one another like lovers to gain what little warmth their bodies can still produce. For many, the hours of glacial cold have dried out their bodies, producing a kind of colic, and the room is filled with the sound of raspy coughing. Some women are crying from the agony of blood returning to frozen fingers and toes; some cry from hunger, or out of simple misery. It is almost impossible to sleep amid such pain and despair.

There are no restrooms in the factory, only slop buckets; to get to the buckets the women have to step over bodies in the darkness, and they do the best they can, but fatigue makes them unsteady and they often stumble over one another. Howls of protest rise up from the floor, accompanied by insults in several languages. More than anything the prisoners are howling at their own hunger, at their pain and exhaustion and powerlessness, at the hovering presence of death that crowds the room, but the shouting back and forth is directed at indi-

viduals, and before long, some of the German common-law prisoners have begun to shove and threaten the French and Belgian NN
prisoners, until finally one young German communist stands up and
makes a plea for calm and discipline. Her words are translated into
French by Elisabeth Dussauze, the former Paris chief of the Combat
resistance network, who is fluent in three languages. *We are all prisoners,* the young German exhorts her countrywomen; *there are no longer
Germans, nor Poles, nor Russians or French or Belgians, but only prisoners, only unfortunates who have to fight together and help one another.*
Her passionate appeal is received with applause all around, and with
that, order is restored.

In the morning, the women set out once again on the line of
march. This is their life now, they are coming to understand: walking
hour after hour, one day upon the next, until it seems that this is
what they have always done, what they will always do. In the mornings, they receive a cup of ersatz coffee with a small piece of bread,
sometimes accompanied by a bit of margarine; at noon, a clear soup
in which one can find traces of rutabaga or cabbage; at night, again,
coffee and bread. They sleep in whatever shelter the Germans can
find along the way, usually a barn or some other outbuilding. The
nights are a kind of inventory of suffering. The intense cold has laid
siege to their bodies: Fingernails are falling off, the skin on their legs
tears off in shreds, ulcerated blisters cover their feet. Hips and backs
ache, toes and ankles are bloodied. One night, the Belgian poet
Rosemonde Peeters removes her boots and discovers that her stockings have stuck to her feet.

Each day their number decreases slightly: Some of the women
have died, a few seem to have escaped. After four days of marching,
the common-law prisoners are led off in another direction, and the
NN prisoners continue the route on their own. One night they stay
on a working farm, where they are given the luxury of bedding down
in the warm straw with the sows and their piglets.

The landscape here is pristine, austere, marked by great white ex-
panses, majestic firs heavy with snow: Under other circumstances, it
could be seen as beautiful. Sometimes, in the distance, a clock tower
or a set of small houses will come into view; passing through the vil-

lage, the women try to barter with the inhabitants, trading whatever they have left for food. This is the new mathematics of starvation: One silk dress is equal to one loaf of bread.

Over time, hunger and thirst and fatigue give rise to hallucinations. One afternoon some of the women see the strangest spectacle of all: a pair of camels walking calmly through the snow, with soldiers singing behind them. Yet this is not a hallucination; this is the evacuation of a local circus.

On another day in February, when the women have been on the road for nearly two weeks, a *résistante* from Lorraine, Lucie Primot, is walking alongside a young Parisienne named Andrée. Passing behind a farmhouse, they see a dead pigeon lying on a pile of manure. Half-crazed with hunger, Andrée rushes for the bird and begins to devour it without even removing the feathers. The pigeon has already begun to decompose, and Lucie Primot shouts at her not to eat it, but Andrée, oblivious or uncaring, does not stop. In a matter of days she has grown feverish and delirious, and black spots have appeared on her body, like those from a medieval plague; within the week she is dead.

Finally, in the town of Löbau in eastern Germany, the women are led to a train station, where they are put aboard a train bound southwest to Bavaria. More than two hundred women are crowded into three third-class carriages; those of the first and second class are reserved for German soldiers and civilians. As there is not a place for everyone, the younger and sturdier prisoners are hoisted into the baggage nets overhead; others pile under the benches or stand crammed together in the aisles. The third-class carriages contain only bare wooden benches, and sitting on them is difficult, as by now the women are so thin that their bones seem to pierce their skin. The train windows are locked shut, and as time goes on the air inside the carriage becomes nearly unbreathable.

The train rolls on, day after day, through a seemingly endless progression of little stations. Many of the women are suffering from dysentery and run a high fever; they moan, cry out for water, but the water in the bathroom is unclean and must be boiled before drinking. Some begin to hallucinate; it seems they will die of thirst amid a landscape covered with snow. "To survive," Lucie Primot recalls, "we commit the unthinkable: We drink our own urine, gathered in our cupped hands, as if in offering." Finally, at one of the stations, the women are given bread and cups of hot water in which float indefinable bits of roots and leaves; some are no longer able to swallow the bread, and others sit beside them, providing sips of water.

One afternoon, passing along a hillside, a siren unexpectedly sounds and without explanation the train comes to a halt. Fifteen minutes pass with no movement. The women are locked inside their carriages, but many of the Germans aboard the train become impatient and step down onto the platform. Suddenly a low purring can be heard in the sky, almost indefinable at first but growing steadily louder; in a few moments five planes have appeared in the distance. They are American fighter planes, and as they draw nearer they begin to descend. All at once the earth around the train explodes; the air is filled with shouts and cries and the shriek of shredding metal. The Germans on the platform make a dash for a nearby copse of fir trees, but the strafing pursues them from the air. Piled atop one another in their third-class carriages, the women lie petrified in terror; it is almost impossible to believe that after enduring so much suffering, they will be killed by their own men. They hear bursts of machine-gun fire, the high-pitched whistle of bullets, the bang of antiaircraft guns coming from the woods. Three times the planes circle back to continue the attack; finally, after what seems an eternity, they roar off and the air is silent once more.

Later, after the medical personnel have arrived, it is possible to survey the damage. The three third-class carriages are the only ones to have been spared; attached to the locomotive at the front of the train, they were shielded by the hillside, while the cars to the rear were all hit, their roofs badly pockmarked by bullet holes—"transformed into colanders," one of the NN prisoners will observe. Not a single injury is recorded among the French and Belgians, but ten Germans lie dead, with dozens more wounded.

The next afternoon, the damaged train rolls into the station at Aichach, a town in central Bavaria. At last the carriage doors are opened and the women, nearly paralyzed by stiffness, stagger down onto the platform. No trucks or other trains are waiting for them. The SS guards arrange the women into ranks of four, and once more—they cannot believe this is true—they are ordered to set off into the snow.

The inhabitants of Aichach shake their heads in pity at the sight of what Louise de Landsheere, a Belgian *résistante*, will call "our cortege of misery." Haggard, emaciated, arms and legs wrapped in shreds of blanket, the women drag themselves through the streets as best they can. Nearly a mile on, they arrive at another walled fortress, this one made of pale yellow stone with a steeply arched red roof: the women's prison of Aichach. It is four o'clock in the afternoon, February 22, 1945; their long journey has finally come to an end.

Two hundred fifty Nacht und Nebel prisoners had set out from Jauer in the early-morning hours of January 28, 1945; twenty-six days later, two hundred twenty-two women arrived at Aichach. Five had died en route; eight were left in the lazaretto of Görlitz; fifteen managed to escape.

In all, the women walked nearly 200 kilometers—about 125 miles— through snow and ice and the bitterest cold, under armed guard, with little sleep and almost nothing to eat and drink, all the while consumed by pain and ravaged by illness. The Aichach women's prison was liberated by American troops on April 28; after the liberation, several of the prisoners gave testimonies to interrogators, and in the years to come a few would even publish memoirs of their experiences. Still, the extraordinarily difficult and courageous march of the women of Jauer was little known even then and today is scarcely remembered at all, other than among the families of the survivors. Five decades later, one of those survivors, Simone Monier, née Harrand— the very woman with whom Kate Bonnefous spent Christmas Day 1942—would produce a wartime memoir entitled *Un grain de sable* [*A Grain of Sand*], in which she noted that she now had ten grandchildren: They were, she said, her revenge against the Nazis.

28

K ATE BONNEFOUS IS ONE of about one hundred prisoners left behind at Jauer, some two dozen of them French and Belgian Nacht und Nebel prisoners and the rest common-law prisoners from Germany and other nations. After the evacuation of Jauer on January 28, the remaining NN prisoners are removed from the infirmary and taken to their own workroom. Though little work remains to be done, the women must sit at the worktables under the surveillance of one of the few guards who have not yet left the castle.

The women spend their days idle in the workroom, their nights locked inside the freezing attic of the nearly empty prison. "We were living in a fever of waiting," one of the NN prisoners, Jeanne Valentin, will recall later that year. By February 12, it has been sixteen days since the prison cleared out, sixteen days of an existence poised somewhere between liberation and death. That night, the lights in the attic suddenly go out: The electricity for the castle has been cut. Then the walls begin to shake from the concussive force of nearby explosions; it seems that the roof will collapse, that the women will be buried alive inside that ancient castle, their bodies to be unearthed one day, Pompeii-like, trapped in anguished postures of terror and disbelief. Soon a handful of guards storm into the room; barking commands—"*Schnell! Schnell!*"—they herd the prisoners down into one of the cellar workrooms, then lock the doors behind them. The common-law prisoners have been locked in the room next door; the NN prisoners can hear shouts in German coming from there. After some time, they realize that the noises above them have died out, the last of the guards having abandoned the castle.

All that night, the NN prisoners huddle together under the worktables, listening to the rolling thunder of the bombs. Although it is cold and damp and dark, unmistakably tomb-like inside that room dug into the earth, and though their bodies are racked by hunger and illness and exhaustion, it is impossible for the women not to feel a sense of anticipation, even hope, in thinking of the transports that will soon be speeding them homeward. Sometime after daybreak, the silence of the castle is broken by a great crash; then they hear the thud of boots above them, unintelligible voices, the sounds of glass smashing and heavy furniture being overturned. The Red Army has entered Jauer Castle. At once the women begin calling for help, pounding their wooden clogs against the workroom door, doing whatever they can to speed their moment of liberation.

A group of soldiers clomp down the stairs to the cellar, the noise stopping at the room in which the common-law prisoners are being held. The NN prisoners can hear locks being smashed with rifle butts, followed by a roar of excitement as the doors open and the soldiers pour into the workroom. They await the joyful sounds of rescue, but somehow that is not what emerges, as shortly the men's shouts and laughter are joined by higher-pitched cries of pain and confusion and terror, a sustained, anguished howling that Madeline Dubois would later describe as "Dantesque." The NN prisoners listen helplessly, and with growing horror, to the unfolding of a scenario that they had not previously contemplated, one in which the liberators themselves are the victimizers; and in despair the women realize that they will have to defend themselves once more, and they take cover as best they can beneath worktables and in whatever distant corners of the room they can find, and wait in the darkness, barely breathing, for whatever new horrors may lie in store, while still clinging to the hope that the Russian soldiers will not treat them as they have the common-law prisoners. The women next door, after all, are mainly German, and despite their status as prisoners, might still be viewed by the Russians as the enemy; they, on the other hand, are Allied citizens and political prisoners of the highest classification, who had fought the Nazis just as the Russians had, who had risked their lives and sacrificed their bodies for freedom, which after so long seems finally within their grasp.

Then there is a banging at their own workroom doors, and after some moments the doors are flung open and with whoops of triumph the shock troops of Marshal Ivan Konev's 52nd Army surge into the room. They look nothing like the clean-cut, strong-jawed heroes of the Soviet propaganda posters; these soldiers are, for the most part, unshaven and ill-clad, wearing oil-soaked, mismatched uniforms (including some looted bowlers and top hats, which add a surrealistic touch to the scene) with submachine guns strapped around their chests, and they reek of sweat and smoke and especially of alcohol, some of them still swigging from bottles of Silesian vodka and schnapps they have picked up along the way.

The majority of the soldiers are of Mongolian origin, and they speak neither French nor English nor German; nor do they have an interpreter with them, but that seems not to matter, as they have no interest in communication. There may be dozens of them, there may be hundreds, it's impossible to tell amid the frenzied, chaotic scene, but together they form a wild throng apparently bent on some sort of vengeance, and they pull the women out from their hiding places, disregarding their shrieks and cries or simply laughing at them, tearing clothes and slapping and beating those who offer any resistance, throwing themselves on their victims as in a hideous grotesquerie of love and combat. From the hallway, crude torches made from burning rags cast an eerie flickering light on the bodies thrashing about on the floor. In one part of the room Soeur Élisabeth is struggling with the man on top of her, trying to fight him off with one hand while brandishing a crucifix with the other; Osithe Docquier is doing everything she can to protect Henriette, finally locking her inside a closet, in the vain hope that her daughter might escape the attentions of the rampaging liberators.

"We had long dreamed of such a beautiful deliverance," Madeline

Dubois would later observe, "and now here we were before the atrocious reality."

None of the NN prisoners are to be spared, neither the ill nor the aged—indeed, that comprises all the women there, the ones whom the Nazis had deemed unfit to take part in the evacuation of the castle, the weakest tenth of the prison population as a whole. Kate Bonnefous herself is fifty-eight years old, and she has been a prisoner for more than three years. In that time her foot has been broken, her teeth shattered, vertebrae and internal organs damaged, and she has been reduced to something of a walking skeleton. "They arrived absolutely dead drunk," she will attest at war's end, "and for eight days, the elderly women were violated along with the young ones."

In all, Kate Bonnefous is in the hands of the Soviet army for three weeks; later, she will say that she would rather have been a prisoner of the Germans for another six months.

Eyewitness accounts of Soviet war crimes in Silesia are legion, and while each has its own particular horrors, they all share the dreadful, surreal, disjointed quality of a nightmare. The stories are saturated with blood, lit by flames, strewn with corpses, filled with the keening of grief-stricken women, the wailing of children wandering dazed and alone in the snow. That terrible period has been called the "Silesian inferno," and Dante's journey into the underworld does provide a ready analogy for what must have seemed, to those who experienced it, a visitation of hell on earth.

It was a terror spree that ultimately stretched all the way to Berlin, a lawless outpouring of rape and murder and pillage that beggars even the lowest imagination. Often whole families were slaughtered if any of them offered the slightest bit of resistance in acquiescing to the soldiers' demands (in an especially cruel flourish, at some of the more remote farmhouses the soldiers would leave a single infant or old man alive to fend for himself); often every woman and girl in a village was raped, with no exception made for the ill or the incapacitated, or the very old, or the very young. In one village, when a desperate mother refused to hand over her thirteen-year-old daughter, a

Soviet soldier promptly shot dead thirty-six of her neighbors. In the town of Kanth, near Breslau, a woman was raped for hours by Russian soldiers. "I kept wanting to hang myself," she would later attest, "but I didn't have the chance because Russians kept coming in and out of the house." In Rogau, more than sixty men were shot against the wall of the church; the priest's cook, who was sixty-eight years old, was then raped by a group of soldiers in broad daylight in the town square. In Dyhernfurth, nuns were raped in their convent; the coffins in the church vault were broken open and the bones scattered everywhere. In Schiedlow, a group of twenty soldiers stood in line to rape the corpse of an elderly woman. "They were shouting and laughing their heads off while waiting to satisfy themselves over a lifeless body," reported one observer. "It was the most horrible thing I have ever seen."

Alcohol is present in virtually all of these accounts. "There's schnapps and spirits," a 1st Ukrainian Front soldier wrote home cheerfully, "we drink each day, each man as much as he needs and as much as his heart desires." Like a swarm of locusts methodically stripping a field of its corn or potato plants, the advancing Soviet soldiers plundered all the taverns, inns, beer halls, shops, and wine cellars in their path—even seizing alcohol-based chemicals from laboratories and factories. "The worst mistake of the German military authorities had been their refusal to destroy alcohol stocks in the path of the Red Army's advance," the British historian Antony Beevor observed in *The Fall of Berlin 1945*, which amply documented war crimes committed by Soviet armies in Europe. "This decision was based on the idea that a drunken enemy could not fight. Tragically for the female population, however, it was exactly what Red Army soldiers seemed to need to give them courage to rape as well as to celebrate the end of such a terrible war."

"Courage to rape," of course, is a deeply problematic phrase; it might instead be said that the widespread abuse of alcohol among Soviet soldiers helped to remove the social constraints that would otherwise have deterred such behavior, while also inflaming a sense of bloodlust and giving vent to their rage over German crimes committed against fellow Russians. "From the individual soldier's point of view," the German historian Miriam Gebhardt wrote in *Crimes Unspoken: The Rape of German Women at the End of the Second World War,*

> there were immediate grounds for justifying such behavior. One such ground was the motive of revenge for crimes committed by the German Wehrmacht and the entire Nazi system: revenge for the invasion of their homeland and the attacks on their families; revenge for their own dead soldiers, for shot partisans, murdered prisoners of war and slave laborers; revenge for the other victims like Jews and other persecuted groups whom the Red Army soldiers encountered as they liberated the camps; revenge for the pain and horror experienced by the soldiers themselves, particularly in the last weeks of senseless resistance by the Germans; and of course revenge for rapes by German soldiers.

So men inflict violence on women as revenge for the violence inflicted by other men on other women.

In her essay "Rape as a Weapon of War," the philosopher Claudia Card observed that "martial rape"—that is, rape during wartime—is an ancient practice, meant to display, produce, and maintain dominance not only over female victims but also over the men socially connected to them. "Martial rape," she wrote, "is a practice defined by unwritten rules (for example, the rules that only females are 'fair game,' that age does not matter, that soldiers who rape 'enemy women' are not to be reported for it, that anonymous publicity of it may be desirable)." All of these criteria apply to the case of the Soviets in 1945; still, revenge against Germany can by no means explain the full scope of the savagery. It is reliably estimated that more than one million women were raped by Soviet soldiers in the regions of East Prussia, Pomerania, and Silesia. By no means were they all of German extraction—nor did Soviet soldiers evince much interest in ascertaining a potential victim's origins before raping her or pay much attention when a woman protested that she was, say, Polish rather than German. Nor would revenge explain the rape of non-German prisoners liberated from concentration camps or, as at Jauer, from fortress prisons. Antony Beevor acknowledged that he was "shaken to the core" when he discovered the existence of such rapes, as it "completely undermined" the all-encompassing notion that Soviet soldiers were simply using rape as a form of revenge against the Germans.

While Soviet leaders did issue perfunctory orders against such atrocities (although the NKVD, the Soviet secret police, punished soldiers far less often for committing rape than for contracting a venereal disease as a result of it), they also took pains to minimize their seriousness or even to excuse them as the harmless, predictable revelry of war-weary soldiers. Once, after a Yugoslav communist protested to Joseph Stalin about rapes and looting in his country, Stalin exploded to an aide, "Can't he understand it if a soldier who has crossed thousands of kilometers through blood and fire and death has fun with a woman or takes some trifle?" While acknowledging to a British journalist that rape was widespread in the newly conquered territories, a Soviet army major attributed it simply to soldiers having been too long without female companionship. "Our fellows were so sex-starved," he explained, "that they often raped old women of sixty, seventy, or even eighty—much to these grandmothers' surprise, if not downright delight."

"The men in the first wave barely had enough time to collect the watches and jewelry," wrote another Soviet officer, Capt. Mikhail Koriakov, describing the pillage of Silesia. "The second wave, supporting the advance, was less in a hurry—the men had time to go in for the girls. The men in the third wave never found any jewelry or untouched girls, but they combed the town and packed suitcases." Indeed, this notion—that the first wave gets the valuables, the second wave gets the women, and the third gets whatever is left—was something of a standing joke among the Red Army soldiers in the region. In that formulation, of course, women are seen merely as objects, another class of war booty—less precious than watches or jewelry, perhaps, but desirable nonetheless, and available by simple right of conquest. Regardless of their background or their age or anything else, the women are there to be taken, with no need of explanation and by no authority other than an unchallengeable assertion of power; so too might soldiers burn down a house for their own amusement or slit the throat of a crying child or kill every animal on a farm.

The greater the scale of the violation—the more it deviates from the norms of civilized behavior—the greater the sense of power that might be gained, the reckless, dizzying freedom of no longer having to justify one's actions, the almost godlike privilege of exempting oneself from the terms of the human contract.

For days the NN prisoners remain in Jauer, captive to their liberators; their only nourishment, Madeline Dubois would recall, is "a few pieces of bread tossed to us by the Russians." Although the women have been freed, at least nominally, it's clear that the conquering armies have made no plans to transport them home. Beyond the town the battle with the Germans still rages, and from inside the castle they can hear regular bursts of artillery fire. Russian fighting units come in and out, making use of the women as they wish, such that Kate Bonnefous would later describe the prison during that period as a kind of brothel.

After several days, the supplies in the castle have run out, and the women are informed that if they want to eat, they can go into town and loot some of the stores. The center of Jauer is only a few minutes from the castle; most of the shops there have already been ransacked, their doors broken, windows smashed. Foraging for food, Kate and a companion meet a young Czech soldier who speaks some French; they advise him of what is going on inside the prison, and before long armed sentries have been placed at the castle gates. One day an interpreter for the army arrives; he is sympathetic to the women's plight and suggests that they make their way to the larger town of Liegnitz, where they might find transportation elsewhere. Liegnitz is twelve miles away, and even in their weakened condition, the women have no choice but to walk; still, as Madeline Dubois observes, "Anything would be better than to remain in this hell."

The next morning Kate and several other women set out for Liegnitz, carrying the few belongings they have left. Fortunately, along the way they encounter an ambulance belonging to the Russian Red Cross, and in two trips the ambulance takes the women to Liegnitz, passing through battlefields covered with corpses and stinking of death. In Liegnitz they are taken to a gathering camp for foreign prisoners that has been set up in a former customs house; there Kate manages to talk herself aboard a truck bound for Breslau. It is forty miles back to the east, but in Breslau she at least has the possibility of getting a train out of Silesia.

In January 1945, Breslau had been the site of ferocious fighting between German and Russian forces, and now, two months later, the city lies gutted, ruined buildings everywhere, their windows shattered, façades broken and smoke-blackened and with great gashes torn out of them like gaping wounds, the streets still strewn with piles of bricks and rubble and the charred hulks of overturned cars. Wandering through this desolate landscape, Kate is delighted to come across a group of five freed British prisoners of war, who have been living in an apartment lent to them by the local Russian commandant; she will remain with them in this apartment for five days, after which they are all put aboard a train bound for Odessa, the great port city on the Black Sea.

The terrain is immense and flat, an unvarying, endless horizon; occasionally the train passes an isolated station house for a village with an unpronounceable name. Farther south, the snow has begun to melt, exposing vast tracts of mud. On the outskirts of Odessa is a field overgrown with clumps of weeds, gray specters seeming to peek out from behind them. As the train draws closer, the specters are transformed into stones; some have flat tops, others are rounded, but all have Hebrew characters engraved on them. This is an old Jewish cemetery that seems to have been vandalized. The great slabs lean this way and that, tottering, resting against each other, as though the earth itself were heaving.

The train moves slowly past, the barely living gazing upon the dead.

Outside the train station in Odessa, a crowd of ragged people wanders aimlessly through the streets, looking to obtain whatever items might be available for sale or trade—a pair of pajamas, perhaps, for a bit of food or a bottle of vodka. The soldiers from the train take Kate to the British Mission in the city, where, to her astonishment, she finds that the officers on duty already have her name on a list of prisoners for whom they are searching. They take down Kate's information and offer to cable her brother in England to let him know that she is alive.

Kate remains in Odessa for several days, until she is able to secure passage to France on the Norwegian steamship *Bergensfjord*. Launched in 1913 for the Norwegian-America Line, operating between Oslo (then Kristiania) and New York, the *Bergensfjord* was requisitioned by the British Ministry of War in 1940 and converted into a troop ship; its luxurious interiors were torn out and refashioned into giant dormitories hung with hammocks to accommodate 2,000 troops at a time. Over the course of the war, the *Bergensfjord* would transport some 165,000 soldiers, ultimately spending nearly three full years at sea. Now, at war's end, it is being used as a mercy ship, and on April 2, 1945, Kate Bonnefous is among the crowd of people who pass through the large customs building at the port of Odessa and then make their way to the docks, just beyond the gigantic Potemkin steps immortalized in the Eisenstein film, to board the great ship with its twin masts flying the blue Nordic cross.

At the top of the gangway, the Norwegian crew stands beaming at attention, welcoming the travelers aboard. There are 2,388 of them; they are English and French and Belgian and Dutch, former prisoners of war, political prisoners, refugees, even a few who have managed to emerge from concentration camps. Decades later, one such passenger, Joseph Bialot, a French writer of Polish Jewish origin who had been deported to Auschwitz, would write in his memoir *Votre fumée montera vers le ciel* [*Your Smoke Will Rise to Heaven*] of "all these voyagers without bags, whose heads are full of shocks, of bombs, of cadavers, of pleas, of cries, of tears, of blood, of ruins, of sadism, of famines, of wounds, of fires, of wrecked tanks in which the metal with its peeling paint seems to be bleeding as well."

A long howl from the ship's siren announces the impending departure; then the moorings are released and the *Bergensfjord* slips slowly away from the land.

Belowdecks, the dining hall is a large, low-ceilinged room full of long wooden tables. Dressed with white ceramic plates and a large water jug, each table has a pair of wooden benches and is set for fourteen people; they are reminiscent of the worktables of Jauer, yet at the same time utterly different. At lunchtime, attendants in snow-white uniforms bring out tureens full of steaming vegetable soup, accompanied by slices of white bread that seem as soft and sweet as cake. In the large room the only sound is the clinking of silverware, as the passengers concentrate on the food set before them (surely some are willing themselves not to devour it like starving animals), eating in a kind of silent communion, as if in tacit agreement that this otherwise unexceptional meal is a dream from which they cannot bear to awaken.

After dark, down in the hold, the passengers lie wrapped in their military hammocks like rows of giant cocoons. Kate writhes uncomfortably through the night. She has become, like Job, skin and bones. All night long, passengers scream in their sleep; some vomit from seasickness in the nearby lavatories. Beneath her, she has an old overcoat and a few articles of clothing stuffed into a bag. It is a far cry from the last time she was aboard a great steamship such as this one, when she sailed solo for New York. That ocean crossing was a week-long whirl of laughter and Champagne and cigarette smoke—the female passengers were even permitted to smoke in the ship's public rooms. Her memory remains clear, but she has no sense of what the future might hold, cannot even bring herself to imagine it: Like a broken-down automobile, her mind seems now to have only one available gear.

In the morning, the sun is shining on the turquoise waters of the Bosphorus; already cold Odessa feels very far away. The *Bergensfjord* glides through the narrow strait, sailing past white villages nestled in greenery and flowers, lemon trees heavy with fruit, gnomish olive trees sprouting long, gnarled branches. Asia is at the port side, Europe at starboard. Graceful minarets of blue and white rise over the harbor of Istanbul; a stone fortress at Cape Helles looks like something from biblical times, but it is less than three hundred years old, and Kate herself is old enough to remember the Allied landing there during the Gallipoli campaign. Thirty thousand British boys died on that rocky peninsula—how tiny it seems close up—and even more of the Turks. That was a time, not so many years earlier, when a world war was simply referred to as "great," not yet given a number.

On the fourth day they reach the Mediterranean; there in the distance is mighty Etna, its summit still covered with snow, the coast-line of Sicily blazing white under a deep blue Technicolor sky. Early on the morning of the sixth day, a slight blip interrupts the endless flat line of the horizon: It is the coast of France, France at last. Before long, a pair of small naval boats has arrived to accompany the *Bergensfjord* into the harbor of Marseille. The harbor is gently curved, the shape of an embrace.

As the ship pulls up to its berth, a unit of French soldiers stands at attention. The dockside is crowded with happy, cheering onlookers, many of them waving berets or miniature flags; somewhere a band is playing martial music. The morning sun seems to polish everything it touches: bicycles, lampposts, trolley rails embedded in the street. Finally, gangways are lowered and the disembarkation begins. Red Cross workers are on hand to direct the passengers to the reception center, a set of white prefabricated buildings, where they are handed cards to be mailed to family members. They have only to provide the address and the signature, as the message has already been printed: *Suis Marseille. Bonne santé. Arrive bientôt. Baisers* [In Marseille. Good health. Arriving soon. Kisses]. Behind small tables, young men in uniform receive them with clipped courtesy. They are questioned—with a greater firmness than many had expected—about the circumstances of their deportation to Germany. The questioning is especially pointed for the few women among the arrivals: if married, whether they might have voluntarily followed a husband who had been deported; if single, whether they had followed a German boyfriend. After the initial questioning, the passengers are directed to the medical building. An X-ray is taken of their lungs; a dentist inspects their teeth; then they receive a shower and their hair, skin, and clothing are deloused with a white powder called DDT.

According to her medical report, Kate Bonnefous stands five feet six inches tall and weighs thirty-three kilograms—about seventy-three pounds.

When the physical examinations have been completed, a Carte de Rapatrié is filled out: name, date of birth, place of birth, nationality, marital status, parents' names, home address, last place of detention in Germany; on Kate's card, a note is made that she can receive a new set of clothing at one of the *vestiaires* run by the Red Cross. At another table, the arriving passengers are given a *prime* [gratuity] of 1,000 francs; additionally, those fortunates who are carrying German marks are given francs in exchange. Everyone receives, as well, a travel voucher for a train heading home.

For her part, Kate does not receive the 1,000 francs, likely because of her status as a married woman. With few chairs available in the reception center, she sits for hours at the end of a bench, her bag at her feet, waiting for her train to be announced. As she waits, she is handed a telegram that has just arrived for her, sent from Oran, Algeria:

RECEIVED YOUR LETTER ODESSA STOP AM PAINFULLY MOVED TO LEARN OF THE ABUSES OF WHICH YOU WERE THE OBJECT STOP BE ASSURED OF MY MOST AFFECTIONATE THOUGHTS SEND MY WISHES FOR SPEEDY RECOVERY STOP BUT TRUST YOUR USUAL ENERGY TO RESPOND TO YOUR CURRENT TROUBLES PAINFUL CONSEQUENCE OF CRUEL VICISSITUDES YOU HAVE BORNE WITH AN HONORABLE COURAGE TENDERLY HENRI BONNEFOUS

As the hours pass, Kate sits in growing annoyance and impatience; she doesn't understand how the arriving passengers here are not provided even a hot beverage. Eventually she decides to head outside to find a coffee and inquire about departure times of the trains to Paris. When she returns, she discovers to her horror that her bag is gone; it seems to have been stolen, but no one can say for certain. The bag contained everything that she had managed to hold on to during three and a half years in captivity: She will be returning to Paris with nothing.

Finally the passengers for Paris are put aboard trucks to take them to the nearby Gare Saint-Charles. In line at the train station, a French railway official comes by to check their vouchers; the train, the passengers learn to their chagrin, will *"faire le taxi"*—that is, it will stop at every destination along the line, even the smallest, even if only a single passenger is to be let off there.

The train rolls through the night and into the next day. Jubilant crowds wait at nearly every station stop; strangers come aboard bearing coffee, wine, sandwiches, flowers. The train takes on the air of a triumphal procession bound for the capital. At last the slender white clock tower of the Gare de Lyon appears in the distance. Stepping onto the train platform, the stunned arrivals are met by an enormous crush of people, crying, laughing, shouting out names, collapsing in joy into the arms of their loved ones.

From every direction, people call out: "Where are you coming from?" These are family members of the disappeared, who haunt the returning trains in search of information.

"From Odessa."

"No, before that!" A photograph is thrust forward, in hopes that one of the arriving passengers might recognize that person, might know something of his fate. The photos show happy people, well fed, with clean faces, full cheeks, styled hair; it has been a very long time since they saw anyone like that.

Kate is met at the station by her daughter-in-law, Mireille; Len will see her back at their apartment. Slowly they navigate their way through the crowd, regularly approached by porters asking about their bags. She has no bags, not even an overcoat, nothing but some shabby clothes draped on her matchstick frame.

"I came back to Paris to find a son who didn't recognize me," is all she will say later. "I was in rags and tatters."

Her apartment on rue Balny-d'Avricourt, which had been requisitioned by the Gestapo, is now being lived in by a married couple named Godet. All of her furnishings are long gone, confiscated along with her car, clothing, money, and valuables by order of the Nazi military tribunal. In 1939, Kate had rented the apartment on a standard Parisian 3-6-9 lease, under which the tenant is entitled to remain for a minimum of nine years, with the option of terminating after three years if notice is given six months in advance. On May 2, 1945, three weeks after Kate's return to Paris, Capt. Gilles Lefort of the French intelligence service sends a letter on her behalf to the head of the Service de la France combattante indicating her strong desire to return to her apartment and asking that she "be permitted to exercise her rights" as provided for by current legislation.

This was the Ordinance of November 14, 1944, issued by the provisional French government, which decreed that a person who was compelled to leave a residence as a result of the war "may request, against any tenant or occupant, even one of good faith, his reinstatement in the rented location if he was evicted without his consent." However, there was a complication: According to the terms of the ordinance, this provision did not apply when the residence "has subsequently accommodated therein a disaster victim, an evacuee, or a refugee." Monsieur Godet had been living at 2 rue Balny-d'Avricourt since October 1, 1944; although Godet was not a disaster victim, evacuee, or refugee, he had given asylum in the apartment to a Mlle Blanche Someck, who had been evicted from her own apartment by the Nazis—and whom, as it happens, Godet married on December 7, twenty-three days after the ordinance went into effect. Thus, when Kate Bonnefous files a claim for her former apartment, the Godets resist, and the issue goes to court; ultimately, a court of appeals will decide against her, ruling that Madame Godet, having been evicted once, cannot be evicted again.

For now, Kate is living in temporary housing at 16 rue François 1er, in the eighth arrondissement, in an apartment provided by the French government. (She is not precisely living alone; happily enough, she has been able to retrieve her black-haired cocker spaniel Winkie, the sole surviving dog of the original three.) That is where, on May 8, she receives a visit from a dark-haired, rather severe-looking woman in her middle years, who introduces herself as Betty Winkler.

Betty Winkler is living nearby, on rue de la Paix, after having spent the majority of the war in New York City. She has recently returned to Paris, where she is now working as a war correspondent for the International News Service. It is not in that capacity, however, that she wants to meet Kate Bonnefous; instead, she has come to hand-deliver a copy of a recent, highly successful book on which she and her husband had worked. It is called *Paris-Underground*, and it is dedicated to Kate (specifically, "To Kitty").

Kate reads the book that very night; the next day she appears in the Paris office of a high-ranking British intelligence official, Maj. Donald Darling, to inquire about the possibility of suing her friend Etta Shiber.

29

MAJOR DARLING IS ALREADY familiar with the particulars of
Kate Bonnefous's case. Two weeks earlier, on April 26, Kate
had arrived at the Hôtel Lutetia, the luxury hotel in Saint-Germain-
des-Prés that is serving as a temporary repatriation center. During
the war, the hotel had been requisitioned by the Abwehr, the Nazi
counterintelligence agency; now it is where the Ministère des Prisonniers, Déportés et Réfugiés is registering and processing the claims
of untold thousands of former prisoners and other deportees—some
of whom, undoubtedly, had been tortured in the special interrogation
room right upstairs, the one with the balcony overlooking Cherche-
Midi prison, where many others, including Kate Bonnefous herself,
had been held while they awaited their judgment.

At the Lutetia, Kate and a French ministry official fill out a questionnaire about her activities during the war. It is a routine procedure, mainly following along the lines of the questioning already
done at Marseille, although a greater emphasis is given to the circumstances of her arrest, trial, and detention. There is, as well, a notable addendum: Asked the reasons for her arrest, she answers,
"Évasion et espionnage au profit de l'Intelligence Service"—that is, "espionage for the benefit of the Intelligence Service."

That very day, in another part of Paris, Maj. Donald Darling of the

British intelligence division IS9 (AB) sends a memo to a French colleague providing a brief résumé of Kate Bonnefous's activity. He explains that she had helped supply British servicemen with "food, clothes, accommodation and money," and then lists by name thirteen of these servicemen, followed by the catchall phrase "and numerous others."

IS9 (AB) had been established by the British intelligence agency MI9 to identify and reward civilian helpers of Allied soldiers. In close cooperation with the intelligence services of the United States and France, officials of the Awards Bureau—thus the AB in the name—interview those who had helped British and American evaders (Darling's memo about Kate Bonnefous is in preparation for an eventual interview); investigate various claims and counterclaims; and make recommendations of decorations and monetary awards for helpers. By the middle of 1945, the original clerical staff of sixteen has grown to sixty-five, working out of the Grand Hôtel du Palais Royal, at 4 rue de Valois, just north of the Louvre. That is where Kate Bonnefous appears on May 9, 1945; she is received in the lobby and taken to the first-floor offices of Maj. Donald Darling, the intelligence officer who serves as the head of the Awards Bureau.

Sturdily built in his khaki army uniform, Darling is a rather dashing individual, known as a charming, witty raconteur, with romantic dark eyes under heavy brows, hair swept back in a lustrous black pompadour. Fluent in French and Spanish, he had spent much of the war ostensibly working for the British consulate in Lisbon but actually supervising the establishment of escape routes for Allied evaders through the Iberian Peninsula, using the code name Sunday; in that capacity, he had worked closely with Capt. Ian Garrow, the young Scotsman who succeeded Capt. Charles Murchie—whom Kate Bonnefous sheltered in her apartment for two weeks—as head of the Marseille escape line in 1941.

He and Kate, then, surely have much to talk about before she presents the reason for her call. With that, Darling takes her to the office of an English colleague of his (unnamed, but likely one of the Awards Bureau's legal counsels), and the discussion continues there among the three of them.

Kate explains that a Mrs. Winkler of 5 rue de la Paix has just given her a copy of the book *Paris-Underground,* published by the American company Scribner's in 1943. Apparently the book has been a great bestseller and will soon serve as the basis of a Hollywood movie. Although *Paris-Underground* carries the name of her former flatmate Etta Shiber as its primary author, Mrs. Winkler had represented herself to Kate as the book's ghostwriter. The central character in the book, Kate continues, is undoubtedly herself; "Kitty" is the name by which she is known among her friends, and while her surname has been changed slightly in the book, her exact home address is given, as is the true name of her housemaid, Margot. Other people described in the book would also be easily recognized, such as, for example, the curate of the northern village of Conchy-sur-Canche, which is also mentioned by name.

Her husband, Henri, now working with the Free French Forces in Algeria, is named as well, along with compromising information on his assistance with evasion activities.

Once the Gestapo found out about the book—which was not difficult to do, as portions of it were serialized in the *Daily Mail*—Kate had been beaten and tortured in an effort to extract additional information. This beating resulted in numerous injuries—the absence of her front teeth bears stark witness to that—that now require medical attention. Furthermore (as Donald Darling's colleague bluntly summarized it in his memorandum of the meeting), "the consequences of this book were that after two years of captivity and hard labour, she was suddenly condemned to death by the Germans and was to have her head chopped off."

Major Darling explains that he has brought in Madame Bonnefous to ask what actions she might take against Etta Shiber, who is a longtime friend of hers; she has been inquiring about the possibility of suing Mrs. Shiber for endangering her own safety and that of her comrades.

After some consideration, Darling's colleague suggests that Madame Bonnefous might put her objections in writing to Etta Shiber. In the event that she does not "obtain satisfaction" from her friend, "she could, of course, sue her, but it is a lengthy and annoying business."

Thus the meeting draws to a close. Discouraged by the advice,

Kate ultimately decides not to pursue the matter. Her sense of personal betrayal, however, would only have been heightened by conversations with her brother, Leonard (with whom she stays in London for much of the following month), when she learns that he had objected to the publication of *Paris-Underground* while Kate was still in the hands of the Nazis—so much so that he had immediately gone to the British Foreign Office to complain about it, receiving a reply from Etta Shiber nearly two months later in which she attempted to explain her motives for having written the book and included several favorable reviews.

Kate is sufficiently disturbed by the whole matter that she seems not to have written to Etta at all, not even to share the news that she is alive: Etta's long handwritten letter from the Catskills, in which she notes that she has just heard the news about Kate's liberation, is dated August 10—three months and one day after the meeting with Major Darling.

The day after the meeting in the Awards Bureau, Kate Bonnefous speaks again with government officials; this time the officials are French and belong to the Direction générale des Études et Recherches, a division of the intelligence agency founded by Charles de Gaulle during his exile in London. The result of the meeting is a typed, three-page single-spaced account of her forty months as a German prisoner. Marked "confidential," the declaration eventually makes its way to the British War Office, and then to the Foreign Office, where Sir David Scott Fox of the War Crimes section sends it on to Sir Thomas Barnes, the Treasury solicitor; he attaches a cover letter of his own, noting that Madame Bonnefous would likely be able to give evidence regarding the mistreatment of other Britons imprisoned in Germany, while adding (with an almost astonishing level of British reserve), "She was eventually liberated by the Russians—as you will see, a not very edifying experience which has already been the subject of diplomatic action."

"Briefly, the facts are these," Sir David writes by way of introduction: "Madame Bonnefous, who is a British-born woman married to a French citizen, was used by our military authorities after the German occupation of France. She was eventually caught by the Germans on 30th November 1940 and sentenced to death for helping British prisoners of war to escape. The death sentence was commuted into one of life imprisonment."

One cannot help but note the phrase "was used by our military authorities." This would seem to indicate that Kate Bonnefous's activities were not unknown to British military intelligence. Indeed, military officials might well have seen Kate's unusual access to British prisoners and German prison camps in the Occupied Zone as an opportunity for her to observe and pass along information on German military activity—as was done, for instance, by Kate's contact in Lille, Sally Siauve-Evausy, another Red Cross worker who (as Capt. Derek Lang would later write) "regularly sent reports to England of troop movements and positions." Kate herself, after all, had described her activities to the French ministry official in the Hôtel Lutetia not just as "evasion," but also as "espionage for the benefit of the Intelligence Service."

After the war, in her application to receive a government pension, one of Kate's co-defendants before the German military tribunal, Jeanne Monier, mentioned that part of her resistance work in the fall of 1940 involved "regular transmission to an agent of the IS [British Intelligence Service], contacted during my service, of information of a military nature that was brought to me by colleagues and friends." Another defendant, Gustave Rackelboom, attested to something similar in his own application, except that he specifically cited "*une Anglaise de l'IS*"—an Englishwoman of the Intelligence Service. Other than Kate Bonnefous, no Englishwoman has ever been identified as having worked with Gustave Rackelboom.

Rackelboom, then, might well have been providing more than just forged identification papers to Kate Bonnefous; like Jeanne Monier, he might also have been passing along military information that had been brought to him "by colleagues and friends." In that event, the likely recipient of Kate's information would have been Col. Cecil A. Shaw, the retired British intelligence officer in the American embassy, who was in contact with London via diplomatic channels (and was the source of the money that Kate gave to Lt. Colin Hunter and Cpl. Gordon Hood-Cree before their escape to the Unoccupied

Zone). What, after all, had Kate even been doing in the American embassy on the afternoon of October 19, 1940, when she happened to meet Hunter and Hood-Cree, two escaped British servicemen?

In her own 1954 application for a military pension, Kate Bonnefous would cite two organizations in which she served during the war. The first was the Croix-Rouge, for which she attested she drove ambulances; that much is known to be true. The other was MI9, the British intelligence service charged with aiding in the escape of British prisoners.

The year before that, in her signed and sworn application to receive the title of Déporté Résistant [Deported Resister], Kate was asked to summarize the acts for which she was deported. She wrote: "Belonging to MI9, Ministry of War (London). Escape of allied soldiers and officers. Sabotaging telephone lines between Doullens and Paris. Information provided to London. Shelter of escapees from the camps in my apartment in Paris."

While she was in prison, on more than one occasion, Kate had been beaten by Gestapo agents who believed that she was associated with MI9 and who hoped to extract information from her about British intelligence; this, though, they were never able to obtain. "They poured petrol on her hands, ignited it, and then broke the blisters," the wire service Reuters reported after her return to France. "They ground burning cigarettes on the back of her hands. They beat her to try to make her say she worked for the British Intelligence Service. But she always kept her secrets."

In June 1945, when Kate Bonnefous's case is to come up before the Awards Bureau, Maj. Donald Darling sends a memorandum to his French counterpart, Capt. Gilles Lefort, a former military reconnaissance officer and intelligence officer with the French Resistance; he sends a copy as well to their American colleague, Maj. John White of the U.S. Air Force. "This lady's excellent work is well known to us," he writes in the memo. "We agree to award Grade 3."

Monetary payments to helpers were shared by the three nations, and as such, recommendations had to be approved by all three representatives. In his 1975 memoir, *Secret Sunday,* Donald Darling recalled, "We had long weekly meetings to decide upon gradings for large numbers of commendations. The Americans at times were difficult to convince as to gradings, arguing that a person might, or might not, deserve a higher or lower award."

Such is the case here. The Grade 3 designation, as proposed by Darling, indicated that a person had sheltered between twenty and forty evaders; it would be given to only a few hundred of the many thousands of helpers investigated by the Awards Bureau. However, regarding Kate Bonnefous, the American delegation objects: In a memo to Donald Darling, Major White writes: "This lady's activity was before the time of the U.S. entry into the war. Under these circumstances, it appears inadvisable for us to give an award."

In the end, a decision is made to award a Grade 5, the lowest grade, given to those who had helped one airman after a landing or who had given help to six or seven men for a brief period of time. Kate will receive 10,000 francs as a direct award, plus another 458,000 francs (slightly less than $100,000 in today's currency) for expenses incurred during the war.

Decorations for heroism were awarded by individual countries, and by the following year Kate Bonnefous had received two. The first, from Great Britain, is an honorary membership in the Order of the British Empire. "Madame Bonnefous," concludes the long citation that accompanies the designation, "has shown at all times a superb courage, loyalty, and a true devotion to the Allied Cause." The second, from France, is the Croix de guerre avec étoile d'argent [Croix de Guerre with Silver Star], a medal awarded for heroism in one of the world wars.

Afterward, on official letters, she will add beneath her signature the honorifics "X de guerre" and "O.B.E."

"Not one of my boys was caught," Kate proudly tells a *Daily Mail* reporter in 1947, "and not one of my colleagues shot." This was, she had always felt, her truest reward. By then she has been working for more than a year at the Welfare Centre of the British Army Staff, on boulevard des Capucines; she has inquired about a posting with British troops in Burma, or perhaps Germany, but that request never comes through, presumably due to concerns about her age and physical condition.

At the end of the year Kate moves out of Paris, to the fishing village of Saint-Jean-Cap-Ferrat, on a peninsula just a few miles up the coast from Nice. The house, called Villa Mady, has been provided to her by the British government; it is very much the house by the seaside of which she has always dreamed. On the French Riviera she begins to dress more casually, in slacks and open-necked shirts, and she lets her hair grow out a bit, in soft waves. Her brother, Leonard, and sister Maggie often come to visit from London, and on summer vacations her two grandsons, Yann and Thierry, arrive from Paris with their mother and an English governess. She has, astonishingly, turned sixty years old. She buys a car, smaller than her old Peugeot, the better to negotiate the narrow, twisting roads that run through the pine forests and along the hillsides above the shoreline. The clus-

Kate Bonnefous with her cocker spaniel Winkie at
Saint-Jean-Cap-Ferrat in the South of France

ters of pink and yellow and orange houses rise along the shore like gigantic bouquets, the sea somehow every shade of blue at once; here, in the southern sun, it seems finally possible to warm herself again. She is trying to recover whatever she can of her health: She undergoes a series of dental procedures to replace the teeth that were knocked out by blows from a heavy key ring. Her damaged appendix is removed in a hospital in Nice. She receives a prescription for Librium to ease her nerves; bismuth seems to help with her stomach ulcers. Little by little, she manages to get her weight back up to one hundred pounds.

That article in the *Daily Mail* had indicated that Kate was eager for "her boys" to receive news of her, especially the ones whom she met in the Doullens hospital, where her resistance activities had begun. After the war, her new red-leather-bound address book contains numerous addresses and phone numbers for British soldiers whom she had sheltered in her apartment, as well as for her compatriots in the escape line. One of them, Edouard Régniez, the former curé of Conchy-sur-Canche, is now living in Saint-Maur-des-Fossés, a suburb southeast of Paris—like Kate, he is still alive despite having been sentenced to death by the Nazis in 1941. Indeed, Kate is the one who provides Régniez's name and address to Major Darling, recommending him as someone who merits official recognition.

After leaping from the train that was transporting him to Germany, Edouard Régniez had found refuge with the brother-in-law of one of his parishioners, in the farming village of Châlons-sur-Vesle. Once he had managed to procure civilian clothing and fake identity cards, he made his way south to the Auvergne, across the demarcation line, where he joined Charles de Gaulle's Forces françaises de l'Intérieur (FFI). For the remainder of the war he served as a trusted *agent de liaison* for Colonel Pontcarral, chief of the Secret Army; using the noms de guerre Christian Rémy and Claude Leroy, he was involved in a number of high-risk missions, including the armed rescue of resistance leader Yvette Baumann from a hospital in Blois. On one occasion he crossed the line of demarcation to bring to Paris a team of British radio agents who had parachuted in from London, and in the closing days of the war, he commanded an FFI assault group in the attack on the École militaire of Paris, headquarters of

the German 1st Guards Regiment. He finished the war as a lieutenant, and afterward, in recognition of his heroism, he was awarded the
Croix de guerre and named a chevalier of the Légion d'honneur.
The war had changed him in countless ways, perhaps most notably in
the realization that he was at heart a soldier, not a priest: He left the
priesthood at the end of the war and married in January 1945.

When officials from IS9 (AB) approach him about receiving a
monetary award, Régniez refuses, saying that he will not accept payment for services rendered to his country.

Most sorrowfully, the *passeur* Elie Teyssier died in 1943, at the age
of forty-eight, having suffered a badly fractured jaw and hemorrhag-
ing of his mouth and nose after a German guard in Fresnes prison
struck him in the face with the butt of a rifle. The medical report,
filed after the war by a doctor in Castillon, indicated that he had died
"in a state of cachexia"—a general wasting condition resulting from
an inability to eat—"that was by all evidence the consequence of
poor food and poor treatment in a captivity of two years." Teyssier's
widow, Jeanne, is awarded 100,000 francs for her late husband's aid
to escaped and evading servicemen.

On November 9, 1947, Henri Bonnefous dies in Oran at the age
of sixty-two; he and Kate are still married at the time, despite not
having lived together in a decade. After his death, Kate uses a calling
card bearing the title *Madame Vve.* [Widow] *Bonnefous, O.B.E.,* followed by pictures of her two medals; she will wear her wedding ring
for the rest of her life.

Kate never sees Etta Shiber again. The address that she has for
Etta is the apartment on West Seventy-third Street, where Etta lived
upon moving back to New York in 1944; just beneath it is the address for the Press Alliance, Inc. At some point Kate strikes a line
through both addresses in her book, as she does after a person has
died. Among her possessions, she has saved several news clippings
about herself, including the *Daily Mail* story that identified her as
"this war's Nurse Cavell"; among the others is one with the headline,
"'Paris Underground' Author Dies at 70."

········

At the age of sixty-five, Kate leaves Saint-Jean-Cap-Ferrat for Neuilly, an affluent suburb of Paris, where she has been given lodging in a home for elderly British women. Opened in 1887, the Victoria Home was a product of British charity, in the fashion of the privately endowed infirmaries and orphanages of the time, its goal to provide "a bright home with peaceful and happy surroundings for the aged and helpless of our countrywomen in France, who have been less favored than their fellows in the unequal 'struggle for life.'" She shares an apartment and garden with two other Englishwomen, but despite her age and wobbly health, she yearns to live on her own again, in an apartment that she can decorate and tend to as she likes. After three years at the Victoria Home she returns to the seventeenth arrondissement, moving to 50 avenue de Wagram, a five-story honey-colored stone building just five blocks from her old apartment on rue Balny-d'Avricourt.

She has a two-bedroom apartment on the top floor, which offers light, quiet, and space for extended family visits; Len has recently divorced and remarried, and Kate, making herself useful as always, steps in to help care for her two grandsons. Once, when Mireille falls ill, the boys stay with her for an entire month. Decades later, Thierry Sales will remember Kate as a caring and attentive grandmother, their visits together marred only by her regular fits of coughing. The boys assume that the coughing is somehow related to Granny's time in the war; they know that she had been imprisoned, and suffered as a result, but they have not learned the details. Occasionally one of them asks about it, but she just smiles and says lightly, *"Ça ne te regarde pas"* ["That doesn't concern you"].

They were still young, after all; they didn't need to know of such things. The coughing is due to chronic bronchitis that she attributes to the promenades in the rain and snow at Jauer, aggravated by the onset of emphysema, surely the result of a lifetime of Player's cigarettes. (After her return from prison, and against the firm advice of her doctors, she had given herself the pleasure of smoking once again; she had been denied so much for so long.) Like the web of cracks that can develop in concrete after an earthquake, none of which seems ruinous in itself but together make a structure uninhabitable, her body is failing now, in countless ways, most of which the doctors trace to her treatment in German prisons and which account for the disability pension she receives from the French government. There is the rheumatism that attacks the vertebrae in her neck and spine, giving her constant headaches and making driving long distances impossible; the drowsiness and burning in her stomach after meals, and the distressing bouts of colitis; the too-rapid beating of her heart; the ulceration of her ankles, and the edema in her feet that gets worse in the evenings and often prevents her from wearing shoes.

It had all been worth it, though, all the suffering—that much she knows. Quietly she revels in the success of their rescue work. The boys whom they saved had gone back to the war, fought bravely in subsequent campaigns. Lt. Colin Hunter received two Military Cross decorations, the first for his courage during the retreat at Saint-Valery-en-Caux and the second for his distinguished service at Kohima, in India, one of the decisive battles in the war against Japan. Capt. Charles Murchie started an escape line out of Marseille that ultimately carried hundreds of British soldiers to safety; in 1945 he was awarded the Croix de guerre avec étoile d'argent, as she had been. Second Lt. John Buckingham, one of the two escaped British servicemen she had unexpectedly encountered in the American embassy, received the Military Cross for valor shown in Sicily. Capt. Derek Lang, the other serviceman in the embassy, was awarded the Military Cross for his remarkable escape from France into Spain and then Palestine before returning to England; later in the war he was made commanding officer of the 5th Battalion of the Queen's Own Cameron Highlanders and fought in Normandy after the D-Day landings, for which he received the Distinguished Service Order. Eventually Captain Lang would become Lieutenant-General Lang, and then Sir Derek Lang, Knight Commander of the Order of the Bath.

Kate remains especially close with Colin Hunter and Derek Lang and their families, and as the years go by, she writes to them often and sometimes visits with them in London and Scotland; they share lots of cigarettes, and whiskey-and-sodas, and warm, cheerful conversation in wood-paneled rooms. Her once firm handwriting has grown spidery; her voice has deepened, roughened over time, though she still speaks in the plummy tones she learned in finishing school in Kent, back in the nineteenth century, when proper English girls were trained mostly in the arts of domesticity. Derek Lang's daughter Sarah Hunt remembers her as having "quite a deep voice, but a very robust voice. There was nothing querulous about Kitty." In old age, her hair has become entirely gray; she draws on her eyebrows in upward-tilting lines that give her face a permanent expression of surprise. Her hands still bear the scars of cigarette burns.

Kate Bonnefous, then seventy-four years old, with
her teenaged grandsons Yann and Thierry, during a 1960
vacation at the home of Brig. Derek Lang
and his family in Alyth, Scotland

In 1964, Great Britain and West Germany sign the Anglo-German Agreement for Compensation to Victims of Nazism. West Germany agrees to provide £1 million (worth about $32 million in today's U.S. currency) for British citizens "who were victims of National-Socialist measures of persecution and who, as a result of such measures, suffered loss of liberty or damage to their health or, in the case of those who died in consequence of such measures, for the benefit of their dependents." To determine which victims will receive compensation, the claims department of the British Foreign Office establishes a point-based system in which applicants are "allocated units according to the length of imprisonment and gravity of health damage." Ultimately, 1,015 applications are approved and another 3,045 rejected; the average payout is just a bit under £1,000 (about $30,000 today).

In support of her claim, Kate submits a personal statement tracing her time as a prisoner of the Nazis, from her arrest in November 1940 to her arrival in Odessa in March 1945. She names nine prisons through which she passed during that time; after the mention of Lübeck, she adds, "where I was sentenced to be shot after the publication of the book 'Paris Underground,' published by my friend." The Parisian doctor who examines Kate for the application duly records the litany of her physical ailments, as well as her chronic insomnia and nervousness. She "looks older than her age," he observes—a particularly striking comment in relation to a woman who is seventy-eight years old. In the section of the form reserved for general remarks, he jots down: "Woman very brave, but still has her life spoiled by her gastric troubles due to ulcer and colitis, on top of psychoneurosis due to 4 years of deportation in camps."

The evaluator from the claims department is brief in his assessment of Kate's application, noting at the front of the file: "Since Mme. Bonnefous was consistently beaten and tortured to extract information, there is a good case for saying that she suffered Nazi persecution throughout. Her case is well known and it may be possible to accept her without further checking." In August 1965, Kate is awarded £2,293 (about $70,000 today); she receives an initial payout of £1,000, and the remainder is sent to her son in 1968.

Asked in her later years how she had managed to carry on her underground work during the war, Kate replies simply, "You got worked up to such concert pitch that you didn't know what you were doing. You could do almost anything." It is a typically self-effacing observation, and the use of the second person adds another layer of modesty, deflecting attention from herself, as though anyone in her situation might have done what she did. She thought of herself not as a heroine but rather as a kind of soldier, serving her native and adopted homelands as best a civilian woman in her midfifties might do—whether that meant patrolling the Paris streets with rubber suit and gas mask, or driving a Red Cross ambulance loaded with supplies, or opening her home to servicemen on the run, or passing information to a countryman in an embassy, or, if the opportunity arose, stopping by the side of the road to cut an enemy telephone line. These were all eminently practical tasks, and she had always been a practical woman, sturdy, who had run two businesses and raised a child on her own, and over the course of her life had acquired a number of skills, one of which was recognizing when she could be of use. She had never seen herself as especially courageous, but she had always kept, she knew, a strong sense of purpose.

More and more she can feel her life thinning out; the pages of her address book are increasingly filled with crossed-out entries. She visits with her brother, Leonard, at his home in Hendon; with her niece Jocelyn in Sevenoaks, Kent, not far from Margate, where, at Thanet Hall, as a long-haired girl in a high-necked dress and button boots, she had learned to sew and paint and, most helpfully, how to speak French. By 1965 she is spending as much time in England as in France, as much time, it seems, in the hospital as out. There are pulmonary troubles, respiratory troubles, optic inflammation, recurrent ulcers. In November her cough worsens, her breathing grows faint; she enters London Hospital for the last time.

The cause of death is reported as "cor pulmonale plus purulent bronchitis and emphysema." She has lived for seventy-nine years and three months. Etta used to say that it was good to be able to live to eighty; remarkably enough, Kate had just about made it. One of the London papers will run a brief notice of her death. "Recently," it begins, "there died in her eightieth year, in the London Hospital, unrecognized and almost alone, a very gallant lady." In the hospital that day, and all through the city, people are wearing crimson poppies on their chests like medals in honor of the fallen war dead; in Paris, they wear pins of brilliant cornflower blue. It is the eleventh of November: Remembrance Day in England and France.

Appendix

BRITISH SOLDIERS KNOWN TO HAVE BEEN
AIDED BY KATE BONNEFOUS

Sergeant Thomas Boyle, Royal Army Service Corps
Second Lieutenant John F. N. Buckingham, Royal Field Artillery
Private W. J. Clark, Gordon Highlanders
Sergeant Interpreter Henry K. Clayton, Royal Air Force
Gunner Francis S. J. Croose, Royal Artillery
Private Robert Dundas, Royal Army Service Corps
Private Reginald T. Emmott, Royal West Kent Regiment
Private Joseph Fagan, Royal Warwickshire Regiment
Sergeant Thomas E. Guthrie, Argyll and Sutherland Highlanders
Corporal Gordon Hood-Cree, Royal East Kent Regiment
Lieutenant Colin D. Hunter, Queen's Own Cameron Highlanders
Sergeant Rupert E. Knight, Royal Army Service Corps
Private Reginole W. Krahn, Royal West Kent Regiment
Captain Derek B. Lang, Queen's Own Cameron Highlanders
Private George Lindsay, Durham Light Infantry
Captain Charles P. Murchie, Royal Army Service Corps
Private William A. Sheldon, Royal Warwickshire Regiment
Private Ronald W. Squires, Royal West Kent Regiment
Gunner William H. Taylor, Royal Artillery
Private George R. West, Royal Warwickshire Regiment

Acknowledgments

MUCH OF THE RESEARCH for this book was conducted at a time of quarantine, when international travel was impossible, and as a result I relied heavily on numerous talented researchers in France, England, and Italy to navigate for me the often-byzantine byways of their local archives; I thank them all most heartily for their perseverance and ingenuity on my behalf. I am especially indebted to Ishtar Mejanes, who took on this project as if it were her own, tracking down like a detective the historical records of Kate Bonnefous and her associates in archives and libraries in Paris and surrounding regions. Her research, and her commentary on its deeper meanings, is imbued with a singular erudition, curiosity, and intellectual rigor, and I never fail to marvel at it; for me, one of this book's great pleasures is the opportunity it afforded me to become friends with Ishtar. Also in France, the historian Christophe Woehrle delved deeply into multiple repositories throughout the country (he was the one who, in a folder buried in the departmental archives in Caen, found the trial report of the Nazi military tribunal that convicted Kate, Etta, and the others), and in our extensive email correspondence he helped to shape my emerging sense of the story, his insights informed by his own important work on prisoners of war and other victims of Nazism. In the Gironde region of France, the local historian Maurice

Friot became as fascinated as I was by the story of Elie Teyssier, and worked doggedly to unearth the traces of this courageous but unsung *métayer;* ultimately Maurice and his colleague Françoise Villechenoux wrote a book, *Vivre dangereusement sous l'Occupation à Castillon,* that has nobly rescued, as much as is possible, the lives of Elie and his fellow *passeurs.*

I am grateful, as well, for research assistance provided by Manal Alyedreessy and Linda Hammond in France and Mariel Lëmail in Portugal; at the outset of this project, Nina Staehle offered helpful research suggestions and translated various documents from their original German. In England, Phil Tomaselli and Steven Kippax located scores of files for me from the National Archives of the United Kingdom, including numerous wartime testimonies that British escapers and evaders gave to interviewers from MI9, as well as Kate Bonnefous's own account of the crimes committed against her by the Nazis and Soviets. Also in England, the highly skilled genealogist Maxine Willett located relatives of the British servicemen aided by Kate Bonnefous, as well as background information on Kate herself, including the record of her early marriage to James Walsh. Lisa Tucci and Simona Giordano provided fascinating information on the English community in Rome in the early years of the twentieth century, and after a good deal of searching discovered the birth records for Leonardo Sales, born to a mother identified simply as "Caterina Robins."

Numerous librarians and archivists gave me invaluable assistance with this project, chief among them Cate Brennan at the National Archives and Records Administration in College Park, Maryland; Rebecca Erbelding (an estimable historian in her own right) at the United States Holocaust Memorial Museum in Washington, D.C.; Abigail Altman at the American Library in Paris; Emma Sarconi in the Special Collections archive at Princeton University; and Kimberly Sulik at the New York County Surrogate's Court. Several members of Yahoo's Special Operations Executive group helpfully responded to my query about Edouard Régniez and the Richard Coeur de Lion escape line; one of them, John Clinch, additionally sent me a copy of a Nazi-era report on the castle prison at Jauer, as well as several contemporary photographs of it. Keith Janes, proprietor of the Conscript Heroes website, shared much useful information about escape lines in general and the Richard Coeur de Lion line in particular; for anyone interested in the subject, Conscript Heroes also provides a chronological listing of the more than three thousand British escape-and-evasion reports that are now held in the National Archives of the United Kingdom. In that regard, I am also indebted to Franck Signorile for his work in creating a searchable online database of French helpers of escaped Allied servicemen.

Thanks, as well, to the historians and other authors who took time to respond to my (mostly unsolicited) queries: Antony Beevor, Saul David, Hanna Diamond, Charles Glass, Ellen Hampton, René Lesage, Robert Lyman, Marie-José Masconi, Sherri Ottis, Sarah Rose, Anne Sebba, Jacky Tronel, Richard Weisberg, and Ben Yagoda. I thank particularly Peter Hore, who over the course of a most interesting email correspondence shared with me his ideas about Cecil Shaw, Edward Sutton, and much else regarding the wartime activities of the British Interests Section at the American consulate in Paris, a subject to which he has given much thought.

Many relatives of Etta Shiber and Kate Bonnefous—Gillie Crick, Humphrey Crick, Martin Crick, Judi Keim, Thierry Sales, Linda Smith, and Angela Umpleby—offered cheerful and exceedingly generous help to a stranger asking about their beloved ancestors; this would have been a far poorer book without their assistance. I owe a special debt to Laurie Dart (Etta Shiber's great-grandniece), who gave me copies of never-before-seen letters that Etta wrote to her brother and sister-in-law in America before and during the German occupation of France; Etta was a splendidly lucid correspondent, and these letters afford an intimate understanding of the daily lives and activities of the two women living at 2 rue Balny-d'Avricourt. Similarly, Erik Sales shared with me a wealth of materials that he had saved from his grandmother Kate Bonnefous, including newspaper clippings, personal and official correspondence, medical reports, photographs, passports, her postwar address book, and Kate's own handwritten notes about her years of imprisonment. Many relatives of servicemen rescued by Kate Bonnefous spoke with me as well, and I thank them for their recollections, which were fond, often poignant, and unfailingly illuminating: Charlotte Beddoe, James Buckingham,

Henry Clayton, Sheena Gilmour, Jacqui Hood-Cree, Karen Hood-Cree, Terry Hood-Cree, Jonathan Hunt, Sarah Hunt, Alasdair Hunter, Andrew Hunter, Simon Lang, Michele Rist, Kate Squires, Jill Zorab.

Jean-Marie Burguburu (himself a very distinguished attorney in Paris) graciously shared with me memories of his father, Jehan Burguburu, while also providing insight into Jehan Burguburu's legal career, particularly his work on behalf of those accused under Nazi military law. I am deeply grateful as well to Michel Guénaire, a partner in the Parisian law firm of Gide Loyrette Nouel, who sent me a copy of Jehan Burguburu's case file on Etta Shiber—a file that had surely not been inquired about for many decades but was still faithfully preserved in the firm's archives.

At Ballantine Books, I'm privileged to have been able to work once more with Susanna Porter. She is an exemplary editor—intelligent, discerning, enthusiastic, and possessed of a salutary calm. Also at Ballantine, Anusha Khan handled myriad technical details with attentiveness and good cheer. Production editor Loren Noveck and copy editor Emily DeHuff carefully scrutinized the manuscript for solecisms of every kind; any errors that may remain belong, of course, solely to me. Many thanks, too, to Kathleen Quinlan and the Ballantine marketing team, and to the production team that so deftly turned a plain manuscript into a gorgeous book: Carlos Beltrán (who designed the cover), Daniel Christensen (who came up with the title), Caroline Cunningham, and Katie Zilberman. For their continued support of my work, I offer heartfelt gratitude as well to Ballantine's president Kara Welsh, deputy publisher Kim Hovey, and editor-in-chief Jennifer Hershey.

Henry Dunow has unfailingly supported my work for many years, and I'm eternally grateful that he agreed to take me on at an early stage of my career as an author; he is both a talented literary agent and, in and out of the world of publishing, a mensch among mensches.

Much of the research material for this book, from history books to newspaper articles and personal testimonies, was written in French. I could never have managed to absorb it all without Sarah Audu, French tutor extraordinaire, who over long years, with her characteristic patience, enthusiasm, and warmth, has helped transform my grasp of the language from nearly hopeless into something just beyond passable. *C'est ouf!*

This book (and frankly, much else in my life) has benefited immeasurably from the good conversation, good food and drink, and general goodwill given to me by many friends, among them Lenny Benardo, Josh Broder, Marty Dobrow, Pagan Kennedy, Karen Leiner, John Sanbonmatsu, Deborah Schupack, Adam Sexton, Tim Sommer, and Jennifer Weiss, as well as my comrades in the Power Broker Poker Club (Ada Calhoun, Dan Conaway, Kevin Hogan, Abbott Kahler, Gilbert King, and Simon Lipskar), with whom I have spent countless happy evenings kibitzing around the table of honor.

Finally, I send love and thanks to my most wonderful family: my wife, Cassie Schwerner, and our children, Ezra and Vivian. To them I offer this book, but for them, my gratitude is beyond all words.

Notes

PROLOGUE

3 **1,500 metric tons:** Max G. Tretheway, "1,046 Bombers but Cologne Lived," *New York Times,* June 2, 1992.

4 **Entering the harbor:** The description of the *Drottningholm*'s voyage is drawn primarily from Atcheson, 482–83, 500; "908 Home with Tales of 'V'-Hungry Europe," New York *Daily News,* June 2, 1942; "'Diplomat Ship' In," *New York Times,* June 2, 1942; "Diplomatic Exchange Ship Docks at Jersey City Pier," Associated Press wire story, June 1, 1942. Newsreel footage of the arrival can also be seen at gettyimages.com/detail/video/drottningholm-arriving-in-the-new-york-harbor-people-news-footage/502852393 and collections.ushmm.org/search/catalog/irn1003843.

4 **"grandmotherly":** See, for instance, Stewart Robertson, "Secret Passage," *Family Circle* 24:13 (March 31, 1944): 4–5; "Etta Shiber," *Current Biography: Who's News and Why 1943* (New York: H. W. Wilson, 1943), 690–92.

5 **She had lost more than twenty-five pounds:** Gilbert Swan, "American Woman, 65, Nabbed by Gestapo for Aiding British, Fleeing France, Home After Escaping Death by a Firing Squad," *The Times* (Munster, Indiana), January 12, 1944.

5 **but simply butter:** Mary Braggiotti, "Mrs. Shiber Surprised Even Herself," *New York Post,* September 21, 1943. In a letter to her sister-in-law Helen, Etta Shiber also noted, "The rationing of butter would hit me more because I eat quite a lot."

6 **"and without them I was lost":** Shiber, 10.

8 **("What could I have told them"):** Etta Shiber, "The Green Dress," *Evening Star* (Washington, D.C.), December 12, 1943.

10 **"It is not only literally, factually true":** "Paris-Underground," *Reader's Digest,* October 1943, 119.

CHAPTER 1

15 sixteen streets and three avenues: Census records show that Etta Shiber lived (in chronological order) at 306 East Fifty-eighth Street (between Second and Third avenues), 640 Lexington Avenue (between Fifty-fourth and Fifty-fifth streets), 156 East Fifty-second Street (between Third and Lexington avenues), and 315 East Sixty-eighth Street (between First and Second avenues).

15 "For almost thirty-five years": Inez Whiteley Foster, "Home Again After 18 Months Under Nazis," *Christian Science Monitor,* October 19, 1943.

16 "One thing I have learned": Ibid.

17 had named her Jennett: This (with slight spelling variations) is how she was identified in early census forms.

17 in accordance with the Jewish tradition: A good deal of evidence exists to indicate that Etta Shiber was Jewish. In Europe, both Kahn and Weil (her cousin Irving's last name) were identifiable as Jewish, as was her paternal grandmother's maiden name of Lowe, and her own mother's maiden name of Roth. (Kahn is a variation of Cohen; the name Weil traces back to a fifteenth-century rabbinic family originally from the German town of Weil.) Etta's great-aunt Jeanne was born in the Jewish Hospital of Eguisheim in 1828 and later married a Jewish man. Etta was named after her late grandmother Jeannette; naming a child after a deceased ancestor is a Jewish tradition. An article in *The American Israelite* from 1943 refers to Etta Shiber as "the middle-aged American Jewish widow whom the Nazis captured in France." One of Etta Shiber's fellow prisoners in Cherche-Midi, a British woman named Mary Lindell, referred to her, not entirely accurately, as "a German Jewess married to an American." When Etta's nephew Harry Kahn crossed the border into Canada in 1925, he filled out an entry form in which he listed his nationality as "Jewish" and his religion as "Hebrew." Etta Shiber's funeral director came from the Riverside Memorial Chapel, a Jewish funeral home in New York. In an interview with the author, Linda Smith, Etta Shiber's grandniece, stated unequivocally, "Etta was Jewish on both sides."

18 only the second optician in the city: Lewis Francis Byington, *The History of San Francisco in 3 Volumes* (Chicago: S. J. Clarke, 1931), II: 434; "New York," *Optical Review and Journal of Optometry* (March 2, 1911): 593.

19 seven doors south of her: William Shiber's address at the time was 626 Lexington Avenue. ancestry.com/discoveryui-content/view/66990733:7602?tid=&pid=& queryId=e17dad9a-e229-4197-9d2b-de786afa117a&_phsrc=yQB1&_phstart= successSource.

19 the manager of the telegraph room: "W. N. Shiber Dies; Head Telegrapher for Over 40 Years," *New York American,* April 25, 1936; "William Shiber," *New York Times,* April 25, 1936.

19 "Shiber is one grand fellow": "New York Local No. 16," *Commercial Telegraphers' Journal,* February 1911, 310.

19 Adler himself had performed the ceremony: City of New York marriage certificate no. 3884, April 2, 1901.

20 "The ideal of the school": Adler, 4.

21 Irving Weil: See, for instance, "Irving Weil, Music Critic of Journal, Dies in Paris," *New York Evening Journal,* August 29, 1933; "Irving Weil, 55, Dies Here of Long Illness," *New York Herald* (European edition), August 29, 1933; "Irving Weil, Noted Music Critic, Dies," *Chicago Daily Tribune* (European edition), August 29, 1933.

22 **hired at Public School 147:** The starting salary was $600 a year. *City Record* (New York), November 11, 1902, 7617.

22 **"unusually sheltered":** Inez Whiteley Foster, "Home Again After 18 Months Under Nazis," *Christian Science Monitor,* October 19, 1943.

22 **"just a sheltered housewife":** "American Woman Saves 200 Fighters for Allies," *Pittsburgh Press,* October 2, 1943.

22 **to purchase the entire library:** William N. Shiber folder, General Correspondence, William Randolph Hearst papers, Bancroft Library, University of California, Berkeley.

22 **"A deep sympathy developed":** Shiber, 9.

23 **the Hôtel Splendide-Royal:** "'New' Aix-les-Bains Nearly Done; Visitors Filling Leading Hotels," *New York Herald* (European edition), June 14, 1933.

23 **to the Hôtel Bristol:** Shiber, 10; "Majestic Brings Horde of Tourists, 160 Barrels Gold," *New York Herald* (European edition), September 7, 1933.

24 **"It was a privilege and a stimulus":** Robert A. Simon, "Musical Events," *New Yorker,* September 9, 1933.

24 **on the SS *Paris:*** The complete passenger list for that voyage can be found here: catalogs.marinersmuseum.org/media/Media/00001/MS15.04471%20Paris 00635822369119661316.pdf.

24 **Etta imagined that she could still hear:** Etta Shiber describes many of these details in letters from Paris to her brother, Chester, and sister-in-law, Helen; the letters were provided to the author by Etta's great-grandniece, Laurie Dart.

CHAPTER 2

26 **Player's Navy Cut:** Thierry Sales email to author, October 16, 2020.

27 **The name on her birth certificate:** Kate Robins entry of birth, Brentford, August 5, 1886, General Register Office, London. Kate Robins Bonnefous file, AC21P713027, Archives Départementales du Calvados.

27 **a country squire's wife:** Reginald Eason, "German Soldiers Slept at German Military HQ," *Daily Mail* (London), October 11, 1943.

28 **wasted on the female mind:** James C. Albisetti, Joyce Goodman, and Rebecca Rogers, eds. *Girls Secondary Education in the Western World from the 18th to the 20th Century* (New York: St. Martin's Press, 2010), 3–4.

29 **the experience would embitter her:** Angela Umpleby email, January 18, 2021.

30 **"While it would be an insincerity":** "Death of Mr. James Walsh," *Oxford Times,* March 21, 1947.

31 **"from his natural union with a woman":** Translations from the Italian are by Lisa Tucci and Simona Giordano.

33 **2,588 divorces:** "Divorce Rates Data, 1858 to Now: How Has It Changed?" *The Guardian,* Datablog, theguardian.com/news/datablog/2010/jan/28/divorce-rates -marriage-ons#data.

33 **"a fascinating companion":** Shiber, 113.

34 **"it was ill considered to have a wife who worked":** Weber, 81.

34 **could not maintain a bank account in her own name:** Olson, 27; Sebba, 19.

34 **director of the American Business College:** "News Jottings," *New York Herald* (European edition), November 29, 1932; "Business College Takes New Quarters," *New York Herald* (European edition), February 11, 1933.

35 **"They seemed deeply in love":** Shiber, 113.

36 **a hunting ground for royalty:** Olson, 64.

CHAPTER 3

38 **one thousand per day:** Weber, 11.

38 **one in four was permanently disabled:** Ousby, 7.

38 **"all the anonymous, demonic":** McAuliffe, 35.

38 **France's population grew by only 3 percent:** Weber, 13.

39 **"The gunners settled down in the Maginot Line":** Dutourd, 13.

40 **for only 23,000:** Contemporaneous advertisements priced the Peugeot 402 at 22,900 francs.

40 **Sandbags were piled around the building:** Bove, 209.

41 **Ambulance and Transport Service:** *Ambulance and Transport Service: The American Hospital of Paris in the Second World War* (France: 1940), 14; "Women Drivers of Hospital Unit Help Evacuate Brussels Helpless," *New York Herald* (European edition), May 19, 1940.

41 **helping the nurses on their rounds:** Otto Gresser, "A History of the American Hospital of Paris," 3, Archives of the American Hospital of Paris.

41 **Dozens of groups:** Office central des Oeuvres de Bienfaisance, *La France charitable pendant la guerre,* No. 1, November 1939.

44 **thousands of huge balloons:** Bove, 213.

44 **gas mask boxes in leather or satin:** Sebba, 29.

45 **four times as much on horse feed:** Weitz, 22.

45 **wild rumors began to appear:** Lottman, 39.

45 **A group of younger military officers:** Ibid.; Schoenbrun, 11; Kladstrup and Kladstrup, 32.

46 **"you could reach out and grab":** Lottman, 266.

46 **were seen burning papers:** Sherman, 2.

46 **hurriedly arranged trains rolled south:** Thornton, 4.

CHAPTER 4

48 **of the twenty-six drivers:** *Ambulance and Transport Service: The American Hospital of Paris in the Second World War* (France: 1940), 26.

48 **"The work of the women ambulance drivers":** Ibid., 15.

49 **"Occasionally a tiny baby cries":** Marion Conger, "Refugees Arrive, Soldiers Leave on Adjoining Nord Station Lines," *New York Herald Tribune* (European edition), May 16, 1940.

50 **The Special Division, a newly established office:** Russell, 28–29; Stuart, *American,* 7–9; Stuart, "Special War Problems," 3. War History, General Records of the Department of State, Special War Problems Division, Records Group 59, National Archives and Records Administration.

50 **"proved rather contentious":** Williams, 10.

51 **exchanged addresses, updated wills:** Lottman, 303.

51 **more than 1.2 billion francs:** Josephs, 17.

51 **Albert Camus:** Lottman, 259.

52 **"There never has been anything like":** Lyman, 155.

52 **"The creatures were hungry":** Walter, 12.

53 **a black Peugeot 402:** Lang, 129. For more on the Peugeot 402, see: Patrick Lesueur, *La Peugeot de mon père* (Boulogne: E.T.A.I., 2000), 48–77; René Bellu, *Toutes les voitures françaises 1939* (Lausanne: Edita, 1982), 60–67; "1935–1940

Peugeot 402," auto.howstuffworks.com/1935-1940-peugeot-402.htm; "Peugeot 402," en.wikipedia.org/wiki/Peugeot_402.

53 **the dashboard trimmed with chrome:** See the diagram in Peugeot, *Voiture Type 402: Notice d'Entretien*, 6th ed. (1937), 52.

54 **A line of refugees was already stretched out:** The description of the exodus is drawn from numerous sources, including Diamond, 53–79; Amouroux, 9–13; Sebba, 46–50; Saint-Exupéry, 57–72; Barber, 64–66; and Shiber, 13–26, as well as Etta Shiber's letters describing their personal exodus. The first section of Irène Némirovsky's novel *Suite Française* also contains a long and vivid description of the exodus.

55 **"a Dantesque vision":** Vidalenc, 272.

55 **"a great boot had smashed":** Saint-Exupéry, 57.

55 **the largest migration in recorded history:** Diamond, 2.

56 **Hans and Margret Rey:** The story of the Reys' flight from France is told in Louise Borden's book *The Journey That Saved Curious George: The True Wartime Escape of Margret and H. A. Rey* (Boston: Houghton Mifflin Harcourt, 2005).

56 **"They are so tired":** Liebling, 94.

57 **more sun in France that June:** Lottman, 165.

57 **"an atmosphere of riot":** Le Maner, 475.

58 **"Base men show their baseness":** Saint-Exupéry, 72.

58 **The Châteauroux field hospital:** Otto Gresser, "A History of the American Hospital of Paris," 3–4, Archives of the American Hospital of Paris; *Ambulance and Transport Service: The American Hospital of Paris in the Second World War* (France: 1940), 22–23. Gresser indicates that the field hospital had forty beds; *Ambulance and Transport Service* notes that the hospital was opened in February 1940 with thirty.

58 **Dr. Thierry de Martel:** On the death of Dr. Martel, see: Glass, 66–67; Schoenbrun, 32; Lottman, 355.

59 **Fourteen residents of Paris committed suicide:** Sebba, 46. The historian Richard Vinen puts the number at sixteen. Vinen, 14.

59 **"It is with a heavy heart that I say":** Freeman and Cooper, 291.

59 **"a skeleton with a chill":** Ousby, 59.

59 **"We had all heard the same speech":** Freeman and Cooper, 292.

60 **sixteen people were dead:** Dallot, 21.

62 **"After the flow of the exodus":** Amouroux, 58.

63 **"two middle-aged respectable women":** Shiber, 37.

CHAPTER 5

64 **"a dead planet":** Amouroux, 67.

65 **a Parisian shopping spree:** Peabody, 208.

66 **while wearing the uniform:** Lottman, 259; Flanner, 54.

66 **ninety thousand children:** Josephs, 17; Drake, 55.

67 **1.8 million more had been taken prisoner:** The number of French prisoners is inexact; it has been estimated at anywhere from 1.5 to 1.9 million. The number 1.8 million is from Quinn, 59, as is the following observation about the number of prisoners as a percentage of the general French population.

67 **"the new border that separates France from France":** Amouroux, 84.

69 by dimming the lights: "Soirée de Paris en 1940," *Le Matin,* August 10, 1940, 3.

70 "a poorly lit room": Hughes, 180.

70 "French women who were not nurses": "Rappel Historique," "Croix-Rouge fran-çaise: Direction des conductrices ambulancières (1939–1991)," Reference Code 20200063, Archives Nationales de France, Paris.

70 "oozed improvisation": Dutourd, 150.

71 "When one reaches an advanced stage": Quinn, 91.

71 killed while trying to escape: Ibid., 88.

71 "were in the first rank": Jean Lacouture, *Le témoignage est un combat: Une biogra-phie de Germaine Tillion* (Paris: Seuil, 2000), 100.

71 treated colonial troops far more harshly: See the discussion in Quinn, 94–100.

72 "You see, my son is handsome": Hughes, 181.

72 On July 18, 1940: This scene is drawn primarily from Shiber, 64–66; Etta Shiber's letters to her brother, Chester Kahn; Escape report, Lieutenant C. D. Hunter, Cameron Highlanders, WO 208/3301/172, National Archives of the United Kingdom; Colin Hunter interview, 1994. The notice appeared in the "Annonces Classées" section of *Le Matin,* July 18, 1940, 2.

73 *"Allo! Allo!":* "Soirée de Paris en 1940," *Le Matin,* August 10, 1940, 3.

CHAPTER 6

74 Second Lt. Colin D. Hunter: The description of Hunter's capture and intern-ment is drawn primarily from Lang, 25–42; Shiber, 67–85; Escape report, Lieu-tenant C. D. Hunter; Colin Hunter interview, 1994; interviews by the author with Andrew Hunter, Alisdair Hunter, and Sheena Gilmour.

75 "Colin, are you down there?": Colin Hunter interview, 1994.

75 "for you the war is over": Andrew Hunter interview, April 19, 2021.

78 less than two-thirds of a tank: The Peugeot 402 main gas tank had a capacity of sixty-six liters; the smaller reserve tank could hold another five liters. Peugeot, *Voiture Type 402: Notice d'Entretien,* 6th ed. (1937), 72.

78 Kate managed to procure extra gasoline: Shiber, 57.

78 arranged a deal with the German commandant: "Many Allied Servicemen Owe Life to Elderly Englishwoman in Paris," *Montreal Gazette,* November 6, 1945.

78 "She even used to go to the German aerodromes": The prisoner was Gordon Hood-Cree. Reginald Eason, "Mrs. Beaurepos Saved Me, Says Corporal," *Daily Mail* (London), October 10, 1943.

78 she loved to go out and "kid": Reginald Eason, "British Soldiers Slept at German Military HQ," *Daily Mail* (London), October 11, 1943.

78 "German soldiers could not get chocolate": "Report on Escape After Being Taken Prisoner of War, by Captain D. B. Lang," WO 208/3301/174, National Archives of the United Kingdom.

80 the nightly curfew began at nine: First-hand accounts of the German occupation from residents of the Pas-de-Calais can be found in Michelsen.

81 bore the same relation: Dejonghe, 487.

81 *l'exode* had begun on May 17: Guerville, 71.

81 The Hôpital-Hospice of Doullens: Ibid., 168–71.

82 Jules Ponthieu: "Succès universitaire," *Le Progrès de la Somme,* November 5, 1938; "Revue générale de clinique et de thérapeutique," *Journal des praticiens,* 1923, 487.

82 Kate and Etta found Lt. Colin Hunter: The description of the meeting with Colin Hunter is drawn primarily from Shiber, 71–76; Colin Hunter interview,

1994; interviews by the author with Andrew Hunter, Alisdair Hunter, and Sheena Gilmour. An account of the life of wounded British soldiers in a French military hospital in 1940 can also be found in Langley, 60–68.

82 **served as the standard garb:** Langley, 61.

84 **"cold terror":** Shiber, 75.

84 **to put Lieutenant Hunter entirely out of her mind:** In his book *Beautiful Souls*, Eyal Press notes of rescuers, "One characteristic they did share was a level of awareness that made it hard for them to put the faces of the victims out of mind." Press, 27.

85 **"Such an infinitely important thing it is":** Adler, 11.

86 **knew how to get this young man out:** Eva Fogelman has noted that rescuers felt capable, competent—having what psychologists call "internal locus of control." She writes, "Rescuers strongly believed they could influence events . . . that made them feel that what they did, or failed to do, mattered a great deal." Fogelman, 59.

CHAPTER 7

87 **"a magnificent amount of food":** Escape report, Lieutenant C. D. Hunter.

87 **round metal-rimmed military glasses:** The description of Gordon Hood-Cree is from an author interview with Terry Hood-Cree, Jacqui Hood-Cree, and Karen Hood-Cree, April 22, 2021.

87 **the French tradition of the *marraine de guerre:*** See the discussion in Darrow, 77–79; Bergin, 51–56.

88 **"the pen is heavier than the rifle":** Darrow, 78.

89 **On the morning of Wednesday, August 28:** Escape report, Lieutenant C. D. Hunter.

89 **the Germans had begun to seize privately owned automobiles:** Thornton, 21.

89 **(Leonard was a Freemason):** Like his father, Charles, Leonard was a member of St. Thomas's Lodge No. 142, one of London's oldest lodges, founded in 1775. Ultimately, he would rise to the third degree of Masonry, becoming a Master Mason. Email to the author from Angela Umpleby, March 27, 2021.

90 **all foreigners over the age of fifteen:** Drake, 111; Rosbottom, 117.

90 **had not received any rain:** "Résumé mensuel du temps en France: Années 1940 à 1944," *La Météorologie Nationale* (1951), 25.

91 **striking up a conversation:** "American woman who lived with Mme. Bonnefous spoke German and discussed points with soldiers when accompanying Mme. Bonnefous on her visits." Appendix, "Report on Escape After Being Taken Prisoner of War, by Captain D. B. Lang."

91 **the pro-Nazi German American Bund:** Federal Writers' Project, 251; Russell, 98–99. Film footage of the 1939 Madison Square Garden rally can be seen in the short documentary *A Night at the Garden,* anightatthegarden.com/.

91 **"Camp Siegfried Specials":** Aaron Short, "New York's Nasty Old Nazi Problem," *Daily Beast,* thedailybeast.com/new-yorks-nasty-old-nazi-problem.

92 **their intense hatred for the British:** "Predominant points arising from conversations were general depression at failure of invasion, coupled with unbelievable hatred of the British." Appendix, "Report on Escape After Being Taken Prisoner of War, by Captain D. B. Lang."

92 **On the officers' ward:** The description of the escape is drawn primarily from Shiber, 75–78; Escape report, Lieutenant C. D. Hunter; Colin Hunter interview, 1994; interviews by the author with Andrew Hunter, Alisdair Hunter, and Sheena

Gilmour. Colin Hunter never said exactly how he escaped from the hospital grounds; in his escape report, he said simply, "On 28th August she [Kate Bonnefous] brought me civilian clothes, hid me in the luggage boot of her car and took me to her flat in Paris." The account of climbing the tree comes from Etta Shiber, and a photograph of the back wall of the hospital, taken during the period, does appear to show a single tree in the spot she describes.

95   **vacationed with Etta's brother, Chester:** The trip took place in April 1939; Etta Shiber refers to it in a number of her letters to Chet and Helen the following year, including one in which she says that she wishes she could live in Nice.

CHAPTER 8

98   **"I don't know":** Blumenson, 66.

98   **"Will the people who produced":** Humbert, 14.

99   **"The Anglophiles hoped":** Gilliam, 194.

100 **buildings had been requisitioned by the Germans:** Desprairies, 580–602.

101 **reduced solely to Gruyère:** Drake, 109.

101 **Even the Bois de Boulogne had been closed:** Peabody, 184; Hughes, 214.

101 **"was British to the backbone":** Reginald Eason, "British Soldiers Slept at German Military HQ," *Daily Mail* (London), October 11, 1943. In this article, published during the war, Colin Hunter is identified simply as "X," and Gordon Hood-Cree as "Y."

101 **In a joke told widely that year:** Blumenson, 88.

102 **sometimes at such short intervals:** Etta Shiber describes herself doing exactly this in other tense circumstances. Shiber, 269.

102 **all six foot two of him:** Author interview with Terry Hood-Cree, Jacqui Hood-Cree, and Karen Hood-Cree, April 22, 2021.

102 **his right foot turned in noticeably:** Ibid.

102 **the clothing that Kate had procured for him:** Hood-Cree would provide differing accounts of how he obtained the civilian clothing. To a reporter from the *Daily Mail,* he mentioned "Yvonne, a good-looking French girl of about 18," who passed articles of clothing to his window on a piece of string; "I never met her except to talk to her from my window," he said. In his essay "Escape from France," Hood-Cree wrote that "contact was made with a girl who passed the prison [by which he meant prison hospital] daily," but he did not indicate whether it was he or Kate Bonnefous who made the contact with her; he said again that "by night my 'civvy' clothes arrived piece by piece on the end of a length of string hung from the second floor." In the report provided to interrogators from MI9, he said simply, "Mme. B. (an Englishwoman married to a French wine merchant and actively engaged in welfare work on behalf of the French Prisoners Aid Society) found me a suit of civilian clothes." It is possible that after Colin Hunter's escape Kate Bonnefous no longer felt comfortable bringing clothes into the hospital, and that she managed to initiate contact with "Yvonne" and arranged for her to deliver the clothes she had obtained. See Hood-Cree, 259; Reginald Eason, "British Soldiers Slept at German Military HQ," *Daily Mail* (London), October 11, 1943; Escape report, Corporal Gordon Hood-Crees [*sic*], 5th Royal East Kent Regiment, WO/3301/219, National Archives of the United Kingdom.

102 **"Mme. B's flat in the town":** Escape report, Corporal Gordon Hood-Crees [*sic*].

103 **to ask loudly in French:** According to Gordon Hood-Cree, "The arrangement was

that I should stop the car and ask for a lift as though I was a Frenchman." Reginald Eason, "Mrs. Beaurepos Saved Me, Says Corporal," *Daily Mail* (London), October 10, 1943.

CHAPTER 9

108 ("besieging the Embassy"): Cecil M. P. Cross, undated memorandum, 4, Elizabeth Deegan folder, Central Decimal File 1940–1944, Record Group 59, General Records of the Department of State, Box 308, National Archives and Records Administration.

109 Born in 1871: For biographical information on Cecil Shaw, see Hore, 34–35, 252.

109 "a tower of strength": "Death of a Great Soldier," *Liverpool Echo*, June 30, 1950.

110 "In 1940 . . . he used his close connection": Ibid.

111 a watercooler: John Forbes Christie testimony, 30, Record 88/47/1, Imperial War Museum.

111 well and "with friends": Escape report, Lieutenant C. D. Hunter.

111 brought back 1,750 francs: Ibid. In her testimony before the German military tribunal, Bonnefous stated that the money had come from Cecil Shaw.

111 a new system of food rationing: Sebba, 62; Drake, 125.

111 "a rather sordid-looking garage and store": Walter, 82.

112 "Any responsible, good-natured French citizen": Ibid.

112 "Nobody crosses his vegetable store owner": Ibid., 89.

112 "set fire to my grocer's store": Ibid., 87.

112 ("prewar sugar"): Ibid., 84.

113 "She had a colossal sense of humor": Reginald Eason, "British Soldiers Slept at German Military HQ," *Daily Mail* (London), October 11, 1943.

113 "To 'find' is when": Ousby, 129.

114 "Food in Paris was extremely short": Reginald Eason, "British Soldiers Slept at German Military HQ," *Daily Mail* (London), October 11, 1943.

114 yet another errand that Kate had to run: There is some disagreement in the accounts regarding this incident. In his 1952 essay "Escape through France," Gordon Hood-Cree claims that the two men did not have identification papers, and were only able to get past the German guards at the railroad station after having noticed that the guards only checked one passenger out of every three—an observation made after having "spied on the procedure of the German guards" at the various entrances to the station "for three days or more." (Hood-Cree, 260.) However, Colin Hunter never spoke of such observations—and indeed, he specifically stated that the only time he left the apartment was to get his photograph taken at a large department store downtown. (Colin Hunter interview, 1994.) It is difficult to imagine that the two servicemen would have relied for their safety on German guards only checking one passenger out of every three—a system that has not been established in other accounts—or that Kate Bonnefous would have sent off the two servicemen with no identification. Furthermore, in an interview conducted with his son years later, Colin Hunter recalled of his trip with Hood-Cree, "Eventually we got on a train with false identity papers."

115 "perfect dignity of the passersby": Henri Michel, *Paris Allemand* (Paris: Albin Michel, 1981), 50.

115 six small black-and-white photographs: Thus the Photomaton slogan: "6 different photos for 5 francs in 8 minutes."

115 had shaved their mustaches: Colin Hunter interview, 1994.

115 "It was terrifying": Ibid.
116 "I consider that about 2,500 British soldiers": "Helpers, Details of Evasion and Notes on Marseilles," Lieutenant J. M. Langley, Coldstream Guards, WO 208/3301/13, National Archives of the United Kingdom.
116 at stationery shops: Ibid.; Schoenbrun, 76.
116 with a small box camera: John Forbes Christie testimony, 23.
116 Rackelboom, a World War I veteran: Biographical information is drawn from the Gustave Rackelboom file, Côte GR 16 P 496941, Archives of the Service Historique de la Défense.
116 a razor blade in the rubber heel: John Forbes Christie testimony, 23.
116 a cold hard-boiled egg: Langley, 82.
117 he sought assistance from another government office: Jeanne Monier attestation for Gustave Rackelboom, ibid.; Gustave Rackelboom attestation for Jeanne Monier, Jeanne Monier file, Archives of the Service Historique de la Défense.
117 Henri Grimal: Information on Grimal is drawn from the Léon-Henri Grimal file, Archives of the Service Historique de la Défense.
118 the letter arrived from Henri Bonnefous: "This lady [Kate Bonnefous] then tried to find a route to Marseille for us. Eventually her husband, who was a wine merchant, wished to go south to Marseille and found a route through between Libourne and La Reole. On his arrival in Unoccupied France he wrote us full details." Escape report, Lieutenant C. D. Hunter.

CHAPTER 10

119 a multitude of fantastic creatures: Galet, 147.
119 born in 1895 in the southwestern town of Castillon-sur-Dordogne: Autobiographical details about Elie Teyssier are primarily drawn from Elie Teyssier, matricules 841 and 6269, Côte 1 R 1554 841, Archives Départementales de la Gironde; Elie Teyssier file, Côte GR 16P 566481, Service Historique de la Défense; Elie Teyssier file, AC21P543527, Archives Départementales du Calvados; Friot and Villechenoux, unpaged.
120 more than twenty thousand *métayers:* In 1885, the Périgord had 24,893 *métayers.* Rocal, 209.
120 a contract minutely detailed: The relevant section in an agricultural economics textbook of the period notes in part: "Whilst grain is usually divided equally, in some places the lessor takes a third of the wheat and rye and a quarter of the oats and barley; in the latter event the *métayer* would be expected to provide seed corn and two-thirds or three-quarters of the manure. Potatoes almost invariably go to the tenant, but in [the] Périgord, anything up to a third is the lessor's perquisite. Even manure heaps, fodder, and standing grass in temporary meadows, if they escape an annual division, are yet subject to valuation on the termination of a lease, and any increase in their value is divisible." The explanation continues for some time in this vein. J. A. Venn, *The Foundation of Agricultural Economics* (Cambridge, U.K.: University Press, 1933), 87–90.
120 he had bought himself a boat: Michel Charles Ganipeau affidavit, Elie Teyssier file, Service Historique de la Défense.
122 no more powerful and humiliating symbol of defeat: Rolli, 36.
122 requisitioned to cut down trees: Ibid., 40.
123 about four-fifths of the *passeurs* were men: Alary, 145.
123 a taste for adventure: Ibid., 132.

123 **a payment of 250 francs might suffice:** Souleau, 187.

123 **only 50 francs per passenger:** Jehan Burguburu trial notes, Etta Shiber case file, Archives of Gide Loyrette Nouel, Paris.

123 **"worked for us purely free of charge":** Gaston Melet affidavit, Elie Teyssier file, Service Historique de la Défense.

123 **On September 26, 1940:** Escape report, Lieutenant C. D. Hunter.

123 **The train trip was passed mostly in darkness:** The description of the train trip and subsequent journey is drawn primarily from ibid.; Escape report, Corporal Gordon Hood-Crees [*sic*]; Hood-Cree, 261; Colin Hunter interview, 1994; author interview with Terry Hood-Cree, Jacqui Hood-Cree, and Karen Hood-Cree, 2021.

124 **"dismantled and inspected":** Rolli, 54.

125 **"Listen," he murmured:** Reginald Eason, "British Soldiers Slept at German Military HQ," *Daily Mail* (London), October 11, 1943.

125 **"The place . . . was stiff with Germans":** Ibid.

125 **"We went to see a Frenchman in Libourne":** Escape report, Lieutenant C. D. Hunter.

125 **the second man was Elie Teyssier:** Colin Hunter's name appears on an MI9 list of British soldiers transported by Elie Teyssier. After the war, MI9 compiled questionnaires as well as other supporting information to determine possible monetary awards for individuals who had aided evading British and American servicemen; these files are now held by the National Archives and Records Administration in College Park, Maryland. Elie Teyssier folder, Case Files Relating to French Citizens Proposed for Awards for Assisting American Airmen, 1945–1947, National Archives and Records Administration, Record Group 498, Box 1176.

126 **Perhaps twenty-five hundred German soldiers:** Vinen, 103; Rolli, 56.

126 **"the line of demarcation was neither":** Alary, 133.

126 **where the German control posts had been established:** A map of the control posts in the immediate area, with descriptions, can be found in Gaillard et al., 82–83.

126 **the safer route was instead to head downstream:** There are gaps in both Hunter's and Hood-Cree's descriptions of this leg of the journey. In his escape report, for instance, Colin Hunter recalled simply, "In the morning we left hurriedly and went to see a Frenchman in Libourne, who put us in touch with another man, who helped us to cross the line of demarcation, where we met a woman and her young son who walked us through the vineyards and so we arrived in Unoccupied France." In his escape report, Hood-Cree stated: "We remained in Paris for three weeks and then left by train for Libourne, 18 miles ENE of Bordeaux. Five days later we walked to La Reole and from there by train to Marseille." Neither one specifically mentioned being transported by boat—or by any other mode of transportation. However, the Dordogne River did separate Saint-Pey-d'Armens from the line of demarcation, and the bridges across the river were heavily guarded; the authors of *Castillon à l'heure allemande* noted that the great majority of *passeurs* in the area were those who had their own boat (Gaillard et al., 92); and, according to an affidavit given after the war by a resistance comrade, Michel Charles Ganipeau, "Teyssier had a boat at Castillon and made transports from one zone to the other" (Michel Charles Ganipeau affidavit, Elie Teyssier file, Service Historique de la Défense). Another escaper helped by Kate Bonnefous, 2nd Lt. John F. N. Buckingham, did mention crossing the Dordogne River.

126 **downstream on the Dordogne, toward Civrac:** The debarkment near Civrac is an estimation based on the local topography, the position of the line of demarcation, and the subsequent arrival on foot of Hunter and Hood-Cree at Pujols-sur-

Dordogne. Another British serviceman sent by Kate Bonnefous to Libourne, John Buckingham, noted in his escape report that he "cross[ed] the line 20 kilometers east of Libourne, across the river Dordogne and so through Pujols." Civrac is approximately twenty kilometers southeast of Libourne. Escape report, 2nd Lieutenant J.F.N. Buckingham, Royal Field Artillery, WO 208/3304/355, National Archives of the United Kingdom.

126   "They were a link in a network": Gaillard et al., 92.

127   "Soon she turned": Hood-Cree, 261.

127   a German soldier rode by on a bicycle: Colin Hunter interview, 1994.

127   "Colin was a few yards away": Hood-Cree, 261.

128   the village of Pujols-sur-Dordogne: Escape report, Lieutenant C. D. Hunter.

128   where they could stay overnight: The hotel in which they stayed was l'Hôtel Central. Patrick Dihars email to author, May 16, 2021.

CHAPTER 11

129   "unacceptable" authors such as Shakespeare: Drake, 124.

129   posted their combat medals: Ibid., 133.

130   a "special census" of the Jewish community: Poznanski, *Jews,* 32–33; Poznanski, "Le fichage," 250; Josephs, 24.

130   the Vichy definition of a Jew: Weisberg, 39; Gildea, 221.

131   Only 477 Levys: Weisberg, 320.

131   149,734 Parisian Jews: Poznanski, *Jews,* 33.

132   British evaders and escapers: Helen Fry, 3; Neave, 21.

133   Sally was thirty-five years old: Biographical information on Sally Siauve-Evausy is drawn primarily from the Sally Siauve Evausy folder, Case Files Relating to French Citizens Proposed for Awards for Assisting American Airmen, 1945–1947, National Archives and Records Administration, Record Group 498, Box 1169; see also Lang, 93–109.

133   Her husband, Georges, a distinguished surgeon: Lang, 93.

133   "America was not yet in the war": Ibid., 120.

134   His deputy consul had been arrested: His name was Edward John Sutton. Information on Sutton's arrest and imprisonment is contained in his September 10, 1965, letter to the British Foreign Office, Nazi Persecution Claim: Mr. John Sutton, FO 950/1757, National Archives of the United Kingdom.

134   no one left to countersign the receipts: Cecil M. P. Cross, supplemental memorandum on ED case, December 10, 1940, Elizabeth Deegan folder, Central Decimal File 1940–1944, Record Group 59, General Records of the Department of State, Box 308, National Archives and Records Administration.

134   "I hear that you are escapers": Lang, 127.

134   "Kitty had an air of directness": Ibid., 126.

135   At three o'clock the bell rang: This is an approximation. Lang and Buckingham arrived at the American embassy immediately as it opened; Lang then reports that they had "six hours to kill" before their appointment at Kitty's flat. Ibid., 127.

135   just a bit under six feet tall: Sarah Hunt interview, April 22, 2021.

135   wearing a slouch beret: Lang, 110.

135   a pinkish complexion: Ibid., 78.

135   "You must be starving!": Ibid., 129. The lunch is described on pages 129–31.

136   French officer . . . showed up unexpectedly: Escape report, Lieutenant C. D. Hunter.

136 "She was a bundle of nerves": Lang, 129.

137 "These tales of her various activities": Ibid., 131.

137 "bullied it out of an American official": Ibid.

137 Kate Bonnefous was "heroic": Ibid., 129.

137 "another Nurse Cavell": "Report on Escape After Being Taken Prisoner of War, by Captain D. B. Lang."

138 "If anything ever happens to me": Shiber, 10.

138 "into a new course": Ibid., 30.

CHAPTER 12

139 Georges Siauve-Evausy had confided: Escape report, Lieutenant C. D. Hunter.

141 "one of those Frenchmen whose classic profiles": Shiber, 132.

141 He stood five foot ten: Edouard Régniez file, AC21 P 649111, Archives Départementales du Calvados.

141 had been named curé of Conchy-sur-Canche: M. Beirnaert et al., *Dictionnaire du monde religieux dans la France contemporaine* (Volume 11, Arras: Artois–Côte d'Opale) (Paris: Beauchesne, 2013), 666.

141 "He was welcomed with a delirious joy": *Histoire de la paroisse de Conchy-sur-Canche, Monchel et Aubrometz,* unpaged handwritten manuscript, Archives Historiques du Diocèse, Arras.

141 piloted a Potez 60: "Aero-Club de la Somme," *Le Progrès de la Somme,* May 3, 1938.

141 Edouard had been born in Carvin: Biographical information is drawn primarily from the Edouard Régniez file, Côte GR 16 P 503622, Archives of the Service Historique de la Défense; Edouard Régniez file, Archives Départementales du Calvados; M. Beirnaert et al., *Dictionnaire du monde religieux dans la France contemporaine* (Volume 11, Arras: Artois–Côte d'Opale) (Paris: Beauchesne, 2013), 666; *Histoire de la paroisse de Conchy-sur-Canche, Monchel et Aubrometz,* unpaged handwritten manuscript, Archives Historiques du Diocèse, Arras.

142 a tin can filled with water: Hilaire, 121.

142 Convoys of French prisoners of war: "La vie quotidienne à Carvin sous l'occupation allemande," archivespasdecalais.fr/Recherche-par-commune/Lettre -C/Carvin/La-vie-quotidienne-a-Carvin-sous-l-occupation-allemande.

143 "Without a doubt": Villate, 205.

143 "No matter the cost": Ibid., 186.

143 only about fifteen hundred remained alive: Ibid., 204.

143 "are being sacrificed like glasses of water": Saint-Exupéry, 4.

143 "an end-of-the-world spectacle": Jean Malaquais, *Jean Malaquais' War Diary,* translated by Peter Grant (Garden City, N.Y.: Doubleday, 1944), 193.

144 everything had been taken from them: McPhail, 92–93.

144 "go out into the woods": Ibid., 85.

144 like working the lock on a safe: This was the analogy used by the British escaper John Forbes Christie of the 51st Highland Infantry Division. John Forbes Christie testimony.

144 "[He] always volunteered for missions": Edouard Régniez file, Archives of the Service Historique de la Défense.

145 the very day he arrived back in Conchy-sur-Canche: Ibid.

145 eight escaped British servicemen: MI9 escape reports indicate that the eight were likely Capt. Charles P. Murchie, Sgts. Thomas Boyle and Rupert Knight, Driver

S. D. Boyd, and Pvts. Harry H. Kimble, M. Allen, C. E. Camgee, and one identified only as "Poole."

145 **one of the local parishioners had seen:** This information was related by Régniez to a clerical colleague while he was in Cherche-Midi prison. Letter from the vicar of Saint Germain to Monseigneur Dutoit, March 15, 1941, Archives Historiques du Diocèse, Arras.

145 **had set off for Lille:** This was Capt. Charles P. Murchie. Clutton-Brock, 27.

145 **taking such risks:** According to the French captain Albert Girardon, a fellow prisoner in Cherche-Midi, Régniez had told his parishioners, "It is not for you, caring for children, to run such risks. Entrust your prisoners to me." Girardon, 256.

146 **"is in general respected and sometimes venerated":** Decroix, unpaged.

146 **Mondays and Fridays:** July Boulanger testimony, December 17, 1945, July Boulanger folder, Service Historique de la Défense.

147 **"dangerous merchandise":** This was the *passeur* Jeanne Huyge of Wattrelos, a town in the Nord-Pas-de-Calais. Murphy, 36.

147 **"The network was in the process of being established":** Testimony of Dr. Alphonse Poteau, June 27, 1947, 72 AJ 173, Archives Nationales de France, Paris.

147 **a retired typesetter:** Arthur Richards folder, Côte 16 P 509982, Archives of the Service Historique de la Défense; Lesage, "La Résistance précoce," 505; René Lesage email to author, July 10, 2020.

148 **"artisanal stage":** Dejonghe, *Le Nord-Pas-de-Calais,* 179.

148 **more than twelve thousand civilian helpers:** Neave, 16.

148 **"I regret nothing at all":** Eliane Méplaux-Hermant folder, GR 16P 291537, Service Historique de la Défense.

149 **"While [Bonnefous's] efforts":** Bergin, 62.

CHAPTER 13

150 **"haunted by the memory of its grandeur":** Sartre, 6.

150 **gray sheets pulled over them:** Peabody, 197.

151 **"The silence caught you by the throat":** Rosbottom, xix.

151 **"listen in on all suspected wires":** Kernan, 24.

151 **or released a pigeon:** Drake, 145.

151 **"accustomed to expressing themselves without fear":** Michel, 166.

151 **"The phrase on everybody's lips":** Ousby, 48.

152 **an escaped soldier named Harry Clayton:** Information on Clayton is primarily drawn from Escape report, Acting Sergeant Interpreter H. K. [Henry Keith] Clayton, Royal Air Force, WO 208/3308/701, National Archives of the United Kingdom; Clutton-Brock, 27–28; Michelle Clayton Rist interview with author, April 23, 2021; Henry Clayton email to author, April 29, 2021.

152 **Capt. Charles P. Murchie:** Information on Murchie is primarily drawn from: Escape report, Capt. C. P. Murchie, Royal Army Service Corps, WO 208/3308/681, National Archives of the United Kingdom; Clutton-Brock, 27–28; Baynac, 166; Murphy, 53.

152 **didn't mind flashing money around:** See the description of Murchie in "Helpers, Details of Evasion and Notes on Marseilles," Lieutenant J. M. Langley.

153 **they made contact with Elie Teyssier:** Murchie's name appears on a postwar list of nine British servicemen aided by Teyssier. Elie Teyssier folder, Case Files Relating to French Citizens Proposed for Awards for Assisting American Airmen,

1945–1947, National Archives and Records Administration, Record Group 498, Box 1176.

153 "I was advised": Escape report, Lt. J. M. Langley, Coldstream Guards, WO 208/3301/213, National Archives of the United Kingdom.

153 "arrested daily by the French": Letter from Charles P. Murchie to Sir Samuel Hoare, August 15, 1941, "Treatment of British Service Personnel Detained in Spain," Code 41 File 17, FO 371/26949A, National Archives of the United Kingdom.

153 The line that Murchie had established: Regrettably, the enormous contributions made by Charles Murchie have been effaced in some accounts of the Pat O'Leary line, with all credit for the early work given to Ian Garrow. In part, this may be due to the fact that some of the leading figures in MI9, such as Jimmy Langley and Airey Neave, knew Garrow better than they did Murchie. The absence might also derive from Murchie's having been a somewhat unsavory character—and in particular a controversy that arose near the end of his time in Marseille, when he lost a large sum of money (perhaps as much as 2 million francs) that he had hidden in the hotel room of his girlfriend, a cashier in a nightclub owned by a pair of Corsican gangsters. Murchie insisted that the money had been stolen at gunpoint, but that claim was never proved. See, for instance, the discussion in Baynac, 166–67.

153 rescuing some six hundred soldiers: This estimate, which is generally accepted, came from Airey Neave, a British escaper during World War II who went on to become MI9's contact with the Pat O'Leary line. Neave, 22. See also Foot and Langley, 75.

154 would arrive only on Fridays: July Boulanger testimony, December 17, 1945.

154 "If we didn't want people": Shiber, 175.

155 "My dear, how glad I am": Ibid.

155 November 11 was Armistice Day: The account of the events of November 11, 1940, is drawn primarily from: Cobb, 43–46; Schoenbrun, 89–91; Drake, 146–51.

157 "There were no difficulties": Shiber, 164.

158 "We arranged it": Mary Braggiotti, "Mrs. Shiber Surprised Even Herself," *New York Post,* September 21, 1943.

CHAPTER 14

161 "The drain that purchases on the black market made": Shiber, 161.

161 Etta had sent for $1,500: Stuart, 9; "Woman Held by Nazis Has Brother Here," *Syracuse Herald-Journal,* December 14, 1940.

161 one pair each: July Boulanger testimony, December 17, 1945.

161 Kate "reproached" her: Ibid.

162 another overcast day in Paris: November 26, 1940: "The sky has been gray for several days." Girardon, 217.

163 At noon the doorbell rang: This scene is drawn primarily from Shiber, 191–94; "Special War Problems," War History, General Records of the Department of State, Special War Problems Division, RG 59, National Records and Archives Administration, 11; Etta Kahn Shiber file, 362.1121/47, Records Group 59: General Records of the Department of State, Central Decimal Files, National Archives and Records Administration; July Boulanger testimony, December 17, 1945.

165 containing money and other valuable goods: Célerse, 39.

166 the driver turned onto the rue de Varenne: This scene is drawn from excerpts from the fifty-four-page transcript of the interview Etta gave to Paul Winkler's Press Alliance, included in Aladar A. Farkas affidavit, "Record on Appeal, in the Matter of the Arbitration Between Aladar A. Farkas and Paul Winkler, Betty Winkler, Press Alliance, Inc., Etta Shiber, and Charles Scribner's Sons," New York Supreme Court, Appellate Division—First Department, 1944, "Etta Shiber, 1943," Box 236, Folder 7, Archives of Charles Scribner's Sons, 1786–2004, Special Collections, Princeton University Library; as well as Shiber, 195–200; July Boulanger testimony, December 17, 1945; and other accounts from women arrested by the Gestapo during the same period, among them Mary Lindell's in Wynne, 94–97, and Bessy Myers's in Myers, 166–72.

166 had been requisitioned by the Germans: Lottman, 371; Mark Seal, "Paris' Hotel Lutetia Is Haunted by History," *Smithsonian*, April 2019.

169 long-standing fault lines in French society: Wobick-Segev, 19.

169 an old French pamphlet about the Dreyfus affair: Shiber, 205.

CHAPTER 15

170 one wall lined with empty bookshelves: Myers, 118.

171 She was in her cell: Descriptions of the cell and of the prison routine are drawn from Shiber, 208, 234–38, as well as accounts by other female prisoners held at Cherche-Midi at the time, including Humbert, 55–56; Myers, 133–37; and Wynne, 98; also Sherwill, 158–59.

172 She had not cried so intensely: Shiber, 208.

173 Her name was Mary Bird: Ibid., 209. See also Bell, 38–40; Durand, *Guernsey*, 62; frankfallaarchive.org/people/mary-bird-later-bichard/.

173 seventeen machine-gun positions: Bell, 12.

174 in their stockinged feet: Testimony of Henriette Docquier, memoresist.org/rencontre/conference-exposition-sur-la-prison-militaire-du-cherche-midi-un-trou-noir-de-lhistoire/.

174 or do manual work of any kind: Humbert, 62.

175 "bread orderly": Sherwill, 163.

175 "allowing me to lie in its silence": Shiber, 209.

176 his name was Captain Liebgott: Girardon, 166. In his unpublished memoir, *Peace in Our Time*, Josiah Marvel refers to him simply as Captain L.

176 "a tall, handsome gentleman": Marvel, "Notes," 4.

176 Marvel came from a family: Biographical information on Josiah P. Marvel is drawn from Henry Beckett, "The Too-Unselfish Friend," *New York Post*, August 19, 1948; "Joseph P. Marvel (1896–1959)," Quaker Emergency Service Records, 1942–1965, Friends Historical Library of Swarthmore College. As it happens, Josiah Marvel was a devotee of classical music; his wife, Eleanor Jacobs, was a musicologist with a specialty in modern American and French classical music and would surely have been familiar with the writings of Irving Weil, Etta Shiber's cousin.

177 "to be arrested by the Gestapo": Marvel, "Notes," 4.

177 "I find myself running a large laundry service": "Former Local Man in France Learns Worth of Liberty," *Palladium-Item* (Richmond, Indiana), January 19, 1941.

177 "Did the American Embassy send you over?": Shiber, 225.

178 kept a storeroom of clothing: Wynne, 102.

178 "almost lightheartedly": Shiber, 226.

CHAPTER 16

179 **"in relation to the arrest"**: Maynard B. Barnes memo, January 17, 1941, Etta Shiber file, 362.1121/47, Record Group 59: General Records of the Department of State, Central Decimal Files, National Archives and Records Administration.

179 **a longtime Foreign Service officer**: "Further Correspondence Respecting Morocco, Part 3: January to December 1949," *Foreign Office: Confidential Print Morocco and North-West Africa 1839–1957,* 20; prabook.com/web/edwin_august .plitt/326559.

180 **who held a coveted *Ausweis***: Josiah P. Marvel scrapbook, HC.MC.975.04.017, Quaker and Special Collections, Haverford College.

180 **"he entered by a ruse"**: Stuart, *American,* 181–82.

180 **Plitt had made contact with an attorney**: Stuart, "Special," 9.

180 **A native of Strasbourg**: Guénaire, 106.

180 **to speak French without a German accent**: Jean-Marie Burguburu email to author, February 20, 2021.

180 **advised him to get in touch with her**: Barnes memo, January 17, 1941.

180 **Marvel had brought her woolen underwear**: Inez Whiteley Foster, "Home Again After 18 Months Under Nazis," *Christian Science Monitor,* October 19, 1943.

180 **she indicated that it was Henri Bonnefous**: Shiber, 226, 245.

181 **the Special War Problems Division**: Russell, 28.

181 **Originally called simply the Special Division**: Ibid.; Stuart, "Special," 7.

181 **the division's organizational history**: The history of the Special War Problems Division was produced as part of the U.S. State Department's *Histories of Organizational Units and Functions During World War II,* the working papers and source materials for which are now held by the National Archives and Records Administration.

181 **"The American Embassy first learned"**: "Special War Problems Division," Record Group 59: General Records of the Department of State, Drafts of Histories of Organizational Units and Functions During World War II, 1943–1949, National Archives and Records Administration.

181 **the ongoing routines of the prison**: Accounts of daily life inside Cherche-Midi can be found in Shiber, 215, 237–38; Humbert, 55–59, 73; Myers, 133–34; Hanley, 87; Sherwill, 158–59.

181 **Frau Blümelein**: prisons-cherche-midi-mauzac.com/des-hommes/frau-blumelein -matonne-a-la-prison-allemande-du-cherche-midi-11766; Humbert, 59. Blümelein was so brutal that in September 1941 one of the prisoners, Jane Jeunet Darboy, took the great risk of writing directly to the prison commandant to complain of *"le sadism tortionnaire"* and warning that suicides would become numerous if he did not intervene.

183 **worked as a clerk and receptionist**: Elizabeth Deegan can be seen in footage of the American embassy taken in July 1938 for the newsreel series *The March of Time.* collections.ushmm.org/search/catalog/irn1000862.

183 **"a comfortable hotel in Paris"**: This was the Hotel Avenida, at 41 rue du Colisée. Information on the arrest and detention of Elizabeth Deegan is drawn from Elizabeth Deegan folder, Central Decimal File 1940–44: 123, Record Group 59: General Records of the Department of State, Box 308, National Archives and Records Administration; Classified General Records, 1940–1942, Record Group 84: Department of State, U.S. Embassy, France, National Archives and Records Administration.

183 an "underground railway": "Embassy Clerk's Arrest Stirs New U.S.-Nazi Rift,"
     New York *Daily News,* December 7, 1940.

183 had stayed in the home of an American embassy official: Escape report, Private
     S. G. C. Park, Argyll and Sutherland Highlanders, WO 208/3301/218, National
     Archives of the United Kingdom.

184 "watching the matter closely": "U.S. Protests to Germany in Deegan Case," *Wash-
     ington Post,* December 7, 1940.

184 "relief has been refused": [H. Freeman] Matthews telegram, December 24, 1940,
     Elizabeth Deegan folder, Central Decimal File 1940–44: 123, Record Group 59:
     General Records of the Department of State, Box 308, National Archives and
     Records Administration.

184 "Mrs. Deegan gave me another 250 francs": Escape report, Private A. A. L. Lang,
     Argyll and Sutherland Highlanders, WO 208/3301/167, National Archives of the
     United Kingdom.

185 "was given 500 francs by an American lady": Escape report, Sergeant-Major
     Charlie Fullerton, Gordon Highlanders, WO 208/3299/73, National Archives of
     the United Kingdom.

185 "and there found Colonel Shaw": Escape report, Driver G. J. Thibaut, Royal
     Army Service Corps, WO 208/3299/46, National Archives of the United King-
     dom.

185 they wished to see "Mrs. Deacon": John Forbes Christie testimony, 30.

185 "the recipients of such payments": William Leahy telegram, December 30, 1940,
     Classified General Records, 1940–1942, Record Group 84: Department of State,
     U.S. Embassy, France, National Archives and Records Administration.

186 on Saturday, December 14: Shiber, 240; Barnes memo, January 17, 1941.

186 an Unteroffizier handed her a release form: A photo of the signed release form
     can be seen in Shiber, 241.

CHAPTER 17

188 arrived at the embassy on Tuesday, December 17: Barnes memo, January 17,
     1941.

188 he "strongly advised" her: Ibid.

189 set into motion the various bureaucratic processes: Ibid.

189 had not heard from his sister since August: Ibid. "Nazis Seize Second American
     Woman in Occupied France," *Washington Post,* December 14, 1940.

189 "I take pleasure in informing you": Cecil M. P. Cross letter, December 19, 1940,
     Etta Shiber file, 362.1121/47, Record Group 59: General Records of the Depart-
     ment of State, Central Decimal Files, National Archives and Records Adminis-
     tration.

189 its basement shelter was the only one: Glass, 37.

190 paper soaked for twenty-four hours: Shiber, 177–78; Ousby, 122.

190 made from the pelts of dogs: Kershaw, 50.

190 the Gestapo had stationed a man: July Boulanger testimony, December 17,
     1945.

192 On the evening of December 22: Barnes memo, January 17, 1941.

193 "I seemed to re-enter immediately": Shiber, 273.

193 a young engineer named Jacques Bonsergent: See Blumenson, 123–27; Hanley,
     86–89; Ousby, 208; Drake, 166.

194 "an act of violence": Glass, 164.

194 he waved away the appeal: Hanley, 86.

194 At dawn on December 23: This scene is described in ibid., 88–89.

194 he was "transfixed" by the news: Ousby, 208.

194 midnight mass in Paris was celebrated at five P.M.: Blumenson, 127.

194 she began to sing the Latin hymn: Etta Shiber, "Pangs for Victims of War Grip the Heart at Yuletide," *Chicago Tribune*, December 5, 1943.

195 "I was no sadder": Ibid.

195 "One of the most moving moments": Bell, 45.

195 "It occurs to me": Shiber, 277.

196 introduced herself as Mrs. Symes: For more on Rachel Symes, see frankfallaarchive .org/people/rachel-symes-nee-tostevin/.

196 "wrote messages on the window": frankfallaarchive.org/people/mary-bird-later -bichard/.

196 a difference of opinion: See, for example, frankfallaarchive.org/people/louis -morin-symes/; Sherwill, 163.

196 "was not a concentration camp": Nazi Persecution Claim: Mrs. Rachel Symes, FO 950/2068, National Archives of the United Kingdom.

197 evacuated to Great Britain: Ralph Durand, 14; "Evacuees from Guernsey Recall Life in Scotland," bbc.com/news/uk-scotland-11708270.

198 dug out a tiny hole in the wall: "L'Appartement de Mme. Bonnefous," Kate Bonnefous file, Côte GR 28 P 4 290 83, Archives de la Service Historique de la Défense; Montague Taylor, "British Heroine of 60 Who Defied Gestapo," *The People* (London), November 4, 1945.

CHAPTER 18

199 "to see how we were getting on": Escape report, Lieutenant C. D. Hunter.

199 a five-person international medical board: Ibid.; Reginald Eason, "British Soldiers Slept at German Military HQ," *Daily Mail* (London), October 11, 1943.

199 "Georges François": Escape report, Corporal Gordon Hood-Crees [*sic*].

199 "the most violently pro-British Frenchman": Reginald Eason, "British Soldiers Slept at German Military HQ," *Daily Mail* (London), October 11, 1943.

200 to provide 35,000 francs: Escape report, Lieutenant C. D. Hunter.

200 "I am going back": This and the subsequent quotations are from ibid.; Reginald Eason, "British Soldiers Slept at German Military HQ," *Daily Mail* (London), October 11, 1943.

201 she donned a wig: Wynne, 103. In his escape report, Colin Hunter said only that she "altered her appearance a certain amount."

201 On November 30: After the war, a pension claim filed by Elie Teyssier's wife, Jeanne, states that he was arrested with Kate Bonnefous on December 25, 1940, but this date is incorrect. Bonnefous was arrested on November 30, and a confidential report of the local special commissar to the director general of national security, dated December 16, 1940, indicates that Teyssier was already in custody by then: "The German authorities have also arrested certain cross-border workers functioning as 'passeurs' and among whom are those named B. André and B. René, who had already been reported previously, as well as Teyssier, who has already been the subject of several reports." "Rapport du commissaire spécial au director général de la sûreté nationale," December 16, 1940, AD 24: 1 W 1800, Archives Départementales de la Gironde.

201 near Castillon-sur-Dordogne: Kate Bonnefous questionnaire, April 26, 1945,

Ministère des Anciens Combattants, Documentation et Témoignages, F/9/5583, Archives Nationales de France, Paris; "War Crimes: Declaration Made by Madame Bonnefous," June 8, 1945, FO 371/50978, National Archives of the United Kingdom; Escape report, Lieutenant C. D. Hunter.

201 a "man most steeped in villainy": David Wingeate Pike, *In the Service of Stalin: Spanish Communists in Exile, 1939–1945* (New York: Oxford University Press, 1993), 170.

201 converted into a torture chamber: Déogracias, 89.

202 thrown into the dungeon: Nazi Persecution Claim: Mrs. Kate Bonnefous, June 7, 1965, FO 950/3106, National Archives of the United Kingdom.

202 The dungeon was where: The description is primarily drawn from Bordes, 82–83; Déogracias, 89–90.

203 She remained there until January 3, 1941: "War Crimes: Declaration Made by Madame Bonnefous," June 8, 1945.

203 warmed by powerful arc lights: Wynne, 101.

203 they brutalized her: "I was interrogated every day from January 10 until the middle of February. According to their mood, they brutalized me or offered me cigarettes." Ibid.

203 ground lit cigarettes into the backs of her hands: The tortures suffered by Kate Bonnefous are described in "War Crimes: Declaration Made by Madame Bonnefous," June 8, 1945, as well as various newspaper articles, e.g., Montague Taylor, "British Heroine of 60 Who Defied Gestapo," *The People* (London), November 4, 1945. Handwritten notes made by Bonnefous, perhaps in anticipation of filing her Nazi persecution claim, contain the following: "Very badly treated Cherche Midi prison Paris, burnt my hands to get information from me, beaten and kicked, very little food." Another female political prisoner at Cherche-Midi, Monique Sisich, has also written of "being under questioning every day by the Abwehr, slapped, tortured with cigarette burns, and other duress." Sisich, 38.

204 tracked down her son, Len: "War Crimes: Declaration Made by Madame Bonnefous," June 8, 1945.

204 Edouard Régniez had been arrested on December 24: Girardon, 256; July Boulanger testimony, December 17, 1945. In an autobiographical poem entitled "In Memory of the Hours Spent in Prison," written by Régniez after the war, he notes, "On Christmas Eve, I entered prison." memoire14-45.eu/fr/notice/2013-1 -33-poeme-musee-de-la-resistance-bondues-e0217c6a-4c7a-4547-b9f0 -ef8f77b6977f.

204 Abbé Julien Berteloot was arrested two weeks later: Julien Berteloot folder, Case Files Relating to French Citizens Proposed for Awards for Assisting American Airmen, 1945–1947, Record Group 498, Box 928, National Archives and Records Administration; July Boulanger testimony, December 17, 1945.

204 in front of the Gare Saint-Lazare: Gustave Rackelboom file, Archives of the Service Historique de la Défense.

204 a young Alsatian named Alfred Noëppel: Jeanne Monier file, Archives of the Service Historique de la Défense. Gustave Rackelboom would remember him only as "Moëppel/Noëppel." Gustave Rackelboom file, Archives of the Service Historique de la Défense.

205 "He didn't make a good impression": "Activité de Madame Bonnefous," Kate Bonnefous file, Archives of the Service Historique de la Défense.

205 arrested in the same sweep: Léon-Henri Grimal file, Archives of the Service Historique de la Défense.

205 **a payment of 10,000 francs:** "Activité de Madame Bonnefous," Kate Bonnefous file, Archives of the Service Historique de la Défense. See also Shiber, 189. Years later Bonnefous raised the total to 30,000 francs. "Speaking Personally," *Courier and Advertiser* (Dundee, Scotland), August 16, 1960.

205 **"As it has, so far, been impossible":** Barnes memo, January 7, 1941. Etta Shiber file, 362.1121/47, Record Group 59: General Records of the Department of State, Central Decimal Files, National Archives and Records Administration.

205 **"In reply to the American Embassy's letters":** German embassy memo (translated from German), January 15, 1941. Ibid.

206 **in a French courtroom, on French soil:** See Blumenson, 8.

CHAPTER 19

208 **to meet with Jehan Burguburu:** Jehan Burguburu trial notes, Etta Shiber case file, Archives of Gide Loyrette Nouel, Paris.

208 **of Basque origin:** Jean-Marie Burguburu email to author, February 20, 2021.

208 **"displayed an impressive activity":** Guénaire, 106.

208 **his work with German military tribunals:** The French legal profession itself was not exempt from anti-Semitic discrimination. A Vichy statute of October 3, 1940, had set a quota of 2 percent on Jewish participation in a number of professions, including the law, and hundreds of attorneys were expelled from the Bar of Paris simply for being Jewish. The practice of law in Vichy France was carried on within an overarching system of repression and anti-Semitism; and while some individual attorneys, Jehan Burguburu among them, were occasionally able to win meaningful legal victories for their clients, it is also the fact that, collectively, l'Ordre des avocats de Paris never raised any protest against anti-Jewish Vichy legislation that was inhumane on its face and itself violative of settled French law. Weisberg, "Hermeneutic," 1884; Weitz, 30. See also Drake, 135; Gildea, 220.

208 **a panel of three judges:** *"Feldurteil,"* March 9, 1941, Etta Shiber case file, Archives of Gide Loyrette Nouel, Paris; Shiber, 291; Blumenson, 7.

208 **The procedures that were to be followed:** "The German military courts were tough but not arbitrary, and they worked according to set procedures." Gildea, 41.

208 **Germanophones:** Burguburu email, February 20, 2021.

208 **thirty-five years old:** Biographical information on Jehan Burguburu is drawn primarily from Jean-Marie Burguburu email, February 20, 2021. A photograph of Burguburu can be found in Perrault, 296.

209 **Burguburu's notes for the session:** Jehan Burguburu trial notes, Etta Shiber case file, Archives of Gide Loyrette Nouel, Paris.

209 **the Hôtel de Brienne:** Lehrer, 87.

210 **The grand entrance hall:** The description of the tribunal is drawn primarily from Jehan Burguburu trial notes, Etta Shiber case file, Archives of Gide Loyrette Nouel, Paris; Shiber, 290–312; Blumenson, 3–8; Monier, 11; Wynne, 106; Rossel-Kirschen, 29–30.

210 **"the swastika swimming in blood":** Blumenson, 6.

211 **the head judge, Maj. Hans Dotzel:** Biographical information on Dotzel is drawn from Hans Dotzel file, Côtes PERS-6/41089 and PERS-6/253207, Bundesarchiv-Militärarchiv, Freiburg.

211 **"We have received affirmations":** *Je suis partout,* April 25, 1941.

213 **by way of Colonel Shaw:** In Jehan Burguburu's handwritten trial notes, the name is spelled "Col. Shot"—as it would have been heard by Gallic ears.

214 **"I listened to Kitty":** Shiber, 295.

214 **"Madame . . . if I had a hat":** "Many Allied Servicemen Owe Life to Elderly Englishwoman in Paris," *Montreal Gazette,* November 6, 1945. In their appeal of the death sentence, Kate Bonnefous's attorneys also made reference to her having "favorably impressed the Tribunal" with her attitude.

214 **"The judge began":** This statement is drawn from the fifty-four-page transcript made from the interview Etta gave to Paul Winkler's Press Alliance. It is included in Farkas affidavit.

215 **"It wasn't so much that I was frightened":** Shiber, 307.

215 **Great Britain would award him the King's Medal:** The citation for the medal attests that "between June 1940 and January 1941, Monsieur Berteloot worked in close cooperation with other helpers in the Pas de Calais area, feeding and sheltering evaders, arranging for their safe evacuation and providing them with funds and fake identity cards where necessary. It is estimated that an approximate total of thirty to forty evaders passed through his hands during this period."

216 **The accused Rackelboom:** The sentences are listed in the "field judgment": "*Feldurteil,*" March 9, 1941, Etta Shiber case file, Archives of Gide Loyrette Nouel, Paris.

216 **"a calm and silent demeanor":** "Recours en Grâce," Kate Robins Bonnefous file, Archives Départementales du Calvados.

216 **sixty-two death sentences:** Schoenbrun, 118.

217 **"I broke down completely":** "U.S. Woman Bares Horror of Jail Under Nazi Rule," *San Francisco Examiner,* June 7, 1942.

217 **wrapped a chain around the wrists:** See, for example, Humbert, 72.

217 **the first woman in Paris to be condemned to death:** This point was also noted by the French *résistante* Simone Harrand (later Monier), who met Kate Bonnefous when they were both in the Lübeck prison camp: "Catherine [Kate] had certainly been the first Parisian woman condemned to death." Monier, 39.

CHAPTER 20

218 **The tribunal's decision was affirmed:** "*Feldurteil,*" March 9, 1941, Etta Shiber case file, Archives of Gide Loyrette Nouel, Paris.

218 **Recours en Grâce:** Kate Robins Bonnefous file, Archives Départementales du Calvados.

219 **frantically reached out to others:** "War Crimes: Declaration Made by Madame Bonnefous," June 8, 1945.

219 **contacted by Achille Cardinal Liénart:** Letter to Monseigneur Dutoit, bishop of Arras, March 18, 1941, Edouard Régniez file, Archives Historiques du Diocèse, Arras.

220 **the führer had rejected her appeal:** "War Crimes: Declaration Made by Madame Bonnefous," June 8, 1945.

220 **by an intermediary of the pope:** Ibid.

220 **Blanche Paugan was arrested:** Dejonghe, *Le Nord-Pas-de-Calais,* 187.

220 **was shot in Rouen:** Yagil, 37.

221 **the telephone line between Royan and La Rochelle:** Ibid., 38.

221 **"all damage of means of transmission":** "Sabotage d'une installation télephonique allemande," museedelaresistanceenligne.org/media6481-Sabotage-dune-installation-tA.

221 copper wires no more than ten millimeters: Ibid.

221 she had cut telephone lines: Kate Bonnefous, "Demande d'attribution du titre de déporté résistant," February 27, 1953, FO 371/50978, National Archives of the United Kingdom.

221 Alone in cell 119: Letter to Monseigneur Dutoit, bishop of Arras, March 15, 1941, Edouard Régniez file, Archives Historiques du Diocèse, Arras.

221 the newly appointed prison chaplain: The description of Franz Stock is drawn from Closset, 15.

221 willing to pass covert messages: Ibid., 81; Sisich, 119.

222 exactly the age his father had been: Letter to Monseigneur Dutoit, bishop of Arras, March 15, 1941, Edouard Régniez file, Archives Historiques du Diocèse, Arras.

222 the three refugees: July Boulanger testimony, December 17, 1945.

222 How he had hated this prison: Some of the ideas in this passage were drawn from an unpublished, undated poem, "*En souvenir des heures passées en prison*" ["In Memory of Hours Spent in Prison"], written by Edouard Régniez. It is now held by the Musée de la Résistance et de la Déportation and can be viewed online at memoire14-45.eu/fr/notice/2013-1-33-poeme-musee-de-la-resistance-bondues -e0217c6a-4c7a-4547-b9f0-ef8f77b6977f.

222 "physical and emotional exhaustion": Sisich, 119.

223 "[I] call out 'Régniez'": Girardon, 317.

223 interrogated while in a weakened state: Inez Whiteley Foster, "Home Again After 18 Months Under Nazis," *Christian Science Monitor,* October 19, 1943.

223 "in very modest financial circumstances": State Department memorandum, April 10, 1941, Etta Kahn Shiber file, 362.1121/47, Records Group 59; General Records of the Department of State, Central Decimal Files, National Archives and Records Administration.

224 the sound of heavy boots: Humbert, 59.

224 most often children's songs: See Michel Lemoine, "Paroles de Femmes," Conférence-Exposition sur la "Prison Militaire du Cherche-Midi, un trou noir de l'histoire." memoresist.org/rencontre/conference-exposition-sur-la-prison-militaire-du -cherche-midi-un-trou-noir-de-lhistoire/.

224 atmosphere of a boarding school: Ibid.

224 having her children slip messages: Blumenson, 188. See also Humbert, 67.

224 still had a wristwatch: Humbert, 67.

224 "In the communal cells": Ibid.

225 "I hadn't realized there were so many of us": Ibid., 68.

225 "We inform you that in the case": Letter to Alexandre Strelnikoff, April 22, 1941, Kate Robins Bonnefous file, Archives Départementales du Calvados.

225 Burguburu sent a letter: Letter to the Commandant of the Tribunal of Greater Paris, May 9, 1941, Etta Shiber case file, Archives of Gide Loyrette Nouel, Paris.

226 "The inspector informs me that my request is rejected": Ibid.

CHAPTER 21

227 In May 1941, Etta Shiber was transferred: In a letter to Jehan Burguburu, Etta Shiber indicated that she arrived at Fresnes on May 16, 1941. Etta Shiber case file, Archives of Gide Loyrette Nouel, Paris.

227 there was no "hard labor": Shiber, 314.

227 the food at Fresnes was even worse: Shiber, 315; Hany-Lefèbvre, 35.

228 riddled with worms: Hanley, 121.

228 "I am sure": Shiber, 315.

228 only in the medical register: Calet, 35.

228 "Very often," Etta wrote: Shiber, 315.

229 aboard a regular passenger train: Email from Christophe Woehrle to author, May 26, 2021.

230 curved track: "In the course of the transfer to Germany, as the train slowed for a curve, he took the opportunity to jump." Biographical description, Edouard Régniez file, Archives Historiques du Diocèse, Arras.

230 and he leaped: The account of Régniez's leap from the train can be found in sources including M. Beirnaert et al., *Dictionnaire du monde religieux dans la France contemporaine* (Volume 11, Arras: Artois–Côte d'Opale), Paris: Beauchesne, 2013, 666; *Histoire de la paroisse de Conchy-sur-Canche, Monchel et Aubrometz,* unpaged handwritten manuscript, Archives Historiques du Diocèse, Arras; Girardon, 318. In *Paris-Underground,* Etta Shiber incorrectly describes the escape as the product of a British intelligence operation. Shiber, 385.

230 to receive one book per week: Hany-Lefèbvre, 35.

230 "This letter is to let you know": Shiber letter to Jehan Burguburu, August 30, 1941. Etta Shiber case file, Archives of Gide Loyrette Nouel, Paris.

231 "I rejoice in noting": Burguburu letter to Etta Shiber, September 6, 1941. Ibid.

231 felt her health beginning to slip: Shiber, 359.

231 led to an oral infection: Ibid., 282. Shiber's entrance papers to the hospital identified her as "Ettah Shiber," the discharge papers as "Itta Schiper." Ibid., 283, 285.

232 six hundred calories per day: Hanley, 121.

232 were ordered to assemble: Shiber, 343.

233 Hauts-Clos prison: A photo of the prison as it appeared at the time can be seen at   lest-eclair.fr/id57049/article/2019-04-10/annees-40-le-noir-passe-des-hauts -clos#popin-newsletters-form.

234 Etta could discern no heating system: Shiber, 349.

235 "Under these conditions": Shiber, 351.

CHAPTER 22

237 she lined up with the others: Shiber, 368.

238 where she filled out a form: "U.S. Woman Bares Horror of Jail Under Nazi Rule," *San Francisco Examiner,* June 7, 1942.

238 Davis wrote a memorandum: Stuart, "Special," 7.

238 issued Departmental Order 810: Ibid.

238 would serve the Axis powers as agents: Russell, 39.

238 "legal attachés": Ibid.

239 fifteen Latin American countries handed over: Max Paul Friedman, "Private Memory, Public Records, and Contested Terrain: Weighing Oral Testimony in the Deportation of Germans from Latin America During World War II," *The Oral History Review* 27:1 (Winter-Spring 2000): 1.

239 German Jewish victims of Nazi persecution: Ibid.

239 back-channel negotiations were begun: Williams, 7, 10–11.

239 Thirty of these voyages would take place: Ibid., 7, 21.

239 "The numbers of persons for exchange": Ibid., 10.

240 contacted the State Department: Joseph Green memorandum to Breckinridge Long, January 16, 1942, Johanna Hofmann file, Records Group 59, Central Dec-

imal Files 1940–1944, 862.20211, Box C286, National Archives and Records Administration.

240 **Johanna Hofmann:** The spelling of Hofmann's last name is inconsistent. In *Paris-Underground,* for instance, it is spelled "Hoffmann."

240 **"There is a somewhat parallel case":** Joseph Green memorandum to Breckinridge Long, January 16, 1942.

240 **"This Government," he wrote:** Sidney K. Lafoon memorandum, January 27, 1942. Ibid.

241 **"furnish the Department of State":** Long memorandum to Francis Biddle, February 4, 1942. Ibid.

241 **"do not contain any record of a memorandum":** Green memorandum to Breckinridge Long, April 20, 1942. Ibid.

242 **a friend of hers, Marguerite Boë:** Ibid.

242 **to close the bathroom door and fill the tub:** John Selby, "Author of 'Paris Underground' Still Amazed at Own Exploits," Associated Press wire story, November 22, 1943.

242 **"It is almost too good to be true":** Shiber letter to Jehan Burguburu, May 11, 1942. Etta Shiber case file, Archives of Gide Loyrette Nouel, Paris.

243 **"Dear Madame":** Burguburu letter to Etta Shiber, May 12, 1942. Ibid.

243 **that metal statues be removed:** Photographs of some of the destroyed statues can be seen at messynessychic.com/2016/01/07/where-the-statues-of-paris-were-sent-to-die/.

243 **put on a major exhibition:** Drake, 219–20; Sebba, 91.

244 **"what should be done with the Jews":** Drake, 165.

244 **arrested 3,710 Jews of foreign birth:** Sebba, 89.

244 **a half-finished apartment complex:** Vinen, 143.

244 **signed a new decree:** See ibid., 41; Poznanski, *Jews,* 238; Sebba, 125.

244 **five thousand meters of yellow cloth:** Josephs, 41.

245 **A slim, elegant triple-screw steamship:** Williams, 32.

245 **its interior had been designed:** William H. Miller, *The First Great Ocean Liners in Photographs* (New York: Dover Publications, 1984), 116–17; Frank O. Braynard and William H. Miller, *Fifty Famous Liners* (New York: W.W. Norton, 1982), 29–31.

245 **had transported 948 Axis deportees:** Williams, 75.

245 **"As usual," remarked a State Department official:** "Diplomatic Exchange Ship Docks at Jersey City Pier," Associated Press wire story, June 1, 1942.

245 **the typewriters of the C Deck writing room:** Atcheson, 482.

246 **was carrying 908 passengers:** "908 Home with Tales of 'V'-Hungry Europe," New York *Daily News,* June 2, 1942.

246 **"a floating cross-section of melting-pot America":** "Diplomatic Exchange Ship Docks at Jersey City Pier," Associated Press wire story, June 1, 1942.

246 **"She had a German nurse":** "908 Home with Tales of 'V'-Hungry Europe," New York *Daily News,* June 2, 1942.

246 **the white-uniformed Swedish crew:** Atcheson, 482.

247 **"Oh, please take me home":** Russell Miller, *The House of Getty* (New York: Bloomsbury USA, 2011), 305.

248 **most of those donated:** "U.S. Woman Bares Horror of Jail Under Nazi Rule," *San Francisco Examiner,* June 7, 1942.

248 **Her nephew John would be at the pier:** "Mrs. Shiber Visited Brother in Syracuse," *Syracuse Herald Journal,* July 20, 1943.

CHAPTER 23

254 called the book "poignant": Hilary St. George Saunders, "The Scarlet Pimpernel of 1942," *New York Times,* September 19, 1943.

255 "No spy story could be half as exciting": Orville Prescott, "Books of the Times," *New York Times,* September 20, 1943.

255 "a strange and inordinately thrilling story": The quotations in this paragraph are drawn from: Percival R. Knauth, "France Under the Occupation," *Saturday Review of Literature,* September 25, 1943; "Lady Pimpernels," *Newsweek,* September 20, 1943; Paul Kennedy, "Middle-Aged Women Outwit the Gestapo," *Boston Globe,* September 23, 1943; "Briefly Noted," *The New Yorker,* September 25, 1943; Lewis Gannett, "Books and Things," *New York Herald Tribune,* September 20, 1943.

255 "are present in full measure": Diana Trilling, "What Has Happened to Our Novels?," *Harper's Magazine,* May 1, 1944.

256 offered $100,000 for the film rights: Leonard Lyons, "Times Square Tattle," *Washington Post,* October 15, 1943.

256 "Well, he was wrong there": The "Paris-Underground" episode of *Words at War* can be heard at jimramsburg.com/uploads/1/0/7/4/10748369/words_at_war___10-12-43.mp3.

257 "Her appearance, her composure": Harry Hansen, "Some Writers Make Hoopla and Some an Impression," *New York World-Telegram,* November 21, 1943.

258 "urged that lend-lease arms be smuggled": "Ottley Says Army 'Jim Crowism' Abroad Is a Blow to Democracy," *New York Herald Tribune,* January 12, 1944.

258 "I never saw a plainer": The quotations in this paragraph are drawn from Harry Hansen, "Some Writers Make Hoopla and Some an Impression," *New York World-Telegram,* November 21, 1943; Harry Hansen, "The First Reader," *New York World-Telegram,* May 10, 1943; Orville Prescott, "Books of the Times," *New York Times,* September 20, 1943; John Selby, "Author of 'Paris Underground' Still Amazed at Own Exploits," Associated Press wire story, November 22, 1943; Gilbert Swan, "American Woman, 65, Nabbed by Gestapo for Aiding British, Fleeing France, Home After Escaping Death by a Firing Squad," Central Press wire story, January 12, 1944; and "Etta Shiber," *Current Biography: Who's News and Why 1943* (New York: H. W. Wilson, 1943).

259 "15–20 anglais": Jehan Burguburu trial notes, Etta Shiber case file, Archives of Gide Loyrette Nouel, Paris.

259 consistent with the admissions made: Ibid.

260 Yet *Paris-Underground* includes a scene: Shiber, 180.

260 "More than 150": Stewart Robertson, "Secret Passage," *Family Circle,* 24:13 (March 31, 1944): 12.

260 "nearly 200 British soldiers": Winkler, 8.

260 "over 250 British soldiers": Harry Hansen, "Some Writers Make Hoopla and Some an Impression," *New York World-Telegram,* November 21, 1943.

261 (fifty-seven personal war narratives): Neel, 34.

261 "Two women less likely to get involved": Orville Prescott, "Books of the Times," *New York Times,* September 20, 1943.

261 "no author of fiction would dare": The quotations in this paragraph are drawn from Hilary St. George Saunders, "The Scarlet Pimpernel of 1942," *New York Times,* September 19, 1943; Gerard Hopkins, "Two Brave Women," *Sunday Times*

(London), July 2, 1944; and Edward Barry, "Adventure and Psychological Story Combined in One Book," *Chicago Daily Tribune,* September 19, 1943.

262 **"This absorbing record":** "Paris-Underground," *Reader's Digest,* October 1943, 119.

262 **"Names and places have been changed":** "Soldier Snatcher," *Time,* September 27, 1943.

264 **"Catherine Bonnefous, Etta Shiber":** conscript-heroes.com/Art54-Kate-Bonnefous .html.

267 **("He'll have a better chance"):** Shiber, 30.

267 gradations of inaccuracy: See, for example, the discussion in Yagoda, 267–69.

267 **"Etta Shiber, American":** Anne Thoraval, *Paris, les lieux de la Résistance: La vie quotidienne de l'armée des ombres dans la capitale* (Paris: Parigramme, 2007), 246.

CHAPTER 24

268 **Aladar Anton Farkas:** Biographical information on Aladar Farkas is drawn primarily from "Aladar Farkas 1940–1941," Folder 11, Box 1, Emergency Rescue Committee Records 1936–1956, German and Jewish Intellectual Émigré Collection, M. E. Grenander Special Collections and Archives, University at Albany, State University of New York.

268 **His most recent manuscript:** The history of Farkas and Winkler's business relationship is described in pages 3–6 of Aladar Farkas's affidavit, submitted as part of Aladar A. Farkas, Plaintiff, against Paul Winkler, Betty Winkler, Press Alliance, Inc., Etta Shiber, and Charles Scribner's Sons, Defendants, before the State Supreme Court of the State of New York, County of New York, filed October 5, 1943, Shiber, Etta (Box 236), Archives of Charles Scribner's Sons, 1786–2004, Manuscripts Division, Special Collections, Princeton University Library.

268 **Paul Winkler:** Biographical information on Paul Winkler is drawn primarily from Thierry Desjardins, "Paul Winkler," *Revue des Deux Mondes,* December 1982, 572–75; Herbert R. Lottman, "Opera Mundi: The Many Facets of a Versatile Firm," *Publishers Weekly,* June 28, 1971, 33–35; "Eighth Wonder Syndicated," *Time,* September 15, 1941; and Joel E. Vessels, *Drawing France: French Comics and the Republic* (Jackson: University of Mississippi Press, 2010).

269 **"an office, a telephone, and an assistant":** Vessels, 61.

269 **he and the children arrived in New York:** The children were named Liliane, Serge, and Claude. *Passenger and Crew Lists of Vessels Arriving at and Departing from Ogdensburg, New York, 5/27/1948–11/28/1972,* Microfilm Serial or NAID: T715, 1897–1957, National Archives and Records Administration, Washington, D.C.

270 **His sister, Roza (Ray):** The information in this paragraph is drawn from the Aladar Farkas file in the Emergency Rescue Committee archives.

270 **Emergency Rescue Committee:** See, for example, Laurel Leff, "Rebuffing Refugee Journalists: The Profession's Failure to Help Jews Persecuted by Nazi Germany," *Journalism and Communication Monographs* 17:3 (2015), 149–218.

271 **Farkas lost no time in looking up Paul Winkler:** The information on how Aladar Farkas came to work on the Shiber material is drawn from Farkas's affidavit in Aladar A. Farkas, Plaintiff, against Paul Winkler, Betty Winkler, Press Alliance, Inc., Etta Shiber, and Charles Scribner's Sons, Defendants, 6–12.

271 **a large furnished apartment:** "Head of Syndicate Leases Suite Here," *New York Times,* November 21, 1940.

273 "I am writing these lines on the deck": Shiber, Etta (Box 236), Archives of Charles Scribner's Sons, 1786–2004, Manuscripts Division, Special Collections, Princeton University Library.

274 "I said no good-bye to Europe": Shiber, 1.

274 they hired an émigré writer: Joseph Szebenyei affidavit, Aladar A. Farkas, Plaintiff, against Paul Winkler, Betty Winkler, Press Alliance, Inc., Etta Shiber, and Charles Scribner's Sons, Defendants; Farkas affidavit, 9.

274 Over the coming months, Farkas inquired: Information about Farkas's conflict with Winkler about the book is drawn primarily from the Farkas affidavit, 6–17.

275 the contract had been signed many months earlier: Maxwell Perkins letter to Paul Winkler, October 15, 1942; Paul Winkler letter to Maxwell Perkins, October 16, 1942, Shiber, Etta (Box 236), Archives of Charles Scribner's Sons.

276 Farkas sent a long, anguished letter: Farkas affidavit, Exhibit "C" ("Translation of Hungarian Letter Sent by Aladar Farkas to Paul Winkler of the Press Alliance, July 24, 1943").

276 "the few persons referred to": Farkas affidavit, 14.

277 "a literal reproduction": Szebenyei affidavit, 4. Szebenyei amended this observation slightly regarding the first chapter of the book, which he called "substantially the same as my translation except for editorial revisions and changes of style."

277 "according to the time-honored system": "Authorship of 'Paris Underground' Subject of Litigation," *Publishers Weekly,* May 27, 1944, 2000.

277 the case was settled out of court: Exhibit A, Annexed to Foregoing Affidavit (October 19, 1943), Aladar A. Farkas, Plaintiff, against Paul Winkler, Betty Winkler, Press Alliance, Inc., Etta Shiber, and Charles Scribner's Sons, Defendants.

277 "Despite the efforts by Mr. Farkas": Frederick Woltman, "Writing Syndicate Describes How Shiber Best Seller Was Ghosted," *New York World-Telegram,* May 16, 1944.

278 "I always intended that my work be published": Farkas affidavit, 25.

278 "There cannot be the slightest doubt": Winkler letter to Maxwell Perkins, July 13, 1943, Shiber, Etta (Box 236), Archives of Charles Scribner's Sons.

279 "Everything that could be done": "Authorship of 'Paris Underground' Subject of Litigation," *Publishers Weekly,* May 27, 1944, 1999–2000.

279 "disjointed, and inconsecutive": Perkins letter to Harry Hansen, May 10, 1944, Shiber, Etta (Box 236), Archives of Charles Scribner's Sons.

279 "As I told you over the telephone": Plitt letter to Harry Scherman, July 23, 1943. Ibid.

280 "I understand perfectly Mr. Plitt's reaction": Winkler letter to Maxwell Perkins, July 24, 1943. Ibid.

281 "[I] have every reason to feel complete confidence": Perkins letter to Edwin A. Plitt, July 27, 1943. Ibid.

281 it was further decided to withdraw: Ibid.

282 "I just mentioned vaguely": Winkler letter to Maxwell Perkins, July 29, 1943. Ibid.

282 "Helping the British soldiers": Ibid.

282 an estate valued at $7,830: Estate of William N. Shiber, Schedule A, May 23, 1936; New York County Surrogate's Court.

283 Etta resisted Winkler's initial advances: Paul Dupre (Winkler) letter to Maxwell Perkins, July 13, 1943, Shiber, Etta (Box 236), Archives of Charles Scribner's Sons.

283 An additional $485.18 remained: Edwin A. Plitt letter to Etta Shiber, June 30, 1942, Etta Kahn Shiber file, 362.1121/47, Records Group 59: General Records of

the Department of State, Central Decimal Files, National Archives and Records Administration.

283 **Etta wrote to Edwin Plitt:** Shiber letter to Edwin A. Plitt, June 21, 1942. Ibid.

285 **Etta was "overjoyed":** Winkler letter to Maxwell Perkins, July 29, 1943, Shiber, Etta (Box 236), Archives of Charles Scribner's Sons.

285 **"I suddenly realized":** Ibid.

285 **suggested using a composite character:** Thomas Kunkel, *Man in Profile: Joseph Mitchell of* The New Yorker (New York: Random House, 2015), 226.

286 **"The hesitation of the Book-of-the-Month Club":** Ibid.

CHAPTER 25

287 **The backstory presented for Kate Bonnefous:** Shiber, 9.

288 **"the xenophobic, anti-Semitic mood":** Goodwin, 102.

288 **national polling on the subject:** See ibid.; Breitman and Kraut, 88, 208; Rosen, 63.

289 **would eliminate immigration entirely:** Rosen, 62–63.

289 **"warmongering international Jewry":** This was John B. Rankin of Mississippi. Ibid., 168.

289 **"capped the number of immigrants":** Erbelding, 9.

290 **"go to war for the sake of protecting Jews":** Julian M. Pleasants, *Buncombe Bob: The Life and Times of Robert Rice Reynolds* (Chapel Hill: University of North Carolina Press, 2000), 142.

290 **"Ever since 1933":** Joseph W. Bendersky, *The "Jewish Threat": Anti-Semitic Politics of the U.S. Army* (New York: Basic Books, 2000), 286.

291 **"on some country hotel porch":** Jerome M. Dreifuss, "She Licked the Gestapo," *Boston Post,* October 17, 1943.

291 **ordered a second printing:** "Shiber—Paris Underground," notarized sales statement, July 30, 1945, Shiber, Etta (Box 236), Archives of Charles Scribner's Sons.

291 **the names being bandied about:** Hugh King letter to Robert Fellows, October 13, 1943, Myron Selznick Estate, 1944–1963, Subseries 1A14, David O. Selznick Collection, Harry Ransom Center, University of Texas at Austin.

291 **"building up an informed public opinion":** "Ideas for Americans at War Spread by Council on Books," *Publishers Weekly,* December 25, 1943, 2000–2013.

291 **"In discussing the book with friends":** Claudine Gray letter to Charles Scribner, November 15, 1943, Shiber, Etta (Box 236), Archives of Charles Scribner's Sons.

292 **"I think no other American woman":** Adela Rogers St. Johns letter to Etta Shiber, undated. Ibid.

292 **the amenities included maid service:** Beacon Hotel file, George B. Corsa Hotel Collection, New-York Historical Society Library.

293 **remembered seeing** *Aida* **with Irving:** "With her brother [cousin], she went almost daily to concerts and the opera, and the highlights of her life were the first appearances in America of Toscanini, Heifetz, Menuhin, and other luminaries of the concert stage." Winkler, 7.

293 **"and I will go back to live with her":** Stewart Robertson, "Secret Passage," *Family Circle,* 24:13 (March 31, 1944): 22.

294 **Battle of the Somme:** Email to the author from Leonard Robins's grandson Martin Crick, February 8, 2021.

294 **"Our worth as human beings":** Adler, 11.

295 **in a village highly regarded:** The Riverview was located in Roscoe, New York, with a population of under one thousand.

297   **"I am so sorry to have to tell you":** Barbara J. Mousley letter, February 10, 1953, Shiber, Etta (Box 236), Archives of Charles Scribner's Sons.

297   **she had suffered a fall:** "Etta Kahn Shiber, Survivor of Nazis," New York *Daily News*, December 25, 1948.

297   **She died in her room:** Etta Kahn Shiber Certificate of Death, Certificate No. 27843, December 23, 1948; New York City Municipal Archives.

297   **assessed at a value of $95:** Etta Kahn Shiber probate file, Schedule A; New York County Surrogate's Court.

297   **"My investigation disclosed":** "In the Matter of the Appraisal of the Estate of Etta K. Shiber, Deceased," Byrd D. Wise notarized affidavit, December 11, 1950. In ibid.

298   **cauterized their memories:** See the discussion in Fogelman, 282.

CHAPTER 26

301   **taken aboard in handcuffs:** This and many other details of Kate Bonnefous's imprisonment are taken from "War Crimes: Declaration Made by Madame Bonnefous," June 8, 1945; Nazi Persecution Claim: Mrs. Kate Bonnefous, June 7, 1965; and handwritten notes made by Kate Bonnefous, perhaps in support of her Nazi restitution claim, a copy of which was provided to the author by Erik Sales.

302   **some 140 will be incarcerated there:** Henriette Roosenburg, "I Taste Freedom," *Knickerbocker Weekly*, February 10, 1947.

302   **Inside the prison, she is directed:** See the description of intake procedures in ibid.; Monier, 23; Sisich, 48–49.

304   **constantly mocked and insulted:** Details of Kate Bonnefous's escape and punishment are from "War Crimes: Declaration Made by Madame Bonnefous," June 8, 1945.

305   **She remains in solitary confinement:** "Kitty, Twice Condemned to Die, Carries On," *Daily Mail* (London), October 3, 1947.

305   **wonderful family house:** Descriptions of the house are from Leonard Robins's grandson Martin Crick, in an email to the author, February 8, 2021.

306   **"This woman must be transported to Germany":** La Martinière, *Les N.N.*, 5.

306   **he instructed Field Marshal Wilhelm Keitel:** Majer, 368.

306   **"into the night and fog":** La Martinière, *Les N.N.*, 5; Rose, 65–66; Calet, unpaged.

307   **"The Führer desires":** La Martinière, *Les N.N.*, 41.

307   **"The decree meant":** Sisich, 47.

307   **"In September 1942":** La Martinière, *Nuit et Brouillard*, 43.

308   **the train makes stopovers at prisons:** France's Fondation pour la Mémoire de la Déportation has recorded Kate Bonnefous's prison record at bddm.org/liv/details .php?id=I.7.#BONNEFOUS. See also Nazi Persecution Claim: Mrs. Kate Bonnefous, June 7, 1965; "War Crimes: Declaration Made by Madame Bonnefous," June 8, 1945; Montague Taylor, "British Heroine of 60 Who Defied Gestapo," *The People* (London), November 4, 1945.

308   **the women are stripped naked:** For a description of the entry procedures, see Sisich, 52.

308   **a devastating raid on the city:** Richards, 120; Whiting, 12; Grayling, 51.

308   **"A fiery parasite":** Whiting, 12.

308   **the prison of Lübeck-Lauerhof:** Témoignage de Léone Bourgineau, November 1971, Archives of La Contemporaine, Nanterre; Le Boulanger, 35–39; Monier, 34–39.

309 **to speak to one another through the toilets:** Monier, 37.

309 *"Mais, Madame . . . je ne vous connais pas?":* This scene is described in ibid., 39. For more on Simone Harrand, see also museedelaresistanceenligne.org/media10637 -Simone-Harrand-epouse-Monnier.

310 **"Lacking Champagne":** Monier, 39.

311 **Gestapo agents are waiting:** This scene is drawn from several sources, including "War Crimes: Declaration Made by Madame Bonnefous," June 8, 1945; Nazi Persecution Claim: Mrs. Kate Bonnefous, June 7, 1965; and handwritten notes made by Kate Bonnefous, perhaps in support of her Nazi restitution claim, provided to the author by Erik Sales. Gestapo torture of a female political prisoner is also described in Rose, 173.

311 **like pearls dropping from a broken string:** This image is presented, in a different context, in Shiber, 201.

313 **decapitated by guillotine:** Between 1933 and 1945, nearly five hundred men and women were decapitated in the courtyard of the Holstenglacis prison in Hamburg. Quella-Villégerm, 225.

314 **the trees turned into torches:** Monier, 46.

314 **through their cell windows they see:** Sisich, 58.

314 **officially declared an NN prisoner:** "According to the German archives in my possession, it appears that Madame Bonnefous was interned October 30 1942 in LUBECK-Lauerhof, condemned to prison, 'Night and Fog,' by decision of the General Commandant of the Tribunal of Kiel on the date of April 28 1944." Letter from le Ministre des Ancient Combattants et Victimes de la Guerre, January 22, 1954. Kate Bonnefous file, Archives of the Service Historique de la Défense. See also Majer, 368.

314 **The women who are to be transported:** The names of the women transported from Lübeck-Lauerhof to Jauer on May 9, 1944, are contained in the file "Women's prison Lübeck-Lauerhof—state Schleswig-Holstein," in the Arolsen Archives, online at collections.arolsen-archives.org/en/archive/1-2-2-1_8169100/?p =1&doc_id=11305057.

315 **"Working today at the train station of Stettin":** Kate Robins Bonnefous file, Archives Départementales du Calvados.

CHAPTER 27

316 **the castle of Jauer:** For descriptions of Jauer prison, see Berthe Bernard, "Rapport sur la Forteresse (Zuchthaus) de Jauer," Archives of Cegesoma (Research and Documentation Centre for the History of the Second World War in Belgium), Brussels; "Témoignage d'Elisabeth Ingrand, née Dussauze, recuilli par Marie Granet," May 16, 1955, Archives Nationales de France, Paris, 72AJ/46, no. 3; Dossier Aïleen Schoofs, Archives de La Contemporaine, Nanterre; De Landsheere, 144–62; Peeters, 97–98; Masconi, 50–52.

316 **the castle could hold 471 prisoners:** Jonca and Konieczny, 164.

317 **"especially distinguished by her sadism":** Berthe Bernard, "Rapport sur la Forteresse (Zuchthaus) de Jauer," Archives of Cegesoma (Research and Documentation Centre for the History of the Second World war in Belgium), Brussels, unpaged. The Belgian deportee is identified only as "Mme. Razel."

317 **"Numerous women are suffering from dysentery":** Masconi, 51.

317 **"We had to adjust our intestines":** Dossier Aïleen Schoofs, Archives de La Contemporaine, Nanterre.

318   "After a few days of this regime": Monier, 53.

318   on Sunday evenings: Peeters, 100–102; Témoignage de Léone Bourgineau, 5.

318   "There was a real spirit of camaraderie": Ibid.

319   develops bronchitis: Nazi Persecution Claim: Mrs. Kate Bonnefous, June 7, 1965.

319   "looked for every opportunity to push us": "War Crimes: Declaration Made by Madame Bonnefous," June 8, 1945.

320   Nacht und Nebel prisoners must never: La Martinière, *L'évacuation*, 94.

320   A list of 121 French and Belgian prisoners: Ibid., 10.

320   tossing papers into a bonfire: Ibid.

321   a valise full of warm clothing: Masconi, 52.

321   A Norwegian prisoner shows the others: Her name was Dagny Dingstad. Monier, 67.

321   "It is heartbreaking to abandon them": De Landsheere, 166.

321   The prison chaplain addresses them: Ibid., 163; La Martinière, *L'évacuation*, 28.

321   Kate Bonnefous is still upstairs: "War Crimes: Declaration Made by Madame Bonnefous," June 8, 1945.

321   with some two dozen other: Estimates of the number of female political prisoners left behind at Jauer range from twenty to thirty. A list of some of them can be found in ibid., 92.

322   "this poor cohort": Masconi, 53.

322   "We were twenty or so women": La Martinière, *L'évacuation*, 28.

322   A ragged line: The description of the march from Jauer is drawn primarily from accounts by participants, including: De Landsheere, 163–75; Sisich, 70–71; Peeters, 141–61; Masconi, 52–66; and the participant accounts contained in La Martinière, *L'évacuation*, 28–84.

326   a pair of camels: Jacqueline Wiener-Henrion, "Geneviève Janssen-Pevtschin," *Les Cahiers de la Mémoire contemporaine* (2002), 154. See also La Martinière, *L'évacuation*, 38.

326   they see a dead pigeon: Masconi, 60, 64; also La Martinière, *L'évacuation*, 47.

326   "To survive . . . we commit the unthinkable": Masconi, 64.

327   They are American fighter planes: La Martinière, *L'évacuation*, 50; Masconi, 66. Louise de Landsheere identified them as British planes. De Landsheere, 174.

328   "our cortege of misery": De Landsheere, 175.

328   Two hundred fifty Nacht und Nebel prisoners: The statistics about the march are from La Martinière, *L'évacuation*, 66.

328   her revenge against the Nazis: Monier, 81.

CHAPTER 28

329   about one hundred prisoners left behind: The description of this period at Jauer is drawn primarily from accounts of those left behind, including "War Crimes: Declaration Made by Madame Bonnefous," June 8, 1945; "La libération au bagne," testimony of Jeanne Chevalier née Valentin, October–November 1945, Forteresse de Jauer file, Guerre de 1939–1945, Archives du Comité d'histoire de la Deuxième Guerre mondiale et fonds d'origine privée, Archives Nationales de France, Paris; Témoignage de Henriette Docquier, from Marie-José Masconi email to author, November 14, 2021; and accounts contained in La Martinière, *L'évacuation*, 85–90.

331   Soeur Élisabeth is struggling: Madeline Dubois account in La Martinière, *L'évacuation*, 87.

331 "We had long dreamed": Ibid.

332 "They arrived absolutely dead drunk": "War Crimes: Declaration Made by Madame Bonnefous," June 8, 1945.

332 she would rather have been a prisoner: Editorial letter, December 9, 1946, Archives of Charles Scribner's Sons, Box 236, Folder 8, Manuscripts Division, Special Collections, Princeton University Library.

333 shot dead thirty-six of her neighbors: Grau, 42.

332 "I kept wanting to hang myself": Hargreaves, 237.

333 more than sixty men were shot: Grau, 48.

333 "They were shouting and laughing": Thorwald, 86.

333 "There's schnapps and spirits": Hargreaves, 245.

333 "The worst mistake of the German military authorities": Beevor, 409.

333 "From the individual soldier's point of view": Gebhardt, 96.

334 "martial rape": Claudia Card, "Rape as a Weapon of War," *Hypatia* 11:4 (Autumn 1996): 10.

334 more than one million women were raped: Antony Beevor, for instance, suggests that 2 million German women were raped, of whom 1.4 million were from the regions of East Prussia, Pomerania, and Silesia. Beevor, 410.

334 "shaken to the core": Daniel Johnson, "Red Army Troops Raped Even Russian Women as They Freed Them from Camps," *Daily Telegraph* (London), January 24, 2002.

335 "Can't he understand it": Ibid.

335 "Our fellows were so sex-starved": Beevor, 31.

335 "The men in the first wave": Hargreaves, 245; Richard Collier, *The Freedom Road: 1944–1945* (New York: Atheneum, 1984), 234.

336 as a kind of brothel: Lang, 187.

336 loot some of the stores: "War Crimes: Declaration Made by Madame Bonnefous," June 8, 1945.

336 "Anything would be better": La Martinière, *L'évacuation*, 87.

337 five freed British prisoners of war: "War Crimes: Declaration Made by Madame Bonnefous," June 8, 1945.

337 This is an old Jewish cemetery: This view from the train is described in Bialot, 247.

338 There are 2,388 of them: Ed Reid, "Norwegian Ship Set for Dash from Brooklyn Pier to—?" *Brooklyn Daily Eagle*, April 18, 1940.

338 "all these voyagers without bags": Bialot, 51–52. Joseph Bialot took the *Bergensfjord* one month after Kate Bonnefous did, boarding the ship in Odessa on May 2, 1945.

338 Dressed with white ceramic plates: Laloux, 151.

340 a set of white prefabricated buildings: The disembarkation process is described in ibid., 161–62.

340 a white powder called DDT: Bialot, 249; Sisich, 96.

340 According to her medical report: "Examen Médicale," Kate Robins Bonnefous file, Archives Départementales du Calvados.

340 Carte de Rapatrié: Ibid.

341 RECEIVED YOUR LETTER: Kate Bonnefous kept this telegram for the rest of her life; it was included among the personal effects of which copies were given to the author by Kate's grandson, Erik Sales.

341 in growing annoyance and impatience: "They arrived at a reception center which was distinguished by its lack of hygiene having only a few chairs. Madame Bonne-

fous had to spend all night sitting on the end of a bench, nothing was prepared to restore them, not even a hot beverage." "Statement by Madame Bonnefous," April 26, 1945, Kate Bonnefous file, Archives of the Service Historique de la Défense.

341 **her bag is gone:** "Everything that Madame Bonnefous was able to bring back from captivity was stolen from her at the reception center, while the latter had gone to Marseille to have a hot drink and to inquire about the departure times of the trains to their destination of Paris." Ibid.

341 *"faire le taxi":* Laloux, 163.

342 **"Where are you coming from?":** Ibid.

342 **Kate is met at the station:** Thierry Sales email to author, March 15, 2021.

342 **"I came back to Paris to find a son":** "Speaking Personally," *Courier and Advertiser* (Dundee, Scotland), August 16, 1960.

342 **In 1939, Kate had rented the apartment:** "L'Appartment de Mme. Bonnefous," May 2, 1945. Kate Bonnefous file, Archives of the Service Historique de la Défense.

342 **"be permitted to exercise her rights":** Ibid.

343 **"has subsequently accommodated therein":** *Revue des loyers, de la propriété commerciale et des fonds de commerce,* January 1, 1946, 763–64.

343 **Monsieur Godet had been living:** The details of the case, *Godet c[ontre] Bonnefous,* are given in ibid. The decision was handed down on June 28, 1946.

343 **16 rue François 1er:** Kate Bonnefous questionnaire, April 26, 1945, Archives Nationales de France, Paris.

343 **able to retrieve her black-haired cocker spaniel:** "Kitty, Twice Condemned to Die, Carries On," *Daily Mail* (London), October 3, 1947.

343 **who introduces herself as Betty Winkler:** In the memorandum of the meeting among Kate Bonnefous and the two English officials from IS9 (AB), she is incorrectly identified as "Claude Winkler." Claude Winkler was Paul and Betty Winkler's daughter, and she was only thirteen years old at the time. Betty Winkler was the war correspondent, and the one who would have identified herself as the book's ghostwriter. Either Kate or the official who recorded the meeting misremembered this detail, confusing the daughter's name with the mother's.

CHAPTER 29

344 **fill out a questionnaire:** Kate Bonnefous questionnaire, April 26, 1945, Archives Nationales de France, Paris.

345 **sends a memo to a French colleague:** Donald Darling memo to Capt. [Gilles] Lefort, April 26, 1945, Kate Bonnefous file, Archives of the Service Historique de la Défense.

345 **IS9 (AB) had been established:** For more on the creation and functioning of the Paris Awards Bureau, see Darling, 152–66; also ww2escapelines.co.uk/article/donald-darling/.

345 **and the discussion continues there:** "Visit of Madame Bonnefous," May 9, 1945, Kate Bonnefous file, Archives of the Service Historique de la Défense.

346 **"the consequences of this book":** Ibid.

346 **"obtain satisfaction":** Ibid.

347 **three-page, single-spaced account:** "War Crimes: Declaration Made by Madame Bonnefous," June 8, 1945.

347 **"She was eventually liberated by the Russians":** David Scott Fox letter to Thomas Barnes, June 13, 1945. In ibid.

348 **"regularly sent reports to England":** Lang, 103.

348 **"regular transmission to an agent of the IS":** Jeanne Monier file, Archives of the Service Historique de la Défense.

348 *"une Anglaise de l'IS":* Gustave Rackelboom file, Archives of the Service Historique de la Défense.

349 **In her own 1954 application:** On October 30, 1954, Kate Bonnefous submitted an application to the French government for a medical pension. In the section labeled "Memberships," Bonnefous wrote: "La X Rouge" (meaning the French Red Cross) and "M.I.S.9 (Anglais)." Kate Bonnefous file, Archives of the Service Historique de la Défense.

349 **in her signed and sworn application:** "Demande d'attribution du titre de déporté résistant" ["Request for attribution of the title of Deported Resistant"], February 27, 1953, Kate Robins Bonnefous file, Archives Départementales du Calvados.

349 **"They poured petrol on her hands":** Reuters wire service story, November 4, 1945.

349 **Capt. Gilles Lefort:** His real name was Didier Faure Beaulieu; Gilles Lefort was a nom de guerre that he had been using since 1942.

349 **"This lady's excellent work":** Major Darling memo to Capt. Lefort, June 29, 1945, Kate Bonnefous file, Archives of the Service Historique de la Défense.

350 **"We had long weekly meetings":** Darling, 161.

350 **The Grade 3 designation:** See Victor Schutters, "Awards Given to Persons Having Helped Evading Allied Airmen," evasioncomete.be/TxtAwards2.html. Individual awards can be found on the "French Helpers A-Z" searchable database compiled by Franck Signorile: wwii-netherlands-escape-lines.com/helpers-of-allied-airmen/french-helper-list/french-helper-database/.

350 **"This lady's activity was before the time":** John F. White, Jr., memo to Donald Darling, June 19, 1945. Kate Bonnefous file, Archives of the Service Historique de la Défense.

350 **Kate will receive 10,000 francs:** "Mme. Bonnefous," wwiinetherlandsescapelines.files.wordpress.com/2013/10/p1220383.jpg.

350 **"Madame Bonnefous," concludes the long citation:** Citation, Madame Bonnefous, British Foreign Office, Kate Robins Bonnefous file, Archives Départementales du Calvados. The citation was apparently written by Donald Darling.

350 **the Croix de guerre avec étoile d'argent:** "Decision No. 1309," Le Général de Gaulle, Président du Gouvernement Provisoire de la République Française, February 21, 1946. Ibid.

350 **"Not one of my boys was caught":** "Kitty, Twice Condemned to Die, Carries On," *Daily Mail* (London), October 3, 1947.

350 **she has inquired about a posting:** Ibid.

351 **The house, called Villa Mady:** "Bordereau d'Envoi," April 22, 1954, Kate Robins Bonnefous file, Archives Départementales du Calvados; Thierry Sales email to author, November 21, 2021; Erik Sales interview, conducted by Mariel Lëmair, Portimão, Portugal, October 9, 2020.

352 **Kate is the one who provides Régniez's name:** "He was sent to us by Mme. Bonnefous; suggest recognition; does not want money." Edouard Régniez folder, Case Files Relating to French Citizens Proposed for Awards for Assisting American Airmen, 1945–1947, Record Group 498, Box 1152, National Archives and Records Administration.

352 **the brother-in-law of one of his parishioners:** "After a long walk he ended up on the farm of Mr. Paul Loilier-Desruelle (brother-in-law of Antoine Desruelle of Arras), farmer in Châlons-sur-Vesle (in the Marne), borough of Reims." Edouard Régniez file, Archives Historiques du Diocèse, Arras.

352 **south to the Auvergne:** This and the subsequent details on Régniez's activities during the war are drawn from "Services dans La Résistance," August 10, 1953. Edouard Régniez file, Archives of the Service Historique de la Défense.

353 **He left the priesthood:** He married Eveline Honorine Delpierre on January 6, 1945. "État des Services," ibid.

353 **Teyssier died in 1943:** The date of death was June 10, 1943. He had been released from prison shortly before and died at the home of his sister Jeanne Ducom in the town of Flaujagues. Elie Teyssier file, Service Historique de la Défense.

353 **"in a state of cachexia":** Dr. Jean Fournier, Castillon-sur-Dordogne. Ibid.

353 **awarded 100,000 francs:** Elie Teyssier folder, Case Files Relating to French Citizens Proposed for Awards for Assisting American Airmen, 1945–1947, Record Group 498, Box 1176, National Archives and Records Administration.

354 **"a bright home":** "The Victoria Home," *Anglo-American Annual* (1902), 197.

354 **a two-bedroom apartment on the top floor:** Thierry Sales email to author, November 21, 2021.

354 **"Ça ne te regarde pas":** Erik Sales email to author, August 6, 2020.

354 **that she attributes to the promenades:** Nazi Persecution Claim: Mrs. Kate Bonnefous, June 7, 1965.

355 **the disability pension she receives:** By 1962 Kate Bonnefous was receiving a 100 percent disability pension. The ailments mentioned in this passage are among those described in the medical examination performed on her in Paris in February 1962 to support her disability claim. Others included cataracts, conjunctivitis, tooth loss, and Targowla syndrome characterized by fatigue and hypermnesia.

355 **Lt. Colin Hunter received two Military Cross decorations:** Andrew Hunter interview, April 19, 2021.

355 **Capt. Charles Murchie started an escape line:** Bergin, 106.

355 **Second Lt. John Buckingham, one of the two escaped British servicemen:** Jill Zorab interview, May 8, 2021.

355 **Capt. Derek Lang, the other serviceman:** Sarah Hunt interview, April 22, 2021.

356 **"quite a deep voice":** Ibid.

356 **Her hands still bear the scars:** "When I asked how she had been treated by the Germans while in prison, she said, 'Terrible,' and holding out her hands she showed me a number of scars which the Gestapo had made with the burning ends of cigarettes." "Speaking Personally," *Courier and Advertiser* (Dundee, Scotland), August 16, 1960.

356 **Anglo-German Agreement for Compensation:** Information on the agreement is drawn from Schrafstetter, 28–31.

357 **"where I was sentenced to be shot":** Nazi Persecution Claim: Mrs. Kate Bonnefous, June 7, 1965. Here Bonnefous indicates that she was threatened with being shot; in the discussion with Donald Darling two decades earlier, she seems to have indicated that the threat was to be guillotined. The Nazis, of course, executed prisoners via both methods.

357 **"looks older than her age":** Statement by a Dr. Reveillaud of Paris, who examined Bonnefous on July 20, 1965. In ibid.

357 **"Since Mme. Bonnefous was consistently beaten":** Ibid.

357 **Kate is awarded £2,293:** Ibid.

357 "You got worked up to such concert pitch": "Speaking Personally," *Courier and Advertiser* (Dundee, Scotland), August 16, 1960.

358 "cor pulmonale plus purulent bronchitis": Kate Bonnefous entry of death, No. 242, Stepney, November 11, 1965. General Register Office of England and Wales.

358 "Recently," it begins, "there died": "Mme. Kitty Bonnefois [*sic*]," undated newspaper clipping.

Selected Bibliography

ARCHIVES AND LIBRARIES

American Hospital of Paris
American Library in Paris
Archives Départementales de la Dordogne, Périgueux
Archives Départementales de la Gironde, Bordeaux
Archives Départementales de l'Indre, Châteauroux
Archives Départementales du Calvados, Caen
Archives Historiques du Diocèse, Arras
Archives Nationales de France, Paris
Bundesarchiv-Militärarchiv, Freiburg
La Contemporaine, Nanterre
Harry Ransom Center, University of Texas at Austin
Haverford College, Quaker and Special Collections
Hunter College, City University of New York, Archives and Special Collections
Imperial War Museum, London
Margate Library, Kent
Municipal Archives, New York City
Musée de la Résistance et de la Déportation, Besançon
National Archives and Records Administration, College Park, Maryland
National Archives of the United Kingdom, Kew, Richmond upon Thames
New-York Historical Society Library
New York Public Library
Princeton University Library, Special Collections
Service Historique de la Défense, Vincennes, Paris
Swarthmore College, Friends Historical Library
University at Albany, State University of New York, M. E. Grenander Special Collections and Archives

BOOKS AND ARTICLES

Adler, Felix. *The Distinctive Aims of the Ethical Culture Schools: Four Addresses Delivered Before the Teachers of the Schools.* New York: New York Society for Ethical Culture, 1902.

Alary, Eric. *Les français au quotidien, 1939–1949.* Paris: Perrin, 2006.

———. *La ligne de démarcation, 1940–1944.* Paris: Perrin, 2003.

Amouroux, Henri. *La vie des français sous l'occupation.* Paris: A. Fayard, 1961.

Atcheson, George, Jr. "The Second Exchange Voyage of the *Drottningholm,*" *American Foreign Service Journal,* September 1942: 482–83, 500.

Barber, Noel. *The Week France Fell.* New York: Stein and Day, 1976.

Baynac, Jacques. *Présumé Jean Moulin, juin 1940–juin 1943: Esquisse d'une nouvelle histoire de la Résistance.* Paris: Bernard Grasset, 2006.

Beevor, Antony. *The Fall of Berlin 1945.* New York: Penguin, 2003.

Bell, William M. *The Commando Who Came Home to Spy.* Guernsey, U.K.: Guernsey Press, 1998.

Bergin, Catherine Theresa. "Understanding Escape: The Development of the British-Led Escape Organisation, the Pat Line, 1940–1942." PhD thesis, Department of History, Maynooth University, National University of Ireland, 2015.

Berthe, Léon. "Le clergé du diocèse d'Arras sous l'Occupation." *Revue du Nord* (April–June 1978): 405–10.

Besse, Jean-Pierre, and Thomas Pouty. *Les fusillés: Répression et exécutions pendant l'Occupation (1940–1944).* Paris: Les Éditions de l'Atelier, 2006.

Béthouart, Bruno. "Le mouvement Catholique dans le Nord-Pas-de-Calais: Milieu de vie et d'action clandestines sous l'Occupation." *La Clandestinité en Belgique et en Zone Interdite (1940–1944).* Edited by Robert Vandenbussche. Lille, France: Institut de Recherches Historiques du Septentrion, 2008: 89–112.

———. "Les prêtres résistants en zone interdite: Des citoyens au service de la cause patriotique." *Les services publiques et la Résistance en zone interdite et en Belgique,* edited by Robert Vandenbussche. Lille, France: Centre de Recherche sur l'Histoire de l'Europe du Nord-Ouest, 2004: 167–80.

Bialot, Joseph. *Votre fumée montera vers le ciel.* Paris: L'Archipel, 2011.

Blower, Brooke L. *Becoming Americans in Paris: Transatlantic Politics and Culture Between the World Wars.* New York: Oxford University Press, 2011.

Blumenson, Martin. *The Vildé Affair: Beginnings of the French Resistance.* Boston: Houghton Mifflin, 1977.

Bordes, M.-R. *Quartier allemand: La vie au Fort du Hâ sous l'occupation.* Bordeaux, France: Éditions Bière, 1945.

Bove, Charles F. *A Paris Surgeon's Story.* Boston: Little, Brown, 1956.

Boyd, Douglas. *Voices from the Dark Years: The Truth About Occupied France 1940–1945.* Gloucestershire, U.K.: History Press, 2007.

Breitman, Richard, and Alan M. Kraut. *American Refugee Policy and European Jewry, 1933–1945.* Bloomington, Ind.: Indiana University Press, 1987.

Burney, Christopher. *Solitary Confinement.* London: Clerke and Cockeran, 1952.

Calet, Henri. *Les murs de Fresnes.* Paris: Vivian Hamy, 1993.

Caskie, Donald. *The Tartan Pimpernel.* London: Fontana, 1960.

Caudron, André. "Démocrates chrétiens de la région du Nord dans la Résistance." *Revue du Nord* (July–September 1978): 589–628.

Célerse, Grégory. *La traque des résistants nordistes 1940–1944.* Lille, France: Les Lumières de Lille, 2011.

Chauvy, Gérard. *La Croix-Rouge dans la guerre, 1935–1947.* Paris: Flammarion, 2000.

Closset, René. *Franz Stock, aumônier de l'enfer.* Paris: Librairie Arthème Fayard, 1992.

Clutton-Brock, Oliver. *RAF Evaders: The Comprehensive Story of Thousands of Escapers and Their Escape Lines, Western Europe, 1940–1945.* London: Bounty Books, 2012.

Cobb, Matthew. *The Resistance: The French Fight Against the Nazis.* London: Pocket Books, 2009.

Cocula, Anne-Marie, and Bernard Lachaise, editors. *La Dordogne dans la Seconde Guerre mondiale.* Aubas, France: Éditions Fanlac, 2020.

Coilliot, André. *1940–1944, quatre longues années d'occupation: Le récit des événements vécus dans la région d'Arras.* Vols. 1–3. Arras, France: A. Coilliot, 1980–1986.

Dallot, Sébastien. *L'Indre sous l'occupation allemande, 1940–1944.* Clermont-Ferrand, France: De Borée, 2001.

Dancoisne, L. *Le canton de Carvin.* 1877. Paris: Le Livre d'Histoire, 2003.

Darling, Donald. *Secret Sunday.* London: William Kimber, 1975.

Darrow, Margaret H. *French Women and the First World War: War Stories of the Home Front.* Oxford, U.K.: Berg, 2000.

David, Saul. *After Dunkirk: Churchill's Sacrifice of the Highland Division.* 1994. London: Endeavour Ink, 2017.

Decroix, Philippe. *Le Pas-de-Calais autrefois: 1900–1930.* Le Coteau-Roanne, France: Horvath, 1992.

Dejonghe, Étienne. "Le Nord et le Pas-de-Calais pendant la première année d'occupation: Un régime d'exception." *Revue du Nord.* (July–September 1994): 487–99.

Dejonghe, Étienne, et Yves Le Maner. *Le Nord-Pas-de-Calais dans la main allemande.* Lille, France: La Voix du Nord, 1999.

De Landsheere, Louise. *Les mémoires de Louise de Landsheere. De la Résistance à la "Marche de la Mort."* Brussels: J. M. Collet, 1989.

Déogracias, Jean-Jacques. *Le fabuleux destin du Fort du Hâ.* Bordeaux, France: Dossiers d'Aquitaine, 2006.

Desprairies, Cécile. *Paris dans la collaboration.* Paris: Seuil, 2009.

Diamond, Hanna. *Fleeing Hitler: France 1940.* New York: Oxford University Press, 2007.

———. *Women and the Second World War in France, 1939–48: Choices and Constraints.* Harlow, U.K.: Longman, 1999.

Dorland, Michael. *Cadaverland: Inventing a Pathology of Catastrophe for Holocaust Survival.* Waltham, Mass.: Brandeis University Press, 2009.

Drake, David. *Paris at War: 1939–1944.* Cambridge, Mass.: Harvard University Press, 2015.

Duprez, Henri. *1940–1945: Même combat dans l'ombre et la lumière; épisodes de la résistance dans le nord de la France.* Paris: La Pensée Universelle, 1979.

Durand, Ralph. *Guernsey Under German Rule.* London: Guernsey Society, 1946.

Durand, Yves. *Les prisonniers de guerre dans les stalags, les oflags et les kommandos, 1939–1945.* Paris: Hachette, 1994.

Dutourd, Jean. *The Taxis of the Marne.* Translated by Harold King. New York: Simon & Schuster, 1957.

Erbelding, Rebecca. *Rescue Board: The Untold Story of America's Efforts to Save the Jews of Europe.* New York: Doubleday, 2018.

Flanner, Janet. *Janet Flanner's World: Uncollected Writings, 1932–1975.* New York: Harcourt Brace Jovanovich, 1979.

Fogelman, Eva. *Conscience and Courage: Rescuers of Jews During the Holocaust.* New York: Anchor Books, 1994.

Foot, M.R.D. *SOE in France: An Account of the Work of the British Special Operations Executive in France, 1940–1944.* 1966. London: Whitehall History Publishing, 2004.

Foot, M.R.D., and J. M. Langley. *MI9: The British Secret Service that Fostered Escape and Evasion 1939–1945 and Its American Counterpart.* London: The Bodley Head, 1979.

Freedman, Eric, and Richard H. Weisberg. *The Haennig-Nordmann Papers: Two Lawyers in Occupied France.* Cardozo Institute in Holocaust and Human Rights, 2013.

Freeman, Denis, and Douglas Cooper. *The Road to Bordeaux.* London: Cresset, 1940.

Friot, Maurice and Françoise Villechenoux. *Vivre dangereusement sous l'Occupation à Castillon.* Castillon-la-Bataille, France: Les Éditions du GRHESAC, 2024.

Fry, Helen. *MI9: A History of the Secret Service for Escape and Evasion in World War Two.* New Haven: Yale University Press, 2020.

Fry, Varian. *Assignment Rescue: An Autobiography.* 1945. New York: Scholastic, 1968.

Gaillard, Claude, Odile Girardin-Thibeaud, André Gorsse, Paule Landreau, Andrée Luxey, and Jean Richebé. *Castillon à l'heure allemande (1939–1945): Témoignages et archives.* Bordeaux: Éditions Confluences, 2005.

Galet, Jean-Louis. *Le Périgord de bon vieux temps.* Bayonne, France: Éditions Libro-Liber, 1992.

Gebhardt, Miriam. *Crimes Unspoken: The Rape of German Women at the End of the Second World War.* Cambridge, U.K.: Polity, 2017.

Gildea, Robert. *Marianne in Chains: Everyday Life in the French Heartland Under the German Occupation.* New York: Metropolitan Books, 2003.

Gilliam, Florence. *France: A Tribute by an American Woman.* New York: E. P. Dutton, 1945.

Girardon, Jean-Pierre, editor. *Le Capitaine G.: Chevalier sans armure.* Paris: Éditions Thélès, 2006.

Glass, Charles. *Americans in Paris: Life and Death Under the Nazi Occupation 1940–44.* London: Harper Press, 2008.

Goodwin, Doris Kearns. *No Ordinary Time: Franklin and Eleanor Roosevelt: The Home Front in World War II.* New York: Simon & Schuster, 2004.

Grau, Karl Friedrich. *Silesian Inferno: War Crimes of the Red Army on Its March into Silesia in 1945.* 1966. Valley Forge, Pa.: Landpost Press, 1992.

Grayling, A. C. *Among the Dead Cities: Was the Allied Bombing of Civilians in WWII a Necessity or a Crime?* London: Bloomsbury, 2006.

Guénaire, Michel. *Pierre Gide: Une vie d'avocat.* Paris: Perrin, 2020.

Guérin, Alain. *Chronique de la Résistance.* Paris: Omnibus, 2000.

Guerville, André. *La mémoire de Doullens.* Abbeville, France: Imprimerie F. Paillart, 1987.

Hanley, Boniface. *The Last Human Face: Franz Stock, a Priest in Hitler's Army.* CreateSpace, 2010.

Hany-Lefèbvre, Noémi. *Six mois à Fresnes.* Paris: E. Flammarion, 1946.

Hargreaves, Richard. *Hitler's Final Fortress: Breslau 1945.* Barnsley, U.K.: Pen & Sword, 2011.

Hilaire, Yves-Marie. *Histoire du Nord-Pas-de-Calais: de 1900 à nos jours.* Toulouse, France: Privat, 1982.

Hood-Cree, Gordon. "Escape through France." *70 True Stories of the Second World War.* London: Odhams Press, 1952: 258–61.

Hore, Peter. *Lindell's List: Saving British and American Women at Ravensbrück.* London: History Press, 2016.

Hughes, Margaret. *Les lauriers sont coupés . . . : Journal d'une volontaire américaine en France (avril–septembre 1940).* New York: Brentano's, 1941.

Humbert, Agnès. *Résistance: A Woman's Journal of Struggle and Defiance in Occupied France.* 1946. New York: Bloomsbury, 2008.

Jonca, Karol, and Alfred Konieczny. *Nuit et Brouillard: L'opération terroriste Nazie 1941– 1944.* Translated by Teresa Janasz. Draguignan, France: La Dragon, 1981.

Josephs, Jeremy. *Swastika over Paris: The Fate of the Jews of France.* New York: Arcade, 1989.

Jucker, Ninetta. *Curfew in Paris: A Record of the German Occupation.* London: Hogarth Press, 1960.

Kernan, Thomas. *France on Berlin Time.* New York: J. B. Lippincott, 1941.

Kershaw, Alex. *Avenue of Spies: A True Story of Terror, Espionage, and One American Family's Heroic Resistance in Nazi-Occupied Paris.* New York: Crown, 2015.

Kladstrup, Don, and Petie Kladstrup. *Wine and War: The French, the Nazis, and the Battle for France's Greatest Treasure.* New York: Broadway Books, 2001.

Lacour-Astol, Catherine. *Le genre de la Résistance: La Résistance féminine dans le Nord de la France.* Paris: Presses de Sciences Po, 2015.

Laloux, Henri. *Avril 1945, libéré par l'Armée Rouge: L'incroyable odyssée d'un prisonnier de guerre français K.G.* Paris: Éditions Heimdal, 1997.

La Martinière, Joseph de. *L'évacuation et la libération de la prison de Jauer.* 1965. Archives de La Contemporaine, Nanterre, France.

———. *Les N.N.: Le décret et la procédure Nacht und Nebel (Nuit et Brouillard).* 2nd edition. Paris: Fédération Nationale des Déportés et Internés Résistants et Patriotes, 1989.

———. *Nuit et Brouillard à Hinzert: Les déportés N.N. en camp spécial SS.* Tours: Université François-Rabelais, 1984.

Lang, Derek. *Return to St Valéry: The Story of an Escape Through Wartime France and Syria.* London: Leo Cooper, 1974.

Langley, J. M. *Fight Another Day.* London: Collins, 1974.

Le Boulanger, Isabelle. *Henriette Le Belzic, résistante déportée (de novembre 1941 à avril 1945): Mémoires d'une Bretonne dans l'enfer concentrationnaire nazi.* Coop Breizh, 2018.

Lehrer, Steven. *Wartime Sites in Paris 1939–1945.* New York: SF Tafel, 2013.

Le Maner, Yves. "L'invasion de 1940 dans le Nord—Pas-de-Calais." *Revue du Nord.* (July–September 1994): 467–86.

Lesage, René. *La Résistance en Artois occidental (juin 1940–mai 1944).* Lille, France: Revue du Nord, 1998.

———. "La Résistance précoce en Artois occidental." *Revue du Nord.* (July–September 1994): 501–10.

Liebling, A. J. *The Road Back to Paris.* Garden City, N.Y.: Doubleday, 1944.

Long, Helen. *Safe Houses Are Dangerous.* London: William Kimber, 1985.

Longden, Sean. *Dunkirk: The Men They Left Behind.* London: Constable, 2008.

Lottman, Herbert R. *The Fall of Paris: June 1940.* New York: HarperCollins, 1992.

Lyman, Robert. *Under a Darkening Sky: The American Experience in Nazi Europe, 1939– 1941.* New York: Pegasus Books, 2018.

Majer, Diemut. *"Non-Germans" Under the Third Reich: The Nazi Judicial and Administrative System in Germany and Eastern Europe with Special Regard to Occupied Poland, 1939–1945.* London: Johns Hopkins University Press, 2003.

Marino, Andy. *American Pimpernel: The Man Who Saved the Artists on Hitler's Death List.* London: Hutchinson, 1999.

Marvel, Josiah P. *Peace in Our Time.* Typescript manuscript (1942), Quaker Emergency Service Records, 1942–1965, SC/221, Friends Historical Library of Swarthmore College.

Masconi, Marie-José. *La longue nuit de Lucie: Une résistante et ses compagnes dans les bagnes nazis.* Strasbourg: La Nuée Bleue, 2019.

McAuliffe, Mary. *When Paris Sizzled: The 1920s Paris of Hemingway, Chanel, Cocteau, Cole Porter, Josephine Baker, and Their Friends.* Lanham, Md.: Rowman & Littlefield, 2016.

McPhail, Helen. *The Long Silence: The Tragedy of Occupied France in World War I.* London: I. B. Tauris, 1999.

Michel, Henri. "The Psychology of the French Resister." *Journal of Contemporary History* 5:3 (1970): 159–75.

Michelsen, Jean-Paul. "Les habitants de la région de Frévent se souviennent de la guerre 39–45." *Ternesia: Bulletin du cercle historique du Ternois,* 1983: 65–79.

Monier (Harrand), Simone. *Un grain de sable.* Dijon, 1994. Archives of La Contemporaine, Nanterre, France.

Murphy, Brendan M. *Turncoat: The Strange Case of Sergeant Harold Cole, "The Worst Traitor of the War."* New York: Harcourt Brace Jovanovich, 1987.

Myers, Bessy. *Captured: My Experiences as an Ambulance Driver and as a Prisoner of the Nazis.* London: George G. Harrap & Co., 1941.

Naimark, Norman M. *The Russians in Germany: A History of the Zone of Occupation, 1945–1949.* Cambridge, Mass.: Harvard University Press, 1995.

Neave, Airey. *Saturday at M.I.9: A History of Underground Escape Lines in North-West Europe in 1940–5 by a Leading Organizer at M.I.9.* London: Hodder and Stoughton, 1969.

Neel, Hildy Michelle. "Let Us Now Praise Famous Men: A History of the American World War II Personal Narrative, 1942–1945." Doctoral dissertation to the American Studies program, College of William and Mary, 1998.

Nivart-Chatelain, J. H. *Guide-Book to France for Americans.* Liège: A. A. Bénard, 1937.

Olson, Lynne. *Madame Fourcade's Secret War: The Daring Young Woman Who Led France's Largest Spy Network Against Hitler.* New York: Random House, 2019.

Ottis, Sherri Greene. *Silent Heroes: Downed Airmen and the French Underground.* Lexington, Ky.: University Press of Kentucky, 2001.

Ousby, Ian. *Occupation: The Ordeal of France, 1940–1944.* New York: St. Martin's Press, 1998.

Peabody, Polly. *Occupied Territory.* London: Cresset Press, 1941.

Peeters, Rosemonde. *La route sans fin.* Paris: Les Éditions du Scorpion, 1966.

Perrault, Giles. *Paris sous l'Occupation.* Paris: Belfond, 1987.

Pineau, Frédéric. *Les femmes au service de la France: 1919–1940.* Paris: Histoire et Collections, 2006.

Poznanski, Renée. "Le fichage des juifs de France pendant la Seconde Guerre mondiale et l'affaire du fichier des juifs." *La Gazette des Archives,* 1997: 250–70.

———. *Jews in France During World War II.* Translated by Nathan Bracher. Waltham, Mass.: Brandeis University Press, 2001.

Press, Eyal. *Beautiful Souls: The Courage and Conscience of Ordinary People in Extraordinary Times.* New York: Picador, 2013.

Quella-Villégerm, Alain. *France Bloch-Sérazin: Une femme en résistance (1913–1943).* Paris: Des Femmes Antoinette Fouquet, 2019.

Quinn, James. "'We Have No Place': The Captivity and Homecoming of French Prisoners of War, 1939–1947." Master's thesis, University of Kansas, 2006.

Richards, Denis. *The Hardest Victory: RAF Bomber Command in the Second World War.* London: Hodder and Stoughton, 1994.

Richardson, Anthony. *Wingless Victory: The Story of Sir Basil Embry's Escape from Occupied France in the Summer of 1940.* London: Odhams Press, 1950.

Riding, Alan. *And the Show Went On: Cultural Life in Nazi-Occupied Paris.* New York: Alfred A. Knopf, 2010.

Rocal, Georges. *Le vieux Périgord.* Paris: Occitania, 1927.

Rolli, Patrice. *La ligne de démarcation en Dordogne: Passages clandestins, Résistance et répression (1940–1943).* L'Histoire en Partage, 2020.

Roosenburg, Henriette. *The Walls Came Tumbling Down.* 1956. Pleasantville, N.Y.: Akadine Press, 2000.

Rosbottom, Ronald C. *When Paris Went Dark: The City of Light Under German Occupation, 1940–1944.* New York: Little, Brown, 2014.

Rose, Sarah. *D-Day Girls: The Spies Who Armed the Resistance, Sabotaged the Nazis, and Helped Win World War II.* New York: Crown, 2019.

Rosen, Robert N. *Saving the Jews: Franklin D. Roosevelt and the Holocaust.* New York: Thunder's Mouth Press, 2006.

Rossel-Kirschen, André. *Le procès de la Maison de la chimie, 7 au 14 avril 1942: Contribution à l'histoire des débuts de la résistance armée en France.* Paris: L'Harmattan, 2002.

Rossiter, Margaret L. *Women in the Resistance.* New York: Praeger, 1986.

Russell, Jan Jarboe. *The Train to Crystal City: FDR's Secret Prisoner Exchange Program and America's Only Family Internment Camp During World War II.* New York: Scribner, 2015.

Saint-Exupéry, Antoine de. *Flight to Arras.* 1942. Translated by William Rees. London: Penguin Books, 1995.

Sartre, Jean-Paul. "Paris Under the Occupation." 1945. *Sartre Studies International* 4:2 (1998): 1–15.

Say, Rosemary, and Noel Holland. *Rosie's War: An Englishwoman's Escape from Occupied France.* London: Michael O'Mara Books, 2012.

Schoenbrun, David. *Soldiers of the Night: The Story of the French Resistance.* New York: E. P. Dutton, 1980.

Schrafstetter, Susanna. "'Gentlemen, the Cheese Is All Gone!': British POWs, the 'Great Escape' and the Anglo-German Agreement for Compensation to Victims of Nazism." *Contemporary European History* 17:1 (February 2008): 23–43.

Sebba, Anne. *Les Parisiennes: How the Women of Paris Lived, Loved, and Died Under Nazi Occupation.* New York: St. Martin's Press, 2016.

Sherman, Andrew. *The Fall of France, 1940.* Harlow, U.K.: Longman, 2000.

Sherwill, Ambrose. *A Fair and Honest Book: The Memoirs of Sir Ambrose Sherwill.* Lulu.com, 2007.

Shiber, Etta (with Anne and Paul Dupre). *Paris-Underground.* New York: Charles Scribner's Sons, 1943.

Sisich, Monique. *A Nightingale in the Storm.* Pittsburgh: RoseDog Books, 2009.

Souleau, Philippe. *La ligne de démarcation en Gironde: Occupation, Résistance, et société, 1940–1944.* Périgueux, France: Éditions Fanlac, 1998.

Stuart, Graham H. *American Diplomatic and Consular Practice.* New York: Appleton-Century-Crofts, 1952.

———. "Special War Problems Division." *Department of State Bulletin* XI: 262 (July 2, 1944): 6–12.

Thornton, Willis. *The Liberation of Paris.* New York: Harcourt, Brace and World, 1962.

Thorwald, Jürgen. *La débâcle allemande.* Paris: Éditions Stock, 1965.

Veillon, Dominique. *Vivre et survivre en France, 1939–1947.* Paris: Éditions Payot et Rivages, 1995.

Vessels, Joel E. *Drawing France: French Comics and the Republic.* Jackson: University of Mississippi Press, 2010.

Vidalenc, Jean. *L'Éxode de mai-juin 1940.* Paris: Presses Universitaires de France, 1957.

Villate, Robert. *Le Lion des Flandres à la guerre.* Paris: Charles-Lavauzelle & Co., 1946.

Vinen, Richard. *The Unfree French: Life Under the Occupation.* New Haven: Yale University Press, 2006.

Walter, Gerard. *Paris Under the Occupation.* New York: Orion Press, 1960.

Weber, Eugen. *The Hollow Years: France in the 1930s.* New York: W. W. Norton, 1994.

Weinberg, David H. *A Community on Trial: The Jews of Paris in the 1930s.* Chicago: University of Chicago Press, 1977.

Weisberg, Richard H. "The Hermeneutic of Acceptance and the Discourse of the Grotesque, with a Classroom Exercise on Vichy Law." *Cardozo Law Review* (1996): 1875–1913.

———. *Vichy Law and the Holocaust in France.* New York: New York University Press, 1996.

Weitz, Margaret Collins. *Sisters in the Resistance: How Women Fought to Free France 1940–1945.* New York: John Wiley and Sons, 1995.

Whiting, Charles. *The Three-Star Blitz: The Baedeker Raids and the Start of Total War 1942–1943.* London: Leo Cooper, 1987.

Williams, David L. *Lifeline Across the Sea: Mercy Ships of the Second World War and Their Repatriation Missions.* Gloucestershire, U.K.: History Press, 2015.

Winkler, Paul. "Etta Shiber." *Book-of-the-Month Club News,* September 1943, 7–8.

Wobick-Segev, Sarah. *Homes Away from Home: Jewish Belonging in Twentieth-Century Paris, Berlin, and St. Petersburg.* Stanford, Calif., Stanford University Press, 2018.

Wynne, Barry. *No Drums . . . No Trumpets: The Story of Mary Lindell.* London: Arthur Barker, 1961.

Yagil, Limore. *Les "anonymes" de la Résistance en France, 1940–1942: Motivations et engagements de la première heure.* Paris: Éditions SPM, 2019.

Yagoda, Ben. *Memoir: A History.* New York: Riverhead Books, 2009.

Photo Credits

Index

White, John, 349–350
Wiley, John C., 247–248
Winkie (dog), 36, 52, 191, 343
Winkler, Betty, 9, 253, 343, 345–346,
　400n
Winkler, Claude, 400n
Winkler, Paul, 9, 253, 260n, 268–286,
　288, 288n, 290, 400n
Woirgny, Louise, 306
Wolfe, Thomas, 254
women
　ambulance drivers, 40–41, 48
　condemned to death, 217, 220–221,
　　388n
　German, in Paris, 150
　inspections by female Vichy agents,
　　124n
　Lübeck-Lauerhof prison, 307–315
　marraines de guerre, 87–89,
　　148–149
　NN prisoners, 307–315, 316,
　　318–328, 329–332
　passeurs, 127n
　Peugeots advertised to, 53, *53*
　pregnancy ruse to cut to front of
　　food shop lines, 114
　prison guards, 170–171, 317–319
　rape of, 332–336
　resisters, 71, 148–149
　in Richard Coeur de Lion, 148n
Wood, Meredith, 281

Woolf, Virginia, 129
Words at War (radio program), 9, 256
Workingman's School, 20
World War I, 45, 64, 67, 121, 211
　American entry into, 235
　Armistice Day, 155, 305
　Cavell's escape aid, 5–6, 115
　end of, 295
　French casualties, 38–39
　German occupation of France, 142
　marraine de guerre tradition, 87–89
World War II
　American entry into, 235, 290
　beginning of, 38
　British escape organizations, 88
　French mobilization, 39
　Maginot Line, 39
　marraine de guerre tradition, 88–89
　personal war narratives published,
　　261

Y

yellow star, 244–245

Z

Zeigenhain Prison, 301–306, *303,* 309,
　310
zone interdite ("forbidden zone"),
　80–81, 102, 139, 147

ABOUT THE AUTHOR

MATTHEW GOODMAN is the author of four previous books of nonfiction. His most recent book, *The City Game: Triumph, Scandal, and a Legendary Basketball Team*, received the New York City Book Award and was a finalist for the National Jewish Book Award. His book *Eighty Days: Nellie Bly and Elizabeth Bisland's History-Making Race Around the World* was a *New York Times* bestseller and has been translated into eight languages. Goodman's work has appeared in *The Wall Street Journal, USA Today, The American Scholar, Bon Appétit*, and numerous other publications. He lives with his family in Brooklyn, New York.

matthewgoodmanbooks.com
X: @MGoodmanBooks
Bluesky: @mgoodmanbooks.bsky.social

ABOUT THE TYPE

This book was set in Caslon, a typeface first designed in 1722 by William Caslon (1692–1766). Its widespread use by most English printers in the early eighteenth century soon supplanted the Dutch typefaces that had formerly prevailed. The roman is considered a "work-horse" typeface due to its pleasant, open appearance, while the italic is exceedingly decorative.